PHILOSOPHICAL
FRAGMENTS

JOHANNES CLIMACUS

KIERKEGAARD'S WRITINGS, VII

PHILOSOPHICAL FRAGMENTS

JOHANNES CLIMACUS

by Søren Kierkegaard

Edited and Translated
with Introduction and Notes by

Howard V. Hong and
Edna H. Hong

PRINCETON UNIVERSITY PRESS
PRINCETON, NEW JERSEY

Copyright © 1985 by Howard V. Hong
Published by Princeton University Press, 41 William Street
Princeton, New Jersey 08540
In the United Kingdom: Princeton University Press, Chichester, West Sussex

Library of Congress Cataloging-in-Publication Data

Kierkegaard, Søren, 1813-1855.
Philosophical fragments, or, A fragment of
philosophy ; Johannes Climacus, or, De omnibus
dubitandum est.

(Kierkegaard's writings ; 7)
Translation of: Philosophiske smuler; and of:
Johannes Climacus.
Bibliography: p.
Includes index.
1. Religion—Philosophy. I. Hong, Howard Vincent,
1912-   . II. Hong, Edna Hatlestad, 1913-
III. Kierkegaard, Søren, 1813-1855. Johannes Climacus.

English.   1985.   IV.   Title.   V.   Series: Kierkegaard,
Søren, 1813-1855.   Works.   English.   1972 ; 7.
BL51.K48713   1985   201   85-3420
ISBN 0-691-07273-6
ISBN 0-691-02036-1 (pbk.)

Preparation of this volume was made possible in part by a grant from
the Division of Research Programs of the National Endowment for the Humanities,
an independent federal agency

http://pup.princeton.edu

Printed in the United States of America

Second Printing, with corrections, 1987

17 18 19 20

ISBN-13: 978-0-691-02036-5

ISBN-10: 0-691-02036-1

CONTENTS

HISTORICAL INTRODUCTION

It is a very strange experience for me to read the third chapter of the third book of Aristotle's *De anima*. A year and a half ago I began a little essay, *De omnibus dubitandum*, in which I made my first attempt at a little speculative development. The motivating concept I used was: error. Aristotle does the same. At that time I had not read a bit of Aristotle but a good share of Plato.

The Greeks still remain my consolation. The confounded mendacity that entered into philosophy with Hegel, the endless insinuating and betraying, and the parading and spinning out of one or another single passage in Greek philosophy.[1]

In this journal entry from late autumn 1843 or early winter 1844, Kierkegaard offers clues to the dating of the composition of *Johannes Climacus, or De omnibus dubitandum est*,[2] and

[1] *JP* III 3300 (*Pap.* V A 98, 1844).

[2] The title comes from the name of a monk (c. 570-649) who became abbot of the monastery of St. Catherine of Alexandria on Mt. Sinai and wrote the celebrated *Ladder of Paradise* (κλῖμαξ τοῦ παραδείσου). The thirty chapters or steps of the ladder of perfection correspond to the age of Christ at his baptism. A number of Latin translations were made in the Middle Ages, and the Traversari Spanish translation was the first book printed in the New World (Mexico, 1532). The two current English translations bear the title *The Ladder of Divine Ascent* (New York: Harper, 1959; Paulist Press, 1982). Kierkegaard uses the common element (Climacus, climax, ladder) of the name and the title to symbolize the structure of logical sequence in both *Johannes Climacus, or De omnibus dubitandum est* and *Philosophical Fragments*. *De omnibus dubitandum est* (Everything must be doubted) epitomizes the Cartesian method and its significance in modern thought. See p. 131 and note 10.

Kierkegaard first mentions Climacus in an entry on Hegel (see Supplement, p. 231; *Pap.* II A 335). References to Climacus appear in W.M.L. de Wette's *Lærebog i den christelige Sædelære*, tr. C. E. Scharling (Copenhagen: 1835), pp. 135, 138, 139. Kierkegaard owned that volume (*ASKB* 871) and used it in preparing for his final university examinations in 1839. Later, he

to an understanding of the nature of the work. The editor's preface to *Either/Or* was completed in November 1842, and the work was published February 20, 1843. On May 16, 1843, *Two Upbuilding Discourses*, by S. Kierkegaard, was published. Five months later, on October 16, 1843, three works appeared, *Fear and Trembling, Repetition,* and *Three Upbuilding Discourses*, by Johannes de Silentio, Constantin Constantius, and S. Kierkegaard, respectively. Although earlier journal entries give some hints to aspects of *Johannes Climacus*,[3] the sketches and perhaps the draft of this unpublished work were most likely written between November 1842 and April 1843, the period between concluding work on *Either/Or* and the intensive writing of the four subsequent publications.

Having completed the writing of *Either/Or*, Kierkegaard became preoccupied with Greek and modern philosophy: metaphysics, epistemology, ethics, political philosophy, and esthetics. The first two issues figure in *Johannes Climacus*. Reading notes in a notebook entitled *Philosophica*[4] (dated December 2, 1842) and in another notebook called *Æsthetica*[5] (dated November 20, 1842) primarily concern works by Aristotle, Descartes, and Leibniz and W. G. Tennemann's his-

---

used the pseudonym Anti-Climacus in *The Sickness unto Death* (1849). At first sight, the prefix "Anti" may mislead a reader in regard to the relation of the two pseudonyms. The prefix does not mean "against." An old form of "ante" (before), as in "anticipate," the prefix denotes a relation of rank, as in "before me" in the First Commandment. In a journal entry, Kierkegaard explains: "Johannes Climacus and Anti-Climacus have several things in common; but the difference is that whereas Johannes Climacus places himself so low that he even says that he himself is not a Christian, one seems to be able to detect in Anti-Climacus that he considers himself to be a Christian on an extraordinarily high level. . . . I would place myself higher than Johannes Climacus, lower than Anti-Climacus" (*JP* VI 6433; *Pap.* X[1] A 517). See also *Kierkegaard: Letters and Documents*, Letter 213, *KW* XXV.

[3] See, for example, Supplement, pp. 231-32 (*Pap.* II A 335; III A 3, 7).

[4] *Pap.* IV C 4-86. Additional loose sheets (*Pap.* IV C 2-3, 87-101) also contain reading notes on philosophical works and issues. See, for example, Supplement, pp. 233-34. See *JP* VII, p. 113, for a list of *JP* entries from *Philosophica*.

[5] *Pap.* IV C 102-27. See *JP* VII, p. 113, for a list of *JP* entries from *Æsthetica*.

tory of philosophy.[6] One section of the reading notes (written on the back pages of the notebook) is entitled *Problemata*[7] and comprises issues (designated *a* through *p*) such as necessity and freedom, past and future, the nature of a category, being, the positive and the negative, experience, the self, collateral thinking, transition, mediation, paradox, quantity and quality, thought and being, logic, interested and disinterested knowledge, thinker and thought, and pathos and dialectic. *Problemata* became the provisional title of *Fear and Trembling*[8] (published October 16, 1843), and some of the issues became the themes of *Johannes Climacus* and especially of *Philosophical Fragments*.

Doubt, the central issue of *Johannes Climacus*, also appears among the themes of writing contemplated or initiated earlier by Kierkegaard. The other subjects of his earliest interest include the master thief and the legends of the Wandering Jew, Don Juan, and Faust. In the published works, the master thief motif found expression only in scattered allusions to criminals and in the more significant appellation "secret agent" or "spy."[9] The Wandering Jew is mentioned only once, in the first volume of *Either/Or*.[10] The interest in Don Juan appears especially in extended treatments of Mozart's *Don Giovanni*,[11] as well as in references to Don Juan as an idea and

[6] Wilhelm Gottlieb Tennemann, *Geschichte der Philosophie*, I–XI (Leipzig: 1798-1819; *ASKB* 815-26).

[7] *Pap.* IV C 62-86, plus extra sheet with IV C 87-96. See, for example, Supplement, p. 234 (*Pap.* IV C 89). See *JP* VII, p. 113, for a list of *JP* entries from *Problemata*.

[8] See *JP* V 5658 (*Pap.* IV B 60).

[9] See, for example, *Either/Or*, II, *KW* IV (*SV* II 292); *Repetition*, p. 135, *KW* VI (*SV* III 176); *The Concept of Anxiety*, pp. 55, 155, *KW* VIII (*SV* IV 326, 422); *Stages on Life's Way*, *KW* XI (*SV* VI 333); *Practice in Christianity*, *KW* XX (*SV* XII 86, 125); *The Point of View for My Work as an Author*, *KW* XXII (*SV* XIII 563, 571, 608); *Christ's Judgment on Official Christianity*, *KW* XXIII (*SV* XIV 143); *The Moment*, *KW* XXIII (*SV* XIV 178). See also *JP* VII, pp. 60, 85.

[10] See *Either/Or*, I, *KW* III (*SV* I 194). See also *JP* VII, p. 100.

[11] See *Either/Or*, I, *KW* III (*SV* I 29-133); "A Cursory Observation Concerning a Detail in *Don Giovanni*," by A., *The Corsair Affair*, pp. 28-37, *KW* XIII (*SV* XIII 447-56). See also *JP* VII, p. 28.

as a character in the works of Byron, Galeotti, Grabbe, Hauch, Heiberg, and Molière.[12] Also projected were lectures on communication,[13] which were sketched and partially written but not delivered and not printed until the posthumous publication of the *Efterladte Papirer* (1869-1881) and the *Papirer* (1909-1948). Lectures on poetry were contemplated in 1842-1843 but were not begun.[14]

The fascination with Faust emerges as early as 1835 in a journal entry in which Faust is characterized as "doubt personified."[15] Scattered entries from 1835-1837 constitute the core of what Emanuel Hirsch has appropriately called "Letters of a Faustian Doubter."[16] This series, Kierkegaard's first writing plan, was not completed, but he picked up the theme again in *Johannes Climacus*.

Furthermore, he followed the early plan of casting the ideas in the form of a character, even though " 'Johannes Climacus' was actually a contemplative piece"[17] and was intended as the first of a series, with Descartes's *Meditations* as the prototype: "For the most part Descartes has embodied his system in the first six meditations. So it is not always necessary to write systems. I want to publish 'Philosophical Deliberations' in pamphlets, and into them I can put all my interim thoughts. It perhaps would not be so bad to write in Latin."[18] Despite the avoidance of a system, *Johannes Climacus* itself is systematic in the sense of coherent contemplation, because to Johannes "coherent thinking was a *scala paradisi* [ladder of paradise]."[19]

The tone and the intention of *Johannes Climacus* are highly polemical versus speculative philosophy in both substance and

[12] See *Either/Or*, I, *KW* III (*SV* I 26, 85, 86, 89-90, 92, 108, 122). See also *JP* VII, p. 28.
[13] See *JP* I 617-81, especially 648-57 (*Pap.* VIII² B 79-89).
[14] See *JP* 5608 (*Pap.* IV C 127).
[15] *JP* V 5092 (*Pap.* I A 72).
[16] See *JP* V, note 245 (in line 15 read: 1835-37).
[17] *JP* VI 6523 (*Pap.* X² A 163).
[18] *JP* V 5574 (*Pap.* IV A 2, 1842). See *Prefaces*, *KW* IX (*SV* V 68), where Kierkegaard mentions this contemplated publication series.
[19] P. 118.

practice. A residue of the polemical approach can be found even in the *Two Upbuilding Discourses* (1843) published shortly after Kierkegaard completed the writing of *Johannes Climacus*: "It is very curious. I had decided to change that little preface [in *Two Upbuilding Discourses*] . . . because it seemed to me to harbor a certain spiritual eroticism, and because it is extraordinarily hard to devote myself so irenically that the polemical contrast is not clearly present."[20]

The polemical tone of the warning note in the text of *Johannes Climacus* (p. 117) is expressed more specifically in a paragraph appended to the draft:

> The plan of this narrative was as follows. By means of the melancholy irony, which did not consist in any single utterance on the part of Johannes Climacus but in his whole life, by means of the profound earnestness involved in a young man's being sufficiently honest and earnest enough to do quietly and unostentatiously what the philosophers say (and he thereby becomes unhappy)—I would strike a blow at [modern speculative] philosophy. Johannes does what we are told to do—he actually doubts everything—he suffers through all the pain of doing that, becomes cunning, almost acquires a bad conscience. When he has gone as far in that direction as he can go and wants to come back, he cannot do so. He perceives that in order to hold on to this extreme position of doubting everything, he has engaged all his mental and spiritual powers. If he abandons this extreme position, he may very well arrive at something, but in doing that he would have also abandoned his doubt about everything. Now he despairs, his life is wasted, his youth is spent in these deliberations. Life has not acquired any meaning for him, and all this is the fault of philosophy.[21]

This explanatory paragraph ends with a parenthetical sentence stating that a draft contains the following concluding lines:

---

[20] *JP* V 5644 (*Pap.* IV A 83).
[21] See Supplement, pp. 234-35 (*Pap.* IV B 16).

Then the philosophers are worse than the Pharisees, who, as we read, impose heavy burdens but themselves do not lift them, for in this they are the same, but the philosophers demand the impossible. And if there is a young man who thinks that to philosophize is not to talk or to write but in all quietness to do honestly and scrupulously what the philosophers say one should do, they let him waste his time, many years of his life, and then it becomes clear that it is impossible, and yet it has gripped him so profoundly that rescue is perhaps impossible.[22]

As a practicing doubter, Johannes Climacus became a "private thinker,"[23] without official appointment and without adherence to any school, because he found no thoroughgoing practitioners, although some claimed to have gone further than Descartes. In the preface to *Fear and Trembling*, written in the same year as the draft of *Johannes Climacus*, Johannes de Silentio seems to crystallize Johannes Climacus's thoughts:

Not only in the business world but also in the world of ideas, our age stages *ein wirklicher Ausverkauf* [a real sale]. Everything can be had at such a bargain price that it becomes a question whether there is finally anyone who will make a bid. Every speculative monitor who conscientiously signals the important trends in modern philosophy, every assistant professor, tutor, and student, every rural outsider and tenant incumbent in philosophy is unwilling to stop with doubting everything but goes further. Perhaps it would be premature and untimely to ask them where they really are going, but in all politeness and modesty it can probably be taken for granted that they have doubted everything, since otherwise it certainly would be odd to speak of their having gone further. They have all made this preliminary movement and presumably so easily that

---

[22] See Supplement, p. 235 (*Pap.* IV B 6).

[23] *Concluding Unscientific Postscript to* Philosophical Fragments, *KW* XII (*SV* VII 47).

they find it unnecessary to say a word about how, for not even the person who in apprehension and concern sought a little enlightenment found any, not one suggestive hint or one little dietetic prescription with respect to how a person is to act in carrying out this enormous task. "But did not Descartes do it?" Descartes, a venerable, humble, honest thinker, whose writings no one can read without being profoundly affected—he did what he said and said what he did. Alas! Alas! Alas! That is a great rarity in our day![24]

Besides becoming more aware of the tension between ideality and actuality, thought and being (and action), Johannes Climacus finds more theoretical issues as he proceeds in Part Two, Chapter I: the origin of doubt, interested and disinterested knowledge, dualism and monism, inner and outer,[25] immediacy, language, possibility, memory, repetition, recollection, and time and eternity. Some of these issues are developed in the draft;[26] others are touched upon in sketch notes for succeeding chapters.[27] Chapter IV was to have had the heading: "Johannes comes to pure being but cannot come back again."[28] However, the draft of *Johannes Climacus* breaks off with Part Two, Chapter I, which is incomplete; envisioned chapters were not begun. The clue both to Johannes's coming back again and to the next writing, *Philosophical Fragments*, appears in sketch entry IV B 13:18: "Doubt is conquered not by the system but by faith, just as it is faith that has brought doubt into the world."[29]

Although *Philosophical Fragments* (as well as *Concluding Unscientific Postscript to* Philosophical Fragments) is also by Johan-

---

[24] *Fear and Trembling*, p. 5, *KW* VI (*SV* III 57).

[25] See the early discussion of inner and outer in *Either/Or*, I, *KW* III (*SV* I, p. v).

[26] See Supplement to *Johannes Climacus, or De omnibus dubitandum est*, passim.

[27] Supplement, pp. 260-66 (*Pap.* IV B 13:5-23).

[28] See Supplement, p. 263 (*Pap.* IV B 13:15).

[29] See Supplement, p. 256 (*Pap.* IV B 13:18).

nes Climacus and was written after *De omnibus dubitandum est*, it is not in direct continuity in substance, tone, and form. These differences are not surprising, inasmuch as the draft of *Fragments* had S. Kierkegaard as the author and was designated as No. 1 in the projected series of philosophical pamphlets.[30] The final copy also had S. Kierkegaard as author and the designation "No. 1. a dogmatical-philosophical issue." That designation was deleted and the author changed to Johannes Climacus, with S. Kierkegaard as the editor.[31] In a marginal addition to a draft[32] of "A First and Last Explanation" appended to *Postscript*,[33] the role of the editor is explained:

> Thus in the pseudonymous books there is not a single word by me. I am as little the Judge in *Either/Or* as I am the book's editor, Victor Eremita, precisely just as little; my name is on the title page of *Philosophical Fragments* as editor, but I am just as little the author of the preface as of the book, since I am merely an unknown person who is the author's author. . . . I, dialectically reduplicated, may be called the author of the authors, not in the eminent sense as the outstanding one, but in the philosophic sense as the ground that goes to the ground.[34]

The title page of *The Concept of Anxiety* (published four days after *Fragments*) underwent similar but more extensive changes. Originally the draft and the final copy named S. Kierkegaard as the author.[35] The bottom half of the title page of the final copy was removed, and Vigilius Haufniensis was substituted as author.[36] Kierkegaard's name was eliminated entirely, including the S. K. under the epigraph.[37]

---

[30] See Supplement, p. 177 (*Pap.* V B 39).
[31] See *Pap.* V B 40:2-4.
[32] *Pap.* VII¹ B 76.
[33] *KW* XII (*SV* VII [545-49]).
[34] A special Hegelian phrase. See p. 39 and note 12.
[35] See *Anxiety*, Supplement, p. 177 (*Pap.* V B 42).
[36] See *Pap.* V B 72:1.
[37] See *Pap.* V B 72:1; *Anxiety*, p. 3, *KW* VIII (*SV* IV 276).

In addition to changes in the stated authorship of *Fragments*, other revisions occurred in the title page.[38] The envisioned common title for a series of short works, which had been changed to "Philosophical Pamphlets, or a Fragment of Philosophy," was further refined to "Philosophical Fragments, or a Fragment of Philosophy." Omitted entirely were a contemplated subtitle, "The Apologetical Presuppositions of Dogmatics or Thought-Approximations to Faith,"[39] and "No. 1," a serial designation. The contemplated subtitle, modified in formulation, is repeated in the introduction to *Postscript*,[40] and the substance of that subtitle links *Fragments* to its companion piece, *The Concept of Anxiety*. In keeping with these deletions, "1st Position" became "Propositio,"[41] and "Position II"[42] (which in substance became *Postscript*) was omitted. The subheading "Historical Costume" in the sketch[43] became part of the text of *Fragments* in references to a possible sequel (*Postscript*).[44]

The changes on the title page are not reflected in the text by significant alterations. The main changes involved the Preface,[45] which was recast to fit the ironic dialectician Johannes Climacus, and the ending,[46] which now anticipates *Postscript*. The relation of *Fragments* and *Postscript* is announced in the full title of the latter: *Concluding Unscientific Postscript to Philosophical Fragments: A Mimical-Pathetical-Dialectical Compilation. An Existential Contribution*. The relation of the two works, as well as a partial explanation of the subtitle, are also presented at the end of *Fragments*: "in the next section of this pamphlet, if I ever do write it, I intend to call

[38] See Supplement, p. 177 (*Pap.* V B 39), also *Pap.* V B 40:2-4.

[39] See *Pap.* V B 7, also 8, variant formulation, Supplement, p. 217.

[40] *KW* XII (*SV* VII 6).

[41] See Supplement, p. 186 (*Pap.* V B 40:6), also p. 185 (*Pap.* V B 1:12, 3:1).

[42] See Supplement, p. 186 (*Pap.* V B 10).

[43] See Supplement, p. 185 (*Pap.* V B 1:12).

[44] See p. 109.

[45] See Supplement, pp. 183-85 (*Pap.* V B 24).

[46] See Supplement, pp. 186-87 (*Pap.* V B 3:2, 40:7).

the matter by its proper name and clothe the issue in its historical costume."[47]

In substance, *Fragments* is dialectically related to the other major pseudonymous works. Judge William in *Either/Or* delineates the richness of human possibilities in the esthetic and ethical spheres. Johannes Climacus in *De omnibus* begins the philosophical journey with the negativity of total doubt. Similarly, *The Concept of Anxiety* treats anxiety and sin, the underside of human life in the individual and the race. In *Fragments*, the copiousness and depths of human life and thought are exemplified by Socrates and Plato.[48] There the assumption is not the possibility of the good, the theory and practice of doubt, or the actuality of sin, but rather the intrinsic possession of the truth by the learner. Going beyond Socrates in *Fragments* thus becomes an elaboration of the first thesis in *The Concept of Irony*— "Similitudo Christum inter et Socratem in dissimilitudine præcipue est posita [The similarity between Christ and Socrates consists essentially in their dissimilarity]"[49] —and of the observation in *Johannes Climacus* that "Christianity's claim that it had come into the world by a beginning that was simultaneously historical and eternal had caused philosophy much difficulty . . . ."[50]

The form of *Fragments* is announced in the title of Chapter I, "Thought-Project," and elsewhere in the work the term "hypothesis" is used.[51] In *Postscript*, Climacus calls *Fragments* an "imaginary construction":[52] "It took its point of departure in paganism in order by imaginatively constructing to discover an understanding of existence that truly could be said to go beyond paganism."[53] In referreing again to *Fragments*, Climacus uses the phrase "poetically constructing,"[54] which

[47] P. 109.

[48] On the lack of distinction in *Fragments* between Socrates and Plato, see *Postscript*, *KW* XII (*SV* VII 172-73).

[49] *The Concept of Irony*, *KW* II (*SV* XIII 99).

[50] Pp. 134-35.

[51] See pp. 17, 22, 100, 101, 109.

[52] On this phrase in its various forms, see *Repetition*, pp. xxi-xxxi, 357-62, *KW* VI.

[53] *KW* XII (*SV* VII 312-13).

[54] Ibid. (*SV* VII 77).

may seem more appropriate to the obviously poetic productions, such as *Repetition* and *Fear and Trembling*, but only if the root meaning of "poet," a maker, is forgotten. Therefore, Climacus calls *Fragments* itself a "poem," a com-position (a making, a putting together). The imaginary, hypothetical character of the work is further emphasized and qualified by Climacus's promise to "be as brief as possible, for we are speaking not historically but algebraically."[55] The most abstract of all Kierkegaard's writings, *Fragments* presupposes the principle of contradiction[56] and, as an imaginary construction of thought, explores logically the if/then implications of the hypothesis of going beyond Socrates-Plato in learning the truth.

The reception of Kierkegaard's works, pseudonymous and signed, was rather quiet (by 1849, only *Either/Or* was printed in a second edition, six years after publication). *Fragments* was no exception.[57] By July 1847, three years after publication, 229 copies had been sold from an edition of 525.[58]

The first Danish review of the work did not appear until two years after publication.[59] It commends the book for its dialectical character but emphasizes that mediation must not be forgotten. In a journal entry about the review, Kierkegaard writes in the vein of his pseudonym Frater Taciturnus addressing the scandal sheet *The Corsair*:[60]

> Johannes Climacus most likely would say: No, thank you, may I ask to be abused instead; being abused does not *essentially* harm the book, but to be praised in this way is to be annihilated, insofar as this is possible for the re-

---

[55] P. 91. See *Anxiety*, pp. 113, 128, 137, *KW* VIII (*SV* IV 382, 395, 403); *Sickness unto Death*, p. 82, *KW* XIX (*SV* XI 194).

[56] See pp. 108–09.

[57] See Preface, *Postscript, KW* XII (*SV* VII v).

[58] See Frithiof Brandt and Else Rammel, *Kierkegaard og Pengene* (Copenhagen: 1935), p. 18.

[59] Under the pseudonym 80 [Johan Frederik Hagen], *Theologisk Tidsskrift, Ny Række*, IV, 1 (vol. X), May 1846, pp. 175–82.

[60] See *Corsair Affair*, p. 50, *KW* XIII (*SV* XIII 435).

viewer, the nice, good-natured, but somewhat stupid reviewer. An author who really understands himself is better served by not being read at all, or by having five genuine readers, than by having this confusion about mediation spread abroad only all too much with the help of a good-natured reviewer, spread with the help of his own book, which was written specifically to battle against mediation.[61]

In *Postscript*, Climacus takes note of the very first review, which appeared in a German journal a year after the publication of *Fragments*.[62] He appreciates the brevity of the review, which, however, consists primarily of an abstract of the book and thereby represents it as didactic direct communication. Climacus's comments constitute the best concise interpretation of the form, content, and intent of *Fragments*:

> His report is accurate and on the whole dialectically reliable, but now comes the hitch: although the report is accurate, anyone who reads only that will receive an utterly wrong impression of the book. This mishap, of course, is not too serious, but on the other hand this is always less desirable if a book is to be discussed expressly for its distinctive character. The report is didactic, purely and simply didactic; consequently the reader will receive the impression that the pamphlet [*Fragments*] is also didactic. As I see it, this is the most mistaken impression one can have of it. The contrast of form, the teasing resistance of the imaginary construction to the content, the inventive audacity (which even invents Christianity), the only attempt made to go further (that is, further than the so-called speculative constructing), the indefatigable activity of irony, the parody of speculative thought in the entire plan, the satire in making efforts as if something *ganz Auszerordentliches und zwar Neues* [altogether extraordinary, that is, new] were to come of them, whereas what always

---

[61] See Supplement, pp. 223-24 (*Pap.* VII¹ A 158).

[62] Anonymous [Andreas Frederik Beck], *Neues Repertorium für die theologische Literatur und kirchliche Statistik* (Berlin), II, 1, April 30, 1845, pp. 44-48.

emerges is old-fashioned orthodoxy in its rightful severity—of all this the reader finds no hint in the report. And yet the book is so far from being written for non-knowers, to give them something to know, that the person I engage in conversation in this book is always knowledgeable, which seems to indicate that the book is written for people in the know, whose trouble is that they know too much. Because everyone knows the Christian truth, it has gradually become such a triviality that a primitive impression of it is acquired only with difficulty. When this is the case, the art of being able to *communicate* eventually becomes the art of being able to *take away* or to trick something away from someone. This seems strange and very ironic, and yet I believe I have succeeded in expressing exactly what I mean. When a man has filled his mouth so full of food that for this reason he cannot eat and it must end with his dying of hunger, does giving food to him consist in stuffing his mouth even more or, instead, in taking a little away so that he can eat? Similarly, when a man is very knowledgeable but his knowledge is meaningless or virtually meaningless to him, does sensible communication consist in giving him more to know, even if he loudly proclaims that this is what he needs, or does it consist, instead, in taking something away from him? When a communicator takes a portion of the copious knowledge that the very knowledgeable man knows and communicates it to him in a form that makes it strange to him, the communicator is, as it were, taking away his knowledge, at least until the knower manages to assimilate the knowledge by overcoming the resistance of the form. Suppose, now, that the trouble with the very knowledgeable person is that he is accustomed to one particular form, "that he can demonstrate the mathematical theorem if the letters read ABC but not if they read ACB"; then the changed form would indeed take his knowledge away from him, and yet this taking away is precisely communication. When an age in systematic, rote fashion has finished with the understanding of Christianity and all the attendant difficulties and jubilantly proclaims how easy it is to understand the difficulty, then, of course, one must harbor a suspicion. In other words, it is better to understand that something is so difficult that it simply cannot be understood than to understand that a difficulty is so very easy to understand; for if it is so very easy, then perhaps there is no difficulty, since a difficulty is indeed recognizable by its being difficult to understand. When in such an order of things the communication does not aim at making the difficulty even easier, the communication becomes a taking away. The difficulty is invested with a new form and thus actually made difficult. This is communication to the person who already has found the difficulty so very easy to explain. If it so happens, as the reviewer suggests, that a reader can scarcely recognize in the presented material that with which he was finished long ago, the communication will bring him to a halt—yet not in order to communicate something new to him, which would be adding to all that knowledge, but in order to take something away from him.[63]

Johannes Climacus manifests the same Socratic irony in an earlier part of *Postscript*—indeed, in the best of all centuries, with everything made easier and easier, he decides there is nothing for him to do except to make things more difficult.[64] This attitude may explain why both *Fragments* and *Postscript*, like David Hume's *A Treatise of Human Nature*, "fell dead-born from the press,"[65] only to be discovered in a later generation. The same discovery has been made of *Johannes Climacus, or De omnibus dubitandum est*, which has been judged "perhaps still the deepest interpretation of Descartes' doubt."[66]

[63] *Postscript, KW* XII (*SV* VII 233-36). For other observations on *Fragments* in *Postscript*, see especially *SV* VII 13, 27, 37, 76-77, 83, 97, 108, 171-73, 176, 178, 232, 238, 241-42, 297, 312-14, 317, 330, 499, 505, 509, 546.

[64] Ibid. (*SV* VII 155).

[65] David Hume, "The Life of David Hume, Esq. Written by Himself. My Own Life," in *An Enquiry Concerning Human Understanding* (Chicago: Open Court, 1930), p. vii.

[66] Hannah Arendt, *The Human Condition* (Chicago: University of Chicago Press, 1959), p. 275 fn.

PHILOSOPHICAL
FRAGMENTS,
OR

A FRAGMENT OF PHILOSOPHY

by Johannes Climacus
Edited by S. Kierkegaard

Can a historical point of departure be given for
an eternal consciousness; how can such a point of
departure be of more than historical interest; can
an eternal happiness be built on
historical knowledge?

Better well hanged than ill wed.
SHAKESPEARE

PREFACE[1]

What is offered here is only a pamphlet, *proprio Marte, propriis auspiciis, proprio stipendio* [by one's own hand, on one's own behalf, at one's own expense],[2] without any claim to being a part of the scientific-scholarly endeavor in which one acquires legitimacy as a thoroughfare or transition, as concluding, introducing, or participating, as a co-worker or as a volunteer attendant, as a hero or at any rate as a relative hero, or at least as an absolute trumpeter. It is merely a pamphlet and will not become anything more even if I, like Holberg's *magister*,[3] were, *volente Deo* [God willing], to continue it with seventeen others. It has as little chance of becoming something more as a writer of half-hour pieces has of writing something else even if he writes folios. The accomplishment is, however, in proportion to my talents, for I do not, like that noble Roman,[4] refrain from serving the system *merito magis quam ignavia* [from justifiable motives rather than from indolence], but I am a loafer out of indolence *ex animi sententia* [by inclination] and for good reasons. Yet I do not want to be guilty of ἀπραγμοσύνη [abstention from public activity],[5] which is a political offense in any age, but especially in a time of ferment, during which, in ancient times, it was punishable even by death. But suppose someone's intervention made him guilty of a greater crime simply by giving rise to confusion—would it not be better for him to mind his own business? It is not given to everyone to have his intellectual pursuits coincide happily with the interests of the public, so happily that it almost becomes difficult to decide to what extent he is concerned for his own good or for that of the public. Did not Archimedes sit undisturbed, contemplating his circles while Syracuse was being occupied, and was it not to the Roman soldier who murdered him that he said those beautiful words: *Nolite perturbare circulos meos* [Do not disturb my circles]?[6] But one who is not that fortunate should look for another prototype. When Corinth was threatened with a siege by Philip and all the inhabitants were busily active—one polishing his weapons, another collecting stones, a third repairing the wall—and Diogenes[7] saw all this, he hurriedly belted up his cloak and eagerly trundled his tub up and down the streets. When asked why he was doing that, he answered: I, too, am at work and roll my tub so that I will not be the one and only loafer among so many busy people. Such conduct is at least not sophistical, if Aristotle's definition of sophistry as the art of making money[8] is generally correct. Such conduct at least cannot occasion any misunderstanding, for it surely would be inconceivable for anyone to dream of regarding Diogenes as the savior and benefactor of the city. And of course it is impossible for anyone to dream of attributing world-historical importance to a pamphlet (something that I, at least, regard as the greatest danger that could threaten my undertaking) or to assume that its author is the systematic Salomon Goldkalb[9] so long awaited in our dear capital city, Copenhagen. For this to happen, the guilty person would have to be singularly stupid by nature, and, most likely, by yelling day in and day out in antistrophic antiphonies every time someone deluded him into thinking that now a new era, a new epoch, etc. was beginning, he would have so completely bellowed the sparsely bestowed *quantum satis* [sufficient amount] of common sense out of his head that he would have been transported into a state of bliss, into what could be called the howling madness of the higher lunacy, symptomatized by yelling, convulsive yelling, while the sum and substance of the yelling are these words: era, epoch, era and epoch, epoch and era, the system.[10] The state of one thus blissfully transported is irrational exaltation, since he lives not as if every day were just one of the *inter*calary days that occur only every four years but as if it were one of those that occur only once in a thousand years, while the concept, like a juggler in this carnival time,[11] has to keep doing those continual flip-flopping tricks—until the man himself flips over.[12] Heaven preserve me and my pamphlet from the meddling of such an uproarious, bustling oaf, lest he tear me out of my carefree contentedness as the author of a pamphlet, prevent a kind and well-disposed reader from unabashedly looking to see if there is anything in the pamphlet he can use, and place me in the tragic-comic predicament of having to laugh at my own ill fortune, just as the fine city of Fredericia must have laughed amid all its ill fortune when it read in the newspaper the news of a local fire: "The alarm drums sounded; the fire engines raced through the streets"—although there is but one fire engine in Fredericia and probably not much more than one street. The newspaper thus compelled one to conclude that the one fire engine, instead of driving straight to the scene of the fire, did considerable side-maneuvering on the street. But, of course, my pamphlet seems to be least reminiscent of the beating of an alarm drum, and its author is least of all inclined to sound an alarm.

But what is my opinion? . . . . . "Do not ask me about that. Next to the question of whether or not I have an opinion, nothing can be of less interest to someone else than what my opinion is. To have an opinion is to me both too much and too little; it presupposes a security and well-being in existence akin to having a wife and children in this mortal life, something not granted to a person who has to be up and about night and day and yet has no fixed income. In the world of spirit, this is my case, for I have trained myself and am training myself always to be able to dance lightly in the service of thought,[13] as far as possible to the honor of the god [14]and for my own enjoyment, renouncing domestic bliss and civic esteem, the *communio bonorum* [community of goods] and the concordance of joys that go with having an opinion. — Do I have any reward for this? Do I myself, like the person who serves at the altar, eat of what is set on the altar?[15] . . . . . That is up to me. The one I serve is good for it, as the financiers say, and good in quite another sense than the financiers understand it. If, however, anyone were to be so courteous as to assume that I have an opinion, if he were to carry his gallantry to the extreme of embracing my opinion because it is mine, I regret his courtesy, that it is extended

IV
178

to one unworthy, and his opinion, if he does not otherwise have one apart from mine. [16]I can stake my own life, I can in all earnestness trifle with my own life—not with another's. I am capable of this, the only thing I am able to do for thought, I who have no learning to offer it, "scarcely enough for the one-drachma course, to say nothing of the big fifty-drachma course" (*Cratylus*).[17] All I have is my life, which I promptly stake every time a difficulty appears. Then it is easy to dance, for the thought of death is a good dancing partner, my dancing partner. Every human being is too heavy for me, and therefore I plead, *per deos obsecro* [I swear by the gods]: Let no one invite me, for I do not dance.

J. C.

The question is asked by one who in his ignorance does not even know what provided the occasion for his questioning in this way.[2]

I

Thought-Project[3]

A.

[4]Can the truth be learned? With this question we shall begin. It was a Socratic question or became that by way of the Socratic question whether virtue can be taught—for virtue in turn was defined as insight (see *Protagoras, Gorgias, Meno, Euthydemus*).[5] Insofar as the truth is to be learned, it of course must be assumed not to be—consequently, because it is to be learned, it is sought. Here we encounter the difficulty that Socrates calls attention to in the *Meno* (80, near the end) as a "pugnacious proposition": a person cannot possibly seek what he knows, and, just as impossibly, he cannot seek what he does not know, for what he knows he cannot seek, since he knows it, and what he does not know he cannot seek, because, after all, he does not even know what he is supposed to seek.[6] Socrates thinks through the difficulty by means [of the principle] that all learning and seeking are but recollecting.[7] Thus the ignorant person merely needs to be reminded in order, by himself, to call to mind what he knows. The truth is not introduced into him but was in him. Socrates elaborates on this idea,[8] and in it the Greek pathos is in fact concentrated, since it becomes a demonstration for the im-

mortality of the soul—retrogressively, please note—or a demonstration for the pre-existence of the soul.*⁹

In view of this, it is manifest with what wonderful consistency Socrates remained true to himself and artistically exemplified what he had understood. He was and continued to be a midwife, not because he "did not have the positive,"** but because he perceived that this relation is the highest relation a human being can have to another. And in that he is indeed forever right, for even if a divine point of departure is ever given, this remains the true relation between one human being and another, if one reflects upon the absolute and does not dally with the accidental but with all one's heart renounces understanding the half-measures that seem to be the inclination of men and the secret of the system. Socrates, however, was a midwife examined by the god[13] himself. The work he carried out was a divine commission (see Plato's *Apology*),[14] even though he struck people as an eccentric (ἀτοπώτατος, *Theaetetus*, 149), and the divine intention, as Socrates also understood it, was that the god forbade him to give birth (μαιεύεσθαί με ὁ θεὸς ἀναγκάζει, γεννᾶν δὲ ἀπεκώλυσεν [the god constrains me to serve as a midwife, but

IV
181

---

* If the thought is thought absolutely—that is, so that the various states of pre-existence are not considered—this Greek idea is repeated in ancient and modern speculation:[10] an eternal creating, an eternal emanating from the Father, an eternal becoming of the deity, an eternal self-sacrifice, a past resurrection, a judgment over and done with. All these ideas are that Greek idea of recollection, although this is not always noticed, because they have been arrived at by going further. If the idea is analyzed in a tallying of the various states of pre-existence, then the eternal "pre's" of that approximating thinking are similar to the eternal "post's" of the corresponding approximation. [11]The contradiction of existence [*Tilværelse*] is explained by positing a "pre" as needed (by virtue of a prior state, the individual has arrived at his present, otherwise unexplainable state) or by positing a "post" as needed (on another planet the individual will be better situated, and in consideration of that, his present state is not unexplainable).

** As it is said in our age,[12] in which one has "the positive" more or less in the way a polytheist would make light of monotheism's negativity, because polytheism, of course, has many gods, the monotheist but one. The philosophers have many ideas—all valid up to a point. Socrates has but one, which is absolute.

has debarred me from giving birth], *Theaetetus*, 150 c), because between one human being and another μαιεύεσθαι [to
deliver] is the highest; giving birth indeed belongs to the
god.[15]

Viewed Socratically, any point of departure in time is *eo
ipso* something accidental, a vanishing point, an occasion. Nor
is the teacher anything more, and if he gives of himself and
his erudition in any other way, he does not give but takes
away. Then he is not even the other's friend, much less his
teacher. This is the profundity of Socratic thinking, this his
noble, thoroughgoing humanity, which does not exclusively
and conceitedly cultivate the company of brilliant minds but
feels just as kin to a tanner, and for that reason he soon "became convinced that the study of nature is not man's concern
and therefore began to philosophize about the ethical in
workshops and in the market-place" (Diogenes Laertius, II,
V, 21)[16] but philosophized just as absolutely with whomever
he spoke. With half-thoughts, with higgling and haggling,
with claiming and disclaiming, as if the individual to a certain degree owed something to another person but then again
to a certain degree did not, with vague words that explain
everything except what is meant by this "to a certain degree"—with all such things one does not go beyond Socrates
or reach the concept of revelation, either, but simply remains
in empty talk. In the Socratic view, every human being is
himself the midpoint, and the whole world focuses only on
him because his self-knowledge is God-knowledge.[17] Moreover, this is how Socrates understood himself, and in his
view this is how every human being must understand himself, and by virtue of that understanding he must understand
his relation to the single individual, always with equal hu-
mility and with equal pride. For that purpose, Socrates had
the courage and self-collectedness to be sufficient unto himself, but in his relations to others he also had the courage and
self-collectedness to be merely an occasion even for the most
stupid person. What rare magnanimity—rare in our day, when
the pastor is little more than the deacon, when every second
person is an authority, while all these distinctions and all this

considerable authority are mediated[18] in a common lunacy and in a *commune naufragium* [common shipwreck], because, since no human being has ever truly been an authority or has benefited anyone else by being that or has ever really managed successfully to carry his dependent along, there is better success in another way, for it never fails that one fool going his way takes several others along with him.

If this is the case with regard to learning the truth, then the fact that I have learned from Socrates or from Prodicus[19] or from a maidservant can concern me only historically or— to the extent that I am a Plato in my enthusiasm—poetically. But this enthusiasm, even though it is beautiful, even though I wish for myself and for everyone else this εὐκαταφορία εἰς πάθος [disposition to passion],[20] which only the Stoic could warn against, although I do not have the Socratic magnanimity and the Socratic self-denial to think its nothingness— this enthusiasm, Socrates would say, is still but an illusion, indeed, a muddiness of mind in which earthly distinction ferments almost grossly. Neither can the fact that the teaching of Socrates or of Prodicus was this or that have anything but historical interest for me, because the truth in which I rest was in me and emerged from me. Not even Socrates would have been capable of giving it to me, no more than the coachman is capable of pulling the horse's load, even though he may help the horse do it by means of the whip.*

My relation to Socrates and Prodicus cannot concern me with regard to my eternal happiness, for this is given retrogressively in the possession of the truth that I had from the beginning without knowing it. If I were to imagine myself meeting Socrates, Prodicus, or the maidservant in another life, there again none of them would be more than an occa-

---

* I cite one passage in *Clitophon* merely as a remark by a third party, since this dialogue is considered to be spurious. Clitophon laments that, with respect to virtue, Socrates is only encouraging (προτετραμμένος),[21] so that from the moment he has adequately recommended virtue in general, he leaves everyone on his own. Clitophon believes that this conduct must have its basis either in Socrates' not knowing more or in his not wanting to communicate more. (See para. 410.)

sion, as Socrates intrepidly expresses it by saying that even in the underworld he would only ask questions,[22] for the ultimate idea in all questioning is that the person asked must himself possess the truth and acquire it by himself. The temporal point of departure is a nothing, because in the same moment I discover that I have known the truth from eternity without knowing it, in the same instant that moment is hidden in the eternal,[23] assimilated into it in such a way that I, so to speak, still cannot find it even if I were to look for it, because there is no Here and no There, but only an *ubique et nusquam* [everywhere and nowhere].

B.

If the situation is to be different, then the moment[24] in time must have such decisive significance that for no moment will I be able to forget it, neither in time nor in eternity, because the eternal, previously nonexistent, came into existence [*blev til*][25] in that moment. With this presupposition, let us now examine the relations involved in the question: Can the truth be learned?

a. The Preceding State

We begin with the Socratic difficulty: How is one able to seek the truth, since it is indeed equally impossible whether one has it or one does not. The Socratic line of thought in effect annulled the disjunction, since it appeared that basically every human being possesses the truth. That was his explanation. We have seen what resulted with regard to the moment. Now if the moment is to acquire decisive significance, then the seeker up until that moment must not have possessed the truth, not even in the form of ignorance, for in that case the moment becomes merely the moment of occasion; indeed, he must not even be a seeker. This is the way we have to state the difficulty if we do not want to explain it Socratically. Consequently, he has to be defined as being outside the truth (not coming toward it like a proselyte, but going away from it) or as untruth. He is, then, untruth. But

how, then, is he to be reminded, or what would be the use
of reminding him of what he has not known and consequently cannot call to mind?

b. The Teacher

If the teacher is to be the occasion that reminds the learner,
he cannot assist him to recollect that he actually does know
the truth, for the learner is indeed untruth. That for which
the teacher can become the occasion of his recollecting is that
he is untruth. But by this calling to mind, the learner is definitely excluded from the truth, even more than when he was
ignorant of being untruth. Consequently, in this way, precisely by reminding him, the teacher thrusts the learner away,
except that by being turned in upon himself in this manner
the learner does not discover that he previously knew the
truth but discovers his untruth. To this act of consciousness,
the Socratic principle applies: the teacher is only an occasion,
whoever he may be, even if he is a god, because I can discover my own untruth only by myself, because only when
I discover it is it discovered,[26] not before, even though the
whole world knew it. (Under the assumed presupposition
about the moment, this becomes the one and only analogy
to the Socratic.)

Now, if the learner is to obtain the truth, the teacher must
bring it to him, but not only that. Along with it, he must
provide him with the condition for understanding it, for if
the learner were himself the condition for understanding the
truth, then he merely needs to recollect, because the condition for understanding the truth is like being able to ask about
it—the condition and the question contain the conditioned
and the answer. (If this is not the case, then the moment is
to be understood only Socratically.)

But the one who not only gives the learner the truth but
provides the condition is not a teacher. Ultimately, all instruction depends upon the presence of the condition; if it is
lacking, then a teacher is capable of nothing, because in the
second case, the teacher, before beginning to teach, must
transform, not reform, the learner. But no human being is

capable of doing this; if it is to take place, it must be done by the god himself.

Now, inasmuch as the learner exists [*er til*], he is indeed created, and, accordingly, God must have given him the condition for understanding the truth (for otherwise he previously would have been merely animal, and that teacher who gave him the condition along with the truth would make him a human being for the first time). But insofar as the moment is to have decisive significance (and if this is not assumed, then we do in fact remain with the Socratic), he must lack the condition, consequently be deprived of it. This cannot have been due to an act of the god (for this is a contradiction) or to an accident (for it is a contradiction that something inferior would be able to vanquish something superior); it must therefore have been due to himself.[27] If he could have lost the condition in such a way that it was not due to himself, and if he could be in this state of loss without its being due to himself, then he would have possessed the condition only accidentally, which is a contradiction, since the condition for the truth is an essential condition. The untruth, then, is not merely outside the truth but is polemical against the truth, which is expressed by saying that he himself has forfeited and is forfeiting the condition.

[28]The teacher, then, is the god himself, who, acting as the occasion, prompts the learner to be reminded that he is untruth and is that through his own fault. But this state—to be untruth and to be that through one's own fault—what can we call it? Let us call it *sin.*[29]

The teacher, then, is the god, who gives the condition and gives the truth. Now, what should we call such a teacher, for we surely do agree that we have gone far beyond the definition of a teacher. [30]Inasmuch as the learner is in untruth but is that by his own act (and, according to what has already been said, there is no other way he can be that), he might seem to be free, for to be on one's own certainly is freedom.[31] And yet he is indeed unfree and bound and excluded, because to be free from the truth is indeed to be excluded, and to be excluded by oneself is indeed to be bound. But since he is bound by himself, can he not work himself loose or free himself, for that which binds me should also be able to set me free at will, and since that is himself, he should certainly be able to do it. But first of all he must will it. But just suppose that he was very profoundly reminded of that for which that teacher became the occasion (and this must never be forgotten) of his recollecting—just suppose that he willed it. In that case (if by willing it he could do it by himself), his having been bound would become a bygone state, one that in the moment of liberation would vanish without a trace—and the moment would not gain decisive significance. He would be unaware that he had bound himself and now set himself free.*

---

* We shall take our time—after all, there is no need to hurry. By going slowly, one sometimes does indeed fail to reach the goal, but by going too fast, one sometimes passes it.[32] We shall discuss this somewhat in Greek fashion. If a child who has received the gift of a little money—enough to be able to buy either a good book, for example, or one toy, for both cost the same—buys the toy, can he use the same money to buy the book? By no means, for now the money has been spent. But he may go to the bookseller and ask him if he will exchange the book for the toy. Suppose the bookseller answers: My dear child, your toy is worthless; it is certainly true that when you still had the money you could have bought the book just as well as the toy, but the awkward thing about a toy is that once it is purchased it has lost all value. Would not the child think: This is very strange indeed. And so it was also once, when man could buy freedom and unfreedom for the same price, and this price was the free choice of the soul and the surrender of the choice. He chose unfreedom, but if he then were to approach the god and ask whether he could make an exchange, the answer presumably would be: Undeniably there was a time when you could have bought what you wanted, but the curious thing about unfreedom is that once it is purchased it has no value whatsoever, even though one pays the same price for it. I wonder if such a person would not say: This is very strange indeed. Or if two hostile armies faced each other, and there came a knight whom both sides invited to join; but he chose the one side, was defeated and taken prisoner. As prisoner he was brought before the conqueror and was foolish enough to offer him his services on the conditions originally offered. I wonder if the conqueror would not say to him: My dear fellow, you are my prisoner now; true enough, at one time you could have chosen differently, but now everything is changed. Would this not be strange indeed! If it were otherwise, if the moment did not have decisive significance, then the child, after all, must indeed have bought the book and merely have been ignorant

Considered in this way, the moment acquires no decisive significance, and yet this was what we wanted to assume as the hypothesis. According to the hypothesis, then, he will not be able to set himself free. (And this is truly just the way it is, for he uses the power of freedom in the service of unfreedom, since he is indeed freely in it, and in this way the combined power of unfreedom grows and makes him the slave of sin.)[35]

What, then, should we call such a teacher who gives him the condition again and along with it the truth? Let us call him a *savior*, for he does indeed save the learner from unfreedom, saves him from himself. Let us call him a *deliverer*, for he does indeed deliver the person who had imprisoned himself, and no one is so dreadfully imprisoned, and no captivity is so impossible to break out of as that in which the individual holds himself captive! And yet, even this does not say enough, for by his unfreedom he had indeed become guilty of something, and if that teacher gives him the condition and the truth, then he is, of course, a *reconciler* who takes away the wrath that lay over the incurred guilt.

A teacher such as that, the learner will never be able to forget, because in that very moment he would sink down into himself again, just as the person did who once possessed the condition and then, by forgetting that God is, sank into unfreedom. If they were to meet in another life, that teacher would again be able to give the condition to the person who had not received it,[36] but he would be quite different for the person who had once received it. After all, the condition was something entrusted, and therefore the receiver was always

---

of it, mistakenly thinking that he had bought the toy; the prisoner, after all, must have fought on the other side, but had not been seen because of the fog, and had really sided with the one whose prisoner he now imagined himself to be. —"The depraved person and the virtuous person presumably do not have power over their moral condition, but in the beginning they did have the power to become the one or the other, just as the person who throws a stone has power over it before he throws it but not when he has thrown it" (Aristotle).[33] Otherwise the throwing would become an illusion, and the person throwing, despite all his throwing, would keep the stone in his hand, since the stone, like the skeptics' "flying arrow,"[34] did not fly.

responsible for an accounting. But a teacher such as that—what should we call him? A teacher certainly can evaluate the learner with respect to whether or not he is making progress, but he cannot pass judgment on him, for he must be Socratic enough to perceive that he cannot give the learner what is essential. That teacher, then, is actually not a teacher but is a *judge.* Even when the learner has most fully put on the condition and then, by doing so, has become immersed in the truth, he still can never forget that teacher or allow him to disappear Socratically, which still is far more profound than all unseasonable punctiliousness and deluded fanaticism—indeed, it is the highest if that other is not truth.

IV
188And, now, the moment. A moment such as this is unique. To be sure, it is short and temporal, as the moment is; it is passing, as the moment is, past, as the moment is in the next moment, and yet it is decisive, and yet it is filled with the eternal. A moment such as this must have a special name. Let us call it: *the fullness of time.*[37]

c. The Follower[38]

When the learner is untruth (and otherwise we go back to the Socratic) but is nevertheless a human being, and he now receives the condition and the truth, he does not, of course, become a human being for the first time, for he already was that; but he becomes a different person, not in the jesting sense—as if he became someone else of the same quality as before—but he becomes a person of a different quality or, as we can also call it, a *new* person.

Inasmuch as he was untruth, he was continually in the process of departing from the truth; as a result of receiving the condition in the moment, his course took the opposite direction, or he was turned around. Let us call this change *conversion,* even though this is a word hitherto unused; but we choose it precisely in order to avoid confusion, for it seems to be created for the very change of which we speak.

Inasmuch as he was in untruth through his own fault, this conversion cannot take place without its being assimilated into his consciousness or without his becoming aware that it was through his own fault, and with this consciousness he takes leave of his former state. But how does one take leave without feeling sorrowful? Yet this sorrow is, of course, over his having been so long in the former state. Let us call such sorrow *repentance,* for what else is repentance,[39] which does indeed look back, but nevertheless in such a way that precisely thereby it quickens its pace toward what lies ahead![40]

Inasmuch as he was in untruth and now along with the condition receives the truth, a change takes place in him like the change from "not to be" to "to be." But this transition from "not to be" to "to be" is indeed the transition of birth. But the person who already *is* cannot be born, and yet he is born. Let us call this transition *rebirth,* by which he enters the world a second time just as at birth—an individual human being who as yet knows nothing about the world into which he is born, whether it is inhabited, whether there are other human beings in it, for presumably we can be baptized *en masse* but can never be reborn *en masse.* Just as the person who by Socratic midwifery gave birth to himself and in so doing forgot everything else in the world and in a more profound sense owed no human being anything, so also the one who is born again owes no human being anything, but owes that divine teacher everything. And just as the other one, because of himself, forgot the whole world, so he in turn, because of this teacher, must forget himself.

[41]If, then, *the moment* is to have decisive significance—and if not, we speak only Socratically, no matter what we say, even though we use many and strange words, even though in our failure to understand ourselves we suppose we have gone beyond that simple wise man who uncompromisingly distinguished between the god, man, and himself, more uncompromisingly than Minos, Aeacus, and Rhadamanthus[42] —then the break has occurred, and the person can no longer come back and will find no pleasure in recollecting what remembrance wants to bring him in recollection, and even less

will he by his own power be capable of drawing the god over to his side again.

But is what has been elaborated here thinkable? We shall not be in a hurry with the answer, for someone who because of prolonged pondering never comes up with an answer is not the only one who fails to answer—so too the one who admittedly manifests a marvelous quickness in answering but not the desirable slowness in considering the difficulty before explaining it. Before we answer, we shall ask who ought to answer the question. This matter of being born—is it thinkable? Well, why not? But who is supposed to think it—one who is born or one who is not born? The latter, of course, is unreasonable and cannot occur to anyone, for this notion certainly cannot occur to one who is born. When one who is born thinks of himself as born, he of course is thinking of this transition from "not to be" to "to be." The situation must be the same with rebirth. Or is the matter made more difficult by this—that the non-being preceding the rebirth has more being than the non-being that precedes birth? But who, then, is supposed to think this? It must, of course, be one who is reborn, for it would be unreasonable to think that one who is not reborn should do it, and would it not be ludicrous if this were to occur to one who is not reborn?

IV
190

If a person originally possesses the condition to understand the truth, he thinks that, since he himself is, God is.[4] If he is in untruth, then he must of course think this about himself, and recollection will be unable to help him to think anything but this. Whether or not he is to go any further, *the moment* must decide (although it already was active in making him perceive that he is untruth). If he does not understand this, then he is to be referred to Socrates, even though his opinion that he has gone much further will cause that wise man a great deal of trouble, as did those who became so exasperated with him when he took away some foolish notion from them (ἐπειδάν τινα λῆρον αὐτῶν ἀφαιρῶμαι) that they positively wanted to bite him (see *Theaetetus*, 151).[44] —In *the moment, a person becomes aware that he was born*, for his previous state, to which he is not to appeal, was indeed one of "not to be." In *the moment*, he becomes aware of the rebirth, for his previous state was indeed one of "not to be." If his previous state had been one of "to be," then under no circumstances would the moment have acquired decisive significance for him, as explained above. [45]Whereas the Greek pathos focuses on recollection, the pathos of our project focuses on the moment, and no wonder, for is it not an exceedingly pathos-filled matter to come into existence from the state of "not to be"?

[46]This, as you see, is my project! But perhaps someone will say, "This is the most ludicrous of all projects, or, rather, you are the most ludicrous of all project-cranks, for even if someone comes up with a foolish scheme, there is always at least the truth that he is the one who came up with the scheme. But you, on the other hand, are behaving like a vagabond who charges a fee for showing an area that everyone can see. You are like the man who in the afternoon exhibited for a fee a ram that in the forenoon anyone could see free of charge, grazing in the open pasture." —"Maybe so. I hide my face in shame. But, supposing that I am that ludicrous, then let me put things right again with a new project. Admittedly, gunpowder was invented centuries ago; so it would be ludicrous of me to pretend that I had invented it. But would it also be ludicrous for me to assume that someone had invented it? Now I am going to be so courteous as to assume that you are the one who has invented my project—more courtesy you cannot expect. Or, if you deny this, will you then also deny that someone has invented it, that is, some human being? In that case, I am just as close to having invented it as any other person. Therefore you are not angry with me because I falsely attribute to myself something that belongs to another human being, but you are angry with me because I falsely attribute to myself something that belongs

to no human being, and you are just as angry when I mendaciously want to attribute the invention to you. Is it not curious that something like this exists, about which everyone who knows it also knows that he has not invented it, and that this 'Go to the next house'[47] does not halt and cannot be halted, even though one were to go to everybody? Yet this oddity enthralls me exceedingly, for it tests the correctness of the hypothesis and demonstrates it. It would indeed be unreasonable to require a person to find out all by himself that he does not exist. But this transition is precisely the transition of the rebirth from not existing [at være til] to existing. Whether he understands it later certainly makes no difference, for simply because someone knows how to use gunpowder, knows how to analyze it into its components, does not mean that he invented it. So go ahead and be angry with me and with any other human being who pretends to have invented it, but you do not for that reason need to be angry with the idea."

II

The God as Teacher and Savior.
(A Poetical Venture)[1]

Let us briefly consider Socrates,[2] who was indeed also a teacher. He was born in a specific situation, was educated among his own people; and when at a more mature age he felt a call and a prompting, he began to teach others in his own way. Having lived for some time as Socrates, he presented himself when the time seemed suitable as the teacher Socrates. Himself influenced by circumstances, he in turn exerted an influence upon them. In accomplishing his task, he satisfied the claims within himself just as much as he satisfied the claims other people might have on him. Understood in this way—and this was indeed the Socratic understanding— the teacher stands in a reciprocal relation, inasmuch as life and its situations are the occasion for him to become a teacher and he in turn the occasion for others to learn something. His relation, therefore, is at all times marked by autopathy just as much as by sympathy.[3] This was also the way Socrates understood it, and therefore he refused to accept honor or honorific appointments or money for his teaching, because he formed his judgments with the unbribability of one who is dead. What rare contentment—how rare today, when no amount of money can be large enough and no laurels splendid enough to be sufficient reward for the gloriousness of teaching, but all the world's gold and honors are the express reward for teaching, since they are equal in value. But our age, after all, has the positive and is a connoisseur of it, whereas Socrates lacked the positive.[4] But notice whether this lack explains his narrowness, which presumably was grounded in his being zealous for what is human and in his disciplining of himself with the same divine jealousy[5] with which he disciplined others and in which he loved the divine. Between one human being and another, this is the highest: the pupil is the occasion for the teacher to understand himself; the teacher is the occasion for the pupil to understand himself; in death the teacher leaves no claim upon the pupil's soul, no more than the pupil can claim that the teacher owes him something. And if I were a Plato in my infatuation, and if while hearing Socrates my heart pounded as violently as Alcibiades',[6] more violently than the Corybantes',[7] and if the passion of my admiration could not be appeased without embracing that glorious man, then Socrates would no doubt smile at me and say, "My dear fellow, you certainly are a deceitful lover, for you want to idolize me because of my wisdom, and then you yourself want to be the one person who understands me best and the one from whose admiring embrace I would be unable to tear away—are you not really a seducer?" And if I refused to understand him, his cold irony[8] would presumably bring me to despair as he explained that he owed me just as much as I owed him. What rare integrity, cheating no one, not even the person who in being cheated would stake his eternal happiness. How rare in this age, in which everyone goes further than Socrates, both in assessing one's own value and in benefiting the pupil, as well as in socializing soulfully and in finding voluptuous pleasure in the hot compress of admiration! What rare loyalty, seducing no one, not even the one who employs all the arts of seduction to be seduced![9]

But the god needs no pupil in order to understand himself, and no occasion can act upon him in such a way that there is just as much in the occasion as in the resolution. What, then, moves him to make his appearance? [10]He must move himself and continue to be what Aristotle says of him, ἀκίνητος πάντα κινεῖ [unmoved, he moves all].[11] But if he moves himself, then there of course is no need that moves him, as if he himself could not endure silence but was compelled to burst into speech. But if he moves himself and is not moved by need, what moves him then but love, for love does not have the satisfaction of need outside itself but within. His

love = basis for God's movement, goal of his mvmt.

resolution, which does not have an equal reciprocal relation to the occasion, must be from eternity, even though, fulfilled in time, it expressly becomes ~~the moment, for where the oc-casion and what is occasioned correspond equally, as equally~~ as the reply to the shout in the desert, the moment does not appear but is swallowed by recollection into its eternity. The moment emerges precisely in the relation of the eternal resolution to the unequal occasion. If this is not the case, then we return to the Socratic and do not have the god or the eternal resolution or the moment.

IV
194

Out of love, therefore, the god must be eternally resolved in this way, but just as his love is the basis, so also must love be the goal, for it would indeed be a contradiction for the god to have a basis of movement and a goal that do not correspond to this. The love, then, must be for the learner and the goal must be to win him, for only in love is the different made equal, and only in equality or in unity is there understanding. Without perfect understanding, the teacher is not the god, unless the basic reason is to be sought in the learner, who rejected what was made possible for him.

Yet ~~this love is~~ basically unhappy, for they are very unequal, and what seems so easy—namely, that the god must be able to make himself understood—is not so easy if he is not to destroy that which is different.

We shall not be in a hurry, and even though some may think that we are wasting time instead of arriving at a decision, our consolation is that it still does not therefore follow that our efforts are wasted. —There has been much talk in the world about unhappy love, and everyone knows what the term means: that the lovers are unable to have each other. And the reasons—well, there can be a host of them. There is another kind of unhappy love: the love of which we speak, to which there is no perfect earthly analogy but which we nevertheless, by speaking loosely for a while, can imagine in an earthly setting. The unhappiness is the result not of the lovers' being unable to have each other but of their being unable to understand each other. And this sorrow is indeed infinitely deeper than the sorrow of which people speak, for

Shaped by experience

this unhappiness aims at the heart of love and wounds for eternity, unlike that other unhappiness, which affects only the external and temporal and which for the high-minded is only something of a jest about the lovers' not getting each other in time. This infinitely deeper sorrow is identified essentially with the superior person, for he alone also understands the misunderstanding. It is identified essentially only with the god, because no human situation can provide a valid analogy, even though we shall suggest one here in order to awaken the mind to an understanding of the divine.

IV
195
Suppose there was a king who loved a maiden of lowly station in life—but the reader may already have lost patience when he hears that our analogy begins like a fairy tale and is not at all systematic. Well, presumably the erudite Polos found it boring that Socrates continually talked about food and drink and physicians and all such silly things Polos never talked about (see *Gorgias*).[12] But did not Socrates still have one advantage, that he himself and everyone else had the prerequisite knowledge from childhood on? And would it not be desirable for me to be able to stick to food and drink (something far beyond my capability) and to have no need to draw in kings, whose thoughts, provided they are kingly, are not always like everybody else's? Is it not, however, excusable for me, who am only a poet who, mindful of Themistocles' beautiful expression, wants to unroll the tapestry of discourse lest the work on it be concealed by being rolled up.[13]

Suppose, then, that there was a king who loved a maiden of lowly station in life. The king's heart was unstained by the wisdom (loudly enough proclaimed) unacquainted with the difficulties that the understanding uncovers in order to trap the heart and that give the poets enough to do and make their magic formulas necessary. His resolution was easy to carry out, for every politician feared his wrath and dared not even to hint at anything. Every foreign country trembled before his power and dared not to refrain from sending a congratulatory delegation to the wedding. And no cringing courtier, groveling before him, dared to hurt his feelings lest his own head be crushed. So let the harp be tuned; let the poets' songs begin; let all be festive while erotic love [*Elskov*] celebrates its triumph, for erotic love is jubilant[14] when it unites equal and equal and is triumphant when it makes equal in erotic love that which was unequal.

Then a concern awakened in the king's soul. Who but a king who thinks royally would dream of such a thing! He did not speak to anyone about his concern, for if he had done so, any one of his courtiers would presumably have said, "Your Majesty, you are doing the girl a favor for which she can never in her lifetime thank you adequately." No doubt the courtier would arouse the king's wrath, so that the king would have him executed for high treason against his beloved, and thereby would cause the king another kind of sorrow. Alone he grappled with the sorrow in his heart: whether the girl would be made happy by this, whether she would acquire the bold confidence never to remember what the king only wished to forget—that he was the king and she had been a lowly maiden. For if this happened, if this recollection awakened and at times, like a favored rival, took her mind away from the king, lured it into the inclosing reserve [*Indesluttethed*] of secret sorrow, or if at times it walked past her soul as death walks across the grave—what would be the gloriousness of erotic love then! Then she would indeed have been happier if she had remained in obscurity, loved by one in a position of equality, contented in the humble hut, but boldly confident in her love [*Kjærlighed*] and cheerful early and late. What a rich overabundance of sorrow stands here as if ripe, almost bending under the weight of its fertility, only awaiting the time of harvest when the thought of the king will thresh all the seeds of concern out of it. For even if the girl were satisfied to become nothing, that could not satisfy the king, simply because he loved her and because it would be far harder for him to be her benefactor than to lose her. And what if she could not even understand him— for if we are going to speak loosely about the human, we may well assume an intellectual difference that makes understanding impossible. What a depth of sorrow slumbers in

IV
196

this unhappy erotic love! Who dares to arouse it! Yet a human being will not suffer this, for we shall refer him to Socrates or to that which in a still more beautiful sense is capable of making unequals equal.

Now if *the moment* is to have decisive significance (and without this we return to the Socratic, even though we think we are going further), the learner is in untruth, indeed, is there through his own fault—and yet he is the object of the god's love [*Kjærlighed*]. The god wants to be his teacher, and the god's concern is to bring about equality. If this cannot be brought about, the love becomes unhappy and the instruction meaningless, for they are unable to understand each other. We probably think that this may be a matter of indifference to the god, since he does not need the learner, but we forget—or rather, alas, we demonstrate—how far we are from understanding him; we forget that he does indeed love the learner. And just as that royal sorrow is found only in a royal soul and most human languages do not name it at all, likewise all human language is so self-loving that it has no intimation of such a sorrow. But the god has kept it to himself, this unfathomable sorrow, because he knows that he can push the learner away, can do without him, that the learner has incurred utter loss through his own fault, that he can let him sink, and he knows how nearly impossible it is to maintain the learner's bold confidence, without which understanding and equality disappear and the love is unhappy. Anyone who does not have at least an intimation of this sorrow is a lumpish soul with as much character as a small coin bearing the image neither of Caesar nor of God.[15]

Thus the task is assigned, and we invite the poet—that is, if he has not already been invited somewhere else, and if he is not the kind of person who, along with the flutists and other noisemakers, has to be driven out of the house of sorrow if joy is to enter at all.[16] The poet's task is to find a solution, a point of unity where there is in truth love's understanding, where the god's concern has overcome its pain, for this is the unfathomable love that is not satisfied with what the object of love might foolishly consider himself blissfully happy to have.

A. The unity is brought about by an ascent. The god would then draw the learner up toward himself, exalt him, divert him with joy lasting a thousand years (for to him a thousand years are as one day),[17] let the learner forget the misunderstanding in his tumult of joy. Yes, the learner would perhaps be very much inclined to consider himself blissfully happy because of this. And would it not be glorious suddenly to score a great success because the god's eye fell upon him, just as it would be for that lowly maiden; would it not be glorious to be of assistance to him in taking the whole thing in vain, deceived by his own heart! That noble king, however, already saw through the difficulty; he was something of a connoisseur of human nature and saw that the girl would be essentially deceived—and one is most terribly deceived when one does not even suspect it but remains as if spellbound by a change of costume.

The unity could be brought about by the god's appearing to the learner, accepting his adoration, and thereby making him forget himself. Likewise, the king could have appeared before the lowly maiden in all his splendor, could have let the sun of his glory rise over her hut, shine on the spot where he appeared to her, and let her forget herself in adoring admiration. This perhaps would have satisfied the girl, but it could not satisfy the king, for he did not want his own glorification but the girl's, and his sorrow would be very grievous because she would not understand him; but for him it would be still more grievous to deceive her. In his own eyes, just to express his love incompletely would be a deception, even if no one understood him, even if reproach sought to vex his soul. *Prob. of Evil?*

In taking this path, then, love does not become happy—well, perhaps the learner's and the maiden's love would seem to be happy, but not the teacher's and the king's, whom no delusion can satisfy. The god does have joy in adorning the lily more gloriously than Solomon,[18] but if understanding

Must humiliate
lowly state

IV
198

were at all plausible here, it certainly would be a tragic delusion on the part of the lily if, in observing the costume, it
considered itself to be the beloved because of the costume.
Instead of standing cheerful in the meadow, playing with the
wind, carefree as the breeze, it presumably would droop and
not have the bold confidence to lift up its head. This was
indeed the god's concern, for the shoot of the lily is tender
and easily snapped. But if the moment is to have decisive
significance, how unutterable his concern becomes! There was
a people who had a good understanding of the divine; this
people believed that to see the god was death.[19] —Who grasps
the contradiction of this sorrow: not to disclose itself is the
death of love; to disclose itself is the death of the beloved.
The human mind so often aspires to might and power, and
in its constant preoccupation with this thought, as if achiev-
ing it would transfigure everything, it does not suspect that
there is not only joy in heaven[20] but sorrow also: how grievous it is to have to deny the learner that to which he aspires
with his whole soul and to have to deny it precisely because
he is the beloved.

Jews (margin)

The teacher has sorrow (margin)

B. Therefore, the unity must be brought about in some other
way. Here we are once again mindful of Socrates, for what
else was his ignorance but the unitive expression of love for
the learner? But, as we have seen, this unity was also the
truth. If, however, *the moment* is to have decisive significance
(—),[21] then this is certainly not the truth, for the learner owes
the teacher everything. Just as the teacher's love, Socratically
understood, would be only a deceiver's love if he let the
pupil go on thinking that he actually owed him something,
whereas the teacher was supposed to assist him to become
sufficient unto himself, so the god's love—if he wants to be
a teacher—must be not only an assisting love but also a procreative love by which he gives birth to the learner, or, as
we have called him, one born again, meaning the transition
from "not to be" to "to be."[22] The truth, then, is that the
learner owes him everything. But that which makes understanding so difficult is precisely this: that he becomes nothing

and yet is not annihilated; that he owes him everything and yet becomes boldly confident; that he understands the truth, but the truth makes him free;[23] that he grasps the guilt of untruth, and then again bold confidence triumphs in the truth. Between one human being and another, to be of assistance is supreme, but to beget is reserved for the god, whose love is *procreative,* but not that procreative love of which Socrates knew how to speak so beautifully on a festive occasion. Such a love does not mark the relation of the teacher to the pupil but the relation of the autodidact to the beautiful as he, ignoring dispersed beauty, envisions beauty-in-and-by-itself and now gives birth to many beautiful and glorious discourses and thoughts, πολλοὺς καὶ καλοὺς λόγους καὶ μεγαλοπρεπεῖς τίκτει καὶ διανοήματα ἐν φιλοσοφίᾳ ἀφθόνῳ [he will find the seed of the most fruitful discourse and the loftiest thought and reap a golden harvest of philosophy] (*Symposium,* 210 d); and of this it holds true that he delivers and brings forth that which he had already borne within himself for a long time (209 c).[24] He has the condition, therefore, within himself, and the bringing forth (the birth) is only an appearing of what was present, and that is why here again in this birth the moment is instantly swallowed by recollection. It is clear that the person who is born by dying away more and more can less and less be said to be born, since he is only reminded more and more clearly that he exists, and the person who in turn gives birth to expressions of the beautiful does not give them birth but allows the beautiful within him to give them birth by itself.

If, then, the unity could not be brought about by an ascent, then it must be attempted by a descent. Let the learner be X, and this X must also include the lowliest, for if even Socrates did not keep company solely with brilliant minds, how then could the god make distinctions! In order for unity to be effected, the god must become like this one. He will appear, therefore, as the equal of the lowliest of persons. But the lowliest of all is one who must serve others—consequently the god will appear in the form of a *servant.* But this form of a servant is not something put on like the king's

Jesus

IV
200

(margin note, handwritten) Jesus is a man

plebian cloak, which just by flapping open would betray the king; it is not something put on like the light Socratic summer cloak,[25] which, although woven from nothing, yet is concealing and revealing—but it is his true form. For this is the boundlessness of love, that in earnestness and truth and not in jest it wills to be the equal of the beloved, and it is the omnipotence of resolving love to be capable of that of which neither the king nor Socrates was capable, which is why their assumed characters were still a kind of deceit.

Look, there he stands—the god. Where? There. Can you not see him? He is the god, and yet he has no place where he can lay his head,[26] and he does not dare to turn to any person lest that person be offended at him. He is the god, and yet he walks more circumspectly than if angels were carrying him[27] —not to keep him from stumbling, but so that he may not tread in the dust the people who are offended at him. He is the god, and yet his eyes rest with concern on the human race,[28] for the individual's tender shoot can be crushed, as readily as a blade of grass. Such a life—sheer love and sheer sorrow. To want to express the unity of love and then not to be understood, to be obliged to fear for everyone's perdition and yet in this way truly to be able to save only one single person—sheer sorrow, while his days and hours are filled with the sorrow of the learner who entrusts himself to him. Thus does the god stand upon the earth, like unto the lowliest through his omnipotent love. He knows that the learner is untruth—what if he made a mistake, what if he became weary and lost his bold confidence! Oh, to sustain heaven and earth by an omnipotent "Let there be," and then, if this were to be absent for one fraction of a second, to have everything collapse—how easy this would be compared with bearing the possibility of the offense of the human race when out of love one became its savior!
But the form of the servant was not something put on.[29] Therefore the god must suffer all things, endure all things, be tried in all things, hunger in the desert,[30] thirst in his agonies, be forsaken in death,[31] absolutely the equal of the

lowliest of human beings—look, behold the man![32] The suffering of death is not his suffering, but his whole life is a
story of suffering, and it is love that suffers, love that gives
all and is itself destitute. What wonderful self-denial to ask
in concern, even though the learner is the lowliest of persons:
Do you really love me? For he himself knows where the
danger threatens, and yet he knows that for him any easier
way would be a deception, even though the learner would
not understand it.

For love, any other revelation would be a deception, because either it would first have had to accomplish a change
in the learner (love, however, does not change the beloved
but changes itself) and conceal from him that this was needed,
or in superficiality it would have had to remain ignorant that
the whole understanding between them was a delusion (this
is the untruth of paganism). For the god's love, any other
revelation would be a deception. Though my eyes were more
flooded with tears than a repentant prostitute's,[33] and though
each and every tear of mine were more precious than the
copious tears of a pardoned prostitute, and though I could
find a more humble place than at his feet and though I could
sit there more humbly than a woman whose heart's only
choice was this one thing needful,[34] and though I loved him
more sincerely than the faithful servant who loves him to his
last drop of blood, and though I were more comely in his
eyes than the purest of women—nevertheless, if I pleaded
with him to change his resolution, to manifest himself in
some other way, to spare himself, then he would look at me
and say: Man, what have you to do with me;[35] go away, for
you are of Satan,[36] even if you yourself do not understand
it! Or, if he just once stretched out his hand to bid it happen,
and if I were to think that I understood him better or loved
him more, I would then very likely see him weep also for
me and hear him say: To think that you could become so
unfaithful to me and grieve love in this way; so you love
only the omnipotent one who performs miracles, not him
who humbled himself in equality with you.

[37]But the form of the servant was not something put on,

IV
201

and therefore he must expire in death and in turn leave the earth. Though my sorrow were deeper than the mother's sorrow when the sword pierces her heart,[38] and though my situation were more terrible than the believer's when the power of faith fails, and though my misery were more moving than that of the person who crucifies his hope and retains only the cross—nevertheless, if I pleaded with him to spare himself and remain, I no doubt would see him grieved unto death,[39] but grieved also for me, because this suffering must be for my benefit; but his sorrow would also be the sorrow that I could not understand him. O bitter cup[40] —more bitter than wormwood is the ignominy of death for a mortal—how must it be, then, for the immortal one! O sour thirst-quencher, more sour than vinegar[41] —to be refreshed by the beloved's misunderstanding! O consolation in distress to suffer as one guilty—what must it be, then, to suffer as one who is innocent!

Thus speaks the poet—for how could it occur to him that the god would reveal himself in such a way as to bring about the most terrible decision?[42] How could it occur to him to play light-mindedly with the god's pain, falsely to poeticize[43] the love away in order to poeticize the wrath in?

And the learner—has he no share or part in this story of suffering, even though his lot is not that of the teacher? Yet it has to be this way, and it is love that gives rise to all this suffering, precisely because the god is not zealous for himself but in love wants to be the equal of the most lowly of the lowly. When an oak nut is planted in a clay pot, the pot breaks; when new wine is poured into old leather bottles,[44] they burst. What happens, then, when the god plants himself in the frailty of a human being if he does not become a new person and a new vessel! But this becoming—how difficult it really is, and how like a difficult birth! And the situation of the understanding—in its frailty, how close it is at every moment to the border of misunderstanding when the anxieties of guilt disturb the peace of love. And the situation of understanding—how terrifying, for it is indeed less terrifying to fall upon one's face while the mountains tremble at the god's voice⁴⁵ than to sit with him as his equal, and yet the god's concern is precisely to sit this way.

⁴⁶Now if someone were to say, "What you are composing is the shabbiest plagiarism ever to appear, since it is nothing more or less than what any child knows," then I presumably must hear with shame that I am a liar. But why the shabbiest? After all, every poet who steals, steals from another poet, and thus we are all equally shabby; indeed, my stealing is perhaps less harmful since it is more easily discovered. But who then is the poet? If I were so polite as to regard you, who pass judgment on me, to be the poet, you perhaps would become angry again. If there is no poet when there nevertheless is a poem—this would be curious, indeed, as curious as hearing flute playing although there is no flute player.⁴⁷ Or is this poem perhaps like a proverb, of which no author is known because it seems as if all humanity had composed it. And was this perhaps why you called my plagiarism the shabbiest ever, because I did not steal from any one person but robbed the human race and, although I am just a single human being—indeed, even a shabby thief—arrogantly pretended to be the whole human race? If that is the case, then if I went around to every single human being and everyone certainly knew about it but everyone also knew that he had not composed it, am I to draw the conclusion that consequently the human race composed it? Would this not be odd? For if the whole human race had composed it, this might very well be expressed by saying that each and every person was equally close to having composed it. Do you not think we have run into some difficulty here, although initially the entire matter seemed to be decided so easily with your short, angry statement that my poem was the shabbiest plagiarism and with my shame in having to hear it. So perhaps it is not a poem at all, or in any case is not ascribable to any human being or to the human race, either. And I do understand you. You called my conduct the shabbiest plagiarism, because I did not steal from any single person, did not rob the human

IV
203

race, but robbed the deity or, so to speak, kidnapped him and, although I am only a single human being—indeed, even a shabby thief—blasphemously pretended to be the god. Now, my dear fellow, I quite understand you and understand that your anger is justified. But then my soul is also gripped with new amazement—indeed, it is filled with adoration, for it certainly would have been odd if it had been a human poem. Presumably it could occur to a human being to poetize himself in the likeness of the god or the god in the likeness of himself, but not to poetize that the god poetized himself in the likeness of a human being,[48] for if the god gave no indication, how could it occur to a man that the blessed god could need him? This would indeed be the worst of thoughts or, rather, so bad a thought that it could not arise in him, even though, when the god has confided it to him, he adoringly says: This thought did not arise in my heart[49] —and finds it to be the most wondrously beautiful thought. Is not the whole thing wondrous, does not this word come to my lips as a felicitously foreshadowing word, for do we not, as I in fact said and you yourself involuntarily say, stand here before *the wonder* [*Vidunderet*]. And since we both are now standing before this wonder, whose solemn silence cannot be disturbed by human wrangling about what is mine and what is yours, whose awe-inspiring words infinitely drown out human quarreling about mine and thine, forgive me my curious mistaken notion of having composed it myself. It was a mistaken notion, and the poem was so different from every human poem that it was no poem at all but *the wonder.*

IV
204

III

The Absolute Paradox[1]
(A Metaphysical Caprice)

Although Socrates did his very best to gain knowledge of human nature and to know himself—yes, even though he has been eulogized for centuries as the person who certainly knew man best—he nevertheless admitted that the reason he was disinclined to ponder the nature of such creatures as Pegasus and the Gorgons was that he still was not quite clear about himself, whether he (a connoisseur of human nature) was a more curious monster than Typhon or a friendlier and simpler being, by nature sharing something divine (see *Phaedrus*, 229 e).[2] This seems to be a paradox. But one must not think ill of the paradox, for the paradox is the passion of thought, and the thinker without the paradox[3] is like the lover without passion: a mediocre fellow. But the ultimate potentiation of every passion is always to will its own downfall, and so it is also the ultimate passion of the understanding [*Forstand*] to will the collision, although in one way or another the collision must become its downfall. This, then, is the ultimate paradox of thought: to want to discover something that thought itself cannot think. This passion of thought is fundamentally present everywhere in thought, also in the single individual's thought insofar as he, thinking, is not merely himself. But because of habit we do not discover this. Similarly, the human act of walking, so the natural scientists inform us, is a continuous falling,[4] but a good steady citizen who walks to his office mornings and home at midday probably considers this an exaggeration, because his progress, after all, is a matter of mediation[5] —how could it occur to him that he is continually falling, he who unswervingly follows his nose.

But in order to get started, let us state a bold proposition: let us assume that we know what a human being is.* In this we do indeed have the criterion of truth,[8] which all Greek philosophy *sought*, or *doubted*, or *postulated*, or *brought to fruition*. And is it not noteworthy that the Greeks were like this? Is this not, so to speak, a brief summary of the meaning of the Greek mentality, an epigram it has written about itself and by which it is better served than by the sometimes prolix works written about it? Thus the proposition is worth assuming, and for another reason as well, since we have already explained it in the two previous chapters, whereas anyone desiring to give an explanation of Socrates different from ours must see to it that he does not fall into the snares of the earlier or later Greek skepticism. If the Socratic theory of recollection and of every human being as universal man is not maintained, then Sextus Empiricus stands there ready to make the transition implied in "to learn" not merely difficult but impossible,[9] and Protagoras begins where he left off, with everything as the measure of man,[10] in the sense that he is the measure for others, but by no means in the Socratic sense that the single individual is for himself the measure, no more and no less.

We know, then, what man is, and this wisdom, the worth of which I, least of all, will denigrate, can continually become richer and more meaningful, and hence the truth also. But then the understanding stands still, as did Socrates,[11] for now the understanding's paradoxical passion that wills the collision awakens and, without really understanding itself,

IV
206

---

* Perhaps it seems ludicrous to want to give this thesis the form of doubt by "assuming" it, for, after all, in our theocentric age[6] everyone knows such things. Would that it were so! Democritus also knew it, for he defines man thus: "Man is what we all know," and continues, "for we all know what a dog, a horse, a plant, etc. are, but a human being is none of these."[7] We shall not be as malicious as Sextus Empiricus, nor are we as witty, for he, as we know, quite correctly concluded from this that man is a dog, for man is what we all know, and we all know what a dog is, *ergo*—. We shall not be as malicious, but I still wonder if in our age the matter has been clarified in such a way that it does not need to feel a bit uneasy about itself at the thought of poor Socrates and his awkward position.

IV
206

wills its own downfall. It is the same with the paradox of erotic love. A person lives undisturbed in himself, and then awakens the paradox of self-love as love for another, for one missing. (Self-love is the ground or goes to the ground[12] in all love, which is why any religion of love [*Kjærlighed*] we might conceive would presuppose, just as epigrammatically as truly, one condition only and assume it as given: to love oneself in order to command loving the neighbor as oneself.)[13] Just as the lover is changed by this paradox of love so that he almost does not recognize himself any more (the poets, the spokesmen of erotic love, testify to this, as do the lovers themselves, since they allow the poets to take only the words from them, not their state),[14] so also that intimated paradox of the understanding reacts upon a person and upon his self-knowledge in such a way that he who believed that he knew himself now no longer is sure whether he perhaps is a more curiously complex animal than Typhon or whether he has in his being a gentler and diviner part (σκοπῶ οὐ ταῦτα, ἀλλ' ἐμαυτόν, εἴτε τι θηρίον ὂν τυγχάνω Τυφῶνος πολυπλοκώτερον καὶ μᾶλλον ἐπιτεθυμμένον, εἴτε ἡμερώτερόν τε καὶ ἀπλούστερον ζῷον, θείας τινὸς καὶ ἀτύφου μοίρας φύσει μετέχον. *Phaedrus* 230 a).[15]

But what is this unknown against which the understanding in its paradoxical passion collides and which even disturbs man and his self-knowledge? It is the unknown. But it is not a human being, insofar as he knows man, or anything else that he knows. Therefore, let us call this unknown *the god*. It is only a name we give to it. It hardly occurs to the understanding to want to demonstrate that this unknown (the god) exists. If, namely, the god does not exist, then of course it is impossible to demonstrate it. But if he does exist, then it is foolishness to want to demonstrate it, since I, in the very moment the demonstration commences, would presuppose it not as doubtful—which a presupposition cannot be, inasmuch as it is a presupposition—but as decided, because otherwise I would not begin, easily perceiving that the whole thing would be impossible if he did not exist. If, however, I interpret the expression "to demonstrate the existence

IV
207

[*Tilværelse*] of the god" to mean that I want to demonstrate
that the unknown, which exists, is the god, then I do not
express myself very felicitously, for then I demonstrate nothing, least of all an existence, but I develop the definition of
a concept. It is generally a difficult matter to want to demonstrate that something exists—worse still, for the brave souls
who venture to do it, the difficulty is of such a kind that
fame by no means awaits those who are preoccupied with it.
The whole process of demonstration continually becomes
something entirely different, becomes an expanded concluding development of what I conclude from having presupposed that the object of investigation exists. [16]Therefore,
whether I am moving in the world of sensate palpability or
in the world of thought, I never reason in conclusion to existence, but I reason in conclusion from existence. For example, I do not demonstrate that a stone exists but that
something which exists is a stone. The court of law does not
demonstrate that a criminal exists but that the accused, who
does indeed exist, is a criminal. Whether one wants to call
existence an *accessorium* [addition][17] or the eternal *prius* [pre-
supposition], it can never be demonstrated. We shall take our
time; after all, there is no reason for us to rush as there is for
those who, out of concern for themselves, or for the god, or
for something else, must rush to get proof that something
exists. In that case, there is good reason to make haste, especially if the one involved has in all honesty made an accounting of the danger that he himself or the object being
investigated does not exist until he proves it and does not
dishonestly harbor the secret thought that essentially it exists
whether he demonstrates it or not.

[18]If one wanted to demonstrate Napoleon's existence from
Napoleon's works, would it not be most curious, since his
existence certainly explains the works but the works do not
demonstrate *his* existence unless I have already in advance
interpreted the word "his" in such a way as to have assumed
that he exists. But Napoleon is only an individual, and to
that extent there is no absolute relation between him and his
works—thus someone else could have done the same works.

Perhaps that is why I cannot reason from the works to ex-istence. If I call the works Napoleon's works, then the demonstration is superfluous, since I have already mentioned his name. If I ignore this, I can never demonstrate from the works that they are Napoleon's but demonstrate (purely ideally) that such works are the works of a great general etc. However, between the god and his works there is an absolute relation. God is not a name but a concept,* and perhaps because of that his *essentia involvit existentiam* [essence involves existence].*[20]

---

* For example, Spinoza, who, by immersing himself in the concept of God, aims to bring being [*Væren*] out of it by means of thought, but, please note, not as an accidental quality but as a qualification of essence. This is the profundity in Spinoza, but let us see how he does it. In *Principia philosophiae Cartesianae, Pars I, Propositio VII, Lemma I,* he says, "quo res sua natura perfectior est, eo majorem existentiam et magis necessariam involvit; et contra, quo magis necessarium existentiam res sua natura involvit, eo perfectior [in proportion as a thing is by its own nature more perfect, it entails a greater and more necessary existence; and, conversely, in proportion as a thing entails by its own nature a more necessary existence, the more perfect it is]."[21] Consequently, the more perfect, the more being; the more being, the more perfect. This, however, is a tautology. This becomes even clearer in a note, *nota II:* "quod hîc non loquimur de pulchritudine et aliis perfectionibus, quas homines ex superstitione et ignorantia perfectiones vocare voluerunt. Sed per perfectionem intelligo tantum realitatem sive esse [we do not speak here of beauty and the other perfections which men have wanted, through superstition and ignorance, to call perfections. By perfection I mean precisely reality or being]."[22] He explains *perfectio* by *realitas, esse* [perfection . . . reality, being]. Consequently, the more perfect the thing is, the more it *is;* but its perfection is that it has more *esse* in itself, which means that the more it is, the more it is. —So much for the tautology. But to go on, what is lacking here is a distinction between factual being and ideal being.[23] The intrinsically unclear use of language—speaking of more or less being, consequently of degrees of being—becomes even more confusing when that distinction is not made, when, to put it another way, Spinoza does indeed speak profoundly but does not first ask about the difficulty. With regard to factual being, to speak of more or less being is meaningless. A fly, when it is, has just as much being as the god; with regard to factual being, the stupid comment I write here has just as much being as Spinoza's profundity, for the Hamlet dialectic, to be or not to be,[24] applies to factual being. Factual being is indifferent to the differentiation of all essence-determinants, and everything that exists participates without petty

IV
209

[26]God's works, therefore, only the god can do. Quite correct. But, then, what are the god's works? The works from which I want to demonstrate his existence do not immediately and directly exist, not at all. Or are the wisdom in nature and the goodness or wisdom in Governance right in front of our noses? Do we not encounter the most terrible spiritual trials here, and is it ever possible to be finished with all these trials? But I still do not demonstrate God's existence from such an order of things, and even if I began, I would never finish and also would be obliged continually to live *in suspenso* lest something so terrible happen that my fragment of demonstration would be ruined. Therefore, from what

IV
210

works do I demonstrate it? From the works regarded ideally—that is, as they do not appear directly and immediately. But then I do not demonstrate it from the works, after all, but only develop the ideality I have presupposed; trusting in that,[27] I even dare to defy all objections, even those that have not yet arisen. By beginning, then, I have presupposed the ideality, have presupposed that I will succeed in accomplishing it, but what else is that but presupposing that the god exists and actually beginning with trust in him.

And how does the existence of the god emerge from the demonstration? Does it happen straightway? Is it not here as it is with the Cartesian dolls?[28] As soon as I let go of the doll, it stands on its head. As soon as I let go of it—consequently, I have to let go of it. So also with the demonstration—so long as I am holding on to the demonstration (that is, continue to be one who is demonstrating), the existence does

---

jealousy in being and participates just as much. It is quite true that ideally the situation is different. *But as soon as I speak ideally about being, I am speaking no longer about being but about essence.* The necessary has the highest ideality; therefore it is. But this being is its essence, whereby it expressly cannot become dialectical in the determinants of factual being, because it is; and neither can it be said to have more or less being in relation to something else. In the old days, this was expressed, even though somewhat imperfectly, as follows: If God is possible, he is *eo ipso* necessary (Leibniz).[25] Then Spinoza's thesis is quite correct and the tautology is in order, but it is also certain that he completely circumvents the difficulty, for the difficulty is to grasp factual being and to bring God's ideality into factual being.

not emerge, if for no other reason than that I am in the process of demonstrating it, but when I let go of the demonstration, the existence is there. Yet this letting go, even that is surely something; it is, after all, *meine Zuthat* [my contribution]. Does it not have to be taken into account, this diminutive moment, however brief it is—it does not have to be long, because it is a *leap*. However diminutive this moment, even if it is this very instant, this very instant must be taken into account. If someone wants to have it forgotten, I will take the occasion to tell a little anecdote in order to show that it does indeed exist. Chrysippus was trying to determine a qualitative limit in the progressive or retrogressive operation of a sorites. Carneades could not grasp the point at which the quality actually made its appearance.[29] Chrysippus told him that one could pause for a moment in the reckoning, and then, then—then one could understand it better. But Carneades replied: Please, do not let me disturb you; you may not only pause but may even lie down and go to sleep— it will not make any difference. When you wake up, we shall begin again where you stopped. And that, of course, is how it really is; trying to get rid of something by sleeping is just as useless as trying to obtain something by sleeping.

IV
211

Therefore, anyone who wants to demonstrate the existence of God (in any other sense than elucidating the God-concept and without the *reservatio finalis* [ultimate reservation] that we have pointed out—that the existence itself emerges from the demonstration by a leap) proves something else instead, at times something that perhaps did not even need demonstrating, and in any case never anything better. For the fool says in his heart that there is no God,[30] but he who says in his heart or to others: Just wait a little and I shall demonstrate it—ah, what a rare wise man he is!* If, at the moment he is supposed to begin the demonstration, it is not totally undecided whether the god exists or not, then, of course, he does not demonstrate it, and if that is the situation in the beginning, then he never does make a begin-

---

* What a superb theme for crazy comedy![31]

ning—partly for fear that he will not succeed because the god may not exist, and partly because he has nothing with which to begin. — In ancient times, such a thing would have been of hardly any concern. At least Socrates, who did indeed advance what is called the physico-teleological demonstration for the existence of God,[32] did not conduct himself in this way. He constantly presupposes that the god exists, and on this presupposition he seeks to infuse nature with the idea of fitness and purposiveness. If he had been asked why he conducted himself in this manner, he presumably would have explained that he lacked the kind of courage needed to dare to embark on such a voyage of discovery without having behind him the assurance that the god exists. At the god's request, he casts out his net, so to speak, to catch the idea of fitness and purposiveness, for nature itself comes up with many terrifying devices and many subterfuges in order to disturb.[33]

The paradoxical passion of the understanding is, then, continually colliding with this unknown, which certainly does exist but is also unknown and to that extent does not exist. The understanding does not go beyond this; yet in its paradoxicality the understanding cannot stop reaching it and being engaged with it, because wanting to express its relation to it by saying that this unknown does not exist will not do, since just saying that involves a relation. But what, then, is this unknown, for does not its being the god merely signify to us that it is the unknown? To declare that it is the unknown because we cannot know it, and that even if we could know it we could not express it,[34] does not satisfy the passion, although it has correctly perceived the unknown as frontier. But a frontier is expressly the passion's torment, even though it is also its incentive. And yet it can go no further, whether it risks a sortie through *via negationis* [the way of negation] or *via eminentiae* [the way of idealization].

What, then, is the unknown? It is the frontier that is continually arrived at, and therefore when the category of motion is replaced by the category of rest it is the different, the absolutely different.[35] But it is the absolutely different in which there is no distinguishing mark. Defined as the absolutely different, it seems to be at the point of being disclosed, but not so, because the understanding cannot even think the absolutely different; it cannot absolutely negate itself but uses itself for that purpose and consequently thinks the difference in itself, which it thinks by itself. It cannot absolutely transcend itself and therefore thinks as above itself only the sublimity that it thinks by itself. If the unknown (the god) is not solely the frontier, then the one idea about the different is confused with the many ideas about the different. The unknown is then in διασπορά [dispersion], and the understanding has an attractive selection from among what is available and what fantasy can think of (the prodigious, the ridiculous, etc.).

But this difference cannot be grasped securely. Every time this happens, it is basically an arbitrariness, and at the very bottom of devoutness there madly lurks the capricious arbitrariness that knows it itself has produced the god. If the difference cannot be grasped securely because there is no distinguishing mark, then, as with all such dialectical opposites, so it is with the difference and the likeness—they are identical. Adhering to the understanding, the difference has so confused the understanding that it does not know itself and quite consistently confuses itself with the difference. In the realm of fantastical fabrication, paganism has been adequately luxuriant. With respect to the assumption just advanced, which is the self-ironizing of the understanding, I shall merely trace it in a few lines without reference to whether it was historical or not. There exists [*existere*], then, a certain person who looks just like any other human being,[36] grows up as do other human beings, marries, has a job, takes tomorrow's livelihood into account as a man should. It may be very beautiful to want to live as the birds of the air live,[37] but it is not permissible, and one can indeed end up in the saddest of plights, either dying of hunger—if one has the endurance for that—or living on the goods of others.[38] This human being is also the god. How do I know that? Well, I cannot know it, for in that case I would have to know the

IV
213

god and the difference, [39]and I do not know the difference, inasmuch as the understanding has made it like unto that from which it differs. Thus the god has become the most terrible deceiver through the understanding's deception of itself. The understanding has the god as close as possible and yet just as far away.

[40]Someone may now be saying, "I know full well that you are a capricemonger, but you certainly do not believe that it would occur to me to be concerned about a caprice so curious or so ludicrous that it probably has never occurred to anyone and, above all, is so unreasonable that I would have to lock everything out of my consciousness in order to think of it." That is exactly what you have to do, but then is it justifiable to want to keep all the presuppositions *you* have in your consciousness and still presume to think about your consciousness without any presuppositions? [41]Most likely you do not deny the consistency of what has been developed—that in defining the unknown as the different the understanding ultimately goes astray and confuses the difference with likeness? But this seems to imply something different, namely, that if a human being is to come truly to know something about the unknown (the god), he must first come to know that it is different from him, absolutely different from him. The understanding cannot come to know this by itself (since, as we have seen, it is a contradiction); if it is going to come to know this, it must come to know this from the god, and if it does come to know this, it cannot understand this and consequently cannot come to know this, for how could it understand the absolutely different? If this is not immediately clear, then it will become more clear from the corollary, for if the god is absolutely different from a human being, then a human being is absolutely different from the god—but how is the understanding to grasp this? At this point we seem to stand at a paradox. Just to come to know that the god is the different, man needs the god and then comes to know that the god is absolutely different from him. But if the god is to be absolutely different from a human being, this can have its basis not in that which man owes to

the god (for to that extent they are akin) but in that which he owes to himself or in that which he himself has committed. What, then, is the difference? Indeed, what else but sin, since the difference, the absolute difference, must have been caused by the individual himself. We stated this in the foregoing by saying that the individual is untruth and is this through his own fault, and we jestingly, yet earnestly, agreed that it is too much to ask him to find this out for himself. Now we have come to the same point again. The connoisseur of human nature[42] became almost bewildered about himself when he came up against the different; he no longer knew whether he was a more curious monster than Typhon or whether there was something divine in him. What did he lack, then? The consciousness of sin, which he could no more teach to any other person than any other person could teach it to him. Only the god could teach it—if he wanted to be teacher. But this he did indeed want to be, as we have composed the story, and in order to be that he wanted to be on the basis of equality with the single individual so that he could completely understand him. Thus the paradox becomes even more terrible, or the same paradox has the duplexity by which it manifests itself as the absolute—negatively, by bringing into prominence the absolute difference of sin and, positively, by wanting to annul this absolute difference in the absolute equality.

[43]But is a paradox such as this conceivable? We shall not be in a hurry; whenever the contention is over a reply to a question and the contending is not like that on the race track, it is not speed that wins but correctness. The understanding certainly cannot think it, cannot hit upon it on its own, and if it is proclaimed, the understanding cannot understand it and merely detects that it will likely be its downfall. To that extent, the understanding has strong objections to it; and yet, on the other hand, in its paradoxical passion the understanding does indeed will its own downfall. But the paradox, too, wills this downfall of the understanding, and thus the two have a mutual understanding, but this understanding is present only in the moment of passion. Let us consider the con-

Offense at the Paradox[2]
(An Acoustical Illusion)

If the paradox and the understanding meet in the mutual understanding of their difference, then the encounter is a happy one, like erotic love's understanding—happy in the passion to which we as yet have given no name and which we shall not name until later. If the encounter is not in mutual understanding, then the relation is unhappy, and the understanding's unhappy love, if I dare call it that (which, please note, resembles only the unhappy love rooted in misunderstood self-love; since the power of chance is capable of nothing here, the analogy stretches no further), we could more specifically term *offense*.

At its deepest level, all offense is a suffering.*[3] Here it is similar to that unhappy love. Even when self-love (and does it not already seem to be a contradiction that love of self is suffering?) announces itself in the rashest exploit, the amazing deed, it is suffering, it is wounded, and the pain of the wound gives this illusory expression of strength that resembles action and can easily delude, especially since self-love conceals this most of all. Indeed, even when it thrusts down the object of love, even when it self-tormentingly disciplines itself to callous indifference and tortures itself in order to show indifference, even when it indulges in triumphant frivolousness over success in doing this (this form is the most deceptive)—even then it is suffering.

* Our language correctly terms an uncontrolled emotional state [*Affekt*] a *suffering* of the mind [*Sinds l i d e l s e*], although when using the word "affect" we usually think of the convulsive boldness that astounds us, and because of that we forget that it is a suffering.[4] For example, arrogance, defiance, etc.

So it is also with offense. However it chooses to express itself, even when it gloatingly celebrates the triumph of spiritlessness, it is always a suffering. No matter if the offended one is sitting crushed and staring almost like a beggar at the paradox, petrifying in his suffering, or even if he arms himself with mockery and aims the arrows of his wit as if from a distance—he is nevertheless suffering and is not at a distance. No matter if the offense came and took the last crumb of comfort and joy from the offended one or if it made him strong—offense is nevertheless a suffering. It has struggled with the stronger, and his posture of vigor has a physical analogy to that of someone with a broken back, which does indeed give a singular kind of suppleness.

We can, however, very well distinguish between suffering offense and active offense, yet without forgetting that suffering offense is always active to the extent that it cannot altogether allow itself to be annihilated (for offense is always an act, not an event), and active offense is always weak enough to be incapable of tearing itself loose from the cross to which it is nailed or to pull out the arrow with which it is wounded.*

But precisely because offense is a suffering in this manner, the discovery, if it may be put this way, does not belong to the understanding but to the paradox, for just as truth is *index sui et falsi* [the criterion of itself and of the false],[5] so also is the paradox, and offense does not understand itself** but is understood by the paradox. Thus, although the of-

---

* Language usage also shows that all offense is a suffering. We say "to be offended," which primarily signifies only the state, but we synonymously say "to *take* offense" (the identity of the suffering [*Lidende*] and the acting). In Greek it is σκανδαλίζεσθαι. This word comes from σκάνδαλον (offense, affront) and thus means to take affront. Here the direction is clear; it is not the offense that affronts but the offense that takes affront, therefore passively [*passivt*], even though so actively that it itself takes affront. The understanding, therefore, has not itself originated the offense, for the paradoxical affront that the isolated understanding develops discovers neither the paradox nor the offense.

** In this way the Socratic principle that all sin is ignorance[6] is correct; sin does not understand itself in the truth, but this does not mean that it cannot will itself in untruth.[7]

fense, however it expresses itself, sounds from somewhere else—indeed, from the opposite corner—nevertheless it is the paradox that resounds in it, and this indeed is an acoustical illusion. But if the paradox is *index* and *judex sui et falsi* [the criterion of itself and of the false], then offense can be regarded as an indirect testing of the correctness of the paradox, for offense is the erroneous accounting, is the conclusion of untruth, with which the paradox thrusts away. The one offended does not speak according to his own nature[8] but according to the nature of the paradox, just as someone caricaturing another person does not originate anything himself but only copies the other in the wrong way. The more deeply the expression of offense is couched in passion (acting or suffering), the more manifest is the extent to which the offense is indebted to the paradox. So the offense is not the origination of the understanding—far from it, for then the understanding must also have been able to originate the paradox. No, the offense *comes into existence* with the paradox; if it *comes into existence*, here again we have the moment, around which everything indeed revolves. Let us recapitulate. If we do not assume the moment, then we go back to Socrates, and it was precisely from him that we wanted to take leave in order to discover something. If the moment is posited, the paradox is there, for in its most abbreviated form the paradox can be called the moment. Through the moment, the learner becomes untruth; the person who knew himself becomes confused about himself and instead of self-knowledge he acquires the consciousness of sin etc., [9]for just as soon as we assume the moment, everything goes by itself.

From the psychological point of view, offense will now have very many shadings within the category of the more active and the more passive. To describe these is not the interest of this deliberation, but it is nevertheless important to maintain that all offense is in its essence a misunderstanding of *the moment*, since it is indeed offense at the paradox, and the paradox in turn is the moment.

The dialectic of the moment is not difficult. From the Socratic point of view, the moment is not to be seen or to be distinguished; it does not exist, has not been, and will not come. Therefore, the learner himself is the truth, and the moment of occasion is merely a jest, like an end-sheet half-title that does not essentially belong to a book. And the moment of decision is *foolishness*,[10] for if the decision is posited, then (see above) the learner becomes untruth, but precisely this makes a beginning in the moment necessary. The expression of offense is that the moment is foolishness, the paradox is foolishness—which is the paradox's claim that the understanding is the absurd but which now resounds as an echo from the offense. Or the moment is supposed to be continually pending; one *waits and watches*, and the moment is supposed to be *something of great importance, worth watching for*, but since the paradox has made the understanding the absurd, what the understanding regards as very important is no distinguishing mark.

The offense remains outside the paradox, and the basis for that is: *quia absurdum* [because it is absurd].[11] Yet the understanding has not discovered this, since, on the contrary, it is the paradox that discovered it and now takes testimony from the offense. The understanding declares that the paradox is the absurd, but this is only a caricaturing, for the paradox is indeed the paradox, *quia absurdum*. The offense remains outside the paradox and retains probability; whereas the paradox is the most improbable. Once again, it is not the understanding that discovers it, but the understanding merely parrots the paradox, however strange that may seem, for the paradox itself says: Comedies and novels and lies must be probable, but how could I be probable?[12] The offense remains outside the paradox—no wonder, since the paradox is the wonder. The understanding has not discovered this; on the contrary, it was the paradox that ushered the understanding to the wonder stool[13] and replies: Now, what are you wondering about? It is just as you say, and the amazing thing is that you think that it is an objection, but the truth in the mouth of a hypocrite is dearer to me than to hear it from an angel and an apostle.[14] When the understanding flaunts its magnificence in comparison with the paradox, which is most lowly and despised, the understanding has not originated it, but the paradox itself is the originator who hands over all the splendor to understanding, even the glittering vices (*vitia splendida*).[15] When the understanding wants to have pity upon the paradox and assist it to an explanation, the paradox does not put up with that but considers it appropriate for the understanding to do that, for is that not what philosophers are for—to make supernatural things ordinary and banal?[16] When the understanding cannot get the paradox into its head, this did not have its origin in the understanding but in the paradox itself, which was paradoxical enough to have the effrontery to call the understanding a clod and a dunce who at best can say "yes" and "no" to the same thing, which is not good theology.[17] So it is with offense. Everything it says about the paradox it has learned from the paradox, even though, making use of an acoustical illusion, it insists that it itself has originated the paradox.

But someone may be saying, "You really are boring, for now we have the same story all over again; all the phrases you put in the mouth of the paradox do not belong to you at all." —"How could they belong to me, since they do indeed belong to the paradox?" —"Please spare us your sophistry! You know very well what I mean. Those phrases do not belong to you but are very familiar, and everyone knows to whom they belong." —"Ah, my dear fellow, what you say does not pain me as you perhaps think it does; no, it pleases me immensely, for I admit that I trembled when I wrote them down. I could not recognize myself, could not imagine that I, who as a rule am so diffident and fearful, dared to write anything like that. But if they are not my phrases, tell me, whose are they?"[18] —"Nothing is easier. The first is from Tertullian; the second from Hamann; the third from Hamann; the fourth, from Lactantius, is often quoted; the fifth from Shakespeare's comedy *All's Well That Ends Well*, II, 3; the sixth is from Luther; and the seventh is a line in *King Lear*. As you see, I do know my business and know how to catch you with the stolen goods." —"Indeed,

IV
220

I see it very well; but tell me this—have not all these men talked about a relation of the paradox to offense, and will you please notice that they were not the offended ones but the very ones who held firmly to the paradox and yet spoke as if they were the offended ones, and offense cannot come up with a more striking expression than that. Is it not peculiar that the paradox thus seems to be taking bread from the mouth of offense and making it an unremunerative art that has no reward for its trouble but is just as odd as an opponent who absentmindedly does not attack the author but defends him? Does it not seem so to you? Yet offense has one advantage: it points up the difference more clearly, for in that happy passion to which we have not as yet given a name the difference is in fact on good terms with the understanding. The difference is necessary in order to be united in some third, but the difference was precisely this—that the understanding surrendered itself and the paradox gave itself (*halb zog sie ihn, halb sank er hin* [she half dragged him, he half sank down]),[19] and the understanding lies in that happy passion that no doubt will receive a name, but this is the least part of it, even though my happiness does not have a name—if only I am happy, I ask no more."

IV
221

IV

IV
221

The Situation of the Contemporary Follower

[1]So, then (to continue with our poem), the god has made his appearance as a teacher. He has taken the form of a servant; to send someone else, someone completely trusted, in his place could no more satisfy him than it could satisfy that noble king to send in his place the most highly trusted person in his kingdom. Yet the god had another reason as well, for between one human being and another the Socratic relationship is indeed the highest, the truest. Therefore, if the god did not come himself, then everything would remain Socratic, we would not have the moment, and we would fail to obtain the paradox. But the servant form is not something put on but is actual, not a parastatic but an actual body, and the god, from the hour when by the omnipotent resolution of his omnipotent love he became a servant, he has himself become captive, so to speak, in his resolution and is now obliged to continue (to go on talking loosely) whether he wants to or not. He cannot betray his identity; unlike that noble king, he does not have the possibility of suddenly disclosing that he is, after all, the king—which is no perfection in the king (to have this possibility) but merely manifests his impotence and the impotence of his resolution, that he actually is incapable of becoming what he wanted to become. Although the god is unable to send anyone in his place, he presumably is able to send someone in advance who can make the learner aware. Of course, this predecessor cannot know what the god wants to teach, because the god's presence is not incidental to his teaching but is essential. The presence of the god in human form—indeed, in the lowly form of a servant—is precisely the teaching, and the god himself must

IV
222

but Jesus did, no?

provide the condition (see Chapter I); otherwise the learner is unable to understand anything. Through a predecessor of this kind, a learner can become aware, but no more than that.

The god did not, however, take the form of a servant in order to mock human beings; his aim, therefore, cannot be to walk through the world in such a way that not one single person would come to know it. Presumably he will allow something about himself to be understood, although any accommodation made for the sake of comprehensibility still does not essentially help the person who does not receive the condition, and therefore it is actually elicited from him only under constraint and against his will, and it may just as well alienate the learner as draw him closer. He humbled himself and took the form of a servant,[2] but he certainly did not come to live as a servant in the service of some particular person, carrying out his tasks without letting his master or his co-workers realize who he was[3]—wrath such as that we dare not ascribe to the god. Thus the fact that he was in the form of a servant means only that he was a lowly human being, a lowly man who did not set himself off from the human throng either by soft raiment[4] or by any other earthly advantage and was not distinguishable to other human beings, not even to the countless legions of angels[5] he left behind when he humbled himself. But even though he was a lowly man, his concerns were not those that men generally have. He went his way unconcerned about administering and distributing the goods of this world; he went his way as one who owns nothing and wishes to own nothing, as unconcerned about his living as the birds of the air,[6] as unconcerned about house and home as someone who has no hiding place or nest[7] and is not looking for such a place. He was unconcerned about accompanying the dead to their graves,[8] was not attracted by the things that commonly attract [9]the attention of people, was not tied to any woman, so enthralled by her as to want to please her, but sought only the follower's love. All this seems very beautiful, but is it also proper? Does he not thereby elevate himself above what is

ordinarily the condition of human beings? Is it right for a
human being to be as carefree as the bird and not even fly
hither and thither for food as the bird does? Should he not
even think of tomorrow? We are unable to poetize the god
otherwise, but what does a fiction prove? Is it permissible to
wander around erratically like this, stopping wherever evening finds one?[10] The question is this: May a human being
express the same thing?—for otherwise the god has not realized the essentially human. Yes, if he is capable of it, he
may also do it. If he can become so absorbed in the service
of the spirit that it never occurs to him to provide for food
and drink, if he is sure that the lack will not divert him, that
the hardship will not disorder his body and make him regret
that he did not first of all understand the lessons of childhood
before wanting to understand more—yes, then he truly may
do it, and his greatness is even more glorious than the quiet
assurance of the lily.[11]

IV
223

This exalted absorption in his work will already have drawn
to the teacher the attention of the crowd, among whom the
learner presumably will be found, and such a person will
presumably belong to the humbler class of people, for the
wise and the learned will no doubt first submit sophistic
questions to him, invite him to colloquia or put him through
an examination, and after that guarantee him a tenured position and a living.

So we now have the god walking around in the city in
which he made his appearance (which one is inconsequential); to proclaim his teaching is for him the one and only
necessity of his life, is for him his food and drink.[12] To teach
people is his work, and to be concerned about the learners is
for him relaxation from his work. He has no friends and no
relatives, but to him the learner is brother and sister.[13] It is
easy to see that very soon a rumor will be fabricated that will
trap the curious crowd in its net. Wherever the teacher appears, the populace flocks about him,[14] curious to see, curious to hear, craving to be able to tell others that they have
seen and heard him. Is this curious crowd the learner? By no
means. Or if one of that city's professional teachers were to

come secretly to the god in order to test his powers in the po-
lemics of debate,[15] is this the learner? By no means. If the
populace or if that professional teacher *learns* something, then
in the purely Socratic sense the god is only the occasion.

The appearance of the god is now the news of the day in
the market square, in homes, in council meetings, in the rul-
er's palace; it is the occasion for much loose and empty talk,
perhaps also the occasion for more serious reflection. But for
the learner the news of the day is not an occasion for something else, not even the occasion for him in Socratic honesty
to immerse himself in himself—no, it is the eternal, the beginning of eternity. The news of the day is the beginning of
eternity! If the god had let himself be born in an inn, wrapped
in rags, laid in a manger[16] —is that more of a contradiction
than that the news of the day is the swaddling clothes of the
eternal, is indeed its actual form, just as in this assumed case,
so that *the moment* is actually the decision of eternity! If the
god does not provide the condition to understand this, how
will it ever occur to the learner? But that the god provides
the condition has already been explicated as the consequence
of *the moment*, and we have shown that the moment is the
paradox and that without this we come no further but go
back to Socrates.

[17]Right here we shall make sure that it becomes clear that
a historical point of departure[18] is an issue for the contemporary follower as well, for if we do not make sure of this
here, we shall face an insurmountable difficulty later (Chapter V) when we deal with the situation of the follower whom
we call the follower at second hand. The contemporary follower, too, obtains a historical point of departure for his eternal
consciousness, for he is indeed contemporary with the historical event that does not intend to be a moment of occasion, and this historical event intends to interest him otherwise than merely historically, intends to be the condition for
his eternal happiness. Indeed (let us reverse the consequences), if this is not the case, the teacher is not the god but
only a Socrates, who, if he does not go about things as Socrates did, is not even a Socrates.

[19]How, then, does the learner come to an understanding with this paradox, for we do not say that he is supposed to understand the paradox but is only to understand that this is the paradox. We have already shown how this occurs. It occurs when the understanding and the paradox happily encounter each other in the moment, when the understanding steps aside and the paradox gives itself, and the third something, the something in which this occurs (for it does not occur through the understanding, which is discharged, or through the paradox, which gives itself—consequently *in* something), is that happy passion to which we shall now give a name, although for us it is not a matter of the name. We shall call it *faith*. This passion, then, must be that abovementioned condition that the paradox provides. Let us not forget this: if the paradox does not provide the condition, then the learner is in possession of it; but if he is in possession of the condition, then he is *eo ipso* himself the truth, and the moment is only the moment of occasion (see Chapter I).

It is easy enough for the contemporary learner to acquire detailed historical information. But let us not forget that in regard to the birth of the god he will be in the very same situation as the follower at second hand, and if we insist upon absolutely exact historical knowledge, only one human being would be completely informed, namely, the woman by whom he let himself be born. Consequently, it is easy for the contemporary learner to become a historical eyewitness, but the trouble is that knowing a historical fact—indeed, knowing all the historical facts with the trustworthiness of an eyewitness—by no means makes the eyewitness a follower, which is understandable, because such knowledge means nothing more to him than the historical. It is at once apparent here that the historical in the more concrete sense is inconsequential; we can let ignorance step in here, let ignorance, so to speak, destroy one fact after the other, let it historically demolish the historical—if only the moment still remains as the point of departure for the eternal, the paradox is still present.

If there was a contemporary who had even limited his sleep to the shortest possible time so that he could accompany that

IV
225

teacher, whom he accompanied more inseparably than the little fish that accompany the shark, if he had in his service a hundred secret agents who spied upon that teacher everywhere and with whom he conferred every night, so that he had a dossier on that teacher down to the slightest particular, knew what he had said, where he had been every hour of the day, because his zeal made him regard even the slightest particular as important—would such a contemporary be a follower? Not at all. If someone charged him with historical unreliability, he could wash his hands,[20] but no more than that. If someone else concerned himself only with the teaching which that teacher occasionally presented, if he cherished every instructive word that came from his mouth more than his daily bread, if he had a hundred others to catch every syllable so that nothing would be lost,[21] if he painstakingly conferred with them in order to obtain the most reliable version of what the teacher taught—would he therefore be a follower? By no means—no more than Plato was anything other than a follower of Socrates.[22] If there was a contemporary who had lived abroad and came home just when that teacher had only a day or two to live, if in turn that contemporary was prevented by business affairs from getting to see that teacher and arrived on the scene only at the very end when he was about to breathe his last, would this historical ignorance be an obstacle to his being able to be a follower if the moment was for him the decision of eternity? For the first contemporary, that life would have been merely a historical event; for the second one, that teacher would have been the occasion for understanding himself, and he will be able to forget that teacher (see Chapter I), because in contrast to an eternal understanding of oneself, knowledge about the teacher is contingent and historical knowledge, a matter of memory. As long as the eternal and the historical remain apart from each other, the historical is only an occasion. If, then, that ardent learner, who did not, however, go so far as to become a follower, spoke ever so frequently and emphatically about how much he owed that teacher, so that his eulogy had almost no end and its gilding was almost price-

IV
226

less—if he became angry with us as we tried to explain to him that the teacher had been merely the occasion—neither his eulogy nor his anger would benefit our reflections, for both would have the same basis, that he, without even having the courage simply to understand, did not want to lack the recklessness to go further. By talking extravagantly and trumpeting[23] from the housetops as he does, a person merely hoodwinks himself and others insofar as he convinces himself and others that he actually does have thoughts—since he owes them to another. Although courtesy generally does not cost anything, that person's courtesy is bought at a high price, because the enthusiastic expression of thankfulness, which may not even lack tears and the capacity of moving others to tears, is a misunderstanding, because such a person owes his thoughts to no one else, and neither does he owe his shallow talk to any one else. Alas, how many there have been who have had sufficient courtesy to want to be very indebted to Socrates, and yet without owing him anything at all! The person who understands Socrates best understands specifically that he owes Socrates nothing, which is what Socrates prefers, and to be able to prefer this is beautiful. The person who thinks that he is so very indebted to Socrates can be quite sure that Socrates gladly exempts him from paying, since Socrates certainly would be dismayed to learn that he had given the person concerned any working capital whatsoever to exploit in this way. But if the whole structure is not Socratic—and this is what we are assuming—then the follower owes that teacher *everything* (which one cannot possibly owe to Socrates, since, after all, as he himself says, he was not capable of *giving birth*),[24] and this relation cannot be expressed by talking extravagantly and trumpeting from the housetops but only in that happy passion which we call faith, the object of which is the paradox—but the paradox specifically unites the contradictories, is the eternalizing of the historical and the historicizing of the eternal. Anyone who understands the paradox any other way may retain the honor of having explained it, an honor he would win by his unwillingness to be satisfied with understanding it.

IV
227

[25]It is easy to see, then (if, incidentally, the implications of discharging the understanding need to be pointed out), that faith is not a knowledge, for [26]all knowledge is either knowledge of the eternal, which excludes the temporal and the historical as inconsequential, or it is purely historical knowledge, and no knowledge can have as its object this absurdity that the eternal is the historical. If I comprehend Spinoza's teaching, then in the moment I comprehend it I am not occupied with Spinoza but with his teaching, although at some other time I am historically occupied with him. The follower, however, is in faith related to that teacher in such a way that he is eternally occupied with his historical existence.

Now if we assume that the structure is as we have assumed (and unless we do, we go back to Socrates), namely, that the teacher himself provides the learner with the condition, then the object of faith becomes not the *teaching* but the *teacher,* for the essence of the Socratic is that the learner, because he himself is the truth and has the condition, can thrust the teacher away. Indeed, assisting people to be able to do this constituted the Socratic art and heroism. Faith, then, must constantly cling firmly to the teacher. But in order for the teacher to be able to give the condition, he must be the god, and in order to put the learner in possession of it, he must be man. This contradiction is in turn the object of faith and is the paradox, the moment. That the god once and for all has given man the condition is the eternal Socratic presupposition, which does not clash inimically with time but is incommensurable with the categories of temporality. But the contradiction is that he receives the condition in the moment, and, since it is a condition for the understanding of eternal truth, it is *eo ipso* the eternal condition. If this is not the structure, then we are left with Socratic recollection.

It is easy to see, then (if, incidentally, the consequences of discharging the understanding need to be pointed out), that faith is not an act of will, for it is always the case that all human willing is efficacious only within the condition. For example, if I have the courage to will it, I will understand

the Socratic—that is, understand myself, because from the
Socratic point of view I possess the condition and now can
will it. But if I do not possess the condition (and we assume
this in order not to go back to the Socratic), then all my
willing is of no avail, even though, once the condition is
given, that which was valid for the Socratic is again valid.

IV
228

The contemporary learner possesses an advantage for which,
alas, the subsequent learner, just in order to do something,
will very much envy him. The contemporary can go and
observe that teacher—and does he then dare to believe his
eyes? Yes, why not? As a consequence, however, does he
dare to believe that he is a follower? Not at all, for if he
believes his eyes, he is in fact deceived, for the god cannot
be known directly. Then may he close his eyes? Quite so.
But if he does, then what is the advantage of being contemporary? And if he does close his eyes, then he will presumably envision the god. But if he is able to do this by himself,
then he does indeed possess the condition. What he envisions
will be a form that appears to the inner eye of the soul; if he
looks at that, then the form of the servant will indeed disturb
him as soon as he opens his eyes. Let us proceed. As we
know, that teacher dies. So now, then, he is dead—what is
to be done by the person who was contemporary with him?
Perhaps he has sketched a portrait of him—perhaps he even
has a whole series of pictures depicting and exactly repro-
ducing every change that age and mental attitude may have
brought about in the external form of that teacher—when he
looks at these pictures and assures himself that this is the way
the teacher looked, does he then dare to believe his eyes?
Well, why not? But is he therefore a follower? By no means.
But then he may indeed envision the god. The god, however, cannot be envisioned, and that was the very reason he
was in the form of a servant. Yet the servant form was no
deception, for if it were, then that moment would not be the
moment but an accidentality, a semblance, which, in comparison with the eternal, infinitely vanishes as an occasion.
And if the learner could envision the god by himself, then
he himself would possess the condition and then he would

only need to be reminded in order to envision the god, which he could very well do, even if he was not aware of it. But if this is the way it is, then this reminder instantly vanishes as an atom in the eternal possibility that was in his soul, which now becomes actual but then again, as actuality, has eternally presupposed itself.

How, then, does the learner become a believer or a follower? When the understanding is discharged and he receives the condition. When does he receive this? In the moment. This condition, what does it condition? His understanding of the eternal. But a condition such as this surely must be an eternal condition. —In the moment, therefore, he receives the eternal condition, and he knows this from his having received it in the moment, for otherwise he merely calls to mind that he had it from eternity. He receives the condition in the moment and receives it from that teacher himself. All extravagant talking and trumpeting from the housetops about being crafty enough, even though he did not receive the condition from the teacher, to discover the god's incognito— that he could detect it in himself, for he felt so strange every time he looked at that teacher, that there was something in that teacher's voice and countenance, etc., etc.—this is blather, by which no one becomes a follower but only mocks the god.

That form was no incognito, and when the god by his omnipotent resolution, which is like his love, wills to be just like the lowliest person, then let no innkeeper or philosophy professor fancy that he is such a clever fellow that he can detect something if the god himself does not give the con-

IV
229

---

* Any qualification that claims to render the god directly knowable is undoubtedly an approximation milestone, but it registers retrogression rather than progress, movement away from the paradox rather than toward the paradox, back past Socrates and Socratic ignorance. Close attention should be paid to this lest the same thing happen in the spiritual world that happened to the traveler who asked an Englishman if the road led to London and was told: Yes, it does—but he never did arrive in London, because the Englishman failed to tell him that he had to turn around, inasmuch as he was going away from London.[27]

dition. And when the god, in the form of a servant, stretches out his almighty hand, the person who gapes at him in amazement is not to fancy that he is a follower because he is amazed and because he is able to gather others around him who in turn are amazed at his story. If the god himself does not give the condition, the learner would know from the very outset the situation regarding the god, even though he would not know that he knew it, and that alternative is not the Socratic but something infinitely inferior.

But for the follower the external form (not its detail) is not inconsequential. It is what the follower has seen and touched with his hands,[28] but the form is not of such importance that he would cease to be a believer if he happened one day to see the teacher on the street and did not immediately recognize him or even walked beside him for a while without becoming aware that it was he.[29] But the god gave the follower the condition to see it and opened for him the eyes of faith. But to see this external form was something appalling: to associate with him as one of us and at every moment when faith was not present to see only the servant form. When the teacher is dead and departed from the follower, memory presumably will produce the form, but he does not believe because of that but because he received the condition from the teacher; therefore, in recollection's trustworthy picture, he again sees the god. So it is with the follower who knows that without the condition he would have seen nothing, inasmuch as the first thing he understood was that he himself was untruth.

But then is faith just as paradoxical as the paradox? Quite so. How else could it have its object in the paradox and be happy in its relation to it? Faith itself is a wonder, and everything that is true of the paradox is also true of faith. But within this wonder everything is again structured Socratically, yet in such a way that the wonder is never canceled— the wonder that the eternal condition is given in time. Everything is structured Socratically, for the relation between one contemporary and another contemporary, provided that both are believers, is altogether Socratic: the one

IV
230

is not indebted to the other for anything, but both are indebted to the god for everything.

Perhaps someone is saying, "Then the contemporary has no advantage whatsoever from being contemporary, and yet if we assume what you have assumed about the god's making his appearance, it seems natural to regard as blessed the contemporary generation that saw and heard him." —"Yes, of course, it is natural, so natural, I think, that no doubt that generation also regarded itself as blessed.[30] Let us assume this, for otherwise it surely was not blessed and our eulogy merely says that someone in the same circumstances could have become blessed by acting differently. But if that is the case, then our eulogy can change considerably if we look at this more closely; indeed, in the end it may become entirely equivocal. Suppose, as we read in old records, that an emperor celebrated his wedding for eight consecutive days with a festiveness the like of which had never been seen. In order to enhance the enjoyment of the choicest dishes offered in richest abundance, the air one breathed was scented with perfume, while the ear perceived it vibrating continually with the music of strings and song. Day and night, for the night was made light as day by torches—but whether seen by the light of day or by the light of torches, the queen was lovelier and more gracious than any mortal woman, and the whole thing was a kind of magic, as wondrous as the boldest wish's even more bold fulfillment. Let us assume that this did happen and that we had to be satisfied with a scant report about its having happened. Why should we not, humanly speaking, regard the contemporaries as fortunate—that is, those contemporaries who saw and heard and touched, for otherwise what is the good of being contemporary? After all, the magnificence of the imperial wedding and the superabundance of enjoyments could be seen and touched immediately and directly—therefore if anyone was, strictly speaking, contemporary, then he no doubt also saw and gave his heart to gladness. But now suppose that the magnificence was of a different kind, something not to be seen immediately—what

IV
231

good would it be to be a contemporary? After all, a person is not thereby contemporary with the magnificence. One certainly could not call such a contemporary happy or praise his eyes and ears, since he would not be contemporary and would see and hear nothing of the magnificence, not because time and opportunity (in the sense of immediacy) were denied him, but because of something else that could be lacking even if his presence had most richly benefited by the opportunity to see and hear, and even if (in the sense of immediacy) he had not left the opportunity unused. But what does it mean to say that one can be contemporary without, however, being contemporary, consequently that one can be contemporary and yet, although using this advantage (in the sense of immediacy), be a noncontemporary—what else does this mean except that one simply cannot be immediately contemporary with a teacher and event of that sort, so that the real contemporary is not that by virtue of immediate contemporaneity but by virtue of something else. Thus, despite his being contemporary, a contemporary can be a noncontemporary; the genuine contemporary is the genuine contemporary not by virtue of immediate contemporaneity; *ergo* the noncontemporary (in the sense of immediacy) must be able to be a contemporary by way of the something else by which a contemporary becomes a genuine contemporary. But the noncontemporary (in the sense of immediacy) is, of course, the one who comes later; consequently, someone who comes later must be able to be the genuine contemporary. Or is this what it means to be contemporary, and is this the contemporary we eulogize, one who can say: I ate and drank in his presence; that teacher taught in our streets;[31] I saw him many times; he was an unimpressive man of humble birth, and only a few individuals believed there was anything extraordinary about him, something I certainly was unable to discover, even though when it comes down to it I was just as contemporary with him as anyone. [32]Or is this what it means to be contemporary, and is this the contemporary to whom the god must say, if they ever should meet in another life and if he should appeal to his contemporaneity, 'I do not

were a conjurer, and thereby give the spectators opportunity to catch on to how it is done. (b) It can be an occasion for the contemporary to concentrate Socratically upon himself, whereby that contemporaneity vanishes as a nothing in comparison with the eternal he discovers within himself. (c) Finally (and this, after all, is our assumption, lest we return to the Socratic), it becomes the occasion for the contemporary as untruth to receive from the god the condition and now to see the glory with the eyes of faith! Blessed indeed is such a contemporary. Yet a contemporary such as this is not an eyewitness (in the sense of immediacy), but as a believer he is a contemporary in the *autopsy*[39] of faith. But in this autopsy every noncontemporary (in the sense of immediacy) is in turn a contemporary. If someone coming later, someone who may even be carried away by his own infatuation, wishes to be a contemporary (in the sense of immediacy), he demonstrates that he is an imposter, recognizable, like the false Smerdis,[40] by his having no ears—namely, the ears of faith— even though he may have the long donkey ears with which one, although listening as a contemporary (in the sense of immediacy), does not become contemporary. [41]If someone who comes later goes on talking extravagantly about the glory of being a contemporary (in the sense of immediacy) and is continually wanting to be away, then we must let him go, but if you watch him you will easily see by his walk and by the path he has turned onto that he is not on the way to the terror of the paradox but is bounding away like a dancing teacher in order to reach that imperial wedding on time. And even though he gives his junket a holy name, and even though he preaches about community to others so that they join the pilgrimage in crowds, he will hardly discover the holy land (in the sense of immediacy), since it is to be found neither on the map nor on earth, but his journey is a spoof, like the game of escorting someone to grandmother's door.[42] And even though he gives himself no rest, neither by night nor by day, and runs faster than a horse can run or than a man can tell lies, he still is only running on a wild-goose chase and misunderstands himself, like the bird catcher, for if the

IV
234

bird does not come to him, running after it with a lime twig is futile. —Only in one respect could I be tempted to regard the contemporary (in the sense of immediacy) as more fortunate than someone who comes later. If we assume that centuries elapsed between that event and the life of the one who comes later, then there presumably will have been a great deal of chatter among men about this thing, so much loose chatter that the untrue and confused rumors that the contemporary (in the sense of immediacy) had to put up with did not make the possibility of the right relationship nearly as difficult, all the more so because in all human probability the centuries-old echo, like the echo in some of our churches, would not only have riddled faith with chatter but would have eliminated it in chatter, which could not happen in the first generation, where faith must have appeared in all its originality, by contrast easy to distinguish from everything else."

Is the Past More Necessary
than the Future?[2]
Or
Has the Possible,
by Having Become Actual,
Become More Necessary than It Was?

My dear reader! We assume, then, that this teacher has appeared, that he is dead and buried, and that an interval of time has elapsed between Chapters IV and V. Also in a comedy there may be an interval of several years between two acts. To suggest this passage of time, the orchestra sometimes plays a symphony or something similar in order to shorten the time by filling it up. In a similar manner, I, too, have thought to fill the intervening time by pondering the question set forth. How long the intervening period should be is up to you, but if it pleases you, then for the sake of earnestness and jest we shall assume that precisely eighteen hundred and forty-three years have passed. You see, then, that for the sake of the illusion I ought to take plenty of time, for eighteen hundred and forty-three years is an uncommon allowance of time, which will quickly place me in a predicament opposite to that in which our philosophers find themselves, whom time usually permits nothing more than to give a hint, a predicament opposite to that in which the historians find themselves, whom time, not the subject matter, leaves in the lurch. Therefore, if you find me rather prolix, repeating the same thing "about the same thing,"[3] you must, please note, consider that it is for the sake of the illusion, and then

you presumably will forgive me my prolixity and account
for it in a far different and more satisfying way than to presume that I let myself think that this matter definitely required consideration, yours as well, inasmuch as I suspected
⁴you of not fully understanding yourself in this regard, although I by no means doubt that you have fully understood
and accepted the most recent philosophy, which, like the most
recent period, seems to suffer from a strange inattention,
confusing the performance with the caption, for who was
ever so marvelous or so marvelously great as are the most
recent philosophy and the most recent period—in captions.⁵

1. COMING INTO EXISTENCE⁶

⁷How is that changed which comes into existence [*blive til*],
or what is the change (χίνησις)⁸ of coming into existence
[*Tilblivelse*]? All other change (ἀλλοίωσις) presupposes the existence of that in which change is taking place, even though
the change is that of ceasing to be in existence [*at være til*].
Not so with coming into existence, for if that which comes
into existence does not in itself remain unchanged in the change
of coming into existence, then the coming into existence is
not *this* coming into existence but another, and the question
leads to a μετάβασις εἰς ἀλλὸ γένος [transition from one
genus to another],⁹ in that the questioner in the given case
either sees a different change along with the change of coming into existence, which confuses the question for him, or
he errs with regard to that which comes into existence and
thus is in no position to ask. If, in coming into existence, a
plan is intrinsically changed, then it is not this plan that comes
into existence; but if it comes into existence unchanged, what,
then, is the change of coming into existence? This change,
then, is not in essence [*Væsen*] but in being [*Væren*]¹⁰ and is
from not existing to existing. But this non-being that is
abandoned by that which comes into existence must also exist, for otherwise "that which comes into existence would
not remain unchanged in the coming into existence"¹¹ unless
it had not been at all, whereby once again and for another

IV
237

reason the change of coming into existence would be absolutely different from any other change, because it would be no change at all, for every change has always presupposed a something. But such a being that nevertheless is a non-being is possibility, and a being that is being is indeed actual being or actuality, and the change of coming into existence is the transition from possibility to actuality.

Can the necessary come into existence? Coming into existence is a change, but since the necessary is always related to itself and is related to itself in the same way, it cannot be changed at all. All coming into existence is a *suffering* [*Liden*], and the necessary cannot suffer, cannot suffer the suffering of actuality—namely, that the possible (not merely the possible that is excluded but even the possibility that is accepted) turns out to be nothing the moment it becomes actual, for possibility is *annihilated* by actuality. Precisely by coming into existence, everything that comes into existence demonstrates that it is not necessary, for the only thing that cannot come into existence is the necessary, because the necessary *is*.

Is not necessity, then, a unity of possibility and actuality?[12] —What would this mean? Possibility and actuality are not different in essence but in being. How could there be formed from this heterogeneity a unity that would be necessity, which is not a qualification of being but of essence, since the essence of the necessary is to be. In such a case, possibility and actuality, in becoming necessity, would become an absolutely different essence, which is no change, and, in becoming necessity or the necessary, would become the one and only thing that precludes coming into existence, which is just as impossible as it is self-contradictory. (The Aristotelian proposition: "It is possible [to be]," "It is possible not [to be]," "It is not possible [to be]."[13] —The doctrine of true and false propositions [Epicurus][14] confuses the issue here, since it reflects on essence, not on being, with the result that nothing is achieved along that path with regard to defining the future.)

Necessity stands all by itself. Nothing whatever comes into existence by way of necessity, no more than necessity comes into existence or anything in coming into existence becomes the necessary. Nothing whatever exists [*er til*] because it is necessary, but the necessary exists because it is necessary or because the necessary is. The actual is no more necessary than the possible, for the necessary is absolutely different from both. (Aristotle's theory of two kinds of the possible in relation to the necessary. His mistake is to begin with the thesis that everything necessary is possible.[15] To avoid contradictory—indeed, self-contradictory—statements about the necessary, he makes shift by formulating two kinds of the possible instead of discovering that his first thesis is incorrect, since the possible cannot be predicated of the necessary.)

The change of coming into existence is actuality;[16] the transition takes place in freedom. No coming into existence is necessary—not before it came into existence, for then it cannot come into existence, and not after it has come into existence, for then it has not come into existence.

IV
239

All coming into existence occurs in freedom, not by way of necessity. Nothing coming into existence comes into existence by way of a ground,[17] but everything by way of a cause. Every cause ends in a freely acting cause. The intervening causes are misleading in that the coming into existence appears to be necessary; the truth about them is that they, as having themselves come into existence, *definitively* point back to a freely acting cause. As soon as coming into existence is definitively reflected upon, even an inference from natural law is not evidence of the necessity of any coming into existence. So also with manifestations of freedom, as soon as one refuses to be deceived by its manifestations but reflects on its coming into existence.

2. THE HISTORICAL

Everything that has come into existence is *eo ipso* historical, for even if no further historical predicate can be applied to it, the crucial predicate of the historical can still be predicated—namely, that it has come into existence. Something whose coming into existence is a simultaneous coming into existence (*Nebeneinander* [side-by-side],[18] space) has no other history than this, but nature, even when perceived in this manner (*en masse*), apart from what a more ingenious view calls the history of nature in a special sense,[19] does have a history.

But the historical is the past (for the present on the border with the future has not as yet become historical); how, then, can nature, although immediately present, be said to be historical—unless one is thinking of that more ingenious view? The difficulty arises because nature is too abstract to be dialectical, in the stricter sense of the word, with respect to time. Nature's imperfection is that it does not have a history in another sense, and its perfection is that it nevertheless has an intimation of it (namely, that it has come into existence, which is the past; that it exists, which is the present). It is, however, the perfection of the eternal to have no history, and of all that is, only the eternal has absolutely no history.

IV
240

Yet coming into existence can contain within itself a redoubling [*Fordobling*],[20] that is, a possibility of a coming into existence within its own coming into existence.[21] Here, in the stricter sense, is the historical, which is dialectical with respect to time. The coming into existence that here is shared with the coming into existence of nature is a possibility, a possibility that for nature is its whole actuality. But this distinctively historical coming into existence is nevertheless within a coming into existence—this must be grasped securely at all times. The more special historical coming into existence comes into existence by way of a relatively freely acting cause, which in turn definitively points to an absolutely freely acting cause.

3. THE PAST

What has happened has happened and cannot be undone; thus it cannot be changed (Chrysippus the Stoic—Diodorus the Megarian).[22] Is this unchangeableness the unchangeableness of necessity? The unchangeableness of the past has been brought about by a change, by the change of coming into existence, but an unchangeableness such as that does not exclude all change, since it has not excluded this one, for all change (dialectical with respect to time) is excluded only by its being excluded at every moment. The past can be regarded as necessary only if one forgets that it has come into existence, but is that kind of forgetfulness also supposed to be necessary?

What has happened has happened the way it happened; thus it is unchangeable. But is this unchangeableness the unchangeableness of necessity? The unchangeableness of the past is that its actual "thus and so" cannot become different, but from this does it follow that its possible "how" could not have been different? But the unchangeableness of the necessary—that it is constantly related to itself and is related to itself in the same way and excludes all change—is not satisfied with the unchangeableness of the past, which, as shown above, is not only dialectical with regard to an earlier change, from which it results, but must be dialectical even with regard to a higher change that nullifies it. (For example, the change of repentance, which wants to nullify an actuality.)

IV
241

The future has not occurred as yet, but it is not, *because of that*, less necessary than the past, inasmuch as the past did not become necessary by having occurred, but, on the contrary, by having occurred, it demonstrated that it was not necessary. If the past had become necessary, the opposite conclusion could not be drawn with respect to the future, but on the contrary it would follow that the future would also be necessary. If necessity could supervene at one single point, then we could no longer speak of the past and the future. To want to predict the future (prophesy) and to want to understand the necessity of the past are altogether identical, and only the prevailing fashion makes the one seem more plausible than the other to a particular generation. The past has indeed come into existence; coming into existence is the change, in freedom, of becoming actuality. If the past had become necessary, then it would not belong to freedom any more—that is, belong to that in which it came into existence. [23]Freedom would then be in dire straits, something to laugh about and to weep over, since it would bear responsibility for what did not belong to it, would bring forth what necessity would devour, and freedom itself would be an illusion and coming into existence no less an illusion; freedom would become witchcraft and coming into existence a false alarm.*[24]

* The prophesying generation disdains the past, refuses to hear the testimony of written records; the generation busy with understanding the necessity of the past does not want to be asked about the future. The conduct in both cases is utterly consistent, for in its opposite each one would find occasion to perceive how foolish its own conduct is. The absolute method, Hegel's invention,[25] is already a difficult issue in logic—indeed, a brilliant tautology that has been at the service of scientific superstition with many signs and wonderful deeds. In the historical sciences it is a fixed idea,[26] and because the method promptly begins to become concrete there—since, after all, history is the concretion of the Idea[27]—Hegel certainly has had occasion to display a rare scholarship, a rare ability to shape the material, in which through him there is turmoil enough. But it has also prompted the learner's mind to become distracted, with the result that he—perhaps precisely because of his respectfulness and his admiration for China and Persia, the thinkers of the Middle Ages, the philosophers of Greece, the four world-historical monarchies (a discovery that, just as it did not escape Gert Westphaler,[28] has also agitated the glib tongues of many later Hegelian Gert Westphalers)—forgot to examine whether there has now appeared at the conclusion, at the end of that enchanted journey, that which was constantly promised at the beginning, that which was, after all, the primary issue, that which all the world's glory could not replace, the only thing that could make up for the misplaced tension in which we were kept—the correctness of the method. Why become concrete at once, why begin at once to construct imaginatively [*experimentere*][29] *in concreto*, or could not this question be answered in the dispassionate brevity of abstraction, which has no means of distraction or enchantment? What does it mean that the idea becomes concrete, what is coming into existence, how is one related to that which has come into existence, etc.? Likewise, in the logic there could already have been clarification of what transition means before starting to write three volumes that demonstrated the transition in the categorical determinants, astounded superstition, and made dubious the position of the person who would gladly owe much to that superior mind and give thanks for all it owes him but on that account still cannot forget what Hegel himself must have regarded as the primary issue.

IV
242

4. THE APPREHENSION OF THE PAST

Nature as spatial determination exists only immediately. Something that is dialectical with respect to time has an intrinsic duplexity [*Dobbelthed*], so that after having been present it can endure as a past. The distinctively historical is perpetually the past (it is gone; whether it was years or days ago makes no difference), and as something bygone it has actuality, for it is certain and trustworthy that it occurred. But that it occurred is, in turn, precisely its uncertainty, which will perpetually prevent the apprehension from taking the past as if it had been that way from eternity. Only in this contradiction between certainty and uncertainty, the *discrimen* [distinctive mark] of something that has come into existence and thus also of the past, is the past understood. Understood in any other way, the apprehension has misunderstood itself (that it is apprehension) and its object (that "something of that kind" could become an object of apprehension). Any apprehension of the past that thinks to understand it thoroughly by constructing[30] it has only thoroughly misunderstood it. (At first glance a manifestation theory[31] instead of a construction theory is deceptively attractive, but in the very next moment there are once again the secondary construction and the necessary manifestation.) The past is not necessary, inasmuch as it came into existence; it did not become necessary by coming into existence (a contradiction), and it becomes even less necessary through any apprehension of it. (Distance in time prompts a mental illusion just as distance in space prompts a sensory illusion.[30a] The contemporary does not see the necessity of that which comes into existence, but when centuries lie between the coming into existence and the viewer—then he sees the necessity, just as the person who at a distance sees something square as round.) If the past were to become necessary through the apprehension, then the past would gain what the apprehension lost, since it would apprehend something else, which is a poor apprehension. If what is apprehended is changed in the apprehension, then the apprehension is changed into a misunderstanding. Knowledge of the present does not confer necessity upon it; foreknowledge of the future does not confer necessity upon it (Boethius);[32] knowledge of the past does not confer necessity upon it—for all apprehension, like all knowing, has nothing from which to give.

One who apprehends the past, a *historico-philosophus*, is therefore a prophet in reverse (Daub).[33] That he is a prophet simply indicates that the basis of the certainty of the past is the uncertainty regarding it in the same sense as there is uncertainty regarding the future, the possibility (Leibniz—possible worlds),[34] out of which it could not possibly *come forth* with necessity, *nam necessarium se ipso prius sit, necesse est* [for it is necessary that necessity precede itself]. The historian once again stands beside the past, stirred by the passion that is the passionate sense for coming into existence, that is, wonder [*Beundring*].[35] If the philosopher wonders over nothing whatsoever (and how, except by a new kind of contradiction, could it occur to anyone to wonder over a necessary construction), then he *eo ipso* has nothing to do with the historical, for wherever coming into existence is involved (which is indeed involved in the past), there the uncertainty (which is the uncertainty of coming into existence) of the most certain coming into existence can express itself only in this passion worthy of and necessary to the philosopher (Plato—Aristotle). Even if what has come into existence is most certain, even if wonder wants to give its stamp of approval in advance by declaring that if this had not occurred it would have to be fabricated (Baader[36]), even then the passion of wonder is self-contradictory if it fools itself and falsely ascribes necessity to what has come into existence. [37]—The very word "method,"[38] as well as the concept, adequately indicates that the progress implied here is teleological, but in any progress of this sort there is in each moment a pause (here wonder stands *in pausa* and waits for the coming into existence), which is the pause of coming into existence and the pause of possibility precisely because the τέλος [end, goal] is outside.[39] If only one way is possible, then the τέλος is not outside but in the progress itself—indeed, behind it, just as in the progress of immanence.[40]

So much for the apprehension of the past. It is presumed, however, that there is knowledge of the past—how is this knowledge acquired? Because the historical intrinsically has the *illusiveness* [*Svigagtighed*] of coming into existence, it cannot be sensed directly and immediately. The immediate impression of a natural phenomenon or of an event is not the impression of the historical, for the *coming into existence* cannot be sensed immediately—but only the presence. But the presence of the historical has the coming into existence within itself—otherwise it is not the presence of the historical.

Immediate sensation and immediate cognition cannot deceive.[41] This alone indicates that the historical cannot become the object of sense perception or of immediate cognition, because the historical has in itself that very illusiveness that is the illusiveness of coming into existence. In relation to the immediate, coming into existence is an illusiveness whereby that which is most firm is made dubious. For example, when the perceiver sees a star, the star becomes dubious for him the moment he seeks to become aware that it has come into existence. It is just as if reflection removed the star from his senses. It is clear, then, that the organ for the historical must be formed in likeness to this, must have within itself the corresponding something by which in its certitude it continually annuls the incertitude that corresponds to the uncertainty of coming into existence—a double uncertainty: the nothingness of non-being and the annihilated possibility, which is also the annihilation of every other possibility. This is precisely the nature of belief [*Tro*],[42] for continually present as the nullified in the certitude of belief is the incertitude that in every way corresponds to the uncertainty of coming into existence. Thus, belief believes what it does not see;[43] it does not believe that the star exists, for that it sees, but it believes that the star has come into existence. The same is true of an event. The occurrence can be known immediately but not that it has occurred, not even that it is in the process of oc-

IV
245

curring, even though it is taking place, as they say, right in front of one's nose. The illusiveness of the occurrence is that it has occurred, and therein lies the transition from nothing, from non-being, and from the multiple possible "how." Immediate sense perception and cognition do not have any intimation of the unsureness with which belief approaches its object, but neither do they have the certitude that extricates itself from the incertitude.

Immediate sensation and cognition cannot deceive. It is important to understand this in order to understand doubt and in order through it to assign belief its place. However strange it may seem, this thought underlies Greek skepticism.[44] Yet it is not so difficult to understand this or to understand how this casts light on belief, provided one is not utterly confused by the Hegelian doubt about everything,[45] against which there is really no need to preach, for what the Hegelians say about it is of such a nature that it seems rather to favor a modest doubt as to whether there really is anything to their having doubted something. Greek skepticism was a withdrawing skepticism (ἐποχή [suspension of judgment]);[46] they doubted not by virtue of knowledge but by virtue of will (deny assent—μετριοπαθεῖν [moderate feeling]).[47] This implies that doubt can be terminated only in freedom, by an act of will, something every Greek skeptic would understand, inasmuch as he understood himself, but he would not terminate his skepticism precisely because he *willed* to doubt. We must leave that up to him, but we must not lay at his door the stupid opinion that one doubts by way of necessity, as well as the even more stupid opinion that, if that were the case, doubt could be terminated. The Greek skeptic did not deny the correctnness of sensation and of immediate cognition, but, said he, error has an utterly different basis—it comes from the conclusion I draw.[48] If I can only avoid drawing conclusions, I shall never be deceived. If, for example, sensation shows me in the distance a round object that close at hand is seen to be square or shows me a stick that looks broken in the water although it is straight when taken out, sensation has not deceived me, but I am

that it has come into existence, but neither can he know with necessity that it has come into existence, for the first mark of coming into existence is specifically a break in continuity. [55]At the moment belief believes that it has come into existence, that it has occurred, it makes dubious what has occurred and what has come into existence in the coming into existence and its "thus and so" in the possible how of coming into existence. The conclusion of belief is no conclusion [*Slutning*] but a resolution [*Beslutning*],[56] and thus doubt is excluded. It might seem to be an inference from effect to cause when belief concludes: this exists, *ergo* it came into existence. But this is not entirely true, and even if it were, one must remember that the cognitive inference is from cause to effect or rather from ground to consequent (Jacobi[57]). This is not entirely true, because I cannot immediately sense or know that what I immediately sense or know is an effect, for immediately it simply is. That it is an effect is something I believe, because in order to predicate that it is an effect, I must already have made it dubious in the uncertainty of coming into existence. But if belief decides on this, then the doubt is terminated; in that very moment the balance and neutrality of doubt are terminated—not by knowledge but by will. Thus, while making an approach, belief is the most disputable (for doubt's uncertainty, strong and invincible in making *du*plicitous—*dis-putare* [double-reckon]—has run aground in it) and is the least disputable by virtue of its new quality. Belief is the opposite of doubt. Belief and doubt are not two kinds of knowledge that can be defined in continuity with each other, for neither of them is a cognitive act, and they are opposite passions. Belief is a sense for coming into existence, and doubt is a protest against any conclusion that wants to go beyond immediate sensation and immediate knowledge. The doubter, for example, does not deny his own existence, but he draws no conclusions, for he does not want to be deceived. [58]Insofar as he uses dialectics in continually making the opposite equally probable, he does not erect his skepticism on dialectical arguments, which are nothing more than outer fortifications, human accommodations;

IV
248

therefore he has no results, not even negative ones (for this would mean the acknowledgment of knowledge), but by the power of the will he decides to restrain himself and hold himself back (φιλοσοφία ἐφεκτική [ephectic philosophy])[59] from any conclusion.

Instead of having the immediacy of sensation and cognition (which, however, cannot apprehend the historical), the person who is not contemporary with the historical has the report of contemporaries, to which he relates in the same manner as the contemporaries to the immediacy. Even if what is said in the report has also undergone change, he cannot treat it in such a way that he does not personally assent to it and render it historical unless he transforms it into the unhistorical for himself. The immediacy of the report, that is, that the report is there, is the immediate present, but the historical character of the present is that it has come into existence, and the historical character of the past is that it was a present by having come into existence. As soon as someone who comes later believes the past (not the truth of it, for that is a matter of cognition, which involves essence and not being, but believes that it was something present by having come into existence), then the uncertainty of coming into existence is there,[60] and this uncertainty of coming into existence (the nothingness of that which is not—the possible "how" of the actual **thus and so**) must be the same for him as for the contemporary; his mind must be *in suspenso* just as the contemporary's. Then he no longer faces immediacy, or any necessity of coming into existence, but only the "thus and so" of *coming into existence*. The one who comes later does indeed believe by virtue of the contemporary's declaration, but only in the same sense as the contemporary believes by virtue of immediate sensation and cognition, but the contemporary cannot believe by virtue of that, and thus the one who comes later cannot believe by virtue of the report.

Thus at no moment does the past become necessary, no more than it was necessary when it came into existence or appeared necessary to the contemporary who believed it—that is, believed that it had come into existence. Belief and coming into existence correspond to each other and involve the annulled qualifications of being, the past and the future, and the present only insofar as it is regarded under the annulled qualification of being as that which has come into existence. Necessity, however, pertains to essence and in such a way that the qualification of essence specifically excludes coming into existence. The possibility from which emerged the possible that became the actual always accompanies that which came into existence and remains with the past, even though centuries lie between. As soon as one who comes later repeats that it has come into existence (which he does by believing it), he repeats its possibility, regardless of whether there may or may not be more specific conceptions of this possibility.

APPENDIX

Application

What has been said here applies to the directly historical, whose contradiction is only that it has come into existence, IV whose contradiction* is only that of coming into existence, 250 for here again one must not be deluded into thinking that it would be easier to understand that something has come into existence after it has come into existence than before it has come into existence. Anyone who thinks this still does not understand that it has come into existence; he has only the sensation and the cognitive immediacy of the present, which do not contain the coming into existence.

We shall now return to our poem and to our assumption

---

* Here the word "contradiction" must not be taken in the volatilized sense into which Hegel has misled himself and others and miscast contradiction itself—namely, that it has the power to produce something.[61] As long as nothing has come into existence, contradiction is merely the impelling urge to wonder, its *nisus* [impulse], not the *nisus* of coming into existence; when something has come into existence, contradiction is once again present as the *nisus* of wonder in the passion that reproduces the coming into existence.

that the god *has* been. With respect to the directly historical, it holds true that it cannot become historical for immediate sensation or cognition, no more for the contemporary than for someone coming later. But that historical fact (the content of our poem) has a unique quality in that it is not a direct historical fact but a fact based upon a self-contradiction (which adequately shows that there is no distinction between an immediate contemporary and someone who comes later, because, face to face with a self-contradiction and the risk entailed in assenting to it, immediate contemporaneity is no advantage at all). Yet it is a historical fact, and only for faith. Here faith is first taken in its direct and ordinary meaning [belief] as the relationship to the historical; but secondly, faith must be taken in the wholly eminent sense,[62] such that this word can appear but once, that is, many times but in only one relationship. One does not have *faith* that the god exists [*er til*], eternally understood, even though one assumes that the god exists. That is improper use of language. Socrates did not have faith that the god existed.[63] What he knew about the god he attained by recollection, and for him the existence of the god was by no means something historical. Whether his knowledge of the god was quite imperfect compared with the knowledge of one who, as assumed, received the condition from the god himself does not concern us here, because faith pertains not to essence but to being, and the assumption that the god exists defines him eternally, not historically. The historical is that the god *has come into existence* (for the contemporary), that he has been one present by *having come into existence* (for one coming later). But precisely here is the contradiction. In the immediate sense, no one can become contemporary with this historical fact (see above), but because it involves coming into existence, it is the object of faith. It is not a question here of the truth of it but of assenting to the god's having come into existence, whereby the god's eternal essence is inflected into the dialectical qualifications of coming into existence.

So, then, that historical fact remains. It has no immediate contemporary, because it is historical to the first power (faith

IV
251

in the ordinary sense [belief]); it has no immediate contemporary to the second power, since it is based on a contradiction (faith in the eminent sense). But for those who are very different with respect to time, this latter equality absorbs the differences among those who are temporally different in the first sense. Every time the believer makes this fact the object of faith, makes it historical for himself, he repeats the dialectical qualifications of coming into existence. No matter how many millennia have passed by, no matter how many consequences that fact elicited in its train, it does not therefore become more necessary (and, viewed definitively, the consequences themselves are only relatively necessary, inasmuch as they rest in that freely acting cause), to say nothing of the most inverted notion of all, that it should become necessary because of the consequences, since consequences as a rule have their basis in something else and do not give the basis for that. No matter how many preparations for that fact, no matter how many hints and symptoms of its coming a contemporary or a predecessor saw, that fact was not necessary when it came into existence—that is, that fact is no more necessary as future than it is necessary as past.

V[1]

The Follower at Second Hand

"My dear reader! Inasmuch as, according to our hypothesis, eighteen hundred and forty-three years intervene between the contemporary follower and this conversation, there seems to be sufficient occasion to ask about a follower at second hand, inasmuch as this situation presumably must have recurred frequently. The question seems imperative, likewise the question's claim on an explanation of the potential difficulties involved in defining the similarity and difference between a *follower* at second hand and a contemporary follower. Despite this, however, should we not first of all consider whether the question is just as proper as it is close at hand? That is, if the question should prove to be improper, or if one cannot raise such a question without talking like a fool and consequently is without justification in charging with foolishness someone who is sensible enough not to be able to answer it—the difficulties seem to be removed."

"Undeniably, for if the question cannot be asked, then the answer causes no trouble, and the difficulty has become a remarkably easy matter."

"But this is not the case, for suppose the difficulty consisted in perceiving that one cannot question in this way. Or have you perhaps already perceived this; was this perhaps what you meant when you said in our last conversation (Chapter IV) that you had understood me and all the consequences of what I said, although I as yet had not completely understood myself?"

"That was not at all my view, no more than it is my view that the question can be dismissed, even less so because it promptly poses a new question as to whether there is not a distinction among the many included in the category of follower at second hand, in other words, whether it is proper to separate such an enormous time span into such unequal parts: the contemporary period—the later period."

"You are thinking that it ought to be possible to speak of a follower at fifth, at seventh hand, etc. But even if, in order to indulge you, this were discussed, would it follow that a discussion of all these distinctions, provided there is no internal discord, should not be subsumed under one rubric in contrast to the category: the contemporary follower? [2]Or would the discussion proceed properly if it went about things as you did, so that it would be simple enough to do what you were crafty enough to do, namely, get the question about a follower at second hand changed into an entirely different question, whereby you found a chance to baffle me with a new question instead of agreeing or disagreeing with my proposal? But since you most likely do not wish to continue this conversation, fearing that it will degenerate into sophistry and bickering, I shall break it off. But from what I intend to enlarge upon, you will see that the comments we have just made to each other have been taken into consideration."

1. DIFFERENCES AMONG THE FOLLOWERS AT SECOND HAND

Here, then, we shall not reflect on the relation of the secondary follower to the contemporary follower, but the difference to be reflected upon is of such a kind that the similarity (in contrast to another group) of those differing among themselves remains, for the difference that is different only within itself remains within the similarity to itself. Therefore, it is not arbitrary to break off wherever one so desires, for the relative difference here is no sorites[3] from which the quality is supposed to appear by a *coup des mains* [sudden stroke], since it is within the specific quality. A sorites would eventuate only if to be contemporary were made dialectical in the bad sense, by showing, for example, that in a certain sense no one at all was contemporary, for no one could be contemporary with all the factors, or by asking when the contemporaneity ceased and when the noncontemporaneity began, whether there was not a *confinium* [border territory] of haggling in which the talkative understanding could say: to a certain degree etc. etc. All such inhuman profundity leads to nothing or in our time may lead to being considered genuine speculative profundity, since the despised sophism has become the miserable secret of genuine speculation (only the devil knows how it happened), and what antiquity regarded negatively—"to a certain degree" (the mocking toleration that mediates everything without making petty distinctions)—has become the positive, and what antiquity called the positive, the passion for distinctions,[4] has become foolishness.

Opposites show up most strongly when placed together, and therefore we choose here the first generation of secondary followers and the latest (the boundary of the given *spatium* [period], the eighteen hundred and forty-three years), and we shall be as brief as possible, for we are speaking not historically but algebraically,[5] and we have no desire to divert or fascinate anyone with the enchantments of multiplicity. On the contrary, in and with the difference we shall remember always to grasp securely the common similarity in the difference vis-à-vis the contemporary (not until the next section shall we see more specifically that the question about the follower at second hand, essentially understood, is an improper question), and we shall also bear in mind that the difference must not mushroom and confuse everything.

a. The First Generation of Secondary Followers

[6]This generation has (relatively) the advantage of being closer to the immediate certainty, of being closer to acquiring exact and reliable information about what happened from men whose reliability can be verified in other ways. This immediate certainty we have already assessed in Chapter IV. To be somewhat closer to it is no doubt deceptive, for the person who is not so close to the immediate certainty that he is immediately certain is absolutely distanced. Nevertheless, we

IV
254

shall make an appraisal of this relative difference (of the first
generation of secondary followers compared with the later
generations). How high should we appraise it? We can appraise it, however, only in relation to the advantage the contemporary has, but his advantage (immediate certainty in the
strict sense) we have already shown in Chapter IV to be dubious (*anceps*—dangerous), and we shall expand on this in
the next section.

IV
255

Suppose there lived in the generation closest to the contemporary generation a person who combined a tyrant's power
with a tyrant's passion, and he had the notion of concerning
himself with nothing but the establishment of the truth in
this matter—would he thereby be a follower? Suppose he
seized all the contemporary witnesses who were still alive
and those who were closest to them, had them sharply in-
terrogated one by one, had them locked up like those seventy translators[7] and starved them in order to force them to
speak the truth. Suppose he most cunningly contrived to have
them confront one another, simply in order to use every de-
vice to secure for himself a reliable report—would he, with
the aid of this report, be a follower? Would not the god
rather smile at him for wanting to obtain under duress in
this manner what cannot be purchased for money but also
cannot be taken by force? Even if that fact which we are
discussing were a simple historical fact,[8] difficulties would
not fail to arise if he tried to reach absolute agreement on
every small detail—a matter of enormous importance to him
because the passion of faith, that is, the passion that is just
as intense as faith, had taken a wrong turn toward the purely
historical. It is well known that the most honest and truthful
people are most likely to become entangled in contradictions
when they are subjected to inquisitorial treatment and an in-
quisitor's fixed idea; whereas non-contradiction in one's lies
is reserved only for the depraved criminal, because of an ex-
actitude sharpened by an evil conscience. But apart from all
this, that fact of which we speak is indeed no simple historical fact—so of what use is all this to him? If he managed to
obtain a complicated report in agreement down to the letter

and to the minute—then beyond all doubt he would be deceived. He would have attained a certainty even greater than that of the contemporary who saw and heard, for the latter would readily discover that he sometimes did not see and sometimes saw wrongly, and so also with his hearing, and he would continually have to be reminded that he did not see or hear the god directly and immediately but saw a human being in a lowly form who said of himself that he was the god—in other words, he would continually have to be reminded that this fact was based upon a contradiction. Would that person be served by the reliability of his report? Viewed historically, yes, but otherwise not, for all talk about the god's physical comeliness (since he was in the form of a mere servant—a simple human being like one of us—the object of offense), all talk about his direct and immediate divinity (since divinity is not an immediate qualification, and the teacher must first of all develop the deepest self-reflection in the learner, must develop the consciousness of sin as the condition for understanding), all talk about the immediate wondrousness of his acts (since the wonder *is* not immediately but is only for faith, inasmuch as the person who does not believe does not see the wonder)—all such talk is nonsense here and everywhere, is an attempt to put off deliberation with chatter.

This generation has relatively the advantage of being closer to the jolt of that fact. This jolt and its vibrations serve to arouse awareness. The significance of such awareness (which can also become offense) has already been appraised in Chapter IV. Assume that it is an advantage to be somewhat closer (compared with later generations)—the advantage is related only to the dubious advantage of the contemporary. The advantage is completely dialectical, just as the awareness is. Whether one is offended or whether one believes, the advantage is to become aware. In other words, awareness is by no means partial to faith, as if faith proceeded as a simple consequence of awareness. The advantage is that one enters into a state in which the decision manifests itself ever more clearly. This is an advantage, and this is the only advantage that means

IV
256

anything—indeed, it means so much that it is terrifying and is in no way an easy comfort. If that fact never falls stupidly and senselessly into the human rut, every succeeding generation will evince the same relation of offense as did the first, because no one comes closer to that fact immediately. No matter how much one is educated up[9] to that fact, it does not help. On the contrary, especially if the one doing the educating is already himself well read along these lines, it can help someone to become a well-trained babbler in whose mind there is neither a suggestion of offense nor a place for faith.

b. *The Latest Generation*

[10]This generation is a long way from the jolt, but, on the other hand, it does have the consequences to hold on to, has the probability proof of the outcome, has directly before it the consequences with which that fact presumably must have embraced everything, has close at hand the probability proof from which there nevertheless is no direct transition to faith, since, as has been shown, faith is by no means partial to probability—to say that about faith would be slander.* If that

---

* Generally speaking, the idea (however more specifically it is to be understood *in concreto*) of seriously wanting to link a probability proof to the improbable (in order to demonstrate: that it is probable?—but then the concept is changed; or in order to demonstrate: that it is improbable?—but to use probability for that is a contradiction) is so stupid that one could deem its occurrence impossible, but as waggery and jest I deem it hilariously funny and very entertaining to use in such a pinch. —In order to come to the aid of humanity, a magnanimous person wants to use a probability proof to help humanity into the improbable. He is immensely successful; deeply moved, he receives congratulations and expressions of gratitude, not only from dignitaries, who really know how to relish the proof but also from the community—alas, and that magnanimous person has in fact spoiled everything. —Or someone has a conviction, the substance of which is the unreasonable, the improbable. This individual is rather vain. This is the way to go about it. As unobtrusively and amiably as possible, one induces him to come out with his conviction. Suspecting no mischief, he propounds it incisively. When he has finished, one pounces on him in a way as irritating as possible to his vanity. He becomes perplexed, embarrassed, is ashamed of himself—"to think that he would adopt something unreasonable." In-

fact came into the world as the absolute paradox, all that comes later would be of no help, because this remains for all eternity the consequences of a paradox and thus just as definitively improbable as the paradox, unless it is assumed that the consequences (which, after all, are derived) gained retroactive power to transform the paradox, which would be just as acceptable as the assumption that a son received retroactive power to transform his father. Even if one considers the consequences purely logically—that is, in the form of immanence—it still remains true that a consequence can be defined only as identical and homogeneous with its cause, but least of all as having a transforming power. To have the consequences in front of one's nose, then, is just as dubious an advantage as to have immediate certainty, and someone who takes the consequences immediately and directly is just as deceived as someone who takes immediate certainty for faith.

IV
258

[12]The advantage of the consequences seems to be that that fact is supposed to have been *naturalized*[13] little by little. If this is the case (if this is thinkable), then the later generation plainly is in a position of advantage over the contemporary generation (and someone would have to be very stupid to be able to talk about the consequence in this sense and yet ro-

---

stead of calmly replying, "The honorable gentleman is a fool, it is unreasonable and must be that; despite all objections, which I myself have fully considered in a form far more terrifying than the fomulations anyone else is capable of posing to me, I nevertheless chose the improbable"—he tries to adduce a probability proof. Now one comes to his aid, lets oneself be convinced, and ends up with something like this: "Aha, now I see it! Why, this is the most probable of all!" One embraces him; if the waggery is carried very far, one kisses him and thanks him *ob meliorem informationem* [for having possessed better information] and on parting from him looks deeply once again into his romantic eyes and parts from him as a friend and foster brother for life and death, as from a kindred soul one has understood for all eternity. —Such waggery is justifiable, for if the man had not been vain, I would have been made to look like a fool in the face of the honest earnestness of his conviction. —What Epicurus says of the individual's relation to death (even though his observation is scant comfort) holds for the relation between probability and improbability: When I am, it (death) is not, and when it (death) is, I am not.[11]

IV
258

manticize about the good fortune of being contemporary with that fact) and can appropriate that fact quite unabashedly, without noticing the ambiguity of the awareness, from which offense can proceed as well as faith. That fact, however, has no respect for domestication, is too proud to desire a follower who joins on the strength of the successful outcome of the matter, refuses to be naturalized under the protection of a king or a professor—it is and remains the paradox and does not permit attainment by speculation. That fact is only for faith.

IV
259

Now faith certainly may become a person's *second nature*, but a person for whom it becomes second nature must certainly have had a *first* nature,[14] inasmuch as faith became the second. If that fact is to be *naturalized*, then with respect to the individual it may be said that the individual is born with faith—that is, with his second nature. If we start our explication on this premise, then every kind of nonsense begins to celebrate, for now the lid is off and the process cannot be stopped. Naturally, this nonsense must be fabricated by going further, for there truly was good sense in Socrates' view, even though we abandoned it in order to discover what was projected earlier, and nonsense of that sort would certainly feel deeply insulted not to be much further ahead than the Socratic view. There is some sense even in the transmigration of souls, but to be born with one's second nature, a second nature that refers to a given historical fact in time, is truly the *non plus ultra* [ultimate] in lunacy. Socratically understood, the individual has existed before he came into existence and recollects himself; thus recollection is pre-existence (not recollection of pre-existence). His nature (the one nature, for here there is no question of a first and second nature) is defined in continuity with itself. Here, however, everything faces forward and is historical; thus to be born with faith is just as plausible as to be born twenty-four years old. If someone born with faith could actually be pointed out, that someone would be a rarity more worthy of seeing than that which the barber in Den Stundesløse[15] tells of being born in the Neuen-Buden, even though to barbers and busybodies that would seem to be the dearest of all little creatures, the supreme triumph of speculation. —Or is the individual perhaps born with both natures simultaneously—not, please note, in such a way that two natures go together to form the common human nature, but with two complete human natures, one of which presupposes something historical in between. In that case, everything we projected in Chapter I is thrown into confusion; we stand not by the Socratic but in a confusion that not even Socrates would be able to terminate. It becomes a forward-oriented confusion that has much in common with the backward-oriented confusion created by Apollonius of Tyana.[16] In other words, unlike Socrates, he was not satisfied with recollecting himself as being prior to his coming into existence (the eternity and continuity of consciousness is the profound meaning and the idea in Socratic thought) but was in a hurry to go further— that is, he recollected who he had been before he became himself. If that fact has been naturalized, then birth is no longer *birth* but is also *rebirth*, such that he who has never been is reborn—when he is born. —For the individual life, this means that the individual is born with faith; for the human race, this means the same thing, so that the race, after the supervention of that fact, became an altogether different race and nevertheless is defined in continuity with the former.[17] In that case, the race ought to take a new name, for faith as we have formulated it certainly is not something inhuman, such as a birth within a birth (rebirth), but it certainly would become a fabulous monstrosity if it were such as we have let the objection want it to be.

The advantage of the consequences is a dubious advantage for another reason, insofar as it is not a simple consequence of that fact. Let us appraise the advantage of the consequences as high as possible; let us assume that this fact has completely transformed the world, has penetrated even the most insignificant trifle with its omnipresence—how did this take place? It certainly did not occur in one single stroke but occurred gradually—and gradually in what way? Presumably by every single generation's relating all over again to that

IV
260

fact? Therefore, this middle term must be inspected, so that the full strength of the consequences can be of benefit to someone only by a conversion. But cannot a misunderstanding also have consequences; cannot an untruth also be powerful? And has this not occurred in every generation? If all the generations were to entrust all the splendor of the consequences to the most recent generation as a matter of course— then the consequences are indeed a misunderstanding. Is not Venice built upon the sea, even though it was built in such a way that a generation finally came along that did not notice this at all, and would it not be a lamentable misunderstanding if this latest generation was so in error until the pilings began to rot and the city sank? But, humanly speaking, consequences built upon a paradox[18] are built upon the abyss,[19] and the total content of the consequences, which is handed down to the single individual only under the agreement that it is by virtue of a paradox, is not to be passed on like real estate, since the whole thing is in suspense.

IV
261

c. Comparison

We shall not pursue further what has been developed here but leave it up to each person to practice coming back to the idea from the most diverse sides, to practice using his imagination to uncover the strangest instances of relative differences and relative situations in order to figure it all out. In this way, the quantitative is limited and will have free range within the boundaries. The quantitative makes for the manifoldness of life and is continually weaving its multicolored tapestry. It is like that one goddess of fate who sat spinning, but then it holds true that thought, like the other goddess of fate, sees to clipping the thread[20]—something (apart from the metaphor) that ought to take place every time the quantitative wants to constitute quality.

The first generation of secondary followers has the advantage of having the difficulty present; for when it is the difficult that I am to appropriate, it is always an advantage, a relief, to have it made difficult for me. If it were to occur to the latest generation, observing the first generation and seeing it almost collapsing under the terror, to say, "This is inconceivable, for the whole thing is not so heavy that one cannot pick it up and run with it"—there no doubt would be someone who would reply, "Please, why do you not run with it; but just be sure that what you are running with is actually what is under discussion. We certainly do not dispute the fact that it is easy enough to run with the wind."

The latest generation has the advantage of ease, but as soon as it discovers that this ease is the very dubiousness that begets the difficulty, then this difficulty will correspond to the difficulty of the terror, and the terror will grip the last generation just as primitively[21] as it gripped the first generation of secondary followers.

2. THE QUESTION OF THE FOLLOWER AT SECOND HAND

IV
262

[22]Before considering the question itself, we shall make a few observations for orientation. (a) If that fact is regarded as a simple historical fact, then being contemporary counts for something, and it is an advantage to be contemporary (understood more explicitly as stated in Chapter IV), or to be as close as possible, or to be able to assure oneself of the reliability of the contemporaries, etc. Every historical fact is only a relative fact, and therefore it is entirely appropriate for the relative power, time, to decide the relative fates of people with respect to contemporaneity. More it is not, and only puerility and stupidity can make it the absolute by overestimation. (b) If that fact is an eternal fact, then every age is equally close to it—but, please note, not in faith, for faith and the historical are entirely commensurate, and thus it is only an accommodation to a less correct use of language for me to use the word "fact," which is taken from the historical. (c) If that fact is an absolute fact, or, to define it even more exactly, if that fact is what we have set forth, then it is a contradiction for time to be able to apportion the relations of people to it—that is, apportion them in a crucial sense, for whatever can be apportioned essentially by time is

eo ipso not the absolute, because that would imply that the absolute itself is a *casus*[23] in life, a status in relation to something else, whereas the absolute, although declinable in all the *casibus* of life, is continually the same and in its continual relation to something else is continually *status absolutus*. But the absolute fact is indeed also historical. If we pay no attention to that, then all our hypothetical discussion is demolished, for then we are speaking only of an eternal fact. The absolute fact is a historical fact and as such the object of faith. The historical aspect must indeed be accentuated, but not in such a way that it becomes absolutely decisive for individuals, for then we are back to (a) (although, understood in this way, it is a contradiction, for a simple historical fact is not an absolute fact and does not have the power for any absolute decision). But the historical must not be removed, either, for then we have only an eternal fact.

IV
263

[24]Just as the historical becomes the occasion for the contemporary to become a follower—by receiving the condition, please note, from the god himself (for otherwise we speak Socratically)—so the report of the contemporaries becomes the occasion for everyone coming later to become a follower—by receiving the condition, please note, from the god himself.

Now we shall begin. The person who through the condition becomes a follower receives the condition from the god himself. If so (and this is what we developed above, where we showed that immediate contemporaneity is only the occasion, yet, please note, not in such a way that the condition was present as a matter of course in the one for whom it was an occasion), then what place is there for that question about the follower at second hand? For one who has what one has from the god himself obviously has it at first hand, and one who does not have it from the god himself is not a follower.[25]

Let us assume something different. Let us assume that the contemporary generation of followers received the condition from the god and that now the succeeding generations are to receive the condition from these contemporaries—what would be the result? We shall not divert attention by reflecting upon the historical pusillanimity with which people in a new contradiction most likely would covet the report of those contemporaries—as if everything depended upon that—and thereby create a new confusion (for if they first begin with this, then the chaos is illimitable). No, if the contemporary gives the condition to one who comes later, then the latter will come to believe in him. He receives the condition from him, and thereby the contemporary becomes the object of faith for the one who comes later, because the one from whom the single individual receives the condition is *eo ipso* (see the foregoing) himself the object of faith and is the god.

Presumably such meaninglessness will be enough to frighten thought away from this assumption. But if the one who comes later also receives the condition from the god, then the Socratic relation will return—but, please note, within the total difference consisting of that fact and the relation of the single individual (the contemporary and the one who came later) to the god. That meaninglessness, however, is unthinkable in a sense different from our stating that that fact and the single individual's relation to the god are unthinkable. Our hypothetical assumption of that fact and the single individual's relation to the god contains no self-contradiction, and thus thought can become preoccupied with it as with the strangest thing of all. That meaningless consequence, however, contains a self-contradiction; it is not satisfied with positing something unreasonable, which is our hypothetical assumption, but within this unreasonableness it produces a self-contradiction: that the god is the god for the contemporary, but the contemporary in turn is the god for a third. Our project went beyond Socrates only in that it placed the god in relation to the single individual, but who indeed would dare come to Socrates with such nonsense—that a human being is a god in his relation to another human being? No, with a heroism that in itself takes boldness to understand, [26]Socrates understood how one human being is related to another. [27]And yet the point is to acquire the same understanding within the formation as assumed—namely, that one human being, insofar as he is a believer, is not indebted to someone else for something but is indebted to the god for everything. That this understanding is not easy will be seen without any difficulty, not easy especially when it comes to preserving this understanding continually (for to understand it once and for all without thinking the concrete objections, that is, fancying that one has understood it, is not difficult); and anyone who begins to exercise himself in this understanding no doubt will frequently enough catch himself in a misunderstanding, and if he wants to become involved with others, he had better take care. But if he has understood it, he will also understand that there is not and cannot be any question of a follower at second hand, for the believer (and only he, after all, is a follower) continually has the *autopsy*[28] of faith; he does not see with the eyes of others and sees only the same as every believer sees—with the eyes of faith.

What, then, can a contemporary do for someone who comes later? (a) He can tell someone who comes later that he himself has believed that fact; this actually is not a communication at all (that there is no immediate contemporaneity and that the fact is based upon a contradiction indicate this) but merely an occasion. Thus, if I say that this and this occurred, I speak historically; but if I say, "I believe and have believed that this happened, *although it is foolishness to the understanding and an offense to the human heart,*"[29] I have in the very same moment done everything to prevent anyone else from making up his mind in immediate continuity with me and to decline all partnership, because every single person must conduct himself exactly the same way. (b) In this form, he can tell the content of the fact, a content that still is only for faith, in quite the same sense as colors are only for sight and sound for hearing. In this form, he is able to do it; in any other form, he is only talking nonsense and perhaps inveigles the one who comes later to make up his mind in continuity with idle chatter.

[30]*In what sense can the trustworthiness of a contemporary be of interest to someone who comes later?* Whether he actually had the faith that he testified he had is of no concern to one who

comes later; it is of no benefit to him and makes no difference to him in coming to faith himself. Only the person who personally receives the condition from the god (which completely corresponds to the requirement that one relinquish the understanding and on the other hand is the only authority that corresponds to faith), only that person believes. If he believes (that is, fancies that he believes) because many good, honest people here on the hill have believed[31] (that is, have said that they have faith, because one person can go no further in checking up on someone else, even if that someone has borne, endured, and suffered everything for the sake of faith; the outsider cannot go beyond what the other says of himself, because untruth has exactly the same range as truth—for human eyes, not for God's), then he is a fool, and essentially it is incidental whether he believes by virtue of his own view and a perhaps widespread opinion about the faith of good, honest people or whether he believes a Münchhausen.[32] If the trustworthiness of the contemporary is to have any interest for him (alas, one can be sure that this is a subject that will cause an enormous sensation and will be the occasion for the writing of many volumes, for this deceptive appearance of earnestness, this deliberating about whether one or another is trustworthy, rather than about whether one has faith oneself, is tailor-made for intellectual laziness and European town talk), his interest must be in regard to something historical. What historical something? The historical that can be an object only for faith and cannot be communicated by one person to another—that is, one person can communicate it to another, but, please note, not in such a way that the other believes it; whereas, if he communicates it in the form of faith, he does his very best to prevent the other from adopting it directly. If the fact of which we speak were a simple historical fact, the historiographer's scrupulous accuracy would be of great importance. This is not the case here, for faith cannot be distilled from even the finest detail. The heart of the matter is the historical fact that the god has been in human form, and the other historical details are not even as important as they would be if the subject were a

latest generation are essentially alike, except that the latter generation has the occasion in the report of the contemporary generation, whereas the contemporary generation has the occasion in its immediate contemporaneity and therefore owes no generation anything. [33]But this immediate contemporaneity is merely the occasion, and the strongest expression of this is that the follower, if he understood himself, would have to wish that it would be terminated by the departure of the god from the earth. IV
267

But someone may be saying, "How very curious! I have read your discussion to the end, and really not without some interest, and I have been pleased to find no slogans, no invisible writing. But how you do twist and turn. Just as Saft always ends up in the pantry,[34] you always mix in some little phrase that is not your own, and that disturbs because of the recollection it prompts. This idea that it is to the follower's advantage that the god depart is in the New Testament, in the Gospel of John.[35] Yet, whether this was deliberate or not, whether or not you wanted to give that comment a particular effect by casting it in this form, as the matter now stands, a contemporary's advantage, which I originally was inclined to rate very high, seems to have been considerably reduced, since there can be no question of a follower at second hand or, what in other words amounts to the same thing, all are essentially alike.[36] Not only this, but, according to what you just said, immediate contemporaneity, considered as an advantage, becomes so dubious that the most that can be said of it is that it seems to become advantageous to terminate it. This means that it is an intermediate state that no doubt has its significance and cannot be omitted without, as you would say, returning to the Socratic, but, nevertheless, it does not have absolute significance for a contemporary. Therefore, he is not divested of the essential by the termination, since, on the contrary, he gains by it, although if it had not been, he would lose everything and return to the Socratic."

—"Very eloquently spoken, I would say, if modesty did not forbid me, for you speak as I myself would speak.

Yes, that is just how it is. Immediate contemporaneity is by
no means a decisive advantage, if one thinks it through and
is not inquisitive or in a hurry, does not wish—indeed, does
not wishfully strain at the leash, like that barber in Greece[37]
—to risk his life at once by being the first to tell the extraordinary news and is not so foolish as to regard such a death
as a martyr's death. [38]Immediate contemporaneity is so far
from being an advantage that the contemporary must expressly wish its termination lest he be tempted to run around
to see with his physical eyes and to hear with his mortal
ears—all of which is wasted effort—a lamentable, yes, a per-
ilous chore. But this, as you no doubt have observed yourself, actually belongs in another exposition, where the question would be what advantage the contemporary believer,
after having become a believer, could have from his contemporaneity; here we are considering only the extent to which
immediate contemporaneity makes it easier for someone to
become a believer. Someone who comes later cannot be
tempted in this way, for he has only the contemporary's report, which, insofar as it is a report, is in the inhibitive form
of faith. Therefore, if one who comes later understands himself, he must wish the contemporary's report to be not too
prolix and above all not to be couched in so many books that
they could fill the whole world.[39] In immediate contemporaneity there is a restlessness that ends only when it is said: It
is finished[40]—without, however, an elimination of the historical by the relaxation, for then everything is Socratic."

"In this way the equality is established, and the contending
parties are recalled to the equality."

"This is my opinion, too, but you must likewise consider
that the god himself is the reconciler. Would he bring about
a reconciliation with some human beings such that their reconciliation with him would make their difference from all
others blatantly flagrant? That would indeed bring conflict.
Would the god allow the power of time to decide whom he
would grant his favor, or would it not be worthy of the god
to make the reconciliation equally difficult for every human
being at every time and in every place, equally difficult be-

IV
268

cause no human being is capable of giving himself the condition (but neither is he to receive it from another human being and thereby produce new dissension), equally difficult, then, but also equally easy—inasmuch as the god gives it. This, you see, is why at the beginning I considered my project (that is, insofar as a hypothesis can be regarded as such) to be a godly project, and I still consider it to be that, without, however, being indifferent to any human objection, since, on the contrary, I once again ask you, if you have any legitimate protest to make, to present it."

"How festive you suddenly become! Even if the subject did not demand it, simply for the sake of the festivity one might decide to make an objection, unless it is more festive to refrain and your solemn invitation is indirectly intended only to bid silence. Lest the nature of my objection disturb the festivity, I shall draw my objection from the festivity with which, so it seems to me, a later generation comes to distinguish itself from the contemporary generation. I am well aware that the contemporary generation must really sense and suffer profoundly the pain involved in the coming into existence of such a paradox, or, as you put it, in the god's planting himself in human life. But gradually the new order of things must succeed in pushing its way through victoriously, and finally will come the happy generation that with songs of joy harvests the fruit that was sown in tears in the first generation. But this jubilant, triumphant generation that goes through life with singing and ringing, is it not quite different from the first and the earlier generations?"

"Yes, undeniably it is different, and perhaps so different that it does not even retain the equality that constitutes the condition for our speaking of it, the condition such that the generation's differences would frustrate my efforts to achieve equality. But is a jubilant, triumphant generation such as this, which, as you say, goes through life singing and ringing—which reminds me, if I remember correctly, of a jaunty, ale-Norse[41] translation of a Bible verse by a popular genius[42] — is a generation such as this actually supposed to be a believing generation? Truly, now, if faith ever has the notion of

IV
269

advancing *en masse* in triumph, it will not need to give anyone permission to sing satirical songs, because it would do no good for it to forbid everyone. Even if people were struck dumb, this mad procession would evoke shrill laughter, similar to the mocking sounds of nature on Ceylon,[43] for the faith that celebrates triumphantly is the most ludicrous of all. If the contemporary generation of believers did not find time to celebrate triumphantly, then no generation finds it, for the task is identical, and faith is always in conflict, but as long as there is conflict, there is the possibility of defeat. Therefore, with regard to faith, one never celebrates triumphantly ahead of time, that is, never in time, for when is there the time to compose songs of victory or the opportune occasion to sing them! If it does happen, then it is as if an army, drawn up to move into battle, were instead to march back to the city barracks in triumph. Even if no one laughed at this, even if the whole contemporary generation sympathized with this abracadabra, nevertheless, would not the smothered laughter of existence break forth where least expected! [44]What the later so-called believer did was even worse than what the contemporary sought in vain from the god (Chapter II) when he did not want the god to have to expose himself to lowliness and contempt, for the so-called believer who came later would himself not even be satisfied with lowly poverty and contempt, with contending foolishness, but no doubt he would be willing to believe if this were done with singing and ringing. Presumably the god would not, could not, say to such a one what he said to that contemporary: So, then, you love only the omnipotent one who does miracles, not the one who abased himself in equality with you.

"But here I shall stop. Even if I were a better dialectician than I am, I would still have my limits. Basically, an unshakable insistence upon the absolute and absolute distinctions[45] is precisely what makes a good dialectician. This is something we in our day have completely disregarded by canceling and in canceling the principle of contradiction,[46] without perceiving what Aristotle indeed emphasized, that the thesis that the principle of contradiction is canceled is based upon the principle of contradiction, since otherwise the opposite thesis, that it is not canceled, is equally true.[47]

"I shall make just one more comment with respect to your many allusions, all of which were aimed at my mixing of borrowed phrases in what was said. I do not deny this, nor shall I conceal the fact that I did it deliberately and that in the next section of this pamphlet, if I ever do write it, I intend to call the matter by its proper name and clothe the issue in its historical costume.[48] If I ever do write a second section—because a pamphlet writer such as I am has no seriousness, as you presumably will hear about me—why, then, should I now in conclusion pretend seriousness in order to please people by making a rather big promise? In other words, to write a pamphlet is frivolity—but to promise the system, that is seriousness and has made many a man a supremely serious man both in his own eyes and in the eyes of others. Yet it is not difficult to perceive what the historical costume of the next section will be. As is well known, Christianity is the only historical phenomenon that despite the historical—indeed, precisely by means of the historical—has wanted to be the single individual's point of departure for his eternal consciousness, has wanted to interest him otherwise than merely historically, has wanted to base his happiness on his relation to something historical. No philosophy (for it is only for thought), no mythology[49] (for it is only for the imagination), no historical knowledge (which is for memory) has ever had this idea—of which in this connection one can say with all multiple meanings that it did not arise in any human heart.[50] To a certain extent, however, I have wanted to forget this, and, employing the unrestricted judgment of a hypothesis, I have assumed that the whole thing was a whimsical idea of my own, one that I did not wish to abandon before I had thought it through. The monks never finished narrating the history of the world because they always began with the creation of the world. If in discussing the relation between Christianity and philosophy we begin by narrating what was said earlier, how shall we ever, not finish, but ever manage to begin, for history just keeps on growing. If we

begin with "that great thinker and sage Pontius Pilate, *executor Novi Testamenti*,"[51] who in his own way merits a good
deal of gratitude from Christianity and philosophy, even if
he did not invent mediation, and if, before beginning with
him, we have to wait for one or two decisive books (perhaps
the system) that have already been announced *ex cathedra* [with
authority] several times, how shall we ever manage to begin?"

[52]This project indisputably goes beyond the Socratic, as is apparent at every point. Whether it is therefore more true than the Socratic is an altogether different question, one that cannot be decided in the same breath, inasmuch as a new organ has been assumed here: faith; and a new presupposition: the consciousness of sin; and a new decision: the moment; and a new teacher: the god in time. Without these, I really would not have dared to present myself for inspection before that ironist who has been admired for millennia, whom I approach with as much ardent enthusiasm as anyone. But to go beyond Socrates when one nevertheless says essentially the same as he, only not nearly so well—that, at least, is not Socratic.

JOHANNES CLIMACUS,

OR

DE OMNIBUS DUBITANDUM EST

A NARRATIVE

Loquor de vera dubitatione in mente, et non de
ea, quam passim videmus contingere, ubi scilicet
verbis, quamvis animus non dubitet, dicit quis se
dubitare: non est enim Methodi hoc emendare,
sed potius pertinet ad inquisitionem pertinaciæ et
ejus emendationem [I speak of real doubt existing
in the mind, not of such doubt as we see exemplified when a man says that he doubts, though
his mind does not really hesitate. The cure of the
latter does not fall within the province of Method,
it belongs rather to inquiries concerning obstinacy
and its cure].

SPINOZA,
De intellectus emendatione
Tractatus. p. 511.

Μηδείς σου τῆς νεότητος καταφρονείτω
[Let no one despise your youth].

I TIMOTHY 4:12.

PLEASE NOTE

Someone who supposes that philosophy has never in all the world been so close as it is now to fulfilling its task of explaining all mysteries may certainly think it strange, affected, and scandalous that I choose the narrative form and do not in my small way hand up a stone to culminate the system.[1]
But someone who has become convinced that philosophy has never been so eccentric as now, never so confused despite all its definitions (much like the weather last winter when we heard simultaneously things never heard before at the same time—shouts of "mussels," "shrimp," and "watercress"—so that someone who was attentive to a particular shout at one moment would think it was winter, then spring, and then midsummer, while anyone who heard them all would think that nature had become confused and that the world would not last until Easter)[2] —that person will surely find it in order that I, too, by means of the form seek to counteract the detestable untruth that characterizes recent philosophy, which differs from older philosophy by having discovered that it is ludicrous to do what a person himself said he would do or had done—he will find it in order and will merely lament, as I do, that the one who here begins this task has no more authority[3] than I have.

Some years ago in the city of H . . . . .[1] there lived a young student by the name of Johannes Climacus,[2] who had no desire whatsoever to become prominent in the world, inasmuch as, on the contrary, he enjoyed living a quiet, secluded life. Those who knew him somewhat intimately tried to explain his inclosed nature, which shunned all close contacts with people, by supposing that he was either melancholy or in love. In a certain sense, those who supposed the latter were not incorrect, although they erred if they assumed that a girl was the object of his dreams. Such sentiments were totally foreign to his heart, and just as his external appearance was delicate and ethereal, almost transparent, his soul was likewise far too intellectual and spiritual to be captivated by a woman's beauty. In love he was, ardently in love—with
thought, or, more accurately, with thinking. No young lover can be more intensely moved by the incomprehensible transition that comes when erotic love [*Elskov*] awakens in his breast, by the stroke of lightning with which reciprocated love bursts forth in the beloved's breast, than he was moved by the comprehensible transition in which one thought connects with another, a transition that for him was the happy moment when, in the stillness of his soul, his presentiments and expectations were fulfilled. Thus, when in thought his head was bowed down like a ripe spike of wheat, it was not because he was listening to his beloved's voice but because he was listening to the secret whispering of thoughts; when he had a dreamy look, it was not because he had intimations of her picture but because the movement of thought was becoming visible to him. It was his delight to begin with a single thought and then, by way of coherent thinking, to climb step by step to a higher one, because to him coherent thinking was a *scala paradisi* [ladder of paradise],[3] and his blessedness seemed to him even more glorious than the an-

gels'. Therefore, when he arrived at the higher thought, it was an indescribable joy, a passionate pleasure, for him to plunge headfirst down into the same coherent thoughts until he reached the point from which he had proceeded. Yet this did not always turn out according to his desire. If he did not get just as many pushes as there were links in the coherent thinking, he became despondent, for then the movement was imperfect. Then he would begin all over again. If he was successful, he would be thrilled, could not sleep for joy, and for hours would continue making the same movement, for this up-and-down and down-and-up of thought was an unparalleled joy. In those happy times, his step was light, almost floating; at other times, it was troubled and unsteady. As long as he labored to climb up, as long as coherent thinking had as yet not managed to make its way, he was oppressed, because he feared losing all those coherent thoughts he had finished but which as yet were not perfectly clear and necessary. When we see someone carrying a number of fragile and brittle things stacked one upon the other, we are not surprised that he walks unsteadily and continually tries to maintain balance. If we do not see the stack, we smile, just as many smiled at Johannes Climacus, not suspecting that his soul was carrying a stack far taller than is usually enough to cause astonishment, that his soul was anxious lest one single coherent thought slip out, for then the whole thing would collapse. He did not notice that people smiled at him, no more than at other times he would notice an individual turn around in delight and look at him when he hurried down the street as lightly as in a dance. He did not pay any attention to people and did not imagine that they could pay any attention to him; he was and remained a stranger in the world.

If Climacus's conduct must have seemed somewhat remarkable to someone who did not know him very well, it was by no means unexplainable to someone who knew a little about his earlier life, for now in his twenty-first year he was to a certain extent the same as he had always been. His natural disposition had not been disturbed in childhood but had been developed by favorable circumstances. His home

IV
B 1
106

did not offer many diversions, and, since he practically never went out, he very early became accustomed to being occupied with himself and with his own thoughts. His father was a very strict man, seemingly dry and prosaic, but underneath this rough homespun cloak he concealed a glowing imagination that not even his advanced age managed to dim. When at times Johannes asked permission to go out, his request was usually refused; but occasionally his father, by way of compensation, offered to take his hand and go for a walk up and down the floor. At first glance, this was a poor substitute, and yet, like the rough homespun coat, it concealed something altogether different. The offer was accepted, and it was left entirely up to Johannes to decide where they should go for a walk. They walked through the city gate to the country palace[4] nearby or to the seashore or about the streets—according to Johannes's wish, for his father was capable of everything. While they walked up and down the floor, his father would tell about everything they saw. They greeted the passers-by; the carriages rumbled past, drowning out his father's voice; the pastry woman's fruits were more tempting than ever. Whatever was familiar to Johannes, his father delineated so exactly, so vividly, so directly and on the spot, down to the most trifling detail, and so minutely and graphically whatever was unfamiliar to him, that after a half-hour's walk with his father he was as overwhelmed and weary as if he had been out a whole day. Johannes quickly learned his father's magic art. What formerly took place as epic narrative now became a drama; they carried on a dialogue on their tour. If they walked along familiar paths, they watched each other lest something be overlooked. If the path was unfamiliar to Johannes, he made associations, while his father's omnipotent imagination was able to fashion everything, to use every childish wish as an ingredient in the drama that was taking place. For Johannes, it was as if the world came into existence during the conversation, as if his father were our Lord and he himself his favored one who had permission to insert his own foolish whims as hilariously as he wished, for he was never rebuffed, his father was never disturbed—

IV
B 1
107

everything was included and always to Johannes's satisfaction.

While life in his paternal home was contributing in this way to the development of his imagination, teaching him to relish ambrosia, the education he received in school was in harmony with this. [5]The sublime authority of Latin grammar and the divine dignity of rules developed a new enthusiasm. Greek grammar in particular appealed to him. [6]Because of it, he forgot to read Homer aloud to himself as he usually did in order to enjoy the rhythms of the poem. The Greek teacher presented grammar in a more philosophical way.[7] When it was explained to Johannes that the accusative case, for example, is an extension in time and space, that the preposition does not govern the case but that the relation does, everything expanded before him. The preposition vanished; the extension in time and space became like an enormous empty picture for intuition. Once again his imagination was engaged, but in a way different from before. [8]What had entertained him on the walking tours was the filled space into which he could not fit snugly enough. His imagination was so creative that a little went a long way. Outside the one window in the living room grew approximately ten blades of grass. Here he sometimes discovered a little creature running among the stems. These stems became an enormous forest that still had the compactness and darkness the grass had. Instead of the filled space, he now had empty space; he stared again but saw nothing except the enormous expanse.

While an almost vegetative dozing in imagination—at times more esthetic, at times more intellectual—was being developed, another side of his soul was also being acutely fashioned—namely, his sense for the sudden, the surprising.[9] This came about not through the magic means customarily used to keep children spellbound but by means of something far superior. His father combined an irresistible dialectic with an omnipotent imagination. [10]Whenever his father on occasion engaged in an argument with someone else, Johannes was all ears, all the more so because everything proceeded with an almost festive formality. His father always let his opponent

IV
B 1
108

say everything he had to say and, as a precaution, always asked him if he had anything more to say before he began his response. [11]Johannes, having followed the opponent's case with keen attention, had in his own way a co-interest in the outcome. Then came the pause; his father's response followed, and—look!—in a twinkling everything was changed. How it happened remained a riddle to Johannes, but his soul delighted in this drama. The opponent spoke again, and Johannes listened even more attentively, lest he lose the thread of thought. The opponent summed up his argument, and Johannes could almost hear his heart beating, so impatiently did he wait to see what would happen. —It did happen. In an instant, everything was turned upside down; the explicable was made inexplicable, the certain doubtful, the opposite was made obvious. When a shark wants to snatch its prey, it has to turn over on its back, since its mouth is on the belly side; its back is dark, its belly silvery white. It is said to be a glorious sight to see this shift in color. It is supposed to gleam so brightly at times that it almost hurts the eyes, and yet they take pleasure in seeing it. Johannes witnessed a similar shift when he listened to his father argue. He forgot what was said by both his father and the opponent, but he never forgot this thrill in his soul. In his life at school, he had similar experiences. He saw how one word could change a whole sentence, how a subjunctive in the middle of an indicative sentence could throw a different light on the whole.[12] The older he grew, the more his father involved himself with him and the more he became aware of that inexplicable quality. It was as if his father had a secret understanding of what Johannes wanted to say and, therefore, with a single word could confuse everything for him. When his father was not acting just as critic but was himself discoursing on something, Johannes perceived how he went about it, how he step by step arrived at what he wanted. He began to suspect that the reason his father could turn everything upside down with a single word had to be that he, Johannes, must have forgotten something in the step-by-step process of thought.

What other children have in the enchantment of poetry

IV
B 1
109

and the surprise of fairy tales, Johannes Climacus had in the repose of intuition and the interchange of dialectic. These delighted the child, became the boy's play, the young man's desire. In this way, his life had a rare continuity, not marked by the various transitions that generally denote the separate periods. As Johannes grew older, he had no toys to lay aside, for he had learned to play with what would be his life's earnest occupation, and yet it did not thereby lose its appeal. A little girl plays so long with her doll that at last it is transformed into her beloved, for woman's whole life is love. His life had a similar continuity, for his whole life was thinking.

Climacus became a university student, took the qualifying examination, reached the age of twenty, and yet no change took place in him—he was and remained a stranger to the world. He did not, however, avoid people; on the contrary, he tried to find like-minded people. But he did not express his views, never betrayed what was going on inside him— the erotic in him was too deep for that. He felt that he might blush if he talked about it; he was afraid of learning too much or learning too little. He was always attentive, however, when others were speaking. Just as a young girl deeply in love prefers not to speak about her love but with almost painful tension listens when other girls talk about theirs, in order to test in silence whether or not she is just as happy or even happier, to snatch every important clue—just so did Johannes silently pay attention to everything. Then, when he came home, he reflected on what the philosophizers had said, for it was their company, of course, that he sought.

To want to be a philosopher, to want to devote himself exclusively to speculation, had not occurred to him. He was still not profound enough for that. It is true that he did not dart from one thing to another—thinking was and remained his passion—but he still lacked the reflective composure required for grasping a deeper coherence. The least significant and the most significant things tempted him alike as points of departure for his pursuits; for him the result was not important—only the processes interested him. At times, he did become aware of how he would arrive at one and the same

IV
B 1
110

result from quite different points, but this did not attract his attention in a deeper sense. His desire at all times was only to press his way through. Wherever he suspected a labyrinth, he had to find the way. Once he began, nothing could influence him to stop. If he ran into difficulty, if he tired of it too early, he usually resorted to a very simple remedy. He would lock himself in his room, make everything as festive as possible, and loudly and clearly say: I *will* do it. From his father he had learned that one can do what one wills,[13] and his father's life had not disproved the theory. This experience had given Johannes's soul an indescribable pride. That there might be something one could not do even though one willed it was intolerable to him. But his pride was not a matter of a weak will, because once he had spoken these dynamic words, he was ready for everything; he then had an even higher goal: with his will to press his way through the windings of the difficulty. This again was an adventure that inspired him. In this way his life was always adventurous. He did not require forests and travels for his adventures but merely what he had: a little room with one window.

IV
B 1
111

Although he was led into ideality at an early age, this by no means weakened his belief and trust in actuality [*Virkelighed*]. The ideality by which he was nourished was so close to him, everything took place so naturally, that this ideality became his actuality, and in turn he was bound to expect to find ideality in the actuality all around him.[14] [15]His father's depression contributed to this. That his father was an extraordinary man was the last thing Johannes came to know about him. That his father amazed him more than any other person did, he already knew; yet he knew so few people that he had no standard of measurement. That his father, humanly speaking, was rather extraordinary, he did not learn in his paternal home. Once in a while, when an older, trusted friend visited the family and engaged in a more confidential conversation with his father, Johannes frequently heard him say, "I am good for nothing; I cannot do a thing; my one and only wish would be to find a place in a charitable institution." This was no jest. There was not a trace of irony in his father's words; on the contrary, there was a gloomy earnestness about them that troubled Johannes. Nor was it a casual comment, for his father could demonstrate that a person of the least importance was a genius compared with him. No counter-demonstration achieved anything, for his irresistible dialectic could make one forget what was most obvious, could compel one to stare fixedly at the observation he made as if there were nothing else in the world. Johannes, whose whole view of life was, so to speak, hidden in his father, since he himself did not get to see very much, became entangled in a contradiction, because it was a long time before it dawned on him that his father contradicted himself— if by nothing else, then by the skill with which he could vanquish any opponent and reduce him to silence. Johannes's trust in actuality was not weakened; he had not imbibed ideality from books that do not leave those they bring up ignorant of the fact that the glory they describe is nevertheless not found in this world. His formative influence was not a man who knew how to propound his knowledge as valuable but was instead one who knew how to render it as unimportant and valueless as possible.

IV
B 1
112

Pars Prima

IV
B 1
112

JOHANNES CLIMACUS BEGINS TO PHILOSOPHIZE WITH THE AID OF TRADITIONAL IDEAS[1]

INTRODUCTION

²Although he had been a student for a few years, Johannes had done relatively little reading, especially for a student. In grammar school, he had become well acquainted with the classics and was happy to go through them again, although their substance had no effect upon what was going on inside him. On occasion, one or another modern work came into his hands, but he had no perception of what significance the reading of it should have for him. Historical works did not engage him, because the preponderant development of his mind had deprived him of a sense for empirical actuality [*Virkelighed*], and just as he was usually indifferent to what other people said and thought if it had no relation to thinking, so, too, he was indifferent to all accounts of what was said and done by those who had lived earlier. If he encountered a recent philosophical work, he of course did not lay it aside before he had read it, but when he had read it, he often felt dissatisfied and discouraged. His whole orientation of mind made him feel uncomfortable about reading. At times, a title would tempt him, and he would go to the book gladly and expectantly, but, lo and behold, it would discuss many other things, least of all that which one would have expected. If at length he worked his way little by little through to what the title had justified his searching for, the thought process would frequently be interrupted and the matter left undecided. He was often annoyed to find so much attention paid to what appeared to him to be incidentals. The investigation would be interrupted in order to correct one or another singular opinion advanced by some author totally unknown to him. For him to understand this digression properly would require a prior reading of that man's book. That in turn perhaps would presuppose others etc. He also thought he observed that the reason for incorporating a particular opinion of a particular author would be a very peculiar one: because

he lived in the same city as the writer, because he wrote in the same journal, etc. He did not always find rigorous, dialectical movement; he sadly missed the wonderful sport of dialectic, its puzzling surprises. After having made several attempts, he gave up reading. He once again devoted himself to his own thinking, even if it did not lead him to anything. [3]He refrained, however, from any hasty judgments about those particular books or about books in general. He heard others make altogether different judgments and concluded that the fault was his own, that his upbringing had been deficient, and that, even if it had not taught him anything else, it still had taught him to draw this conclusion.

In listening to others talk, he also observed that he had not encountered the writings of the great thinkers among the recent philosophers. Again and again he heard these names mentioned with enthusiasm, almost with adoration. It gave him unspeakable joy to hear their names, even though he did not dare to read them, because he had heard that they were so difficult that the study of them would require ages. It was not cowardice or indolence that deterred him but a painful feeling inherent in him from early childhood: he was not like other people. He was far from feeling happy about this difference but instead [4]he felt it as a pressure he probably would have to endure all his life. He felt like a child who was delivered into the world with much pain and who could not forget this pain even if his mother had forgotten it in her joy over his birth.[5]

As for reading, Johannes now experienced a strange contradiction. The familiar books did not satisfy him, but still he did not dare to lay the blame on the books. The outstanding books he did not dare to read. [6]So he read less and less, followed his inclination to ponder in silence, became increasingly shy, fearful that the major thinkers would smile at him if they heard that he, too, wanted to think, just as fine ladies smile at the lowly maiden if she has the audacity of also wanting to know the bliss of erotic love. He was silent, but listened all the more attentively.

[7]When he listened to the others speak, he noted that a par-

IV
B 1
114

ticular main idea came up again and again, whereupon he snatched it and made it the object of his own thinking. Thus fate came to his aid by providing him with subject matter in exactly the way he needed it. The purer, the more virginal, so to speak, the task, the more precious it was to him; the less others had assisted his thinking, the happier he was and the better everything went for him. He seemed to consider it an imperfection that he could do his best thinking about an idea if it came to him as new-fallen snow without having passed through the hands of others. [8]He truly considered it a great thing to be able, as were the others, to toss about in the multiple thoughts of multiple thinkers. Yet he soon forgot this pain in the joy of thinking.

[9]By listening to the conversation of others, he became particularly aware of one thesis that came up again and again, was passed from mouth to mouth, was always praised, always venerated.* [11]He now encountered the thesis that would come to play a decisive role in his life. This thesis became for his life what in other respects a name frequently is in a person's history—everything can be said in all brevity by mentioning this name.

This thesis became a task for his thinking. Whether it would take a long or a short time to think it through, he did not know. But this he did know: until that time came, he would not let go of it, even though it were to cost him his life.

What made him even more enthusiastic was the connection usually made between this thesis and becoming a philosopher. Whether he would be able to become a philosopher, he did not know, but he would do his best. With quiet solemnity, it was decreed that he should begin. He encouraged himself by recalling the enthusiasm of Dion, who, upon going aboard ship with a handful of men to begin the war with Dionysius, said: It is enough for me just to have participated. If I were to die the moment I set foot on land without

IV
B 1
115

In margin: *Many were the times he heard it repeated: *De omnibus dubitandum est* [Everything must be doubted].[10]

having achieved a thing, I would still regard this death as happy and honorable. [12]

He now sought to clarify for himself the connection between that thesis and philosophy. Preoccupation with it would become for him an encouraging prelude; the clearer the connection became, the more enthusiastically he would proceed to the main concern. So he closed himself up in himself with that philosophical thesis, and at the same time he paid careful attention to every clue he could glean. If he perceived that his own thought process was different from that of others, he memorized theirs, went home, and began all over from the beginning. That their thought process was generally very brief did indeed strike him, but he saw that only as a new point to their advantage.

Now he began his operations and immediately juxtaposed the three principal statements he had heard regarding the relation of this thesis to philosophy. These three theses were as follows: (1) *philosophy begins with doubt;*[13] (2) *in order to philosophize, one must have doubted;*[14] (3) *modern philosophy begins with doubt.*[15]

IV
B 1
116

I

Modern Philosophy Begins
with Doubt

[1]What struck him at once in these three theses was that they did not seem to be at all of the same kind. Although in a strict sense the first two, owing to their universality, had to be regarded as philosophical, because they said something universal concerning the philosophy of every age and place or the philosophizer of every age and place, the third one seemed to be a historical report that would have to undergo a transformation before it could claim to be of philosophical nature in the strict sense. Historically, it could indeed be interesting to learn that modern philosophy begins with doubt, in the same way that it could be interesting to learn whether it begins in Germany or in France and with whom. If, however, a transformation did occur, then it probably would be subsumed under one of the previous theses.

In order to check whether this was so, he decided to explore it.

PARA. 1. HOW MUST THE THESIS BE
UNDERSTOOD LITERALLY?[2]

Here he tried to explain the possible significance of adding to "philosophy" the adjective "modern," which is indeed a historical predicate. In that case, the thesis would state something only about a specific historical philosophy. He accepted the thesis as true, for neither his reading nor his development was adequate for an investigation of it. The thesis implied an older philosophy that had not begun in the same way, for otherwise the thesis would be very imperfectly propounded. He then asked whether he could be justified in concluding that a more recent philosophy could in turn begin in another way and therefore that philosophy could begin in various ways and yet continue to be philosophy. To be as brief as possible, he asked whether a later philosophy in turn could begin in the same way as that older philosophy and yet be philosophy, or whether, after modern philosophy had begun with doubt, this would have a decisive influence on the whole future. If so, would modern philosophy also have a retroactive power, so that the extent to which that older philosophy can be called philosophy would become dubious, even though that older philosophy began with something else? That is, if, because of its beginning, modern philosophy has excluded for all future time the possibility of another beginning, this suggests that this beginning is more than a historical beginning, is an essential beginning. In that case, modern philosophy is essential philosophy, and to call that older version philosophy is merely an accommodation. —If the words were to be interpreted in this manner, the thesis would thereby have undergone the transformation by which it would become identical with the first thesis, that philosophy begins with doubt.

Whether this was philosophy's position, he did not know. [3]He sought in vain to find an illuminating clue in the discourse of others. If this was the view, then it seemed strange to him that people talked so imprecisely, that they confused historical and eternal categories in such a way that when they seemed to be saying something historical they were saying something eternal. Why did they not limit themselves to the first thesis, that philosophy begins with doubt, for then nothing is doubtful, then everything that does not begin with doubt, whatever it may be otherwise, is not philosophy. True enough, this would have the odd result that the eternal beginning had begun in time in such a manner that there had been ages in which it had not begun, whereas he pictured the eternal beginning as present in every age. If he had understood correctly, Christianity's claim that it had come into the world by a beginning that was simultaneously his-

IV
B 1
117

torical and eternal had caused philosophy much difficulty; it must, then, be risky for philosophy to want to say the same thing regarding itself.

From another side, also, Johannes Climacus made the words of the thesis an object of deliberation. The thesis states: "modern *philosophy*"; it does not speak of a particular philosopher who is historically reported to have begun with doubting but speaks of modern philosophy as a whole. It does not use a historical tense or a present in the historical style such as one uses in saying "Descartes begins with doubt," although one nevertheless intends to designate this as something past that is a present only in the historical narrative. One uses an eternal present, as if modern philosophy is also something more than a particular philosopher. Up to that point, the thesis seems to be saying more than something merely historical. It must be assumed to do this for another reason as well. Modern philosophy must be assumed to be even yet in the process of becoming; otherwise there already would be something more modern, in relation to which it would be older. Is it not conceivable that modern philosophy, as it advanced and spread, became aware of its wrong beginning, which, regarded as a beginning would prove not to be a beginning? By what authority is this beginning declared a beginning for all modern philosophy? This can be correct only if the beginning itself is the essential beginning for modern philosophy, but, historically speaking, this cannot be decided until modern philosophy is concluded in its entirety. [4]If it is asserted before that time, it must be said and understood eternally—in other words, it must be because this beginning is the essential beginning for all philosophy. In that case, that thesis has once again undergone a transformation whereby it has become identical with the first thesis—namely, that philosophy begins with doubt.

Why, then, did philosophy use two expressions, one of which either says the same as the other and is, according to that assumption, incorrect, or it says something else and, if that is assumed, is obscure?

Although the ambiguity of the thesis, as it had now be-

IV
B 1
118

come apparent to him, could have made him think twice about going further, Johannes nevertheless decided to test its implications by assuming for the time being that it was a historical thesis. As such, then, it would be different from the first thesis, and he would have only the choice of assuming either that it was a total superfluity, which could only have a disturbing effect, [5]or that it was a somewhat oddly expressed historical thesis.

PARA. 2. HOW DID IT HAPPEN THAT MODERN PHILOSOPHY BEGAN WITH DOUBT?[6]

[7]Johannes Climacus assumed that modern philosophy began with doubt and now asked how it happened, whether it was by accident or by necessity, whether this beginning was an accidental or a necessary beginning.

a. Was it by accident that modern philosophy began with doubt?

At this point, Johannes Climacus asked whether it was by an accident like that by which purple was discovered[8]—an accident of such a nature that it would forever remain an accident. If that were the case, then the thesis that modern philosophy begins with doubt would contain a historical accident from which nothing can be concluded with respect to either a prior or a subsequent philosophy or to philosophy in general, no more than one would dare to conclude from what happened to that dog that every dog must discover purple. If so, then that thesis would not only contain a merely historical report but would contradict the first thesis, that philosophy begins with doubt, for if these theses are juxtaposed, it would appear that the essential happened by accident.

He then asked whether the accident by which modern philosophy came to begin with doubt was perhaps of such a nature that it concealed a necessity that in the next moment explained the accidental, whether that accident was of the same nature as the accident by which Newton discovered the

law of gravity, for although it was an accident, yet the law   IV
it discovered immediately explained the accident itself as a   B 1
necessity. If so, then it would only appear to be the case—in   120
a defective historical sense—that modern philosophy had by
accident begun with doubt, since at the same moment modern philosophy would have had to discover the necessity of
its beginning that way. This necessity for modern philosophy as a historical document could not as yet be discovered,
inasmuch as modern philosophy is not as yet concluded. If,
then, this necessity was discovered, it would have to be in
the eternal sense, because modern philosophy would be philosophy in general. This discovery would then be decisive
for the whole future and be retroactive for the whole past
with respect to the beginning of philosophy. To that extent,
then, that thesis would have undergone a transformation
whereby it would become identical with the first thesis.

b. Was it by necessity that modern philosophy began with doubt?

Now he asked what the nature of that which preceded must
have been in order to necessitate modern philosophy's beginning with doubt, whether that which preceded was a philosophy or something else. Answering his own question, he
decided that, according to the wording of the thesis, it had
to be a philosophy. Of what nature must the philosophy
have been that could make it necessary for modern philosophy to begin with doubt? Whether that philosophy, which
by way of its precedence had made it necessary for modern
philosophy to begin with doubt, whether that philosophy
and modern philosophy alone were philosophy, so that if
there formerly had been a philosophy in the world that had
begun some other way, that philosophy would have to reconcile itself to not being philosophy? He inquired further
whether that antecedent philosophy itself was begun by accident or by necessity. Lest he be led too far, he tried to
explain the following: If modern philosophy by necessity begins with doubt, then its beginning is defined in continuity
with an earlier philosophy. Then if we wanted to say some-   IV
                                                               B 1
                                                               121

thing historical about what philosophy begins with, we presumably should rather mention that with which the antecedent philosophy began, inasmuch as the beginning of modern philosophy would be only a consequence within an earlier beginning. (If this is assumed, it would have a disturbing effect on the first thesis—that philosophy begins with doubt.) Moreover, he already perceived here the difficulty he would have to encounter later: namely, that such a consequence would be difficult to think, because the beginning with which modern philosophy began would be defined as a severance. It would have to be a unique kind of consequence—namely, a consequence by which the opposite results from something. This is ordinarily called a leap.[9]

For the time being, however, he clung as well as he could to the thought that it was by way of a necessary consequence that modern philosophy began with doubt. He concluded, then, that the beginning of modern philosophy had to be an essential beginning for philosophy, since one certainly could not be justified—except merely historically and accidentally—in declaring something essential about a development as yet unfinished. After all, the beginning might turn out to be no beginning at all but a misunderstanding, therefore least of all the beginning of a philosophy. The beginning philosopher could never be justified in saying: With me begins modern philosophy. [10]Nor would the sanction of his successor be sufficient unless the declaration itself were something essential about all philosophy. If the statement were understood in this way, then once again the thesis would be transformed and made identical to that first thesis.

PARA. 3. A PRESENTIMENT.

[11]In all this deliberating, Johannes Climacus did not advance one step. This pained him. [12]Since he could not have any confidence in such a disturbing tautology, he could not make up his mind to assume that the third thesis and the first thesis were identical. It was disturbing because it encouraged people to think something different, although what was thought

was the same. If they thought the same thing with regard to both theses, the tautology would be disturbing. He could not maintain the difference without making a little change, by which the thesis became a historical triviality, as if one said: Descartes began with doubt and several other philosophers followed his example. No objection, philosophically speaking, can be made against such a statement. If such a statement evoked difficulties, they would have to be historical in nature—for example, was it actually the case that they themselves said they had done it, or was it actually true that they had done what they said they had done.

In vain did he hope to be enlightened by listening to the discussion of others—in vain. They used the first and the third theses as totally identical; at times they stated the one, at times the other, sometimes both at once. Sometimes in the course of a conversation, one person used the one thesis, the other person responded with the other, and they understood each other and understood that they were saying the same thing. The thesis remained unexplained, but an explanation was precisely what he needed, and his own private thinking had made him more receptive to instruction by others. But the explanation was not forthcoming; on the contrary, at times the thesis was repeated so swiftly by those speaking that he almost became dizzy because of the uniformity. Then he would always return home troubled, because what seemed so easy for others, so that they only needed to outline it vaguely, was so hard for him to think.

He thought through the thesis again and again, tried to forget what he had thought in order to begin again, but, lo and behold, he always arrived at the same point. Yet he could not abandon the thesis; it seemed as if a mysterious power held him to it, as if something were whispering to him: Something is hiding behind this misunderstanding. He then tried to combine what he had separated in thinking that the thesis must be either purely philosophical or purely historical. Presumably it is a mystery that modern philosophy is simultaneously the historical and the eternal, he thought, and what is more, it is aware of this itself. Indeed, it is a union similar to the union of the two natures in Christ. With every move modern philosophy makes, it becomes conscious of the eternal significance of this move, or, better stated, it becomes conscious of the significance before it makes the move, for otherwise it would be conceivable that the move itself was such that it could never acquire eternal significance unless philosophy's historical progress was absolutely identical with the idea's own movement. But then such a step forward would not be a historical movement. Then, in order to be admitted into the system, modern philosophy would not need to undergo any transformation, any retroactive transfiguration, any purification of forgetfulness, but down to the least little detail it would go straight into the system, just as if a historical personage were so poetic that every word, every gesture of his were pure poetry—hence he would not need to undergo any transformation in order to go on stage but could go right on from the street just exactly as he walked and stood, and without the least embarrassment.[13]

But it still did not become clear to him how he was to think such a combination. Restless and troubled, he was full of presentiment. He had the presentiment that it must be something out of the ordinary; he had the presentiment that to be a philosopher these days must be something indescribably difficult. If modern philosophy is like that, it must, of course, be the same for the individual philosopher. Thus, the individual philosopher *must become conscious of himself and in this consciousness of himself also become conscious of his significance as a moment*[14] *in modern philosophy; in turn modern philosophy must become conscious of itself as an element in a prior philosophy, which in turn must become conscious of itself as an element in the historical unfolding of the eternal philosophy.* Thus the philosopher's consciousness must encompass the most dizzying contrasts: his own personality, his little amendment—the philosophy of the whole world as the unfolding of the eternal philosophy.

It was a long time before Johannes managed to think this enormous thought correctly and definitely. Just as a man rolling a heavy load up a mountain is often overcome so that

his foot slips and the load rolls down, so it went with him.
Finally he was confident that he could make the movement
with ease. He then decided to let the thought work with all
its weight, for he made a distinction between the laborious-
ness of thinking and the weight of the thought. As a historical thought, he thought the thought with ease. He had collected new strength, felt himself whole and complete; he put
his shoulder, as it were, to the thought—and look, it overwhelmed him and *he fainted!* When he recovered consciousness, he hardly dared to turn his attention to that thought. It
dawned on him that it could drive a person to madness, at
least someone who did not have stronger nerves than he had.
All the more did he admire those who were able to think
such things as easily as if it were all only a prank.

He became discouraged, but as he sank into discourage-
ment he once again, half against his will, grasped that enormous thought. He was actually too troubled to think properly, but it seemed to him as if that thought, which appeared
to be so extremely positive, actually was a skepticism, [15]since
the individual's knowledge was always merely knowledge
about himself as a moment and about his significance as a
moment. On the presupposition that this was actually possible—something he still could not really grasp, since it was
not clear to him how a moment could become conscious of
itself merely as a moment, inasmuch as this consciousness
was an impossibility without a consciousness that was more
than a consciousness of oneself as a moment, because otherwise my consciousness would have to reside in another—this
knowledge would then become a very relative knowledge
and would by no means be an absolute knowledge. But how
would it be possible for every single moment to become aware
also of its eternal validity as a moment in the whole? That,
after all, would require that the individual be omniscient and
that the world be finished.

That the single individual could become conscious of the
eternal, he could perhaps grasp, and an earlier philosophy
presumably had thought to have grasped it, too—that is, if
there had been any such thing at all. But to become con-

scious of the eternal in the whole historical concretion, indeed, according to the standard that it did not involve only the past, this he believed was reserved for the deity. Neither could he grasp at what instant in time a person would become so transfigured to himself that he, although himself present to himself, became past to himself. He believed that this had to be reserved for eternity and that eternity was only abstractly present in time.

Insofar as there had been an earlier philosophy, the individual philosopher presumably would also have used his predecessors, would have perceived that he could appropriate this, correct that, etc., but it probably would not occur to him to want to see through the eternal necessity by which one philosopher emerged from another and he himself from his predecessors in an eternal continuity. Even though thinking about the past could succeed in gaining an intimation of an inner necessity of this kind (please note that the more distant the past, the greater the possibility of illusion), it seemed to him that, with regard to the present, it was an impossibility. This did not obtain permission to become a present out of an eagerness to become a past, the sooner the better, but in this way it would become neither. He clarified this for himself by considering personal life. When someone looks back over his life, it may appear, particularly the earlier part of it, to be permeated by necessity.[16] However, if someone beginning a specific period of time in his life wants first to become conscious of this in its eternal validity as an element in his life, he will precisely thereby prevent it from acquiring significance, for he will nullify it before it has been by wanting that which is a present to manifest itself to him in that very instant as a past.[17]

It would already be a precarious matter, so it seemed to him, for someone to undertake to prophesy. And yet, just as one could have an intimation of a necessity in the past, was it not also conceivable that one could have an intimation of a necessity in the future. Philosophy, however, wanted to do something even more difficult: it wanted to permeate everything with the thought of eternity and necessity, wanted

IV
B 1
125

to do this in the present moment, which would mean slaying the present with the thought of eternity and yet preserving its fresh life. It would mean wanting to see what is happening as that which has happened and simultaneously as that which is happening; it would mean wanting to know the future as a present and yet simultaneously as a future.

This is as far as Johannes Climacus came in his consideration of that thesis. It did not happen as quickly as the telling of it here. It cost him time and hard work, but he was poorly rewarded for his troubles. If he were to have an opinion about the implications of the thesis under discussion, it would be this—that it was an impossibility. Yet he did not have the courage to believe this.[18]

IV
B 1
126

II

Philosophy Begins with Doubt[1]

First of all, Johannes Climacus juxtaposed this thesis with thesis no. two, that in order to begin to philosophize one must have doubted. He easily perceived that they did not say the same thing, for while the first defined doubt as the beginning of philosophy, the second defined doubt as something that preceded the beginning. Since one of the several reasons for having turned his attention to these theses was that they might shed some light on the connection between the thesis *de omnibus dubitandum est* and philosophy and thereby more or less brighten his prospects of entering into philosophy, thesis no. one naturally made him happy, for it seemed to be the closest way. It did not speak of doubt as something preceding philosophy but taught that in doubt one is at the beginning of philosophy.

PARA. 1. IS THE THESIS IDENTICAL WITH
THESIS NO. THREE?

[2]For him it was a strange idea that doubt is part and parcel of philosophy. It seemed to him that what happened with thesis no. one was the opposite of what happened with thesis no. three. The latter seemed to be a historical thesis but on closer examination proved to be a philosophical thesis, even if he failed to understand it as such. At first glance, thesis no. one appears to be a philosophical thesis, since it speaks of philosophy in general, but on closer examination it seems historical. It states that philosophy begins with a negative principle, but this implies a polemic against not only this or that which lies outside of philosophy but also against a principle in philosophy. Since it plainly would be absurd to po-

lemicize against nothing, this presupposes an antecedent. If this antecedent is not a principle, then the polemic is unworthy of philosophy—indeed, then the thesis is not negative but positive, for if in my polemic I merely rule out the heterogeneous, then my thesis actually is not a polemic but an enunciation of something higher that I have. But the thesis cannot be ignorant of this polemic against something homogeneous, for although a positive principle, as direct and immediate, can be ignorant of what it excludes, a negative principle never can be. Thus the thesis itself admits an antecedent philosophical principle.

If philosophy had begun with a positive principle, it would have been totally impossible to deduce this consequence with respect to the historical. To the best of his knowledge, the Greeks taught that philosophy begins with wonder [*Forundring*].[3] A principle such as that cannot give rise to any historical consequence whatsoever. If a later thinker made the same assumption, we would be utterly unjustified in drawing the conclusion that he thought one should begin with wonder over the fact that Plato and Aristotle had wondered. Wonder is plainly an immediate category and involves no reflection upon itself. Doubt, on the other hand, is a reflection-category. When a later philosopher said: Philosophy begins with wonder—he was straightway in continuity with the Greeks. They had wondered, and he also wondered; they perhaps had wondered about one thing, and he wondered about something else. [4]But every time a later philosopher repeats or says these words: Philosophy begins with doubt—the continuity is broken, for doubt is precisely a polemic against what went before. The more important the person is who repeats the thesis, the more chasmal the break, whereas in the other case the more important the person is who repeats that thesis, the more it is confirmed and strengthened. Admittedly, in the first case as well, the thesis is strengthened by repetition, but it was strengthened explicitly in order to separate.

The more he thought through the thesis, the more historical and the more identical with no. three it proved to be;

IV
B 1
128

thus, by a reverse process, he arrived at the same point as before. But this was not enough; he also discovered a new difficulty. He was well able to comprehend that an individual could take it into his head to doubt, but he could not understand how it could occur to him to say this to another person, least of all as advice (it would be another matter if it were said to deter), for if the other person was not too slow, he might very well say, "Thank you, but please forgive me for also doubting the correctness of that statement."[5] Now, if the first person in his happiness over the second person's expression of gratitude were to tell a third person that they were in agreement about doubting everything, he actually would be making a fool of the third person, since their agreement was nothing more than a wholly abstract expression of their disagreement, unless each was so disrespectful as to consider the other as nothing, which would be a new contradiction, since the one who had advanced the thesis certainly must have considered himself as something but also considered the other as something, since he wanted to initiate him into it. Nor could the first person become angry over the second person's conduct, for he could not, of course, want him to be of a [6]less perfect nature than he himself and above all could not want him to be inconsistent, no more than Anaxarchus of old, who, having fallen into a deep ditch, became angry with Pyrrho, who walked by without helping him out, but on the other hand praised him for it, because it proved that they truly agreed that a philosopher ought to be indifferent and unsympathetic.[7]

IV
B 1
129 Although Johannes could certainly adhere to this, his mental constitution was such that he did not have the courage to be that consistent with regard to acclaimed truths. [8]Even if it would be inconsistent for a genius to require this of someone, it nevertheless was consistent for a poor student to do it. He was well aware of the imperfection in the way he appropriated truth, but he still did not wish to abandon the thesis for that reason. He tried once again to think it over in order to see how he could enter into relation to it. As yet it was not the thesis itself he wanted to think through, for he

first of all had to find out if he could successfully enter into relation to it. Therefore, he did not ask questions like these: Is doubt as the beginning of philosophy a part of philosophy or is it the whole of philosophy? If it is a part, what, then, is the other part? Could it be certainty? Are these parts forever separated? How can we speak of a whole if its parts exclude one another? What Epicurus had sophistically maintained about the fear of death seemed to him to apply here—namely, that one should not concern oneself about it, because when I am, death is not, and when death is, I am not.[9] Was there something that united these two parts into a whole? He did not ask questions such as these but on the contrary asked about the single individual's relation to that thesis.

PARA. 2. HOW DOES THE SINGLE INDIVIDUAL RELATE TO THAT THESIS?[10]

While his soul was pregnantly pondering this question (that is, as long as he could not question, thought twined itself alarmingly around him, but as soon as he began to ask questions, he was happy and extricated himself from thought inasmuch as thought developed for him in dialogue), he one day heard one of the philosophizers, apropos of that thesis, say, "This thesis does not belong to any particular philosopher; it is a thesis from the eternal philosophy, [11]which anyone who wishes to give himself to philosophy must embrace." He noted clearly how these words stirred the listeners; he himself felt blissfully agitated by the communicative vibrations of the enthusiasm. He hurried home happier than Robinson Crusoe when he had found Friday. On the way, he repeated the words to ensure that his memory would not deceive him.

IV
B 1
130

The eternal philosophy, he said to himself, the eternal philosophy—what does that mean? It is a glorious designation, and no designation of philosophy can be too glorious; but the more glorious the designation becomes, the more obvious and clear it presumably becomes. The eternal philosophy. Is it the philosophy that is unconcerned with time? In that case, it is indeed the most abstract philosophy, so abstract that it has neither beginning nor end. Yet it cannot be that, inasmuch as that thesis speaks of a beginning. Is it the philosophy that has history in itself as the blessed transfiguration of philosophy's richly substantial life, a transfiguration best compared to what everyone, once one's life is ended, expects in eternity? If that is what it is, then, strictly understood, one can only expect it. —Already his soul began to be discouraged; those inspiring and powerful words were so faithless! Yet he still had faith in the latter part of the statement: "Anyone who wishes to give himself to philosophy must embrace this (that is, the eternal philosophy)." But the speaker had not said a single word concerning how one is to go about doing this. Of what use was it to find out that there is an eternal philosophy that everyone should embrace if everyone did not learn how to go about doing it or if no one at all learned it, if at least none of the listeners had learned more than he? And yet it pained him; he thought the words to be so beautiful that he could not stop listening to them, just as one sadly gazes after the wild geese flying in the sky. Anyone who wants to belong to that world must join them, and yet no one has ever been seen flying with them.

The words had not helped him to make any advance. On the contrary, after more careful consideration, they seemed to end precisely where he was at the point of beginning before he even heard them; for that was precisely what he wanted to investigate, how the single individual must relate to that thesis, and, consequently, how the single individual must embrace philosophy. He was well aware that this concurrency was scarcely encouraging for him, because the explanation could be that he was standing and was supposed to begin where others had already ended. This accounted for the likeness. In just the same way, the end of a mathematical demonstration fully resembles the beginning. The one who begins says, for example: The square of the hypotenuse of a right-angled triangle is equal to the sum of the squares of the other two sides. The one who ends says exactly the same, only adding: *quod erat demonstrandum* [which was to be dem-

IV
B 1
131

onstrated]. [12]It pained him that the philosophizers behaved in that way. It was shameful of them that they never explained something—there could be someone, after all, who needed it.

Once again he was ready to follow the inclination of his own thinking, and the question was already on his lips when again he heard another call, a seemingly very important observation made by one of the philosophizers. The thesis that philosophy begins with doubt was on the whole a frequent subject of discussion. Now he heard that the beginning of philosophy is threefold:[13] The *absolute* beginning[14] is that concept which is also the end of the system, the concept of absolute spirit;[15] the *objective* beginning is the concept of absolutely indeterminate being,[16] the most simple determinant that exists [*existere*]; the *subjective* beginning is the work of consciousness, by which this elevates itself to thinking or to positing the abstraction.

This observation made a good impression on Johannes. To him it seemed to be dependable and credible, and even if it did not have the intoxicating power of enthusiasm, it seemed to have clarity and level-headedness. Nevertheless, he was struck by the fact that this observation, which was supposed to shed light on that thesis about philosophy's beginning with doubt, to that end explained that the beginning of philosophy was threefold and named each part separately—yet none of these beginnings carried the designation naming it as philosophy's beginning with doubt. If he were to interpret this to mean that philosophy had four beginnings and that the fourth was doubt, then he was in the awkward position of having to assume that the explanation had explained everything but not what he wanted explained. He was well aware that if any of the beginnings mentioned was the one in question, it had to be the third, because reflecting about philosophy's absolute and objective beginning had to be left to those who had already become philosophers. The subjective beginning, however, was certainly the one with which the individual started from not having been a philosopher to become a philosopher. Consequently, this was the one about which he was asking, for he was not, after all, asking about the relation of that thesis to philosophy but about his relation to that thesis and his thereby possible relation to philosophy.

"The *subjective* beginning," it was said, "is the work of consciousness by which this (that is, the consciousness) elevates itself to thinking or to positing the abstraction." This seemed very beautiful to him, particularly very uplifting, but his consciousness still was not lifted up by it. If this was supposed to be the beginning about which he was talking, then it was obscure to him why it now was put in a positive form instead of the usual negative form. He was well aware that one could arrive at the same place by elevation and by doubt, but still the continuity would be altogether different. If, for example, a person elevated himself above sense perception in order to philosophize and someone else for the same reason doubted sense perception, both perhaps would arrive at the same place, but the movements would be different, and the movement, of course, was what he was asking about in particular. Moreover, since to elevate oneself is a positive principle, no historical consequence could be drawn from it with regard to an earlier philosophy, as can be drawn from the principle of doubt. Is the intention, then, that these two expressions—to elevate oneself and to doubt—are supposed to be identical? That would surely be unreasonable, since they are not identical. Why use two expressions, then? Why explain the more difficult expression by an easier expression that also explained something entirely different and consequently did not explain what it was supposed to explain? The expression he heard repeated again and again was: Philosophy begins with doubt. The other expression he heard far less frequently. Must, then, the thesis be a misunderstanding and, on the other hand, the explanation be the thesis? But that would be inconceivable, and even if it were the case, it would presumably have its meaning as a thesis but would itself need an explanation, because to say: The beginning is the act by which one begins—that is not much of an explanation. What kind of act it is and how the single

IV
B 1
133

individual becomes capable of carrying it out must be defined more explicitly.

He decided, then, to begin where he was at the point of
beginning earlier and to follow the wish of the question just
as he sensed it in his soul.

a. How does the single individual who enunciates that thesis relate to it?

To that end, he asked whether that thesis had existed [*existeret*] at all times in the temporal sense so that everyone had
known it in substance, even though no one had enunciated
it as a thesis. Would it hold for that thesis as it holds for the
thesis: Man is mortal? —Did it state something people had
always done without being conscious of it? Was it something
immediately inherent in human nature? For example, if no
one had ever explained what it is to wonder, every human
being would still have done it. —Had the thesis existed in
the eternal sense at all times but had been discovered in time?
Does it hold for that thesis as it holds for mathematical theses—
namely, that when they are discovered they are discovered
in their eternity? —Would it continue to exist in the eternal
sense at all times just as a philosophical thesis does? —Would
the personality of the one who discovered the thesis become
a matter of indifference after the thesis was discovered, as is
the case with mathematical and metaphysical theses? —Would
it be of importance to the thesis that people knew the personality of the one who had enunciated it? For example, we
would still require acquaintance with the personality of the
speaker with respect to religious theses and also, up to a point,
with respect to an ethical thesis, for anyone could state a
religious or an ethical thesis, but it would not necessarily
follow that in everyone's mouth it would become a religious
or an ethical thesis, unless it were assumed that it makes no
difference whether it was Christ who declared that he was
God's son or any human being whatsoever, or that it makes
no difference whether it was a person who actually knew
himself who said "Know yourself" or any human being
whatsoever. The thesis, to be sure, would be the same, and

IV
B 1
134

yet it would become something else—that is, in the one case it would become a thesis, in the other mere chatter—whereas with respect to a mathematical thesis it makes no difference whether it is Archimedes or Arv[17] who enunciates it, provided only that it is enunciated correctly. In the one case, personality does nothing and in the other, everything, just as in civil life anyone may formally be a guarantor, and yet it makes an absolute difference who the guarantor is.

What kind of a personality should the person be who is supposed to enunciate it? Would he have to be a talented person, and would talent be sufficient to authorize that person to enunciate the thesis? To enunciate a mathematical thesis requires mathematical talent. The person who could enunciate it would prove that he had talent, and if the inanity were to be imagined (something that is always inane by reason of the perfect immanence of the talent in the presentation) that someone devoid of talent could do it, the thesis would retain just as much its truth, its mathematical truth—that is, its essential truth—just as in daily life a bond payable to the bearer is just as sound whether a rich man or a poor man holds it, whether a thief or the legitimate owner possesses it. Not so with religious and ethical theses. If a two-year-old child could be taught a mathematical thesis,* it would be essentially just as true in the child's mouth as in the mouth of Pythagoras. If we taught a two-year-old child to say these words, "I believe that there is a God" or "Know yourself," then no one would reflect on those words. [18]Is talent itself, then, not the adequate authority?[19] Do not religious and ethical truths require something else, or another kind of authority, or, rather, what we do actually call authority, for we do, after all, make a distinction between talent and authority? If someone has enough talent to perceive all the implications in such a thesis, enough talent to enunciate it, it does not follow that he himself believes it or that he himself does it, and insofar as this is not the case, he then changes the thesis from

IV
B 1
135

* *In margin:* if a madman recited it.

a religious to a historical thesis, or from an ethical to a metaphysical thesis.

Now it was clear to him that if philosophy was not supposed to have four beginnings (and even in that case the conclusion would remain the same), then this thesis [philosophy begins with doubt] would have to belong to the subjective beginning, as was also clear from the fact that it would be shadowboxing to talk about an objective doubt, for an objective doubt is not doubt but deliberation. Therefore, this thesis, no more than any philosophical thesis, could not make any claim to mathematical necessity, or to philosophical necessity, either, as any thesis in the absolute and objective philosophy does. This thesis, then, had to be of such a nature that the person who was supposed to enunciate it had to discover it, had to have talent, had to have authority.

b. How does the single individual who receives that
thesis relate to the one who enunciates it?

At this point, Johannes Climacus perceived that some questions would turn out to be the other side of the previous questions. With these, he could be brief. So he asked whether that thesis, once it was enunciated, would promptly have validity, whether one intended it or not, just as with the thesis about human mortality? —Would it have validity with such necessity that, by denying it, one would expose oneself to the inverse conclusion, just as someone who denies a mathematical thesis must be prepared for the conclusion that he does not have a head for mathematics? [20]—Was the thesis, just like a mathematical thesis, indifferent to how many enunciated it: did it neither gain nor lose thereby?—

The question to which he gave special attention was: Is the thesis merely to be enunciated, or does it actually need to be received? A mathematical thesis is merely to be enunciated, for only when one has received it in such a way that one can enunciate it oneself, only then has one received it—otherwise it does not exist at all for that person. This he explained by way of the abstract nature of mathematics. Is that thesis not of the same order because of its negativity? Does not the

IV
B 1
136

negative specifically lack continuity, without which no communication and no reception is conceivable? Would it not be an illusion to give negativity the appearance of having continuity? [21]In the sphere of thought, is not the negative what evil is in the sphere of freedom and thus, like evil, without continuity?

Is the thesis, then, not to be received but merely to be enunciated? Does everyone receive it in such a way that, in the moment he enunciates it, it is to him a matter of indifference from whom he had received it or whether he had received it, since he would not have received it until he himself enunciated it? —Can it be received; can the individual receive it through someone else; is it to be believed? That is, when I, believing, receive a thesis, I cannot grasp it immediately or carry it out; nevertheless, I receive it because I trust the person who enunciates it.[22] —Is the thesis perhaps of such a nature that it requires authority in the person who is to enunciate it, trust and submission in the person who is to receive it? —Should it be believed in such a way that the single individual does not do what the thesis says but believes that the other has done it?[23] Perhaps a particular philosopher had doubted for all just as Christ suffered for all,[24] and is one now only supposed to believe it and not doubt for oneself? In that case, of course, the thesis was not enunciated entirely correctly, for then philosophy would not begin for the single individual with doubt but with the belief that philosopher X had doubted for him. —Should the thesis be appropriated believingly in such a way that the single individual does what it says? Did the person who enunciated it doubt everything so completely that the single individual merely repeats his doubt and, thus believing in the enunciator, makes the motions of doubt just as that one prescribed? With every single individual, would a new element of doubt always be added on for the next one? With respect to that which the earlier individual had been able to doubt, should one believe that he had doubted thoroughly, or would one have to doubt again?

The more Johannes thought about this matter, the more

IV
B 1
137

obvious it became to him that this was not the way into philosophy, because that thesis destroyed the very connection. In an old saga, he had read a story about a knight who received from a troll a rare sword that, in addition to its other qualities, also craved blood the instant it was drawn.[25] As the troll handed him the sword, the knight's urge to see it was so great that he promptly drew it out, and then, behold, the troll had to bite the dust. It seemed to Johannes that he must have the same experience with that thesis: when one person said it to another, it became in the latter's hand a sword that was obliged to slay the former, however painful it was for the latter to reward his benefactor in that way.

The very first person who had primitively[26] discovered that one must begin with doubt had not been in that predicament. He presumably had begun as one begins a daring adventure, not knowing whether it would lead him to victory or defeat. But the single individual who is to learn this from another would fall into the predicament, and if his teacher is not quick enough, he is obliged to become a sacrifice to his teaching.

Johannes could not adopt such sanguinary ingratitude, but even if he did gradually acquire the courage for it, he was fully aware that there would be a new difficulty, for as soon as he, against his will (this he dared to say with a good conscience), murdered the master and thus became himself the master, he would not have the slightest benefit from his predecessors but would have either the prospect of becoming the absolute monarch in philosophy (that is, if he were the last to enunciate that thesis and had no successors, consequently absolute monarch over all philosophers, since he himself would be the only one) or the prospect of ending up the same way as his great predecessors. *Aller Anfang ist schwer* [Every beginning is difficult]—he had always agreed with the Germans on that, but this beginning seemed to him to be more than difficult, and to call it a beginning and to designate it by this category seemed to him to be akin to the way the fox classified being skinned in the category of transition.

IV
B 1
138

Although these deliberations were by no means encouraging to him, Johannes could not help smiling now and then, since smiles and tears, after all, lie close to one another in a strange way. When he, who was such an innocent young person that he might rather be taken for a girl instead of a man, who did not have the heart to hurt a fly, considered that he would be changed into a bloodthirsty Bluebeard who would not cut down stems of grain but immortal philosophers instead, he sensed what a ridiculous figure he would be and that the whole thing could come about only by witchcraft. He certainly understood that a transformation had to take place when someone became a philosopher—but such a transformation!

He decided to let the sword remain in the sheath for the time being and to go on being himself rather than to become a philosopher on that condition.

Whatever else was involved in that thesis [philosophy begins with doubt] and its relation to philosophy, he perceived that this beginning was a beginning that kept one outside philosophy, whether it was assumed that philosophy actually continued to endure even if the single individual by means of his beginning excluded himself from it, or whether it was assumed that this beginning annihilated philosophy, thereby preventing one from entering into it.

IV
B 1
139   The beautiful prospect opened up to him by this thesis had disappeared; he had only one recourse—to assume that this beginning was a beginning that preceded the beginning of philosophy. In that case, thesis no. one was identical with thesis no. two.

III

In Order to Philosophize,
One Must Have Doubted

It was, as the reader recalls, actually the thesis *de omnibus dubitandum est* that Johannes wanted to make the subject of his deliberation. Before that, he wanted to encourage himself with the conception of the relation of this thesis to philosophy. What he found out through a rather exhaustive ordeal was not very gratifying, for he was reduced to the feckless statement that this thesis lay outside philosophy and was a preparation. Yet even in this case his efforts would not be without reward, inasmuch as he, through such preparation, would make himself worthy of beginning philosophy later.

In one sense, there was nothing to prevent him now from proceeding to that thesis, for presumably he might learn from it what he had to do in order to be able to carry it out. Yet he thought it worth the trouble to examine what it could mean that philosophy requires such preparation. Thesis no. two provided occasion for that.

That philosophy requires such preparation he found to be entirely in order—indeed, it really appealed to him; his character, which was just as humble as it was bold, heartily approved of it. Even if he had managed to understand thesis no. one and by means of it slip into philosophy, he still would have been uneasy about whether or not he had arrived there too easily, because to obtain something without difficulty was a paradox to his adventuresome soul, which preferred to seek out hardships. [1]He knew that previously a preparation such as this had been customary in the world. He knew that Pythagoras had commanded silence of his followers,[2] that the Egyptian and Indian philosophers had used a similar period of probation; he knew that in the Church catechumens had gone through prolonged schooling before being received into the Church. Indeed, the more important and significant that was into which one was to be initiated, in the same degree the test was more rigorous. The ascetic monastic orders and the gigantic Jesuit order were to him examples of this. No wonder, then, that philosophy in our age also required an ordeal! He also realized that it was unseemly for the follower to criticize the master. What the master saw fit to command must be done with enthusiasm and confidence, be it ever so offensive, ever so humiliating. That Pythagoras demanded silence, he understood, for the follower ought to be silent; that Diogenes insisted that one who wanted to be his follower had to walk behind him carrying a jar,[3] he could very well understand; that the catechumen had to stand outside the door, kneel when the others stood, stand when the others kneeled, that the novice had to do the hardest work— all this he considered to be in order, and he would never have hesitated to obey if it had been required of him. But for another reason he was a bit hesitant about the prescribed preparation—it seemed to him not to be humble and modest enough.

He who doubts elevates himself above the person from whom he learns, and thus there is no frame of mind less appreciated by a teacher in his pupil than doubt. And yet it was doubt that was required of him; it was by doubting that he was supposed to prepare to become a philosopher. Once again he was in a predicament. [4]Perhaps, he thought, this is a pious fraud. Perhaps this is the way to teach the follower to rely upon the master, just as the child is allowed to burn itself in the fire, is not warned against it, but is encouraged to do it because experience is regarded as the best teacher. Yet this explanation did not satisfy him. Then he found another by becoming aware that there is something elevated and noble in the conduct of philosophy. When the master positively orders the follower to do something, it certainly is easier for the follower, because then the teacher assumes the responsibility. The follower, however, thereby becomes a less perfect being, one who has his life in another person.

IV
B 1
141

But by imposing something negative, the teacher emancipates the follower from himself, makes him just as important as himself. The relation of teacher and follower is indeed canceled. Johannes was well aware of this. "I cannot even know whether doubting is actually a preparation," he said. "I am left to myself; I have to do everything on my own responsibility. Even though I could have wished to remain a minor for yet a while longer, even though I could have wished that there would be someone to give me orders so that I might have the joy of obeying, even though I anxiously feel that I have come of age too soon, even though I feel like a girl who marries too young—well, so it must be. [5]The thesis *de omnibus dubitandum est* has once and for all been brought into my consciousness, and I shall endeavor to think it through to the best of my ability, to do what it says with all my passion. Come what may, whether it leads to everything or to nothing, makes me wise or mad, I shall stake everything but shall not let go of the thought. My visionary dreams about being a follower have vanished; before I was allowed to be young, I became old; now I am sailing on the open sea. The prospects I once conjured up about the relation of this thesis to philosophy have been blocked. I do not know a thing about the relation of this thesis to anything else. I can only follow its path; 'like one who rows a boat, I turn my back toward the goal.' "[6]

Pars Secunda[1]

JOHANNES TRIES TO THINK
*PROPRIIS AUSPICIIS**
[ON HIS OWN BEHALF]
DE OMNIBUS DUBITANDUM EST

---

* Note. Out of solicitude for the young Johannes Climacus and lest he seem to be preoccupied with sheer folly, although he obviously is no genius at schematizing paragraphs, nor has he been drilled in the compendiums of the last ten years, I take the opportunity to recall how the issues he touches on have previously been advanced in philosophy.

INTRODUCTION

Just as the fish that has grabbed its prey on the surface of the
water goes to the bottom of the sea, so Johannes now was
alone with that thesis in the depths of his soul. For a time,
he surrendered to the various moods evoked by the mere
possession of something the true meaning of which one still
cannot fathom; he allowed himself to be moved variously by
the many thoughts about the difficulty of the task, about the
complicated inveiglements, about the fruitless attempts, about
the moments of triumph, about the romantic way in which
he would come to exist [*existere*]—in short, he enjoyed the
sweet joys and sorrows of a first love affair, for it is just as
Hippel says somewhere, "es geht mit den Wissenschaften wie
mit der Liebe: die verstohlne ist die angenehmste [science and
scholarship are like love: what is stolen is the most pleas-
ant]." (See *Lebensläufe*, I, p. 200.)[2]
  As he gradually came more and more to himself and increasingly felt the need and the energy to set about defining
the task in a more specific form, he also tried to decide whether
or not something in what he remembered of the philosophizers' discussions could give an instructive clue. One does
not start out on a journey around the world in the same way
one starts out for a stroll. Not knowing the irksome troubles
of a journey, the soul hides in pensive, elevating devotions
as courage and enthusiasm contend in romantic boldness with
a certain anxiety. But even though one relies entirely on oneself in this manner, still nothing is more natural than to heed
the reports of those who have attempted the same thing.
Johannes was well aware at this point that he dared not expect to find as complete information in what the philosophizers said as a sailor has in his chart, but he also knew that
the mind is not subject to multifariousness and that its movement is much more uniform.[3]
  [4]As he now prodded his memory, he began to feel very ill

at ease, for it became clear to him that in the philosophizers' discussions there was scarcely a word about all the fates and adventures in which one must be tried when going forth to doubt everything. And yet one would have expected to hear this; one would think that this would be their favorite topic, just as seafarers love to talk about their close calls, especially if they meet men who have navigated the same ocean. If some of them had wanted to lie about such an experience without actually having had it, he would have understood, but he also hoped to be able to distinguish the experienced man from the parrot by the fervency of what was said. But it was inexplicable that everyone remained silent. Could it be that what they had seen was so terrible that they dreaded to speak of it? Yet they were indeed associated with men who must have seen the same thing.

Admittedly, it was not altogether the case that Johannes had not heard one word from the philosophizers about this matter, but when he refreshed his memory regarding the little he had heard, he nevertheless had to confess that it amounted to nothing and that it was quite in order at the time that the particular statement only discouraged him. [5]When, for example, he once heard a lecture on the importance of having doubted as a preliminary to philosophy, the following statement was made in his presence: "One must not waste time on doubting but should just start out at once in philosophy." The listeners seized this information with the same joy with which Catholics seize the announcement of an indulgence. Johannes, however, was so ashamed on behalf of the speaker that he wished himself far away so that no one could see it on his face. "Even an ordinary person," he said to himself, "tries to do what he says; yet in ignorance it can happen that he does something else because he does not understand himself. But this cannot happen with the philosopher. But to say right out that it is not worth the trouble to do what one at other times assures us one has done, deliberately to leave undone what one as a rule emphatically declares to be a necessary condition—this is to hold both oneself and philosophy in contempt!" [6]—Another time he heard one of the philosophizers, one whose utterances people especially trusted, express himself this way: "To doubt everything is no easy matter; it is, namely, not doubt about one thing and another, about this or that, about something and something else, but is a speculative doubt about everything, which is by no means an easy matter."[7] He recollected how alert he was at the beginning of this lecture, how dejected at the end, since he perceived that not a single word had been said. It would have been better if the speaker had not said more than the first words, for what followed said nothing, although it gave the appearance of saying something, and therefore it was curious that the lecture was not much longer, for when someone talks in that manner he must have enormously much to say.

Johannes then bade the philosophizers farewell forever. Even if he now and then heard a particular observation by them, he decided to pay no more attention to them, inasmuch as he had had so many sad experiences of how deceitful their words were. He now followed the method he was in the habit of following—namely, to make everything as simple as possible.

IV
B 1
144

I[1]

What Is It to Doubt?

1. WHAT MUST THE NATURE OF EXISTENCE BE
IN ORDER FOR DOUBT TO BE POSSIBLE?

As Johannes began his deliberation on this question, he of course perceived that if he demanded an empirical answer to it, life would offer a multifariousness that would only hide a perplexing diffusion over the whole range of extremes. In other words, not only could that which evokes doubt in the single individual be extremely different, but it could also be the opposite, for if someone were to discourse on doubt in order to arouse doubt in another, he could precisely thereby evoke faith, just as faith, conversely, could evoke doubt. Because of this paradoxical dialectic, which, as he had realized earlier, had no analogy in any sphere of knowledge [2]since all knowledge stands in a direct and immanent relation to its
object and the knower, not in an inverse and transcendent relation to a third, he easily perceived that at this point any empirical observation would lead to nothing. He had to take another route if he sought to find an answer to that question. He had to search out *doubt's ideal possibility in consciousness.* This, of course, had to remain the same, however different the occasioning phenomenon was, since it, without itself being explained by the phenomenon, explained the effect of the phenomenon. Then whatever produced doubt in the individual could be as different as it pleased; if this possibility were not in the individual, nothing would be able to evoke it. Moreover, since the difference of the occasioning phenomenon could be one of contrariety, the possibility would have to be total, essential for human consciousness.

[3]He then sought to orient himself in consciousness as it is

in itself, as that which explains every specific consciousness, yet without being itself a specific consciousness. He asked what the nature of consciousness would be when it had doubt outside itself. There is consciousness in the child, but this has doubt outside itself.[4] How, then, is the child's consciousness qualified? It actually is not qualified at all, which can also be expressed by saying that it is immediate. *Immediacy is precisely indeterminateness.* [5]In immediacy there is no relation, for as soon as there is a relation, immediacy is canceled. [6]*Immediately, therefore, everything is true,**[7] but this truth is untruth the very next moment, *for in immediacy everything is untrue.* If consciousness can remain in immediacy, then the question of truth is canceled.

IV
B 1
146

[13]How does the question of truth arise? By way of untruth, because the moment I ask about truth, I have already asked about untruth. In the question of truth, consciousness is brought into relation with something else, and what makes this relation possible is untruth.

[14]Which is first, immediacy or mediacy? That is a captious question. It reminded him of the response Thales is supposed to have given someone who asked whether night or day came into existence first: Night is one day earlier. Ἡ νύξ, ἔφη, μιᾷ ἡμέρᾳ πρότερον [Night, he said, is older by one day] (see Diogenes Laertius, I, 36).[15]

[16]Cannot the consciousness, then, remain in immediacy? This is a foolish question, because if it could, there would be no consciousness at all. But how, then, is immediacy canceled? By mediacy, which cancels immediacy by *pre*-supposing it. What, then, is immediacy? It is reality itself [*Reali-*

---

* *Note.* The Greek Sophists' thesis that everything is true. Plato's attempts to disprove them, especially by showing that the negative exists (cf. *Sophist*).[8] —Schleiermacher's teaching with respect to feelings, that everything is true (see the beginning of his *Dogmatics;*[9] some rejoinders by Erdmann in Bruno Baur's journal,[10] III, Part 1, p. 11). Heraclitus's thesis that everything is and everything is not, which Aristotle interprets to mean that everything is true.[11] See Tennemann's *Geschichte der Philosophie*, I, p. 237, note.[12]

tet].[17] What is mediacy? It is the word. How does the one cancel the other? By giving expression to it, for that which is given expression is always *presupposed.*

[18]Immediacy is reality; language is ideality;[19] consciousness is contradiction [*Modsigelse*].[20] The moment I make a statement about reality, contradiction is present, for what I say is ideality. \

The possibility of doubt, then, lies in consciousness, whose nature is a contradiction that is produced by a duplexity [*Dupplicitet*] and that itself produces a duplexity.

A duplexity of this sort inevitably has two manifestations. The duplexity is reality and ideality; consciousness is the relation. I can either bring reality into relation with ideality or bring ideality into relation with reality. In reality by itself there is no possibility of doubt; when I express it in language, contradiction is present, since I do not express it but produce something else. Insofar as what was said is supposed to be an expression of reality, I have brought this into relation with ideality; insofar as what was said is something produced by me, I have brought ideality into relation with reality.

IV
B 1
147   [21]So long as this exchange takes place without mutual contact, consciousness exists only according to its possibility. In ideality, everything is just as perfectly true as in reality. Therefore, just as I can say that immediately everything is true, so I can also say that immediately everything is actual [*virkelig*],[22] for not until the moment that ideality is brought into relation with reality does *possibility* appear. In immediacy, the most false and the most true are equally true; in immediacy, the most possible and the most impossible are equally actual. So long as this exchange takes place without collision, consciousness does not actually exist, and this colossal fallacy causes no annulments.[23] Reality is not consciousness, ideality no more so. [24]Yet consciousness does not exist without both, and this contradiction is the coming into existence [*Tilbliven*] of consciousness and is its nature.

[25]Before proceeding any further, he considered whether or

not what he at this point called consciousness was what usually was called *reflection*.* He formulated the relevant definition as follows: Reflection is the *possibility of the relation*; consciousness is *the relation, the first form of which is contradiction.* As a result, he also noted, reflection's categories are always *dichotomous*. For example, ideality and reality, soul and body, to know the true, to will the good, to love the beautiful, God and the world, etc. are categories of reflection. In reflection, they touch each other in such a way that a relation becomes possible. The categories of consciousness, however, are *trichotomous*, as language also demonstrates, for when I say, *I* am conscious of *this sensory impression,* I am expressing a triad. Consciousness is mind [*Aand*], and it is remarkable that when one is divided in the world of mind, there are three, never two. Consciousness, therefore, presupposes reflection. If this were not the case, then it would be impossible to explain doubt. [27]Admittedly, language seems to conflict with this, for in most languages, as far as he knew, the term "to doubt" is etymologically related to the word "two." Yet he surmised that this merely suggested the presupposition of doubt, all the more so since it was clear to him that as soon as I as mind become two, I am *eo ipso* three. If there were nothing but dichotomies, doubt would not exist, for the possibility of doubt resides precisely in the third, which places the two in relation to each other. We could not therefore say that reflection produces doubt, unless we would express ourselves in reverse; we must say that doubt *pre*-supposes reflec-

IV
B 1
148

* *Note.* What Johannes is explaining here is not without significance. The terminology of modern philosophy is often confusing. For example, it speaks of *sinnliches Bewusstsein, wahrnehmendes B., Verstand* [sense-consciousness, perceiving-consciousness, understanding], etc., although it would be far preferable to call it "sense perception," "experience," for in consciousness there is more. It would really be interesting to see how Hegel would formulate the transition from consciousness to self-consciousness, from self-consciousness to reason [*Fornuft*]. When the transition consists merely of a heading,[26] it is easy enough.

tion, without, however, this *prius* being temporary. Doubt arises by way of a relation between two, but for this to happen the two must be. Yet doubt, which is a higher expression, precedes and does not come afterward.

Reflection is the possibility of the relation. [28]This can also be stated as follows: Reflection is *disinterested*. Consciousness, however, is the relation and thereby is interest, a duality that is perfectly and with pregnant double meaning expressed in the word "interest" (*interesse* [being between]).[29] Therefore, all disinterested knowledge (mathematics, esthetics, metaphysics) is only the presupposition of doubt. As soon as the interest is canceled, doubt is not conquered but is neutralized, and all such knowledge is simply a retrogression. [30]Thus it would be a misunderstanding for someone to think that doubt can be overcome by so-called objective thinking. Doubt is a higher form than any objective thinking, for it presupposes the latter but has something more, a third, which is interest or consciousness.

In this respect, he considered the conduct of the Greek skeptics far more consistent than the modern overcoming of doubt. They were well aware that doubt is based on interest, and therefore with perfect consistency they thought they could cancel doubt by transforming interest into apathy.[31] In this method there was a consistency, whereas it was an inconsistency, seemingly based on ignorance of what doubt is, that motivated modern philosophy to want to conquer doubt systematically. Even if the system were absolutely perfect, even if the actuality [*Virkelighed*] exceeded the advance reports, doubt would still not be overcome—it only begins— for doubt is based on interest, and all systematic knowledge is disinterested. From this it is apparent that doubt is the beginning of the highest form of existence [*Tilværelse*], because it can have everything else as its presupposition. The Greek skeptics perceived so exceptionally well that it is unreasonable to speak of doubt when interest is canceled, but presumably they would also have perceived that it is a play on words to speak about an objective doubt. Let ideality and reality [*Realitet*] be in conflict forever and a day—as long as

IV
B 1
149

there is no consciousness, no interest, no consciousness that has an interest in this struggle, there is no doubt—but let them be reconciled, and doubt can continue just as actively. Consciousness, then, is the relation, a relation whose form is contradiction. But how does consciousness discover the contradiction? If that fallacy discussed above could remain, that ideality and reality in all naiveté communicated with one another, consciousness would never emerge, for consciousness emerges precisely through the collision, just as it presupposes the collision. Immediately there is no collision, but mediately it is present. [32]As soon as the question of a *repetition* arises, the collision is present, for only a repetition of what has been before is conceivable.

In reality as such, there is no repetition. This is not because everything is different, not at all. If everything in the world were completely identical, in reality there would be no repetition, because reality is only in the moment.[33] If the world, instead of being beauty, were nothing but equally large unvariegated boulders, there would still be no repetition. Throughout all eternity, in every moment, I would see a boulder, but there would be no question as to whether it was the same one I had seen before. In ideality alone there is no repetition, for the idea is and remains the same, and as such it cannot be repeated. When ideality and reality touch each other, then repetition occurs. When, for example, I see something in the moment, ideality enters in and will explain that it is a repetition. Here is the contradiction, for that which is, is also in another mode. That the external is, that I see, but in the same instant I bring it into relation with something that also is, something that is the same and that also will explain that the other is the same. Here is a redoubling [*Fordobling*]; here it is a matter of repetition. Ideality and reality therefore collide—in what medium? In time? That is indeed an impossibility. In eternity? That is indeed an impossibility. In what, then? In consciousness—there is the contradiction. The question is not disinterested, as if one asked whether all existence is not an image of the idea and to that extent whether visible existence is not, in a certain volatilized sense, a repe-

KEY TO REFERENCES

Marginal references alongside the text are to volume and page [IV 100] in *Søren Kierkegaards Samlede Værker*, I-XIV, edited by A. B. Drachmann, J. L. Heiberg, and H. O. Lange (1 ed., Copenhagen: Gyldendal, 1901-06). The same marginal references are used in Sören Kierkegaard, *Gesammelte Werke*, *Abt*. 1-36 (Düsseldorf: Diederichs Verlag, 1952-69). References to Kierkegaard's works in English are to this edition, *Kierkegaard's Writings* [*KW*], I-XXVI (Princeton: Princeton University Press, 1978-). Specific references to the *Writings* are given by English title and the standard Danish pagination referred to above [*Either/Or*, I, *KW* III (*SV* I 100)]. References to the *Papirer* [*Pap.* I A 100; note the differentiating letter A, B, or C, used only in references to the *Papirer*] are to *Søren Kierkegaards Papirer*, I-XI³, edited by P. A. Heiberg, V. Kuhr, and E. Torsting (1 ed., Copenhagen: Gyldendal, 1909-48), and 2 ed., photo-offset with two supplemental volumes, XII-XIII, edited by Niels Thulstrup (Copenhagen: Gyldendal, 1968-70), and with index, XIV-XVI (1975-78), edited by N. J. Cappelørn. References to the *Papirer* in English [*JP* II 1500] are to volume and serial entry number in *Søren Kierkegaard's Journals and Papers*, I-VII, edited and translated by Howard V. Hong and Edna H. Hong, assisted by Gregor Malantschuk (Bloomington: Indiana University Press, 1967-78).

References to correspondence are to the serial numbers in *Breve og Aktstykker vedrørende Søren Kierkegaard*, I-II, edited by Niels Thulstrup (Copenhagen: Munksgaard, 1953-54), and to the corresponding serial numbers in *Kierkegaard: Letters and Documents*, translated by Henrik Rosenmeier, *Kierkegaard's Writings*, XXV [*Letters*, Letter 100, *KW* XXV].

References to books in Kierkegaard's own library [*ASKB* 100] are based on the serial numbering system of *Auktionsprotokol over Søren Kierkegaards Bogsamling* [Auction-catalog of Søren Kierkegaard's Book-collection], edited by H. P. Rohde (Copenhagen: Royal Library, 1967).

In the Supplement, references to page and lines in the text are given as: 100:1-10.

In the notes, internal references to the present volume are given as: p. 100.

Three spaced periods indicate an omission by the editors; five spaced periods indicate a hiatus or fragmentariness in the text.

Smuler.

Philosophiske ~~Smuler~~

eller

En Smule Philosophie.

af

S. Kierkegaard.

———————

No. 1.

Kan der gives?

Hvorledes kan er et historisk Udgangspunkt for min evige Bevidsthed; hvorledes kan et saadant interessere mig mere end blot historisk; "kan man bygge sin en evig Salighed paa en historisk Viden?

et dogmatisk-philosophisk Problem.

Philosophical Pamphlets.
[*changed to:* Fragments.]
or
A Fragment of Philosophy.
by
S. Kierkegaard.

No. 1.

How do I obtain [*changed to:* Can . . . be given] a historical
point of departure for my [*changed to:* an] eternal consciousness; how can such a point of departure be of more than
historical interest [*deleted:* to me]; how can I build my [*changed
to:* can an . . . be built] eternal happiness on historical knowledge?

a dogmatical-philosophical issue.

[*Pap.* V B 39 *n.d.*, 1844]

Philosophiske Smuler

eller

En Smule Philosophi.

Af

Johannes Climacus.

Udgivet

af

S. Kierkegaard.

Kan der gives et historisk Udgangspunkt for en evig Bevidsthed; hvorledes kan et saadant interessere mere end historisk; kan man bygge en evig Salighed paa en historisk Viden?

Kjøbenhavn.

Faaes hos Universitetsboghandler C. A. Reitzel.
Trykt i Bianco Lunos Bogtrykkeri.
1844.

PHILOSOPHICAL FRAGMENTS

or

A Fragment of Philosophy.

By

Johannes Climacus.

Edited

by

S. Kierkegaard.

Can a historical point of departure be given for an eternal consciousness; how can such a point of departure be of more than historical interest; can an eternal happiness be built on historical knowledge?

Copenhagen.
Available at University Bookseller C. A. Reitzel's.
Printed by Bianco Luno Press.
1844.

SELECTED ENTRIES FROM
KIERKEGAARD'S JOURNALS AND PAPERS
PERTAINING TO
PHILOSOPHICAL FRAGMENTS

See 10:1-14 fn.; 40:19:

Just as there is a *futurum* (*ins blaue hinein* [in the deep blue yonder]), an infinite, continued development, which demolishes all more profound speculation, so the contrasting figure is a "prius," a "præ" in regressive infinity, such as the Alexandrian's *pre*-existence of the λόγος [word, reason], *pre*-existence of matter, *pre*-existence of the soul, *pre*-existence of evil—and just as misleading for all more profound thought.
—*JP* II 2088 (*Pap.* II A 448) May 29, 1839

See title page and epigraph:

With regard to the relation between what is right for all times and for particular times, the thesis that Christian doctrine claims—that something is right before God—determines it; see para. 182,[1] Plato's *Euthyphro*.[2]

Incidentally, there is skepticism at this point if the boundary is not scrupulously defined. Leibniz's analogy that the rules for harmony exist before anyone plays (see para. 181)[3] proves nothing. Only abstract truth is proved in this way. But Christianity is a historical truth[4]—how, then, can it be the absolute? If it is the historical truth, then, of course, it appeared at a certain time and in a certain place and thus is valid only for a certain time and a certain place. If we say that it, just as harmony, existed prior to the coming into existence, we are saying no more about it than about any other idea, for it, too, is ἀπάτωρ, ἀμήτωρ, ἀγενεαλόγητος [without father or mother or genealogy];[5] if we strongly insist on it, then we enervate the essence of Christianity, for the historical is precisely its essential aspect, whereas in other ideas this is the accidental.—*Pap.* IV C 35 *n.d.*, 1842-43

See 72:2-7; 74:4-36; 80:4-5, 11-12:

PROBLEMATA.[6]

Is the past more necessary than the future?

This can be significant with respect to the solution of the problem of possibility—how does Hegel answer it? In the *Logic*, in the doctrine of essence. Here we get the explanation that the possible is the actual [*det Virkelige*], the actual is the possible. It is simple enough in a science, at the conclusion of which one has arrived at possibility. It is then a tautology.

This is important in connection with the doctrine of the relation between the future and God's foreknowledge.

The old thesis that knowledge neither takes away nor adds.

See Boethius,[7] pp. 126-27, later used by Leibniz.[8]

—*JP* II 1245 (*Pap.* IV C 62) *n.d.*, 1842-43

From sketch; see title page and epigraph:

How do I obtain a historical point of departure for my eternal consciousness, and how can such a point of departure be of more than historical interest for me; how can I build my happiness on historical knowledge?—*Pap.* V B 1:1 *n.d.*, 1844

From sketch; see title page and epigraph:

This [a historical point of departure for an eternal consciousness] is and remains the main problem with respect to the relation between Christianity and philosophy. Lessing is the only one who has dealt with it.[9] But Lessing knew considerably more what the issue is about than the common herd [*Creti* and *Pleti*] of modern philosophers.—*JP* III 2370 (*Pap.* V B 1:2) *n.d.*, 1844

From sketch:

Lessing uses the word *leap;*[10] whether it is an expression or a thought is a matter of indifference—I understand it as a thought.

Sämtl. W., VI [V].[11]
—*JP* III 2342 (*Pap.* V B 1:3) *n.d.*, 1844

From draft; see 5-8:

Preface

It is by no means my intention with this project to be polemical, to defend something or to combat something. The declaration I herewith *bona fide* give is devoid of all irony (which should make it an objective explanation that even an infant and an animal can manage), is without any mental reservation, and is in *optima forma*, which seems to make it worse for me. "I have not succeeded in joining more profound learning with independent thought in such a way that I can satisfy the requirements of both as I wished to do and as one who has a legitimate claim to be classified under scientific scholarship ought to be able to do." My choice, then, is made in accordance with this consciousness. I pack up my little bundle and declare myself unauthorized to have any scholarly judicative opinion, to which I am not entitled, inasmuch as scientific-scholarly modesty ought to be as virginal as women are zealous in denunciation of looseness, and inasmuch as I, for the sake of my own honor and for the sake of the sanctity of scientific scholarship, would rather lead a modest life outside scientific scholarship than foolishly take part in it. I take my leave, then, recommending myself as best I can, and take my place in pamphlet literature, whereby I relinquish any claim to be a part of the scientific-scholarly

V
B 24
83

enterprise or of acquiring any ever so relative legitimacy as a link or transition, as a concluder, participator, or introducer, as a co-worker. Nor am I in the mood for such, for I feel like a poor lodger[12] who has his little room in the attic of a huge building that is still being expanded and remodeled and with horror thinks he detects that the foundation is crumbling;[*] I feel like a spider that preserves its life by remaining overlooked in its corner, although it shivers and quakes inwardly with presentiments of a storm.[**] So let me go on sitting here. I really do not credit myself with scientific scholarship; I do not fraternize with its devotees; I do not force myself on anyone. My thought and its fate are not of the slightest importance to anyone, with the exception of myself. What I do, I do *proprio Marte, propriis auspiciis, proprio stipendio* [by one's own hand, on one's own behalf, at one's own expense]—in short, I do it as a *proprietarius* [independent owner], insofar as one can be that without owning something, without coveting something. I do it candidly, not sophistically, if Aristotle's definition of sophistry as the art of making money[13] is at all correct. I do it honestly, for it is not my intention to deceive anyone. If to the best of my poor ability I take note of some individual thinker, I shall conscientiously quote him as well as I can.[†] As for stray remarks, I follow my old custom of placing in quotation marks everything I know is not my own and everything of which I do not know the source. My renunciation of learning is not deceitful, and even if it pains me to have to do it, it comforts me in turn that those who want to be learned, just as those who want to be rich, will fall into all kinds of snares and spiritual trials, something I can easily visualize, for if the "one-drachma" course I have taken has already ensnared me in many ways—to what spiritual trials, then,

[*] *In pencil at bottom of page:* thinks he detects a mistake about which no one is concerned.

[**] *In pencil at bottom of page:* fearful presentiments.

[†] *In pencil at bottom of page:* here the difficulty of giving summaries of Plato, Aristotle manifests itself when one does not understand them.

will not the person [*] be exposed who takes the "big fifty-drachma course"?[14]

[*] *In pencil:* the many.

—*Pap.* V B 24 *n.d.*, 1844

From draft; see 7:27-30:

..... the honor of the god. At times I am a foreman, at times a horseman. —If thought wants something investigated speedily and swerves aside with the speed of an arrow, then I am a jockey—if it advances as slowly as a ship of the desert, then I am the little boy who sits with my goad and drives.—*Pap.* V B 36:1 *n.d.*, 1844

From draft; see 8:2-8:

I can stake my own life, not the lives of others. What I offer thought is not learning but a human life, which, whenever a difficulty appears, is willing to lay down life simply in order to solve it.—*Pap.* V B 36:2 *n.d.*, 1844

From draft; see 9:1:

1st position.[15]
—*Pap.* V B 3:1 *n.d.*, 1844

From sketch; see 9:1-6; 109:5-9:

Propositio[16]

Positio[17]

Historical Costume[18]
—*Pap.* V B 1:12 *n.d.*, 1844

From final copy; see 9:1:

Propositio.
[*changed from:* 1st Position.]
—*Pap.* V B 40:6 *n.d.*, 1844

From draft; see 9:3-4:

Position II.

One in ignorance who presumably knows historically what he is asking about but seeks the answer.—*Pap.* V B 10 *n.d.*, 1844

From draft; see 9:5-6; 109:18-110:8:

Chapter I.
Thought-Project.

As is well known, Christianity is the only historical phenomenon that, the historical notwithstanding—indeed, precisely by means of the historical—has wanted to be the single individual's point of departure for his eternal consciousness, has wanted to interest him otherwise than merely historically, has wanted to base his happiness on his relation to something purely historical. No philosophy, no mythology, no historical knowledge has ever had this idea, of which one can therefore say—is it a recommendation or a condemnation?—that it did not arise in any human heart, for these three spheres must provide analogies to this self-contradicting duplexity, if such are to be found. However, we shall forget this, and have forgotten it, as if Christianity had never existed; on the other hand, employing the unrestricted propensity of a hypothesis,[19] we shall assume that this question was a whimsical idea that had occurred to us and that we now in turn do not wish to abandon before finding the answer. The monks never finished narrating the history of the world, because each one started with creation. If in discussing the relation between philosophy and Christianity we begin by narrating what was said earlier, then how shall we ever—not finish—no, ever manage to begin, for this history just keeps on growing. If we begin with that thinker and sage Pontius Pilate, *Executor novi testamenti*, and yet, before beginning, first wait for the decisive book that some assistant professor or publisher has announced—what then?—*Pap.* V B 3:2 *n.d.*, 1844

From final copy; opening portion on 9:5 transferred to 109:18–110:8:

As is well known, Christianity is the only [*same as* 109:18–110:8 *except for a few minor changes*].

In margin: to be placed at the end of Chapter V, so that the first part ends with these words.—*Pap.* V B 40:7 *n.d.*, 1844

Deleted from final copy, replaced by marginal addition; see 10:7-14 fn.:

The contradictions of existence are explained by positing a "pre" as needed (the Alexandrians);[20] contradictions of existence are explained by some "post" or other (wandering on the stars).—*Pap.* V B 40:8 *n.d.*, 1844

From draft; see 12:13-14:

Εὐκαταφορία εἰς πάθος [propensity for passion] (Tennemann, *Geschichte der Philosophie*, IV, p. 129 n.).[21]—*Pap.* V B 3:4 *n.d.*, 1844

From draft; see 15:24–17:20:

That other teacher, then, must be God himself. As the occasion, he acts to remind me that I am untruth and am that through my own fault; as God, he also gives the condition with the truth.

In margin: Savior.
            Deliverer.
            Redeemer.

In margin: If, with the same money, a child could buy a good book—and a toy—if he has bought the toy, could he then buy the good book with the same money.—*Pap.* V B 3:8 *n.d.*, 1844

From sketch; see 15:32–16:13:

It must be some place in the N. T.: the man to whom one is subordinate is the man one must serve; one who sins is a slave of sin??? Where is this found?

Rom. 6:16 John 8:34
—*Pap.* V B 2 *n.d.*,1844

From draft; see 19:26-37:

If, then, the moment is to have decisive meaning (and if not, we speak only Socratically, something we do not want), then the relation will look like this.—*Pap.* V B 3:11 *n.d.*, 1844

From draft; see 20:23-34:

Then he thinks for the second time that God exists since he himself is guilty.[22]—*Pap.* V B 3:12 *n.d.*, 1844

From draft; see 21:7-11:

Whereas in Socratic thought recollection became the proof for the immortality of the soul, forgetting will now be the beginning of the soul's eternal happiness; whereas Socrates had eternity behind him, in the second case one has eternity ahead.—*Pap.* V B 3:13 *n.d.*, 1844

From draft; see 21:12–22:16:

. . . . . did not arise in any human heart—for it is still too much to demand of a human being that he must discover that he does not exist [*er til*]—. . . . . .
and did not occur before year 1.

Like a vagabond who charges a fee for showing what everyone sees, or like that ram that was exhibited for a fee and in the afternoon was out grazing.

Your projects are not just snatched out of thin air—but are borrowed from the mayor's desk.—*Pap.* V B 3:14 *n.d.*, 1844

In margin of draft; see 24:17:

I wonder if Socrates was that cold; I wonder if it did not hurt him that Alcibiades could not understand him.—*JP* IV 4262 (*Pap.* V B 4:3) *n.d.*, 1844

From draft; see 24:31-38:

He must be moved by himself, and how could we define this more specifically than by love.—*Pap.* V B 4:4 *n.d.*, 1844

From draft; see 30:34–31:27:

. . . . . to being. A procreative love.
In margin: to be developed
Compare *Symposium*—Greek love—
Through this love, the teacher gives birth to himself, comes into existence.—*Pap.* V B 4:6 *n.d.*, 1844

From draft; see 33:37–34:16:

He must leave them, and they do not comprehend that this is good.—*Pap.* V B 4:7 *n.d.*, 1844

In margin of draft; see 35:3–36:27:

The Conclusion of the Chapter

Now, if someone were to say that what I have composed is the shabbiest plagiarism ever to appear, since it is nothing more nor less than what any child knows, then I presumably must put up with appearing to be a liar. But may not the composition be true because I have not composed it? And if it is untrue, then it is, after all, a poor composition, and my plagiarizing is not worth talking about. And if it is true?— well, then, any child, after all, knows the same. Who, then, is the author

Proverb—
The Wonder

. . . . . did not arise in any human heart, and therefore should you find fault with me for my presentation . . . . .

—*Pap.* V B 4:2 *n.d.*, 1844

From draft; see 39:4–9:

. . . . . as the page in *Figaro* says[23]. . . . .

—*Pap.* V B 5:2 *n.d.*, 1844

From draft; see 40:12–30:

I never reason in conclusion to existence (for in that case I would be mad to want to reason in conclusion to what I know), but I reason in conclusion from existence and am so accommodating to popular opinion as to call it a demonstrative argument. Thus the connection is somewhat different from what Kant meant—that existence is an *accessorium* [addition][24]—although therein he undeniably has an advantage over Hegel[25] in that he does not confuse.

In margin: eternal presupposition.

—*Pap.* V B 5:3 *n.d.*, 1844

From draft; see 40:31–43:22:

V
B 5:5
60

. . . . . but when I say God's works and proceed from them, I have, of course, presupposed him.

In margin: . . . . . this is the Spinozistic improvement of the Anselmian-Cartesian idea, which no doubt profoundly but nevertheless deceptively permits a shift by suddenly switching from a factual line of demonstration to an ideal one. Ideally viewed, these works demonstrate a corresponding ideal existence (as the poet does also when he poetizes the hero, but no more than that). The whole thing is a sleight of hand, reminiscent of the Cartesian dolls. One wants the idea, standing on its legs, to stand on its head the moment one lets go of it.[*] Absolutely right, but my letting go of it is indeed *unsere Zuthat* [our addition]: I give it up. Make this moment as diminutive as one will, it is still present, and if this is forgotten, I could be tempted to recall Carneades' reply to Chrysippus. Chrysippus thought he could get a sorites to stop or to switch over into a new quality. Carneades rejected this. Then, in order to make it clear, Chrysippus proposed that one could pause for a moment in the reckoning— then one would understand it better. Carneades answered: Go ahead. As far as I am concerned, you may not only pause for a moment but you may lie down and go to sleep.

V
B 5:5
61

(Tennemann, IV, p. 344.)[26]

In other words, Carneades disputed the thesis that two magnitudes are just as great as an equal third—if one is going to draw a conclusion from it. —He is clearly right in this, for the thesis is only a tautology, since three mathematical magnitudes that are absolutely equal are not three but are the same magnitude.

[*] Or it may also be the result of the inability of human thought to stand on its legs at all (stand alone) and its need to stand on its head right away, but then it does not occur by way of a conclusion but by an immediate leap.

V
5:5
60

—*Pap.* V B 5:5 *n.d.*, 1844

Deleted from final copy; see 43 fn.:

Note. It is true that I am not a poet and thus dare not claim to be capable of an opinion, but would it not have an almost madly comical effect to portray a man deluded into thinking that he could demonstrate that God exists—and then have an atheist accept it by virtue of the other's demonstration. Both situations are equally fantastic, but just as no one has ever demonstrated it, so has there never been an atheist, even though there certainly have been many who have been un-

V
B 40:11
92

willing to let what they know (that the god exists) get control of their minds. It is the same as with immortality. Suppose someone became immortal by means of another's demonstrating it*—would that not be infinitely ridiculous. Therefore there has never been a man who has not believed it, but there certainly have been many who have been unwilling to let the truth conquer in their souls, have been loathe to allow themselves *to be convinced*, for what convinces me exists, but the important thing is that I become immersed in it. —With respect to the existence of God, immortality, etc., in short, with respect to all problems of immanence, recollection applies; it exists altogether in every man, only he does not know it, but it again follows that the conception may be very inadequate.

In margin: *(just as Nille became a stone and the deacon a rooster),[27] suppose there was someone who went around as a miracle man, set up his booth, and demonstrated the immortality of the individual for a fee, just as indulgences were sold, and thus only the individual whose immortality he demonstrated became immortal.—*JP* III 3606 (*Pap.* V B 40:11) *n.d.*, 1844

From draft; see 44:17:

Too bad that the Sophists did not concern themselves with such things, for it would have been salutary for our age to hear Socrates converse with them about that.*

In margin: *If Socrates had been acquainted with the section, I think he would have given a banquet in his joy over the opportunity to ask whether they knew something or not.
—*Pap.* V B 5:6 *n.d.*, 1844

Deleted from final copy; see 44:13-17:

At the god's command, he casts out his net,[28] so to speak, to catch fitness and purpose, for nature itself comes up with many terrifying devices and many subterfuges in order to disturb. Too bad that the Sophists did not concern them-

selves with such things, for it would have been very reward-
ing to later ages if Socrates had introduced a little discipline.
If Socrates could have known all the many professors and
student teachers who demonstrate the existence of God, I
think that out of joy over all this magnificence he himself
would have given a banquet merely in order to have the
opportunity of conversing with these wise men.—*Pap.* V B
40:12 *n.d.*, 1844

From sketch; see 45:36:

How difficult it must have been for Christ's disciples that
he did not work etc., did not actualize the ethical in this
sense—that he predicted something that did not happen—
that he hid something from them—.—*Pap.* V B 1:11 *n.d.*,
1844

In margin of draft; see 45:36:

from the standpoint of the god.—*Pap.* V B 5:7 *n.d.*, 1844

From draft; see 46:1-6:

Yes, neither do I know the difference [between the god
and man] as long as I do not stay by the single difference,
nor, if I do not know the difference, can I know whether it
is present. Thus this individual human being has become the
god, for if the understanding holds fast to some distinguishing mark, then it is not because this is the distinguishing
mark but because the understanding is arbitrary enough to
want it to be the distinguishing mark. In this way the understanding has brought the god as close to itself as possible
and yet as far away as possible, and this is the most ironical
thing imaginable—the god himself has become pure negativity. Historically, one can perhaps show this to be the most
fantastic thing conceivable; whether this assumption has ever
been historical or not makes no difference in the case, but in
this way the understanding itself has made the Incarnation a

paradox, which only it itself can produce.—*JP* II 1340 (*Pap.*
V B 5:8) *n.d.*, 1844

In margin of draft; see 46:7–47:25:

the absolute paradox is, then,
(negatively and positively) a duplexity; otherwise it is not
the absolute paradox
—*Pap.* V B 5:9 *n.d.*, 1844

From draft; see 46:16–47:25; 55:4–57:17:

V
B 5:10
62

Let us agree about this difficulty, whether it would not be
necessary for the understanding that the god would reveal
himself only in order to become discernible through difference, for you recall from the foregoing that if the teacher is
to be something other than an occasion (under which assumption man would remain the highest), the learner must
be untruth, and of this he could not be conscious by himself.
It is the same with his knowledge of the god. First he must
know the difference, but this he cannot know by himself.
The difference that he himself provides is identical with likeness, because he cannot get outside himself. If, then, he comes
to know the difference, he comes to know it absolutely and
comes to know the absolute difference, and this is the first
paradox. Now follows the second, that in spite of this absolute difference, the god must be identical with man, and
not with humanity but with this individual human being.
But the moment he comes to know that the god is absolutely
different from him, he also comes to know that he himself
is absolutely different from the god. Therefore, we said that
when the paradoxical passion of self-knowledge is awakened, it would have a disturbing reflexive effect upon the
man, so that he who believed he knew himself would become doubtful as to whether he was a human being or a
more artfully constructed animal than Typhon. But if the
human being is absolutely different from the god, this difference cannot be rooted in what the god himself has given

to him but must be rooted in himself. Therefore we said that the untruth is also self-deserved. The difference, then, becomes sin. But if he is now to become like the god, is this not the absolute paradox?

In the foregoing[29] we have poetized the god as teacher and savior. Thus he did indeed become an individual human being. But his purpose was certainly not to mock men by revealing himself and then dying in such a way that no human being ever came to know his revelation. Every clue of the understanding was in itself no clue, and therefore it would have been no clue at all if he had gone triumphantly through the world and dominated all kingdoms and countries. Therefore in our poem something offensive was included: he was not entirely like other human beings; in little things he was different. This we could easily have developed further if we had extended the poem. He did not labor; in this way he did not concern himself with human affairs. And there was yet another difference: he suffered.

In margin: For the next chapter.—*JP* III 3081 (*Pap.* V B 5:10) *n.d.*, 1844

In margin of draft; see 47:26–48:16:

Suppose this were conceivable, and yet this is what the understanding would have to will, just as erotic love wills its own downfall, even though this is an imperfect metaphor.

In the moment of passion, erotic love does not notice this—.

—*Pap.* V B 5:11 *n.d.*, 1844

From sketch; see 49:1-12; 52:28-29; 53:32:

Chapter IV.
Offense at the Paradox.

See: telegraph message from an effervescent [*mousvoyant*] to a clairvoyant.

Hamann. Lies, comedies, and novels must be probable.[30]
I would rather

V
B 5:10
63

hear the truth from the mouth of a Pharisee
than from an angel and apostle.[31]
—*Pap.* V B 6:1 *n.d.*, 1844

From draft; see 49:23:

Offense at the Paradox

[*deleted:* (manifest in the pathological defense) *changed to:*
conceived as resonance]
an acoustical illusion
—*Pap.* V B 11:2 *n.d.*, 1844

From draft; see 51:28-29:

If the learner does not collide in *the moment* in the collision
of understanding, as we have shown, then the paradox thrusts
him away, and he takes *offense* or is scandalized.—*JP* III 3082
(*Pap.* V B 11:4) *n.d.*, 1844

From sketch; see 55:4–57:17:

In Chapter II, we have poetized the god as teacher and savior. Thus he did indeed become an individual human being.
But his purpose was certainly not to mock men by revealing
himself and then living and dying in such a way that it never
occurred to anyone that it had happened. Every clue of the
understanding was in itself no clue; for him to have marched
triumphantly through the world conquering kingdoms and
countries would have been no clue. Therefore in our poem
something offensive was included: he was not entirely like
other human beings; in little things he was different. This
we could easily have developed further if we had extended
the poem. He did not labor; he did not apply himself to or
concern himself with earthly affairs, and—he *suffered*.
—*Pap.* V B 6:3 *n.d.*, 1844

From sketch; see 55:4–57:17:

The god must draw attention to himself but must not betray anything (John the Baptizer).—*Pap.* V B 6:6 *n.d.*, 1844

In margin of draft; see 56:34–57:17:

All of which certainly could seem inadmissible, and we caution against being unstable in life this way and putting up somewhere when evening draws near, but the person who does not do it for the sake of comfort certainly dares to make himself an exception at this point.—*Pap.* V B 12:1 *n.d.*, 1844

From sketch; see 58:24–38:

The question already pertains to the apostles, for here it is not a matter of a distance of centuries or of the historical in the narrower sense (the traditional), but how do I come to have a point of departure (outside myself) at all for my eternal consciousness—does it all lie in God and in my relationship to him?—*Pap.* V B 1:4 *n.d.*, 1844

From sketch; see 58:24–38:

The contemporary follower is in the very same position as the follower at second hand with respect to obtaining a historical point of departure for his eternal consciousness. This must be heeded unconditionally.—*Pap.* V B 6:4 *n.d.*, 1844

From sketch; see 59:1–18:

The teacher must also give the *condition*—(faith is the condition).—*Pap.* V B 6:2 *n.d.*, 1844

From sketch; see 62:1–66:2:

To have faith (Fantasy? No. Cognition? No! Historical knowledge? No. Tangibility? No!)—*Pap.* V B 6:7 *n.d.*, 1844

In margin of draft; see 62:3-7:

..... all knowledge is concerned either with teaching or with historical knowledge about the teacher.—*Pap.* V B 12:4 *n.d.*, 1844

In margin of draft; see 65:15-16:

..... the two disciples on the road to Emmaus—Mary Magdalene.—*Pap.* V B 12:5 *n.d.*, 1844

From draft; see 67:35–69:30:

Or is this what it means to be a contemporary, and is this the contemporary we eulogize, who is able to say,[*] "We ate and drank before his eyes, and the teacher taught in our streets,"[**] yet without having known the teacher, which, after all, only the believer (the person not immediately contemporary) did, and without being known by the teacher,* and if the situation nevertheless is such that the teacher gives the condition, then one of course cannot know him without being known by him, and one knows him only insofar as one is known.[†]

[*] *Penciled in margin*: Luke 13:26
[**] *In margin*: (to be developed in sketch)
In margin: *Thus he has to say: I do not know you
[†] Luke 13:26 is the reply; he becomes aware that once again I have interpolated one word.—*Pap.* V B 12:7 *n.d.*, 1844

From sketch; see 69:32–71:17:

Therefore in only one respect can I extol those eyes and ears as blissfully happy (for the difficulty is terrible)—in being free from all the drivel with which someone later, for example, 2,000 years later, would be plagued and hindered in *autopsy*, for all faith is autopsy.—*Pap.* V B 6:8 *n.d.*, 1844.

From draft; see 69:35–70:2:

. . . . . one single wonder that baffles explanation;* thus his joy becomes by no means so secure or so glorious as the joy of the one who is contemporary with that imperial wedding.

In margin: *he does not know and cannot historically know whether he should admire it or be secretly indignant at being made a fool, for by having merely historical information about the wonder, a person never comes further—unless he comes to offense, and who will envy him that?—*Pap.* V B 12:8 *n.d.*, 1844

In margin of draft; see 70:21–71:2:

. . . . . and if he were to continue to talk a lot of nonsense about the gloriousness of being contemporary, we would let him go, but the next minute we would also perceive that his path takes him to that imperial wedding, where he feels completely at home, and the more he talks about the gloriousness, the further we see him move from the paradox, past Socrates—until he finally joins the dance at the wedding, and such gloriousness as that is certainly worth running after, but the paradox is not to be run after—and is not τοῦ τρέχοντος [of the one running].[32]—*Pap.* V B 12:9 *n.d.*, 1844

From sketch; see 72:1-3:

Chapter VI [*changed to*: Interlude]
Is the Past More Certain than the Future.

something about this may be found in the tall cupboard in the corner toward Frue Kirke.—*Pap.* V B 6:9 *n.d.*, 1844

From draft; see 73:5-11:

. . . . . that you were so foolish as to understand* the newest philosophy, which on this point has gained for itself a Herostratic[33] unforgettableness. An individual can be called absent-minded (if he is that at all); unfortunately, an entire age cannot be called that, and yet this is what I would like to call the newest philosophy. Now it is not too bad that one cannot very well say it (that is, apply this expression to an entire age); it is worse that the age nevertheless is absent-minded.

In margin: *and to agree with.

—*Pap.* V B 13 *n.d.*, 1844

From draft, continuation of Pap. V B 13; *see 73:11, 78:6 fn.:*

V
B 14
70

V
B 14
71

There is a phrase that, when uttered, pierces the soul with awe-inspiring solemnity; there is a name that, when uttered together with the phrase from which it is inseparable, makes a person take off his hat and bow down. Even a person who does not know the man removes his hat long before he sees the man and stands with hat in hand without seeing the man. It is a phrase that means something and a name that means something: it is the absolute method[*] and Hegel.[35] Nowadays the absolute method is at home not only in logic but also in the historical sciences. O worldly eminence, what are you, after all; ah, loveliest of roses, how sharp your thorns. I would not be the absolute method, never in the world, and have only such a home as Hegel has prepared for it in logic[**], not to mention in the historical sciences. To have to take refuge in wordplay and witticisms, to cram holes with blotting paper, to have to parade with tinsel and be silent about its not hanging together properly—oh, this is a high price to be the absolute method. Cromwell the Protector in all his glory could not be more unfortunate than the absolute method, even when the trumpet blast proclaims its majesty. And yet Hegel was indeed a great logician, certainly something no one will deny him, even if it is not trumpeted abroad, but

[*] *In margin:* this term is *einhaltsschwer* [weighty in substance], and yet it passes with singular ease, as the poet says: *von Munde zu Munde* [from mouth to mouth],[34]

[**] *In margin:* has he not prepared sheer hell for it in logic.

alongside of that he had a great penchant for logical gim-crackeries [*Snurrepiberier*] and the psychological peculiarity of assigning them the highest value and was especially eager to become recognized for these.[*] In the same way, Nero was incensed at Vindex (who had incited rebellion) not because he had said that he was a bad emperor but because he had said that he was a bad zither player, as his words declare: Nero is a bad zither player but an even worse emperor.

But we shall not discuss logic here; we shall merely con-sider the application of the absolute method to the histori-cal.[**] Too bad that Hegel, merely for the sake of illusion, did not have 1843 years at his disposal, for then he presum-ably would have had time to make the test as to whether the absolute method, which could explain all world history, could also explain the life of one single human being. In ancient times, one would have smiled at the kind of wisdom that can explain all of world history absolutely but cannot explain one single human being, for in ancient times the wise man did not go further in such a way that he did not also under-stand what the simple person understood. Of course, I do not know, either, if any wise man in ancient times called his method the absolute method.

We shall not be so arrogant as to do everything on a grand scale. We shall speak of a single individual human life in the way it can be lived out here on earth. All that holds true of the history of the race holds true of such a person. If one can see God in history, one can see him also in the life of the individual; to think that one can do the former and not the latter is to delude oneself by yielding, in regard to the his-torical, to the brutish imbecility that in the observation of nature sees God by being taught that Sirius is 180,000 million miles away from the earth. The sensate man is astounded by this, and when a person does not have a clear conscience, it

[*] philosophic high treason.
[**] *In margin:* Consistent in existence
   Interesting in history

is best to speak of the whole, of the totality, etc. If every single human being is not an individual, himself and the race, simply by being human, then everything is lost and it is not worth the trouble to hear about the great world-historical events or the absolute method. But the world wants to be deceived. Now, it goes without saying that it is a swindle to get all world history instead of one's own insignificant person—if one does not gain in the trade. Yet people are deceived, deceived insofar as they do not come to understand themselves, which is made evident by their supposing that they have understood the whole world without this.

V
B 14
73

The question as we have presented it is simplified as much as possible, and in the treatment of it we shall again strive to simplify everything as much as possible; for even if the something else received instead of the answer to this particular question were something absolutely glorious, it would still be essentially indulgence in a wicked dissipation, and it would be a loss to get to know something else instead of receiving an answer to the perhaps more insignificant question, but, after all, please note, the one that was asked. No doubt this often happens in the most recent science and scholarship precisely because it has the pet idea of becoming concrete immediately.[36] But this concretion often has the seductive effect of depriving thought of peace of mind, the scientific-scholarly contentment that is satisfied with thought itself. This is by no means to say that it is wrong of science and scholarship to assimilate concrete matter, but it simply should not begin with that. The mathematician is delighted with his algebra, which means nothing but the calculation itself. The sensate person may not be content with that, but would it therefore be proper for the mathematician promptly to give up the letters and choose dollars, marks, and shillings merely in order to arouse the sensate person to participation through the stimulation of his passion. This is the way it goes when one begins to make the thought concrete immediately and does not first of all clarify in pure abstraction the thought one wants to make applicable in the concrete. The concrete is the manifold and as such exercises an enchanting power over a person. Suppose it happened—and why should it not happen—that the thought[*] that is to be pointed out in the concrete remained unclear but that the concrete was itself so rich, so variegated, that it captivated the soul so that the learner or the reader, rejoicing in this delight, forgot the thought, was not enraged with the one who really had deceived[**] him, but even considered himself very indebted to him. The historical (concretely understood) inherently has various charms that the philosopher, however, if in general he wishes to be true to himself, ought to reject. The historical to him means only the historical, not this historical, and one who merely wants to satisfy the demands of imagination or curiosity turns to him in vain. If he then wants to demonstrate the relation of the idea to the historical, the historical becomes purely abstract and essentially is temporality.[†] Whether temporality means a single individual's life or the most wonderful world-historical achievement is a matter of indifference to him. The philosopher, therefore, cannot fall into the misunderstanding, which is a result of sensate astonishment[††] and of superstition, that the idea shows itself more clearly in world history than in an individual man's life. It is the philosopher's passion to reject all these distinctions and above all to reject deceiving the reader by them, as if he had said something (*qua* philosopher) because as historian he had

[*] *In margin*: which in the beginning was not clarified for him in the conciseness and unconcern of abstraction but which was supposed to become clear for the first time in the conclusion—that is, after having seen and understood the most diverse things, which are precisely the things that can distract the thought.

[**] *In margin*: had intruded upon him even more than by speaking to him about the highest and the holiest, which requires stillness of soul above all, in Dyrehaugsbakken [amusement park].

[†] *At bottom of page*: (as if a person wanted to show him how one instrument by its entry into the totality first produced the wholeness—and yet would not first perform the passage of that particular instrument for him but began immediately with the whole orchestra).

[††] *In margin*: delusions of fantasy, the indefinable frauds of indefinite feelings.

V
B 14
74

instructed the learner. If this is not the case, then everything
is confused, and the learner is at a loss as to whether he
should thank such a man or not. If the method is concrete
from the very beginning, it is either because he instanta-
neously ventures out in the historical matter or, preoccupied
with the interpretations of others, because he seeks to demonstrate the idea in them. In the *first case*, for example, he
speaks about China. Who would not be happy to know
something about China? He amazes us with his learning; one
is overwhelmed by all the new things to be learned and thanks
him—if one is numbered among those who previously really
did not know anything in particular about the subject and
among those who in their rejoicing over it forget that this
subject is not at all what they were supposed to find out.
Another reader, however, is by chance very familiar with
the Chinese and discovers that there is an error. This is made
known, and there is a controversy. One is curious, reads
both sides, finds out something new—and forgets even more
what it is that one really wants to find out. —In the *second
case* he speaks about Oriental philosophy, Greek, Jewish, etc.
One acquires an indescribable amount of information, but
unfortunately not what one seeks and what one as philosopher should achieve. One falls into a profound dilemma: one
hardly dares to confide one's secret to anyone, for it would
indeed seem as if one were ungracious toward a man who
knows so much about everything. The philosopher wants to
show how the god enters guidingly into the historical. Consequently he settles upon one or another world-historical decision. He intensifies the dramatic interest; the interests of
countries and kingdoms, the fates of millions, are wrapped
up in the conflict—and now the final judgment develops out
of this: it is divine providence. Previously one was not familiar with that determination of the matter; one thanks the
philosopher for the enjoyment one has had, admires his art—
and forgets that this is not at all what one wishes to find out,
forgets that he who can see the god's guidance only in the
world-historical decision (where it can be seen) but not in
the most insignificant person's life—that he is no philoso-

V
B 14
75

pher, that he does not have the philosopher's passion—he is merely superstitious. Soon everyone who knows anything or knows how to talk about it well becomes a philosopher; all unite in dragging men's minds down into multiplicity and, thus immersed, into forgetfulness of what is the philosopher's business and occupation, what Aristotle expresses so beautifully, that philosophy is occupied with that which is related in only one way.[*][37] Since the method has become so concrete, no provisional reflection, of course, is necessary; one passes on at once to the main dish. At the conclusion of the system, it will be seen that the method is correct. At the end—after every means of diversion has been employed to disturb the reader and bribe the judge. Even a logical problem cannot be handled without one side of the historical concretion immediately crowding in as the long-winded report on what others have thought about it etc. An instrument of distraction, nothing but an instrument of distraction.

[*]*In margin:* ἦν ἀεὶ κατὰ ταὐτὰ ὡσαύτως ἔχειν [always unchanged and the same] (Plato)[38]

—*JP* I 50; III 3301 (*Pap.* V B 14) *n.d.*, 1844

Revision of Pap. V B 14, *on separate sheets apparently deleted from final copy:*

There is a phrase that, simply uttered, pierces the soul with awesome solemnity; there is a name that, simply uttered together with the phrase from which it is inseparable, makes the child of the age take off his hat and bow down, even someone who does not know the man: *the absolute method and Hegel.* The absolute method—this phrase is *einhaltsschwer* [weighty in substance], and yet it passes, as the poet says, from *Munde zu Munde* [mouth to mouth],[39] but in every mouth it is equally weighty in substance. Nowadays the absolute method is at home not only in logic but also in the historical sciences. O worldly eminence, what a fraud you are—exclaimed the beggar who had envied that rich lord, until he discovered that His Lordship walked on crutches—just as the

V
B 14
76

V
B 41
94

absolute method does. O worldly eminence, are you not
worthy to aspire to—to be the absolute method, and then to
have such a home as Hegel has prepared in logic,[40] not to
mention in the historical sciences! To have to take refuge in
wordplay and witticisms and evasions, to have to help oneself along by half-untruths, to have to beg all through life
merely to become the absolute, which does not begin *bitt-
weise* [by request], to have to be silent about its not hanging
together properly—oh, this is a high price! Cromwell the
Protector in all his glory could not have been more unfortunate, more fugitive, when he vainly sought a resting place
for the night. And yet Hegel was a great, an outstanding
logician; this in truth no one can deny him. And yet what
he had understood—if only his explanation had been limited
to this—was more than adequate to assure his significance
and to make the young student understand in joyful and
trusting devotion that Hegel was genuinely a teacher. But
the absolute method is a bad conscience in scarlet. And the
absolute method was the superscription—*ergo*, Hegel had also
accomplished this. And the logical gimcrackeries [*Snurrepiberier*] whereby it is supposed to be the object of pious fetish-
worship—to speak ill of them was the prime philosophical
high treason against Hegel. In the same way Nero was incensed at Vindex, not because he incited rebellion, not because he said he was a bad emperor, but because he said Nero
was a bad zither player.

And, now, in the historical sciences! Too bad that Hegel
lacked time; but if one is to dispose of all of world history,
how does one get time for the little test as to whether the
absolute method, which explains everything, is also able to
explain the life of a single human being. In ancient times,
one would have smiled at a method that can explain all of
world history absolutely but cannot explain a single person
even mediocrely, for in ancient days the wise man did not
begin this way and did not go further in such a way that he
never came to understand or he ceased to understand what
the simple person understands. In ancient times, existence
[*Tilværelsen*] was thought to be structured in such a way that

V
B 14
95

anyone who understood a single human being would be in a position to explain history, if he had the requisite knowledge, because the task of reckoning remained essentially the same. Of course, in ancient days there was no wise man who had invented the absolute method. The malpractice in Hegel is easily pointed out. The absolute method explains all world history; the science that is to explain the single human being is ethics. On the one hand, this is quite neglected in Hegel, and insofar as he explains anything, it is usually in such a way that no living being can exist [*existere*] accordingly, and if he were to exist according to the few better things to be found there, then he would instantly explode the absolute method. Hegel can manage much better with the dead, for they are silent. Nevertheless, he had better guard himself against them, for my wish, although I do not know yet whether or not it can be fulfilled, is that Socrates—who, according to his own statement, wanted to ask the wise in the underworld whether they knew something or not—may get hold of Hegel in order to question him about the absolute method. Perhaps it will then become evident that Hegel, who became so extraordinarily absolute in this earthly life, which ordinarily is the life of relativity, would become rather relative in the absoluteness of eternal life.

The question is simplified as much as possible, and in the treatment of it we shall again strive to simplify everything as much as possible, for we do not have such magnificence to offer that we dare to count on it to make recompense for neglecting the simple duty of answering what has been asked. Yet, even if the something else that one gets instead of an answer were marvelously glorious, it would still be essentially indulgence in a dissipation, and it would be a loss to get to know something else instead of receiving an answer to the perhaps insignificant question that nevertheless had the peculiar characteristic of being what one had asked about. It is a dangerous pet idea to want to become concrete immediately in answering an abstract question,[41] whether the concretion consists of a resumé of some earlier philosopher's

V
B 41
96

thought or the particularity of the historical. The concretion often has the effect of seductively depriving thought of the serenity and simplicity that are satisfied with thought itself. The mathematician is delighted with his algebra and does not wish to use dollars, marks, or shillings in order to arouse the sensate person to participation. But even though the concrete is more necessary than it is for the mathematician, one should not begin immediately by making the thought concrete but *in abstracto* clarify the thought one wishes later to point out in the concrete. Thus if a musician wishes to explain to someone that a lead instrument penetrates the rest of the music with its tones and is the basic constituent of the whole, he would probably first play certain passages on that instrument until the learner is familiar with it and can recognize it among a hundred others playing at the same time; only then would he have the entire orchestra play, and he would ask him to be attentive to the way the tone of that instrument is present throughout. If, on the other hand, he were to begin immediately with the music of the full orchestra, he would confuse everything for the listener. The concrete is the manifold and as such exercises an enchanting power over the soul. Suppose it happened that the thought which is to be pointed out in the concrete did not become clear but that the concrete was itself so rich, so variegated, that it captivated the soul and at times became so difficult that in itself it was work enough, so that the learner or the reader, rejoicing in the delight, weary of labor, finally forgot the thought and with unfeigned gratitude felt how much he owed to this teacher. In the beginning, the teacher had not made the thought clear in the passionless brevity of abstraction; perhaps he minimized such a method as being deficient; the thought is supposed to become clear only at the conclusion of the whole, at the conclusion, that is, after the learner has seen and heard various things, has been in various mental states, has again and again admired the teacher's prodigious knowledge, both the profound and the foolish thoughts of the earlier philosophers. —You see, this is why we speak very abstractly. We do not have magical charms; if we do

V
B 41
97

not win the reader simply by speaking honestly about the given question, we shall hardly win him by polished dishonesty that knows how to amaze at the outset.—*JP* II 1606 (*Pap.* V B 41) *n.d.,* 1844

From draft; see 73:13–75:13:

[42]What has happened has happened, cannot be undone— only to this extent is the past changed. But this change is not a change into necessity, which would indeed be a contradiction, since what was not necessary before it became necessary (that is, everything necessary is presupposed as necessary) will never become necessary, since only that can become necessary which was necessary, but consequently was necessary before it became necessary. Therefore, the necessary cannot come into existence [*blive til*], for this is the same proposition that nothing by its coming into existence [*Tilbliven*] or in its coming into existence can become the necessary.

What has happened has happened as it has happened, but could it therefore not have happened otherwise?

In what sense is there change in that which comes into existence; that is, what is the nature of the change of coming into existence; for all other change presupposes the existence [*at det . . . er til*] of that which changes, even when the change consists in ceasing to exist [*at være til*]. That which comes into existence [*det Tilblivende*] certainly does not do this by becoming greater or lesser or, if it consists of parts, by way of some change taking place in these, in their relationship, and thereby in the whole, etc.; for if the subject of coming into existence does not itself remain unchanged in the change of coming into existence, it is not *this* subject of coming into existence that comes into existence but something else, whereby the question is only postponed and is not answered. The subject of coming into existence remains unchanged, therefore, or only suffers or takes upon itself the change of

V
B 15:1
76

V
B 15:1
77

coming into existence, but what is this [change]? Thus, if my plan, for example, is changed in coming into existence, it is then no longer my plan, and it is another plan that comes into existence, but if it comes into existence unchanged, then it is my plan that comes into existence; this constitutes the unchanged, but coming into existence is indeed a change. This change is from not being to being [*ikke at være til at være*]. But this non-being from which it is changed must also be a kind of being [*en Art af Væren*], because otherwise we could not say that the subject of coming into existence remains unchanged in coming into existence. But such a being that is nevertheless a non-being we certainly could call possibility, and the being into which the subject of coming into existence goes by coming into existence is *actuality* [*Virkelighed*]. Therefore the change of coming into existence is the change of actuality. In coming into existence, the possible becomes the actual. But could it not also become the necessary? Not at all, and therefore we still maintain that coming into existence is a change, but the necessary cannot be changed, it is always related to itself in the same way. Therefore everything that can come into existence shows in this very way that it is not the necessary. The necessary[*] is by no means a change in being, as is actuality in relation to possibility, where the essence continues essentially unchanged. But if the possible in becoming the actual did become the necessary, its essence would become changed, and thus one can understand that it cannot become the necessary, for if it became the necessary, it would no longer be itself. The necessary is therefore not a qualification of being, and one says, even though one expresses oneself somewhat differently, one says not that it is necessary but that the necessary is; one does not say that because it is, it is the necessary, but that since it is necessary, therefore it is.[**]

—*JP* I 262 (*Pap.* V B 15:1) *n.d.*, 1844

V
B 15:1
78

[*] *Obliquely in margin*: Necessity is the unity of possibility and actuality.[43]

[**] *In margin*: Nothing whatever comes into existence by necessity, and if, for example, the world had come into existence by necessity, it would never have come into existence. (This has significance for creation—repentance in ethics.)

From draft; see 78:2-8:

This could be explained only in such a way that freedom is an illusion and that it was necessary before it came into existence in freedom, that is, it did not come into existence at all.

In margin: in such a way that freedom was construed as the putative father of what necessity acknowledged as its own.
—*Pap.* V B 15:6 *n.d.*, 1844

In margin of draft; see 79:20:

. . . . . for when in the next moment the manifestation is displaced—or the manifestation itself is regarded as occurring by necessity, then one is still constructing. . . . .—*Pap.* V B 15:7 *n.d.*, 1844

From draft; see 80:3-4:

But apprehension is not able to do it either; *nam sicut scientia præsentium nihil his quæ fiunt, ita præscientia futurorum nihil his, quæ ventura sunt, necessitatis importat* [for just as knowledge of the present does not impart necessity to the present, so foreknowledge of the future imparts no necessity to that which will happen] (Boethius, Liber V[44]).—*Pap.* V B 15:8 *n.d.*, 1844

In margin of draft; see 80:31–81:2:

The word "method" already expresses the teleological—at every moment there must be a pausing.—*Pap.* V B 15:9 *n.d.*, 1844

From draft; see 83:15 and footnote:

Plato[45] and Aristotle[46] acknowledge the same—that sense perception and cognition cannot deceive. Later Descartes (*errores non tam illos ab intellectu quam a voluntate pendere—longe aliud est velle falli quam velle assentiri iis, in quibus contingit er-*

rorem reperiri [errors do not depend so much on intellect as on will . . . there is a great difference between choosing to go wrong, and choosing to assent to something that in fact involves error]. *Principia philosophiae, Pars prima,* XXXI, XLII,[47] and many other places). *In margin:* (in belief, therefore, lies the annulled possibility that it could have been deceived).—*Pap.* V B 15:11 *n.d.,* 1844

From final copy, an unpublished addition; see 83:1 (note):

[Plato and Aristotle.*] *(The error does not lie in cognition or in sensation: ηὔρηκας δὴ ψευδῆ δόξαν, ὅτι οὔτε ἐν ταῖς αἰσθήσεσίν ἐστι πρὸς ἀλλήλας οὔτε ἐν ταῖς διανοίαις, ἀλλ' ἐν τῇ συνάψει αἰσθήσεως πρὸς διάνοιαν [You have made a discovery—that false judgment resides, not in our perceptions, among themselves, nor yet in our thoughts, but in the fitting together of perception and thought]. *Theaetetus.*[48]) —The ideas are the results of the impressions that similar things have made upon men, but the true and the false appear only when men link such ideas with the concept of being and non-being. (Aristotle, Poul Møller.[49])—*Pap.* V B 40:14 *n.d.,* 1844

From draft; see 84:4-20:

Here again no cognition is sufficient by virtue of inference, for cognitive inferences are an *enchainement* [linking together] (Leibniz[50]). The moment belief draws a conclusion from what is present to becoming, this is no cognitive inference but is a decision—an inference from effect to cause (Leibniz[51]), all cognitive inferences are from cause to effect. *In margin:* and I cannot immediately sense or perceive that what I immediately sense or perceive is an effect, because immediately it simply *is.*—*Pap.* V B 15:12 *n.d.,* 1844

From draft; see 84:35–85:5:

Belief concludes that he has come into existence and *wills* to hold fast to this certitude through the uncertainty of doubt.—*Pap.* V B 15:13 *n.d.,* 1844

From sketch; see 89:1-2:

Chapter VII
The Follower at Second Hand
—*Pap.* V B 6:18 *n.d.*, 1844

Deleted from draft; see 90:9-21:

The follower at second hand is indeed a noncontemporary, and this all the subsequent generations have in common over against a contemporary—that they are not contemporary.
In margin: You did not answer my question but elicited a new one.—*JP* I 690 (*Pap.* V B 18) *n.d.*, 1844

From draft; see 91:30–92:8:

It will be deranging if someone has it lodged in his mind that it is easier to be a contemporary.
In both cases a balance sheet is to be drawn up. The various difficulties and advantages.—*Pap.* V B 6:19 *n.d.*, 1844

From draft; see 94:13–96:10:

If this [latest generation] is a long way from the jolt, then it does, however, have the consequences to hold on to, the consequences with which that fact has gradually embraced everything. It should guard itself well against the consequences, for they are just as doubtful an advantage as is immediate certainty; and the person who takes the consequences immediately is deceived, just like the person who took immediate certainty to be the object of faith; the advantage seems to be that that fact must have been gradually *naturalized*. If this is the case, then the later generation even has a clear advantage over the contemporary generation. Unfortunately, this is unthinkable, even though someone or other might consider it to be profound speculation and think it possible to speculate himself to that fact in this way.
—*Pap.* V B 19 *n.d.*, 1844

From sketch; see 95:18–96:16:

From the consciousness of sin emerges faith in the Incarnation, just as from the immediate consciousness [emerges] belief in a god.—*Pap.* V B 6:15 *n.d.*, 1844

Deleted from draft; see 95:18–96:16:

. . . . . that fact has been gradually naturalized. —It certainly can become a person's second nature, but in that case this person has had a first nature—but no one is born with his second nature without having had a first nature; neither is he born with both at the same time . . . . . —*Pap.* V B 17:2 *n.d.*, 1844

From sketch; see 99:16–100:16:

. . . . . it would be an absurdity [*Absurditet*] if a period of time should determine the absolute relation to the absolute, and that fact manifests itself as absolute precisely by its not being dependent on time, even though it is historical. (Yet this is not understood retroactively with regard to their existence before that fact. Pagans before Christianity.)—*Pap.* V B 6:16 *n.d.*, 1844

From sketch; see 100:2:

It is not the case that the status of a contemporary is *status absolutus*[52] and the status of one who comes later is *status constructus*, but that the status of faith is *status absolutus* for both the contemporary and the one who comes later.—*Pap.* V B 6:22 *n.d.*, 1844

From sketch; see 100:17–102:16:

Between one human being and another, the Socratic is and remains the one and only true relation; if understood otherwise, the apostle, if he is the one who gives the believer the condition, will himself be the god, and faith will be in the apostle as in the god.—*Pap.* V B 6:10 *n.d.*, 1844

From sketch; see 100:17–102:16:

The god must also give the condition—therefore he is the god—if the apostle could also give me the condition, he would be the god—but he is only a human being over against another human being and himself can never want anything else if he has understood himself at all . . . . . —*Pap.* V B 6:12 *n.d.*, 1844

Deleted from final draft; see 100:34:

Here the question itself already seems to be a question of misunderstanding, but it also seems that the difficulty is not thereby removed, since the difficulty (see the above) becomes one of perceiving, despite all the difficulties, the illegitimacy of the question.—*Pap.* V B 22 *n.d.*, 1844

From final draft; see 101:35–102:11:

Socrates knew this, and frequently it certainly does take Socratic boldness to see it again, as it took boldness to see it then, as it took boldness to understand then that Alcibiades did not owe Socrates more than Socrates owed him, something that in its presently adopted formulation is easier to grasp—that one human being, insofar as he is a believer, does not owe another human being anything, but both before the god owe him everything.—*Pap.* V B 23:1 *n.d.*, 1844

From sketch; see 102:2-16:

Is this at all conceivable? For the single individual does relate himself absolutely to the absolute teacher—that is, to the god—and all faith, as we said before, is indeed *autopsy*.
—*Pap.* V B 6:17 *n.d.*, 1844

From sketch; see 102:36–104:17:

. . . . . for the one who comes later, the contemporary's report becomes an *occasion*—this again is why it is foolish to waste time on the scrupulous harmonization of historical details, as if thereby to capture it—or on the trustworthiness etc. of those contemporary witnesses, for in relation to this fact every follower is only a witness, but the latest one is just as good as the first.

the one who comes later believes *through* the contemporary, but not in him, stands in just as free a relation to the god as the contemporary does.—*Pap.* V B 6:14 *n.d.*, 1844

From sketch; see 105:5-9:

. . . . . therefore we may even say of the contemporary that it is to his good and advantage that the god goes away and departs from him.[53]—*Pap.* V B 6:13 *n.d.*, 1844

From sketch; see 106:7-12:

(a) The follower at second hand is not tempted to run around constantly looking to see if there is anything to discover with the physical eye, all of which is wasted effort—indeed, a very lamentable chore until one is weaned from it.—*Pap.* V B 6:21 *n.d.*, 1844

From sketch; see 108:20-30, also 32:33–33:36:

(b) If he then refuses to be content with contempt and lowly poverty in the world, the god asks him just as he asked the one with whom he lived (see Chapter II, end): Whom do you love—the Almighty who is supposed to do the miracle on your behalf or the one who on your behalf abased himself?—*Pap.* V B 6:20 *n.d.*, 1844

From draft; see 109:5-9:

Nor will I conceal from you any longer that I intend to name the child by its right name and give the question its historical costume.—*Pap.* V B 20 *n.d.*, 1844

From sketch; see 109:5-9:

The Apologetical Presuppositions of Dogmatics or
Thought-Approximations to Faith[54]
          —*Pap.* V B 7 *n.d.*, 1844

From sketch; see 109:5-9:

The Apologetical Presuppositions of Christian Dogmatics.
or
Approximations to Faith.[55]
Para. 1
An Expression of Gratitude to Lessing.[56]
          —*Pap.* V B 8 *n.d.*, 1844

From sketch; addition to Pap. V B 8:

Feuerbach's indirect service to Christianity as an *offended* individuality.[57] The illusion it takes in our age to become offended, since Christianity has been made as mild as possible, as meaningless as the scrawl a physician makes at the top of a prescription. —The formulation is absolutely correct according to the Hegelian maundering mediation endeavor.—*Pap.* V B 9 *n.d.*, 1844

From sketch; see 109:5-9:

The Modern Position.

The confusion of incessantly mistaking the conflict.
     There is contention about the Bible; it is attacked and defended. But this is only an illusion, for once the whole

Bible has been defended, everything may have been lost, and once it has been lost, everything may have been won.[58]

The apostolic symbol—the sacraments.[59]

Feuerbach nevertheless is consistent and illuminates by his contrast.[60]

This does not mean, however, that one has to go through that Fire Brook[61] (see *Anekdota* by Ruge,[62] an article written by him).—*Pap.* V B 1:10 *n.d.*, 1844

From sketch; see 109:5-9:

The apologetical questions about the Bible and the Church end up as one. It is not denied that the Church exists, but its claim to have existed—indeed, to be apostolic—is certainly a historical question.[63]—*Pap.* V B 1:5 *n.d.*, 1844

From sketch; see 109:5-9:

For a long time now rigid, to-the-letter orthodoxy has reverted to being a counterpart to Don Quixote, whose various ridiculous hairsplitting sophistries will provide excellent analogies.[64]—*JP* III 3047 (*Pap.* V B 1:6) *n.d.*, 1844

From sketch; see 109:5-9:

A whole theory of the Church instead of a theory of the Bible[65] has something deceptive about it, because the latter is not customarily used in the attacks. Otherwise they come to the same thing.* —An introductory science must be developed etc.[66]—*Pap.* V B 1:7 *n.d.*, 1844

From sketch; addition to Pap. V B 1:7:

*The difficulty with the Church theory[67] (Grundtvig) is not that it claims that it exists, for here it is right in saying that this is not to be demonstrated (for existence is never demonstrated); but when it says it is apostolic, it is stating not merely a conceptual definition but something historical, which must be demonstrated. A person standing right in front of me is certainly correct in not needing to demonstrate that he exists; but if he says that four hundred years ago he was king—well, that requires demonstration. —And as soon as the issue is posed in this way, the objections raised are the same as those raised against the Bible.

—*Pap.* V B 1:9 *n.d.*, 1844

From sketch; see 109:5-9:

The same is true of the sacraments.[68] The sacrament itself is a presence, and the presence is not denied, but when the sacrament is supposed to have been instituted by Christ—in short, all the historical—then there must be proofs—*Pap.* V B 1:8 *n.d.*, 1844

From final draft; see 111:2-15:

If such is not the case with what has been developed, then we remain with the Socratic, and it is foolish to give it another name, and it is always better to remain with Socrates than to venture out into something that is supposed to be this something else but still is not what we have propounded.—*Pap.* V B 23:6 *n.d.*, 1844

From draft of Postscript:

". . . . . for when the child is to be weaned, the mother blackens her breast,"[69] and an ethical individual, of course, is not supposed to be a child any longer. Similarly, to recall *Fragments*, if the god wants to reveal himself in human form and is in the least conspicuous,[70] he deceives, and the relationship does not become one of inwardness, which is truth. But if he looks just like this individual human being, just exactly like any other human being, then he deceives only those who think that getting to see the god has something in common with going to Tivoli.[71]

—*Pap.* VI B 40:38 *n.d.*, 1845

The review of my *Fragments* in the German journal[72] is essentially wrong in making the content appear didactic, expository, instead of being imaginatively constructing [*experimenterende*][73] by virtue of its polar form, which is the very basis of the elasticity of irony. To make Christianity seem to be an invention of Johannes Climacus is a biting satire on philosophy's insolent attitude toward it. And then, too, to bring out the orthodox forms in the imaginary construction "so that our age, which only mediates etc., is scarcely able to recognize them"* and believes it is something new—that is irony. But right there is the earnestness, to want Christianity to be given its due in this way—before one mediates.

In margin: *(These are the reviewer's words.)—*JP* V 5827 (*Pap.* VI A 84) *n.d.*, 1845

From draft of Postscript:

The review in the German *Repertorium*[74] (the concluding remark [whether the author in this apologetic dialectic is ironical or in earnest] in the review is silly; if *Fragments* had been pure and simple earnestness, it would have been correct, but there is indeed irony in the book—but that does not mean that the book is irony).—*Pap.* VI B 51 *n.d.*, 1845

From draft of Postscript:

The pamphlet (*Fragments*) was not didactic, nor is what is written here. This is no lecture about Christianity as the truth; I am merely seeking to find a decisive expression for essential Christianity—which certainly can have its significance, inasmuch as in the midst of Christendom we seem to have forgotten what Christianity is.

—*Pap,* VI B 54:31 *n.d.*, 1845

(1)   Logical Issues[75]
       by
       Johannes Climacus.
       First a preface about *Philosophical Fragments.*

(2) Something about the Art of Religious Address[76]
with some Reference to Aristotle's *Rhetoric*
by
Johannes de Silentio.[77]
With the motto from Aristotle's *Rhetoric*, II, chapter 23 (in the little translation, p. 197),[78] about a priestess who forbade her son to become a public speaker.

(3) God's Judgment[79]
A Story of Suffering
Imaginary Psychological Construction[80]

(4) Writing Sampler[81]
Apprentice Test Piece
by
A. W. A. H.   Rosenblad
                               Apprentice Author
—*JP* V 5786 (*Pap.* VI A 146) *n.d.*, 1845

From draft of Postscript:

In relation to the absurd, objective approximation is nonsense; since objective knowledge, in grasping the absurd, has literally gone bankrupt down to its last shilling.

In this case, the way of approximation would be to interrogate witnesses who have seen the god and have either believed the absurd themselves or have not believed it; in the one case I gain nothing, and in the other I lose nothing—to interrogate witnesses who have seen the god perform a miracle, which for one thing cannot be seen, and if they have believed it, well, it is one further consequence of the absurd. —But I do not need to develop this further here; I have done that in *Fragments*. Here we have the same problem Socrates had—to prevent oneself from getting into objective approximation. It is simply a matter of setting aside introductory observations, and reliabilities, and demonstrations based on effects, and pawnbrokers, and all such in order not to be prevented from making the absurd clear—so that one can believe if one will.

If a speculator would like to give a guest performance here

VI
B 42
139

and say: From an eternal and divine point of view there is
no paradox here—this is quite right. But whether or not the
speculator is the eternal one who sees the eternal—this is
something else again. If he then continues his talking, which
does have the eternal in the sense that, like the song, it lasts
for an eternity,[82] he must be referred to Socrates, for he has
not even comprehended the Socratic and even less found time
to comprehend, from that standpoint, something that goes
beyond it.—*JP* II 2287 (*Pap.* VI B 42) *n.d.*, 1845

From draft of Postscript: *see 87:18-19:*

VI
B 45
140

VI
B 45
141

The forgiveness of sin is indeed a paradox inasmuch as the
eternal truth relates itself to an existing person; it is a paradox
inasmuch as the eternal relates itself to the person botched
up in time and by time and who nevertheless is an existing
person (because under the qualification of sin existence is
registered and accentuated a second time). But forgiveness of
sin is really a paradox only when it is linked to the appearance of the god, to the fact that the god has existed [*existeret*].
For the paradox always arises by the joining of existing and
the eternal truth, but the more often this occurs, the more
paradoxical it is.*

*Note: A reference to *Fragments*, in which I said that I do not
believe that God exists [*er til*, (eternally) is] but know it;
whereas I believe that God has existed [*har været til* (the historical)].[83] At that time, I simply put the two formulations together and in order to make the contrast clear did not empha-
size that even from the Greek point of view the eternal truth,
by being for an existing person, becomes an object of faith and
a paradox. But it by no means follows that this faith is the
Christian faith as I have now presented it.—*JP* III 3085 (*Pap.*
VI B 45) *n.d.*, 1845

VII¹
A 158
103

A Note for "The book on Adler"
that was not used.

I see that Johannes Climacus was reviewed in one of the
issues of Scharling and Engelstoft's *Tidsskrift*.[84] It is one of

the usual two-bit reviews, written in "very fine language" with periods and commas in the right places. A theological student or graduate who otherwise is thoroughly incompetent in discussion nevertheless copies the table of contents and then adds his criticism, which is something like this: J. C. is certainly justified in the way in which he emphasizes the dialectical, but (yes, now comes the wisdom) on the other hand one must not forget mediation. Historically, J. C. comes after Hegelianism. J. C. without a doubt knows just as much about mediation as such a theological graduate. In order, if possible, to get out of the spell of mediation, constantly battling against it, J. C. decisively brought the problem to its logical conclusion through the vigor of a qualitative dialectic (something no theological student or graduate or two-bit reviewer can do), and then the book is reviewed in this way—that is, with the help of a bungling laudatory review the book is ruined, annulled, cashiered. And the reviewer even becomes important to himself: for the reviewer to stand loftily over the author in this way looks almost like superiority—with the help of a wretched stock phrase. The reviewer is so insignificant that he would scarcely be able to write a review if the book were taken away from him, for he copies with a suspicious anxiety, and a reviewer like that becomes so self-important at the end. The way an author must work is to use his time and energy strenuously concentrating upon bringing the problem to its logical conclusion, and then along comes a laudatory review and assists in making the issue and the book into the same old hash. And the author is not read, but the reviewer calls attention to himself; the review is read, and the reader must involuntarily believe the review because it is laudatory—the review which by way of praise has annihilated the book. *Mundus vult decipi* [The world wants to be deceived]. But this comes about because to be a genuine author means a sacrificed life and because an intermediate staff of fiddlers has been formed (two-bit reviewers), whose trade flourishes. And since we are accustomed to the coarsest, most boorish guttersnipe tone in the papers, a reviewer presumably thinks that when, as a bonus, he is so nice as to praise the book—he has a right to reduce it to rubbish. Johannes

VII[1]
A 158
104

Climacus most likely would say: No, thank you, may I ask to be abused instead; being abused does not *essentially* harm the book, but to be praised in this way is to be annihilated, insofar as this is possible for the reviewer, the nice, good-natured, but somewhat stupid reviewer. An author who really understands himself is better served by not being read at all, or by having five genuine readers, than by having this confusion about mediation spread abroad only all too much with the help of a good-natured reviewer, spread with the help of his own book, which was written specifically to battle against mediation. But the concept of author in our day has been distorted in an extremely immoral way.—*JP* V 5944 (*Pap.* VII¹ A 158) *n.d.*, 1846

From final copy of Adler; *same as Pap.* VII¹ A 158 *with the following addition:*

Since so many people who are totally unqualified to be authors (no essential idea to communicate, no essential mission, no ethically conscious responsibility) nevertheless become authors, being an author becomes for men a kind of distinction similar to women's adorning themselves: the primary point and the purpose for writing are to become noticed, recognized, praised. A showy, flashy author of this sort has nothing to tell the reader; just like someone taking a graduate examination, he is writing in order to enjoy the social status of taking an examination or of being an author; he is writing to show that he is an expert in beautiful penmanship. It is no trick, of course, for almost anyone to form an estimate of him, for despite being an author he stands utterly *au niveau* [on the level] with the majority. The lie consists in this, that such a scribbler and candidate up for examination is called an author, but as a result of this lie, people are pampered into regarding an author as someone who writes in order to be recognized, or presumably even to be recognized with praise. Is it not conceivable that an author would write in order that the truth he has to communicate may be understood? If so, he in no way benefits by being recognized—even with praise—by someone who misunderstands him. Not so with the examinee; he has nothing to communicate. If he in fact detects that the examiner does not understand him at all but nevertheless says *prae caeteris* [praiseworthy above others], the examinee is deliriously happy, and one can hardly blame him for that. However, it is really odd that to be an author should be anything like that, and even more odd that the examiner in relation to the author is not a professor but some literary bungler in a newspaper. If it were conceivable that one could become an author without writing, could purchase this dignity just as one buys a title, yet, please note, actually enjoying a bit of a reputation—then a great many of the authors of our generation would perhaps stop writing. And if one could, without doing any writing, earn the money one earns by writing, then many other contemporary authors would undoubtedly refrain from writing, and we would see how many genuine authors we do have.—*Pap.* VII² B 235 *n.d.*, 1846-47

VII²
B 235
84

From final copy of Adler:

Note. With regard to all the dialectical problems relevant to this (*the paradox, the moment, the dialectic of contemporaneity,* etc.), I must refer to a pseudonym, Johannes Climacus, to his two books, *Philosophical Fragments* and *Concluding Postscript to* Philosophical Fragments. For something so dialectically composed, it is impossible to give a brief resumé; if the report is to be reliable, it will end up being just as detailed and difficult as the original exposition, for if just one least little middle term is left out, the whole dialectic suffers. Whether what is said of living organisms is completely true—namely, that when one limb suffers, the whole body suffers—I do not know; but I do know that this is exactly the way it is with the dialectical.—*Pap.* VII² B 235, p. 76 *n.d.*, 1846-47

From final copy of Adler:

Note. This dialectic of contemporaneity is set forth in *Fragments*—namely, that an immediate contemporary is not actually a contemporary, and that for this very reason someone who lives 1,800 years later may just as well be able to be a contemporary.[85]—*Pap.* VII² B 235, p. 84 *n.d.*, 1846-47

From final copy of Adler:

But primarily the four books[86] must objectively have a deeper purpose—for example, if possible, maieutically to cover a specific terrain on all sides at the same time. It must then be important to the author of the four books—for him a half-poetic artistic task—that each book, which *essentially in itself* is different from the others, be kept *characteristically* distinct from the others. The author must poetically know how to support the illusion, which consists essentially in the special point of departure in the particular book. By way of the announcement, he himself must see to splitting them up, so that the impact of the four books at the same time actually is a product of the reader's self-activity. Above all, no one is obliged to know that there are four books at the same time. Therefore, the art connoisseur, if he discovers in a roundabout way that there is one author, still can have a certain enjoyment in entering into the illusion that there are not four books by one author but by four authors. Thus, even in the *Advertiser*, the one and same author does not introduce and offer himself as the author of four books at one and the same time.—*Pap.* VII² B 235, p. 129 *n.d.*, 1846-47

Prof. Martensen's Status

It is now roughly ten years since Prof. Martensen returned home from foreign travels, bringing with him the newest German philosophy[87] and creating quite a sensation with this novelty—he actually has always been more of a reporter and correspondent than a primitive thinker.

It was the philosophy of points of view—the demoralizing aspect of that kind of survey—that fascinated young people and opened the prospect of swallowing up everything in half a year.

He makes quite a splash, and in the meantime young students use the opportunity to inform the public in print that with Martensen begins a new era, epoch, epoch and era, etc. (Note: See the Preface to *Philosophical Fragments*.[88]) The demoralizing aspect in allowing young people to do this, thereby turning all relationships around. . . . —*Pap*. X² A 155, p. 117 *n.d.*, 1849

Here is an error in Julius Müller.[89] He is right in maintaining that sin and every manifestation of freedom (the younger Fichte has already repeatedly stressed this[90]) cannot be [deduced] with necessity (no, neither before nor afterward; see *Philosophical Fragments*[91]) but must be experienced.

Fine, now he should have swung directly into the ethical-religious, into the existential, to the *You* and *I*. Earnestness is that I myself become conscious of being a sinner and apply everything in this respect to myself. But, instead of that, he goes into the ordinary problems about the universality of sin etc. But if it is to be experienced, then either I must know all—and in that case, since the world goes on, the whole thing becomes a hypothesis, which perhaps held water until now but does not for that reason hold water (as, I see, Prof. Levy writes in an article about the maternity hospital[92])—or else I must understand what Johannes Climacus has developed in *Concluding Postscript*, that with regard to actuality every individual is essentially assigned only to himself; he can understand every other individual only in possibility.[93]

—*JP* IV 4037 (*Pap*. X² A 482) *n.d.*, 1850

Johannes Climacus

eller

De omnibus dubitandum est.

fu Schelling.

Loquor de vera dubitatione in mente, et non de ea, quam passim videmus contingere, ubi scilicet verbis, quam in animo non habet, dicit quis se dubitare: non est enim Methodi hoc emendare, sed potius pertinet ad inquisitionem pertinaciae et ejus emendationem.

Spinoza de intellectûs emendatione Tractatus. p. 511.

Johannes Climacus.
eller
De omnibus dubitandum est.

En Fortælling.

Loquor de vera dubitatione in mente, et non de
ea, quam passim videmus contingere, ubi scilicet
verbis, quamvis animus non dubitet, dicit quis se
dubitare: non est enim Methodi hoc emendare,
sed potius pertinet ad inquisitionem pertinaciæ et
ejus emendationem.
Spinoza de intellectus emendatione Tractatus.
p. 511.
[*Pap*. IV B 1, p. 103 *n.d.*, 1842-43]

SELECTED ENTRIES FROM
KIERKEGAARD'S JOURNALS AND PAPERS
PERTAINING TO
JOHANNES CLIMACUS, OR
DE OMNIBUS DUBITANDUM EST

See title page:

Hegel is a Johannes *Climacus*[1] who does not storm the heavens as do the giants—by setting mountain upon mountain—but *climbs up* to them by means of his syllogisms.—*JP* II 1575 (*Pap.* II A 335) January 20, 1839

On the whole, one has to say that modern philosophy, even in its most grandiose forms, nevertheless is really only an introduction to making it possible to philosophize. Hegel undeniably completes—but only the development that had its beginning with Kant and was directed toward knowledge. In Hegel one finds in a more profound form, as the outcome, that which earlier philosophy unreflectively assumed as a beginning—that on the whole there is reality [*Realitæt*] in thought. But the whole line of thought proceeding from this assumption (or now happy over this result) was entering into genuine anthropological contemplation, which has not yet been undertaken.

See K.K., pp. 20-21 [*JP* III 3261 (*Pap.* II C 55)].—*JP* I 37 (*Pap.* III A 3) July 5, 1840

It was only by way of an accidental and arbitrary use of his own principle that Socrates did not become positive but remained negative, for the art of questioning is simply the dialectical aspect of the art of answering (and when it is said that a fool can ask more questions than seven wise men can answer, the wise men deserve the apology explaining that they cannot answer because the fool cannot question), but Socrates used his art only polemically in order to show that John Doe could not answer. In this respect it could be a very interesting project to show how the words of Socrates, where he speaks of immortality and, assuming this possibility, of association with Homer in the other life etc.,[2] were also part of his wishing to question them; either this was for the purpose of showing that they knew nothing and thus to plunge every ὕψωμα [height, pretension][3] into the *einfache* [single, simple] empty infinitude of ignorance, or here the positive plays an important role—questioning for the purpose of learning something. What modern philosophy has been so preoccupied with—to get all presuppositions removed in order to begin with nothing—Socrates did in his own way, in order to end with nothing.

—*JP* I 754 (*Pap.* III A 7) July 10, 1840

See 157:29–158:12:

Apollonius of Tyana's development of the motto "Know yourself" is sheer comical pretension.[4] It was regarded as difficult and as the ultimate, and yet he was not satisfied with it but says that Pythagoras not only knew himself but also knew who he had been, which he then would also like to apply to himself. In a curiously comical way, the profundity of the first sentence is thereby dissipated. So it goes in our time with many philosophers: they will say something in addition, and they thereby make it all ridiculous, even though there are always a goodly number who take it to be profound wisdom.

In margin: See book VI, 11, p. 500.[5]—*JP* III 3289 (*Pap.* IV A 19) n.d., 1842-43

See 139:5-11:

Descartes's philosophy has a birthmark. Having eliminated everything in order to find himself as a thinking being in such a way that this very thinking is myself, he then finds that with the same necessity he thinks God. Then, however, his system also calls for the rescue of the finite world in some way or other. The development toward this end is as follows. God cannot deceive; he has implanted all ideas within me, and therefore they are true. Incidentally, it is noteworthy that Descartes, who himself in one of the meditations explains the possibility of error by recalling that freedom in man is superior to thought,[6] nevertheless has construed thought, not freedom, as the absolute. Obviously this is the position of the elder Fichte—not *cogito ergo sum*[7] but I act *ergo sum*, for this *cogito* is something derived or it is identical with "I act"; either it is the consciousness of freedom in the action, and then it should not read *cogito ergo sum*, or it is the subsequent consciousness.—*JP* III 2338 (*Pap.* IV C 11) *n.d.*, 1842-43

It is really extraordinary that Chrysippus uses the statement, "Every statement is either true or false," to prove that everything happens according to fate. Here the idea of mediation seems to be necessary in order to find a providence. (See Tennemann, *Ges. d. Ph.*, IV, p. 272.[8])—*JP* II 1242 (*Pap.* IV C 55) *n.d.*, 1842-43

It is most remarkable that almost all the skeptics have always left the reality [*Realitæt*] of the will uncontested. Thereby they would actually arrive at the point they should reach, for recovery takes place through the will. The manner in which the skeptics usually expressed themselves is very striking. They thought that as far as action is concerned, one might as well be content with probability, just as if it were less important to act rightly than to know rightly.—*JP* II 1243 (*Pap.* IV C 56) *n.d.*, 1842-43

Certainly doubt is halted not by the necessity of knowledge (that there is something one must acknowledge) but by

the categorical imperative of the will, that there is something
one cannot will.[9] This is the will's concretion in itself, by
which it shows itself to be something other than an ethereal
phantom.—*JP* II 1244 (*Pap*. IV C 60) *n.d*., 1842-43

To what extent does the imagination play a role in logical
thought, to what extent the will; to what extent is the conclusion a resolution.

—*JP* III 3658 (*Pap*. IV C 89) *n.d*., 1842-43

From sketch; see 113:

> De omnibus dubitandum est.
> A Narrative.
> —*Pap*. IV B 2:1 *n.d*., 1842-43

From draft; see 113:

> de omnibus dubitandum
> a Narrative.
> *In margin:* Johannes Climacus.
> —*Pap*. IV B 3a:1 *n.d*., 1842-43

From draft; see 113:

The plan of this narrative was as follows. By means of the
melancholy irony, which did not consist in any single utter-
ance on the part of Johannes Climacus but in his whole life,
by means of the profound earnestness involved in a young
man's being sufficiently honest and earnest enough to do
quietly and unostentatiously what the philosophers say (and
he thereby becomes unhappy)—I would strike a blow at
[modern speculative] philosophy. Johannes does what we are
told to do—he actually doubts everything—he suffers through
all the pain of doing that, becomes cunning, almost acquires a
bad conscience. When he has gone as far in that direction as he
can go and wants to come back, he cannot do so. He per-
ceives that in order to hold on to this extreme position of

doubting everything, he has engaged all his mental and spiritual powers. If he abandons this extreme position, he may very well arrive at something, but in doing that he would have also abandoned his doubt about everything. Now he despairs, his life is wasted, his youth is spent in these deliberations. Life has not acquired any meaning for him, and all this is the fault of philosophy. (The concluding lines are found in my papers [*Pap.* IV B 6].)—*Pap.* IV B 16 *n.d.*, 1842-43

From draft, concluding lines; see 113:

Then the philosophers are worse than the Pharisees,[10] who, as we read, impose heavy burdens but themselves do not lift them, for in this they are the same, but the philosophers demand the impossible. And if there is a young man who thinks that to philosophize is not to talk or to write but in all quietness to do honestly and scrupulously what the philosophers say one should do, they let him waste his time, many years of his life, and then it becomes clear that it is impossible,[11] and yet it has gripped him so profoundly that rescue is perhaps impossible.—*JP* III 3291 (*Pap.* IV B 6) *n.d.*, 1842-43

From sketch; see 115:15:

The first essay by Spinoza on Descartes[12] can also be used.
—*Pap.* IV B 2:13 *n.d.*, 1842-43

From sketch; see 118:2:

A young student in Salamanca.
—*Pap.* IV B 2:2 *n.d.*, 1842-43

From draft; see 121:6-10:

Among the various branches of knowledge in which he was instructed, he soon learned to isolate what appealed to him most. That was grammar.
Latin grammar's strict structure.
—*Pap.* IV B 3a:7 *n.d.*, 1842-43

From sketch; see 121:8-11:

However, he acceded modestly. When he heard the enthusiasm of others, he thought that he was at fault. He had admired Homer—Plato and Aristotle—"the modern philosophers" were even greater—even though he thought it remarkable that they should be more difficult to understand, since they were, after all, so much closer to him.—*Pap.* IV B 5:2 *n.d.*, 1842-43

From draft; see 121:18–122:37:

What hovered there before him was a beautiful area overgrown with aquatic plants; there he walked among the rushes. —His father had taught him to see the great in the small. Close to the house where they lived was a knoll with a luxurious growth of grass. When he stood on the flat ground, he was just tall enough to be able to look into it. His father had often shown it to him. Then the grass was an enormous forest; a little animal ran around in it. He himself became so little that he saw himself walking around in it. —Instead of the overgrown space it was before, it now became an enormous space, an expanse, and the scale became the idea with which he partitioned it.—*Pap.* IV B 3a:9 *n.d.*, 1842-43

From draft; see 121:31:

. . . . . —the silent intuition and succession similar to that of the clouds—the sudden, the surprising.
　　　　　　　　　　—*Pap.* IV B 3a:10 *n.d.*, 1842-43

From draft; see 121:35-38:

When his father began to argue, he listened attentively. It was not quarreling or bickering.
　　　　　　　　　　—*Pap.* IV B 3a:11 *n.d.*, 1842-43

From draft; see 122:3-6:

Then when Johannes, having followed the first speaker's argument with keen attention, had mastered its line of reasoning—his father's two or three words struck like lightning and showed everything to be otherwise.—*Pap.* IV B 3a:12 *n.d.*, 1842-43

From draft; see 124:26–125:4:

His father's depression contributed to this. That his father was an extraordinary man, he did not find out; if he had, he would certainly have perceived that actuality usually was not nearly that great. That his father amazed him, this he did know; that no other person did so in this way, he did know, but still he knew only four. But that his father, humanly speaking, was rather extraordinary, he did not learn in his paternal home. His father was very melancholy. Once in a while when an older, trusted friend visited him and they spoke more confidentially to each other, Johannes often heard him say, "Alas! I am good for nothing, I cannot do a thing; my one and only wish would be to find a place in a charitable institution." This was no jest; there was not a trace of irony in his words. On the contrary, there was a gloomy earnestness about them that troubled Johannes. If they continued in the same vein, he could mention a person of the least importance, a hired farmhand, and demonstrate what a genius he was compared with himself. No one could refute him, not only because he would not accept the reasons, but also because his incomparable dialectic was capable of anything. He could make one forget what was most obvious, could make it clearer than daylight that his view of the matter was the only right way to look at it. Johannes had no intimation that it was depression, had no intimation that here again was the dialectic. To be sure, his father did not lose any of his halo, but his words contributed to developing the idea that the rest of mankind must be a kingdom of gods, since even a farmhand was a genius.—*Pap.* IV B 3c *n.d.*, 1842-43

From sketch; see 127:4:

Chapter I[13]

(Danish Philosophy) Traditional Concepts.

Chapter II

Hegel.—

Chapter III

Kant.—

Chapter IV

Descartes—Spinoza.

—*Pap.* IV B 2:18 *n.d.*, 1842–43

From draft; see 129:2–130:12:

He did not like to read; he had not been developed by reading philosophical books. It was something far more original.

—Books did not appeal to him. They discussed so many other matters—incidentals—not the strict order, not the delight of surprise.—*Pap.* IV B 4 *n.d.*, 1842–43

From draft; see 129:2–130:12:

. . . . . philosophical works—did not always deal with what the title suggested, or it came at the end—a strange historical way of thinking about what this one or that one had said. The development suddenly bounded away—without order, without precision, without surprise.—*Pap.* IV B 5:1 *n.d.*, 1842–43

From draft; see 130:7–131:22:

Meanwhile he came to a modest conclusion. When he heard the enthusiasm of others, he thought that the fault lay in him. Homer he had admired—Plato and Arist.—"the modern philosophers" were even greater—even though it was strange to him that they should be more difficult to understand, since they were indeed much closer to him.—*Pap.* IV B 5:2 *n.d.*, 1842–43

From draft; see 130:23-37:

. . . . . he felt a pressure; it was as if forceps had to be used in his youth when he was delivered into the world, as if he were still wanting to slip back; he was not born easily and thus did not come into the world smiling and victorious, as if everything were merely waiting for him.—*Pap.* IV B 7:1 *n.d.*, 1842-43

From sketch; see 130:31-37:

His thoughts (pertaining to all these points) he kept to himself; it was clear to him—although the reason was obscure—that his comments would not meet with sympathy. It was impossible for him to speak as the others did, and, on the other hand, he realized very well that the others would not understand him.—*Pap.* IV B 5:10 *n.d.*, 1842-43

From sketch; see 130:38-131:2:

When he listened to others talk, he heard only a few phrases that he himself could use.—*Pap.* IV B 5:3 *n.d.*, 1842-43

From draft; see 130:38-131:2:

Generally not much was said to explain it, but there was all the more for him to do.—*Pap.* IV B 7:2 *n.d.*, 1842-43

From draft; see 131:10-13:

For a moment it pained him that once again he was not like the others, but he soon forgot the pain in the joy of thinking.—*Pap.* IV B 7:3 *n.d.*, 1842-43

From sketch; see 131:14-17; 144:2, 146:9:

de omnibus dubitandum.

(1)   to doubt the correctness of their statement, who said it. (it was a witticism)

philosophy begins with doubt
one must doubt in order to philosophize;
in that case philosophy presumably must begin with
something else (just as when it began with wonder, it began with explaining the wonderful—here with *faith*).
modern philosophy began with doubt.
(historically speaking).
—*Pap.* IV B 5:4 *n.d.*, 1842-43

From sketch; see 131:17-21:

These words, *de omnibus dubitandum est,* would come to
play a very important role in his life. They were like a name
in a young girl's history, with a multitude of associations.
—*Pap.* IV B 5:5 *n.d.*, 1842-43

From draft; see 133:4:

I shall now give up the narrative style for the time being,
for proper philosophical reflection is indifferent to personality. But, whenever necessary, I shall once again use it, asking
the reader to remember that this is not simply a discussion
of the meaning and content of that philosophical thesis but
that I am also narrating Johannes Climacus's life.—*Pap.* IV
B 7:5 *n.d.*, 1842-43

From draft; see 133:21:

In margin: Para. 1. Grammatical understanding. *Crossed out
in text: Modern philosophy begins with doubt.*—*Pap.* IV B 7:6 *n.d.*,
1842-43

From draft; see 134:24-25:

. . . . . he was continually hoping to hear something on
that subject in the conversations of the philosophers, but in
vain. —If it was a purely historical statement, then it would
be of absolutely no importance to him, and then this thesis

could be no hindrance to his beginning his philosophy as best he could.—*Pap.* IV B 7:7 *n.d.*, 1842-43

From draft; see 135:28-34:

If the aforementioned is to be assumed, then it must be because this beginning is the essential beginning for all philosophy, and thus we are once again back with the prior [thesis].

It surprised him that philosophy used such an ambiguous expression instead of restricting itself to the first thesis and thereby denouncing all earlier philosophy. What was the point, if any, of using two expressions . . . . . —*Pap.* IV B 7:8 *n.d.*, 1842-43

From draft; see 136:7-8:

. . . . . or a historical thesis not accurately expressed. To presuppose that it was a historical thesis was natural for him at this point, for, after all, if he assumed that it was altogether identical with the first thesis, he would certainly come back to it later.

He would then examine it more closely, not in order to learn whether it was true—for that, of course, could not be made an object of interrogation, only an object for reflection—but in order to see what it contained.—*Pap.* IV B 7:9 *n.d.*, 1842-43

From draft; see 136:9-10:

In margin: Para. 2. How it happened that modern philosophy began with doubt.—*Pap.* IV B 7:10 *n.d.*, 1842-43

From sketch; see 136:11-14:

Was it a necessity that philosophy began in this way, or was it an accident.—*Pap.* IV B 5:7 *n.d.*, 1842-43

From draft; see 138:25-31:

. . . . . for this, of course, the future had to decide. If
anything was to be said about that thesis, it would have to
be said essentially about philosophy, and that thesis would
once again be identical with the first one.

With this whole deliberation . . . . .

—*Pap.* IV B 7:11 *n.d.*, 1842–43

From sketch; see 138:31-139:27:

. . . . . he was supposed to doubt in order to begin. The
others had done this, and now it became manifest that he
could not begin.

. . . . . he made use of the second thesis: *cogito ergo sum.*[14]

. . . . . what kind of *I* was it.

—*Pap.* IV B 2:10 *n.d.*, 1842–43

From draft; see 131:32-139:11:

. . . . . for he could not believe philosophy capable of such
a confusing tautology, confusing because it exhorted people
to believe something because of its having been said twice,
although it was the same thing. He could not maintain the
distinction except by altering the thesis a bit, and he felt himself too insignificant for that.—*Pap.* IV B 7:12 *n.d.*, 1842–43

From draft; see 140:18:

. . . . . for his life had nothing accidental that a later consideration could remove.—*Pap.* IV B 7:13 *n.d.*, 1842–43

From draft; see 141:19-30:

. . . . . since each single one was still but an element and
had validity only as an element.

—*Pap.* IV B 7:14 *n.d.*, 1842–43

From draft; see 142:31:

If a person such as this becomes tenacious about it, then he must be considered essentially mad.—*Pap.* IV B 7:15 *n.d.*, 1842-43

From draft; see 143:13:

He decided to shelve this thesis for the time being and turn to the other two.

Chapter II

Philosophy begins with doubt; one must have doubted in order to begin to philosophize.
In margin: He first juxtaposed this thesis and no. 2 to see whether they said the same thing.—*Pap.* IV B 7:16 *n.d.*, 1842-43

From sketch; see 144:2:

Philosophy *begins with doubt.*
                    —*Pap.* IV B 2:17 *n.d.*, 1842-43

In margin of draft; see 144:19-20:

Thus it was merely a matter of embarking upon doubt, and he would now see whether the thesis could help him to do this.—*Pap.* IV B 7:17 *n.d.*, 1842-43

From sketch, addition to Pap. IV B 2:4; *see 145:27-35:*

. . . . . whether he then should also doubt the earlier philosophers.
It did not apply to those who had taught him that, but Hegel certainly must have done it.
                    —*Pap.* IV B 2:6 *n.d.*, 1842-43

From draft; see 146:22-28:

..... of a less perfect nature than he himself, who, unlike himself, was incapable of attaining emancipation through doubt.—*Pap.* IV B 7:19 *n.d.*, 1842-43

From draft; see 146:31-147:13:

He certainly felt the imperfection in the way in which he appropriated these, but he still did not wish for that reason to give up thinking it through as well as possible, and with that objective he began once again to examine the thesis closely, yet not so much to discern what it contained, for he must indeed be assumed to have embarked upon that in a way already, but in order to enter into relation to it himself. Thus he did not ask about its relation to philosophy in the same way as if he were asking whether doubt, as the beginning, is a part of philosophy or is the whole of philosophy; if it is only a part, what then is the other part.

Para. 1.   Whether the thesis that philosophy begins with doubt came into the world in a miraculous manner and in an equally miraculous manner propagates itself.

The potential problems involved in the thesis he did not want to ponder further. He assumed that the thesis was true since it had enjoyed so much honor in the world. To him the only question of importance to reflect upon was how to enter into it, for once he had just entered into it he would, of course, have landed in philosophy.—*Pap.* IV B 7:20 *n.d.*, 1842-43

From draft; see 147:14-15:

Para. 2   [*changed from:* Para. 1] How did this thesis come into the world? How does the single individual relate to it?—*Pap.* IV B 7:21 *n.d.*, 1842-43

From draft; see 149:1-4:

He now grasped why the speaker had behaved in that way; he wanted merely to remind his listeners of familiar things, and therefore no explanation was needed. This pained him; he considered it almost shameful of the philosophers not to explain the least thing—there could always be someone, after all, who needed it—but whenever they came together, they always entertained themselves with their own wisdom, and it never occurred to them to give a little help to the weak.

—*Pap.* IV B 7:22 *n.d.*, 1842-43

From draft; see 152:28-32:

In other words, in order for the religious and ethical thesis to have significance, there must be authority. —Must the one who is supposed to enunciate that philosophical thesis also have authority? Is talent itself not adequate authority? Philosophical talent is adequate authorization for enunciating a philosophical thesis. But something else is required when it involves religious and ethical truths; for if . . . . . —*Pap.* IV B 7:26 *n.d.*, 1842-43

From draft; see 153:27-29:

Is it a matter of indifference to the thesis that someone receives it or not, as is the case with the mathematical thesis, just as it is a matter of indifference with regard to the one who enunciated it?—*Pap.* IV B 7:27 *n.d.*, 1842-43

From draft; see 154:4-6:

Is not the negative like evil, which also lacks continuity, as is the case regarding unity among thieves?—*Pap.* IV B 7:28 *n.d.*, 1842-43

From sketch; see 154:16:

. . . . . then he considers that Descartes is the one who said it; he reads Descartes, understands him, especially the progression, that God must be truthful.[15]
He ends with understanding . . . . . —*Pap.* IV B 2:9 *n.d.*, 1842-43

From sketch; see 132:19; 147:23–148:22; 154:21:

Hegel might explain this. —One single passage in the *Phenomenology*—how shall I go about it, and yet it is the condition for making the beginning. He thought it must be difficult; he thought: I shall not get any further than the beginning.
since nothing is said in explanation, it must be very easy to understand; he was ashamed to ask about it.
Others were of the opinion that Hegel had indeed done it.
now one should begin.
the eternal philosophy.
—*Pap.* IV B 2:4 *n.d.*, 1842-43

From sketch; see 154:22:

He had already been struck by Hegel's and Spinoza's saying that Descartes did not doubt as a skeptic *for the sake of* doubting, but *for the sake of* finding truth[16] . . . . . this *for the sake of.* —*And* why do these men talk about it as if they themselves had not done it? Has Descartes done it for all of us[17] in the same way Christ was crucified—is this a scientific question—or a practical one—. It certainly must be that in Descartes.—*JP* I 734 (*Pap.* IV B 2:16) *n.d.*, 1842-43

From sketch; see 157:28–158:18:

Pythagoras's silence[18]—Apollonius of Tyana[19]—the Middle Ages—   —*Pap.* IV B 2:3 *n.d.*, 1842-43

From sketch; see 157:28–158:18:

. . . . . he indeed found it remarkable that the follower was given work of such distinction—
   Pythagoras: to be silent—
      to wonder . . . . .

                              —*Pap*. IV B 8:2 *n.d.*, 1842-43

From sketch; see 157:28–158:18:

. . . . . to go beyond Hegel—that would be a precarious matter. He feared that it would go with him as with Apollonius of Tyana, who also went beyond Pythagoras, did not merely know himself but knew who he had been before he became himself[20]—whereby all the philosophy in the Pythagorean thesis was annulled.—*Pap*. IV B 8:11 *n.d.*, 1842-43

From sketch; see 158:27-31:

. . . . . would it not be a pious fraud? In the manner of the Carpocratians,[21] it would teach them to rely upon the teacher, just as one allows children to burn themselves in the fire instead of warning them.—*Pap*. IV B 8:4 *n.d.*, 1842-43

From sketch; see 159:12-18:

It would have to lead to something or to nothing; he would have to become wise or go mad—he would stake his life, but let go of the thought he would not— . . . . . —*Pap*. IV B 8:6 *n.d.*, 1842-43

From sketch; see 161:1-10:

Part II.
De omnibus d.
The Preliminary.
                              —*Pap*. IV B 13:1 *n.d.*, 1842-43

From draft; see 161:1-10:

Chapter IV.
De omnibus dubitandum est.
—*Pap.* IV B 9:2 *n.d.*, 1842-43

From draft; see 163:32:

Even if he did not want to do the same, it still would always be good to know the danger and know the way. Indeed, one might even wish the directions to be relatively brief, for in the world of mind one could not designate such specific points—and generally it would easily turn out to be like a peasant's directions: first to the right, then to the left, then to the left again, and then to the right.—*Pap.* IV B 9:3 *n.d.*, 1842-43

From sketch: see 163:33-164:12:

They will probably have to describe accurately what one should do—what shocking sights one will see along the way—not as when a peasant shows someone the way and says: First to the right and then to the left.

Yet he learned very little about this—he heard only that by doubting everything one would arrive at pure being. — He felt as he did in his childhood when he played the game "Going to Grandmother's Door."[22]—

For the particular statement that he usually heard either made him discouraged or sounded to him like mockery.
—*Pap.* IV B 8:13 *n.d.*, 1842-43

From sketch; see 164:21-27:

One must not spend too much time.
One should just begin, and then it would turn out all right.
One should embrace the eternal philosophy.
—*Pap.* IV B 5:9 *n.d.*, 1842-43

From sketch; see 164:21-27:

"One should just begin, not waste time on doubting." This appeared to have just as gratifying an effect on the listeners as when the pope announces an indulgence—on Johannes it made a different impression—*Pap.* IV B 8:5 *n.d.*, 1842-43

From sketch; see 164:21-27:

Preliminary
One must just begin, not waste time on doubting.
It is no easy matter.   —*Pap.* IV B 8:12 *n.d.*, 1842-43

From sketch; see 164:38–165:21:

He thought that it possibly was something one ought to handle carefully, as one handles nitric acid.

When Agnonides ventured to accuse Theophrastus of contempt of religion, he was very close himself to being declared guilty of the same crime;[23] it is a thorough way of demonstrating something.

—*Pap.* IV B 8:10 *n.d.*, 1842-43

From sketch; see 165:2-6:

He could readily perceive that to doubt everything meant to abstract from everything. —But how does this time pass.
—*Pap.* IV B 2:5 *n.d.*, 1842-43

From sketch; see 165:2-6:

Prof. Martensen[24] made an exception. He explains that it is no *easy matter*, that one can understand, if it would only be of some help.—*Pap.* IV B 2:7 *n.d.*, 1842-43

From sketch; see 165:2-6:

> "It is not easy; it is not doubt about this or that, about
> one thing or another, about something and something
> else, but about everything," . . . . .
>
> —*Pap.* IV B 8:9 *n.d.*, 1842-43

From sketch; see 166:1-4:

> To doubt, what is it.
> a determination of the will
> or a necessity of cognition.
>
> —*Pap.* IV B 5:6 *n.d.*, 1842-43

From sketch; see 166:1-4:

Chapter I
What is it to doubt
Para. 1. How does one come to doubt?

—*Pap.* IV B 13:4 *n.d.*, 1842-43

From draft; see 166:1-4:

IV
B 12
173

Chapter I
What is it to doubt?
Para. 1. Is doubting an act of cognition?
How does one come to doubt?[*]

    In order to orient himself psychologically, he provisionally
interpreted the term "to doubt" in its quite ordinary sense.
He asked: What would be the state of one who does not
doubt—not because he had conquered doubt but because he
had never begun to doubt. The animal does not doubt; the
child does not doubt. In what state, then, is the child? In the
state of immediacy. For the child, therefore, everything is
true. Yet he did not stop there; he perceived that this was a
way of expressing that directly and immediately *everything is
true.*** How does the possibility that something can be untrue
arise? It can only occur by bringing immediacy into relation

with something else. Thus as soon as I want to express immediacy, I encounter difficulty. Immediacy does not allow itself to be expressed at all. Thus as soon as I want to express immediacy in language, contradiction is present, for language is ideal. As long as I am defined as merely a sensory being, everything is true; as soon as I want to express sensation, contradiction is present. To take a very simple example, there is contradiction in my merely wanting to see a repetition in sense perception. For example, if I have seen an egg and then see something that resembles an egg and trace what I am seeing now to what I have seen, then what I have seen is defined ideally, because my having it in recollection is a qualification of ideality—it no longer exists. Indeed, even if I place the two objects side by side, the ideality is in the consciousness, because ideality is the relation I establish between them. Therefore, as soon as I bring a reality [*Realitæt*][28] into relation with an ideality, I have doubt. It is the same conversely—when I bring an ideality into relation with a reality. As long as I am only immediately qualified, everything is possible. Just as one, as far as knowledge is concerned, can say of a child that everything, the most true and the most false, is equally true, so is everything, the most impossible and the most possible, equally possible. But as soon as I posit a relation that manifests itself as a consequence—for the person who acts spontaneously does not suspect that there is anything called a consequence—then doubt is present; for even if there is no reflection on the consequence, so that the consequence itself is unimportant to one, this knowledge of the consequence is nevertheless an element of doubt.

IV
B 12
174

This duplexity was also implicit in language usage, that is, in most languages, but not in Greek.

[*]*In margin:* What is the first thing one finds by doubting—it is untruth.—

In margin: **The sophistical thesis in Plato[25]—Schleiermacher's teaching that feelings are true.[26] See Bruno Baur's journal, III(1), p. 11.[27]—*Pap.* IV B 12 *n.d.*, 1842-43

In margin of draft; see 166:15-19:

. . . . . all other knowledge is dichotomous, lies in immanence, not in transcendence.

. . . . . since all knowledge either evoked that which it is supposed to evoke or it is without effect.—*Pap.* IV B 14:1 *n.d.*, 1842-43

From sketch; see 166:31–170:4:

Feeling
Intuition
Recollection
Representation

                                —*Pap.* IV B 10:6 *n.d.*, 1842-43

From draft; see 167:5:

If one were to speak of an animal's consciousness, then it would indeed be a consciousness that would have doubt outside itself. Yet this would always be disputable; therefore he took the child, because there is consciousness in the child.

                                —*Pap.* IV B 14:3 *n.d.*, 1842-43

From sketch; see 167:8–171:3:

As soon as I state the immediate, the statement is first and foremost untrue, for I cannot state anything immediately but only mediately.
    Repetition

Doubt, then, does not arise from and advance with truth. On the contrary, as long as doubt is not present everything is true. Doubt comes through ideality and ideality through doubt.

          The ideas are always dichotomous
[*In pencil*: in reflection every-   In ideality everything is dichotomous.]   thing is dichotomous

to know—truth
to love—the beautiful
to will—the good

The principal pain of existence is that from the beginning I am in contradiction with myself, that a person's true being comes through an opposition. —It may be that one does not perceive this contradiction, for in ideality by itself, just as in reality by itself, everything is true. But it cannot remain hidden from a person since he submits everything to ideality—he then discovers that reality is a deception. It is usually through an illusion that one realizes this. But it is easy to see that if all sense perception is not deception, then there would be no illusion at all. That men persist in the mixed position that sense perception as a rule is true, but now and then deceives, proves nothing, because the fact that something appears to be different under other conditions is, after all, not a deception by sense perception; on the contrary, the opposite would be a deception by sense perception. An eye can be so lazy that it does not detect the change, but in that case it is the particular eye that deceives the individual.

All this demonstrates the possibility of doubt per se. Now he wanted to try to determine more definitely what it is to doubt, for the language had many different expressions to describe this situation, and it is not properly called doubt.

When a judge is uncertain, he conducts an interrogation, pursues every clue, and then pronounces a judgment—that is, he comes to the conclusion: guilty or innocent; but now and then he dismisses the charge. Is then nothing accomplished by that judgment? Indeed there is—the uncertainty is determined. He was uncertain as to how he should judge; now he is no longer uncertain, now his verdict is ready: he judges that he is uncertain. He rests in that, for one cannot rest in uncertainty, but one can rest when one has determined it.—*JP* V 5620 (*Pap.* IV B 10a [Suppl., XI³, pp. xxxvii-xxxviii]) *n.d.*, 1842-43

From sketch; see 167:10–171:13:

When I hold to the point that everything is true, doubt is canceled. This I am able to do by destroying ideality, for example, by saying that what I am looking at now is something else entirely, by making a certain use of the *principium indiscernibilium* [principle of indiscernibility].[29] In this way, every illusion is canceled, for illusion arises through my believing one of the parts and is canceled by my believing none of the parts or both parts. I believe the one is an egg, the other is something resembling an egg; I believe the stick is straight, I put it in the water, I believe it is broken.[30]—*Pap.* IV B 10:1 *n.d.*, 1842-43

From sketch; see 167:10–17:13:

But when the possibility of repetition is posited, then the question of its actuality arises: is it actually a repetition.
Illusion
—*JP* III 3792 (*Pap* IV B 10:9) *n.d.*, 1842-43

From sketch; see 167:6-7 fn.:

Just as actuality precedes possibility, as Aristotle says (it is superior both in time and in worthiness),[31] so also certainty precedes doubt.—*Pap.* IV B 2:15 *n.d.*, 1842-43

From sketch; see 167:14-18:

A distinctive mark of truth. Something like this must naturally be subject to the same dialectic as truth itself: consequently one does not advance beyond it.

The Socratic observation, when someone designated man as a distinctive mark of truth, that he did not know what a human being is.[32]

See Tennemann, *Ges. d. Ph.*, V, p. 302.

—*Pap.* IV B 10:10 *n.d.*, 1842-43

From sketch; see 167:19-24:

Consciousness presupposes itself. The old question of which came first, the tree or the seed—if there were no seed, where did the first tree come from; if there were no tree, where did the first seed come from.—*Pap.* IV B 10:14 *n.d.*, 1842-43

From draft; see 167:25-168:10:

In immediacy, then, everything is true; but cannot consciousness remain in this immediacy? If this immediacy and that of animals were identical, then the problem of consciousness would be canceled, but that would also mean that man is an animal or that man is *inarticulate*. Therefore, it is language that cancels immediacy; if man could not talk he would remain in the immediate.

This could be expressed, he [Johannes Climacus] thought, by saying that the immediate is reality,[33] language is ideality, since by speaking I produce the contradiction. When I seek to express sense perception in this way, the contradiction is present, for what I say is something different from what I want to say. I cannot express reality in language, because I use ideality to characterize it, which is a contradiction, an untruth.

The possibility of doubt, then, is implicit in the duplexity of consciousness. . . . —*JP* III 2320 (*Pap.* IV B 14:6) *n.d.*, 1842-43

From sketch; see 167:25-172:7:

> The Nature of Consciousness.
> Reality[34]   ꓤIdeality.
>   a direct relation
> Dichotomies.
>   a relation of contradiction
> Trichotomies
> Consciousness.

Repetition.
Here the possibility of doubt is posited; the question is

whether it is to be asserted. This possibility of doubt is essential to existence, is the secret of human existence.

This has to be developed further to see whether it is an act of cognition or an act of will.

—*Pap*. IV B 10:11 *n.d*., 1842-43

From sketch; see 168:4-169:2:

Doubt is produced EITHER by bringing reality[35] into relation with ideality
    this is the act of cognition
    insofar as interest is involved, there is at most a
    third in which I am interested—for example, the truth.
OR by bringing ideality into relation with reality
    this is the ethical.
    that in which I am interested is myself.
    it is really Christianity that has brought this doubt into the
    world, for in Christianity this self received its meaning. —
Doubt is conquered not by the system but by faith, just as it is faith that has brought doubt into the world. If the system is to set doubt at rest, then it is by standing higher than both doubt and faith, but in that case doubt must first and foremost be conquered by faith, for a leap over a middle link is not possible.

—*JP* I 891 (*Pap*. IV B 13:18) *n.d*., 1842-43

From draft; see 168:22-23:

Yet consciousness is not clear about this; it believes that it expresses reality.[36] As long as this double movement takes place without mutual friction, consciousness is at rest.—*Pap*. IV B 14:7 *n.d*., 1842-43

From draft; see 168:33:

. . . . . for consciousness is actually the manifestation of this collision, of the thereby conditioned contradiction.—*Pap*. IV B 14:8 *n.d*., 1842-43

From draft; see 168:34–169:2

The coming into existence of consciousness. This is the first pain of existence.
In margin: It was not reflection he had discovered, for consciousness presupposes reflection.

—*Pap.* IV B 14:9 *n.d.*, 1842-43

From sketch; see 168:37–169:9:

Ideality and reality[37] only in relation to each other without contradiction give sheer dichotomies.

soul—body
to love—the beautiful

—*Pap.* IV B 10:5 *n.d.*, 1842–43

From sketch; see 168:37–169:9:

Intrinsically there is already a contradiction between reality and ideality; the one provides the particular defined in time and space, the other the universal.

—*Pap.* IV B 10:7 *n.d.*, 1842-43

From sketch; see 168:37–169:2:

Consciousness is not identical with *reflection*. In reflection everything is dichotomous.

Consciousness is mind; there everything is trichotomous. There are three factors in the most insignificant sensory consciousness. —In the world of mind, one always becomes three.

Consciousness presupposes reflection.

C
*

A.*   *B

or

A*   B*

*
C.

Note. What Johannes is explaining here is not without significance. The terminology of modern philosophy is often confusing—for example, in speaking of *sinnliches B.* [*Bewusstsein*, sense-consciousness], *wahrnehmendes B.* [perceiving-consciousness], *Verstand* [understanding], which even language usage is set against, since I must always say: *I* am conscious of *this*. Therefore, it is really interesting to see how Hegel wishes to formulate the transition from consciousness to self-consciousness, from self-consciousness to reason [*Fornuft*]. When the transition consists merely of a heading, it is easy enough.—*Pap.* IV B 10:12 *n.d.*, 1842-43

From sketch; see 169:18-23:

Doubt arises through my becoming a *relation* between two; as soon as it ceases, doubt is canceled.

and it is remarkable that in the world of mind as soon as one is divided it does not become two but three.—*Pap.* IV B 10:2 *n.d.*, 1842–43

From sketch; see 169:18-23:

Reflection is the possibility of the relation; consciousness is the relation; the first expression of this is contradiction.
						—*Pap.* IV B 10:13 *n.d.*, 1842-43

From sketch; see 169:18-23:

> *dubito (duo). zweifeln (zwei)*
> *tvivle (tve)*
> σκέπτειν [to doubt].[38]
						—*Pap.* IV B 13:2 *n.d.*, 1842-43

From sketch; see 170:5-10:

Disinterested knowledge—with doubt begins the relation in which the question of my interest arises.—*Pap.* IV B 10:15 *n.d.*, 1842-43

From sketch; see 170:13–171:3:

Doubt can never be stopped within itself. —In self-reflection, cognition is led astray, it cannot be stopped by itself—the will must enter in—when the will is misled in a person, then he is healed by letting the feelings enter in etc.—*Pap.* IV B 2:12 *n.d.*, 1842–43

From sketch; see 170:13–171:3:

He realized that in doubt there had to be an act of will, for otherwise doubting would become identical with being uncertain.—*Pap.* IV B 5:8 *n.d.*, 1842–43

From sketch; see 170:13–171:3:

. . . . . genuine skeptics do not doubt for the sake of doubting—the immanental, which ordinarily is recommended—but in order to doubt one must will it[39]—the factor of willing must be taken away if one is to stop—consequently one must will to stop it, but then doubt is not at all conquered by knowledge.—*Pap.* IV B 5:13 *n.d.*, 1842–43

From sketch; see 170:13–171:3:

. . . . . *de omnibus*, in that case I indeed have to know everything.
The skeptics did not do it, but they considered that the trick was to preserve doubt despite all the inveiglements of thinking.[40]—*Pap.* IV B 5:15 *n.d.*, 1842–43

From sketch see 170:13–171:3:

. . . . . so there is just as much basis for the one as for the other; therefore, in a way doubt is not implicit in me—the ancient skeptics fundamentally believed all existence to be so constituted. Here we encounter the indifference that precedes the principle of contradiction.—*Pap.* IV B 13:3 *n.d.*, 1842–43

From sketch; see 170:13–171:3:

μετριοπάθειαν [moderation of the passions] in the intellectual sense, when *pro* and *contra* are equally balanced—then I am not uncertain, for I am that only as long as in that one moment the *pro* seems to mean more than the *contra.*—*Pap.* IV B 10:19 *n.d.*, 1842–43

From sketch; see 171:11-13:

Repetition
. . . . . here doubt could be broken off—one assumes that there is no repetition. But it cannot be done without assuming a repetition.—*JP* III 3792 (*Pap.* IV B 10:3) *n.d.*, 1842–43

From sketch; see 171:11-13:

The Actuality of Repetition
Illusion.[41]
—*JP* III 3792 (*Pap.* IV B 10:4) *n.d.*, 1842–43

From sketch; see 171:11-13:

The first expression for the relation between immediacy and mediacy is *REpetition.*

In immediacy there is no repetition; it may be thought to depend on the dissimilarity of things; not at all, if everything in the world were absolutely identical, there still would be no repetition.—*JP* III 3792 (*Pap.* IV B 10:8) *n.d.*, 1842–43

From sketch for unwritten section:

Para. 2 [*changed from:* 1]. Is it an act of cognition?
    (a) ignorance
    (b) uncertainty
    (c) can cognition deceive[42]
    (d) how does one come to begin
    (e) how to stop.
        —*Pap.* IV B 13:5 *n.d.*, 1842–43

From sketch; addition to Pap. IV B 13:5:

. . . . . developed with respect to one single fact—a human being, my personal relationship to him.—*Pap.* IV B 13:6 *n.d.*, 1842–43

From sketch:

Aristotle[43]—Epicurus in Diogenes Laertius[44]—Descartes[45]—Spinoza[46] after him.
Sextus Emp. Tennemann, V, p. 345.[47]
—*Pap.* IV B 13:7 *n.d.*, 1842–43

From sketch:

        can sensation deceive.
        can experience deceive.
        can the idea deceive.
        —*Pap.* IV B 13:8 *n.d.*, 1842–43

From sketch for unwritten section:

Is it an act of cognition?
  ignorance
  uncertainty
  how do I come to begin
  how do I come to stop.
Can cognition deceive?
  "not *in order to* doubt"*
  but *in order to* find truth.
        —*Pap.* IV B 10:16 *n.d.*, 1842–43

From sketch; addition to Pap. IV B 10:16:

*doubt actually had not done that, for he still clearly recollected that the ancient skeptics taught that the τέλος ἐοτὶ ἐποχή [the end (or aim) is suspension].[48]
    they made a distinction between ἐποχή [suspension] and ἀφασία [speechlessness].—*Pap.* IV B 10:17 *n.d.*, 1842–43

From sketch for unwritten section:

   Ignorance—
      when I am ignorant, I do not doubt.
   Uncertainty—
      I leave the issue alone; I am uncertain whether there are
      ghosts or not.
   Doubt—is it a higher element of uncertainty—
      I determine my relation to the thing
      —I do not determine it in uncertainty.
                              —*Pap.* IV B 10:18 *n.d.*, 1842-43

From sketch for unwritten section:

   Para. 3 [*changed from:* 2] Is it an act of will?
         (a)   Have I, then, a purpose for doubting[*] (*Hegel,
               Spinoza*⁴⁹) for finding truth.
         (b)   how do I come to begin
         (c)   how do I come to stop.
                              —*Pap.* IV B 13:9 *n.d.*, 1842-43

From sketch; addition to Pap. IV B 13:9:

   [*]the skeptics
   therefore philosophy also says: one *must* doubt everything—*Pap.* IV B 13:10 *n.d.*, 1842-43

From sketch for unwritten section:

                           Chapter II
                  What is it to doubt everything.

   The skeptics doubted *everything*, but it was not a finished
result; on the contrary; it was life's task to keep on doubting
despite all the inveiglements of cognition.⁵⁰ Therefore, in a
certain sense they never finished, because to their very last
moment there was a possibility of going astray. It is different
when this doubting everything is supposed to be the beginning.—*Pap.* IV B 13:11 *n.d.*, 1842-43

From sketch; addition to Pap. IV B 13:11:

> Para. 1. is it a succession?
> Para. 2. is it a total act?
> —*Pap.* IV B 13:12 *n.d.*, 1842-43

From sketch for unwritten section:

. . . . . to doubt is to withhold approval;[51] the comical in my withholding approval every time something is presented . . . . . —*Pap.* IV B 13:13 *n.d.*, 1842-43

From sketch for unwritten section:

Chapter III
Johannes begins to doubt.[52]

> Para. 1. about sensation, the historical, about other people.
> at this point the Skeptics' ten theses[53] can be used.
> Para. 2. about oneself.
> (a) sensation
> (b) mathematical knowledge
> (c) philosophical knowledge
> (d) religious knowledge.
> —*Pap.* IV B 13:14 *n.d.*, 1842-43

From sketch:

He came up—cannot come back.
> —*Pap.* IV B 2:8 *n.d.*, 1842-43

From sketch for unwritten section:

Chapter IV

Johannes comes to pure being but cannot come back again.

He becomes almost afraid for himself, as if he had a bad conscience, although he had indeed done no evil. He has become cunning, crafty as a schemer, in his daily conversation could not resist saying and doing and apparently thinking what others thought, and yet he had a private opinion.—*Pap.* IV B 13:15 *n.d.*, 1842-43

From sketch for unwritten section:

Now he could not come back—because he had to use all his energy actually to be at the radical point of doubt. How then could he begin to make any movement—without deceiving himself. —Everything that he should use was put *in dubio* [in doubt]; if he postulated the least little thing about it, everything was changed and he had to begin doubting all over again from the beginning.

—*Pap.* IV B 2:19 *n.d.*, 1842-43

From sketch for unwritten section:

Part III

Johannes philosophizes with the help of traditional philosophical studies.

Para. 1. Hegel
Para. 2. Kant
Para. 3. Spinoza
Para. 4. Descartes
—*Pap.* IV B 13:16 *n.d.*, 1842-43

From sketch for unwritten section:

He regrets that he did not begin immediately with Descartes, all the more so because he recalls that Hegel praises Descartes for his "childlike and simple exposition"[54]—but that was precisely why he did not begin, because it sounded like sarcasm by Hegel, who certainly was a long way from praising the childlike and the simple and who in other passages says of Descartes: *"mit ihm ist weiter nichts anzufangen* [with him nothing more was begun]."[55]—*Pap.* IV B 13:17 *n.d.*, 1842-43

From sketch for unwritten section:

In a *stricter sense,** doubt is the beginning of the ethical, for as soon as I am to act, the interest[56] lies with me inasmuch as I assume the responsibility and thereby acquire significance.—*JP* I 891 (*Pap.* IV B 13:19) *n.d.*, 1842-43

From sketch for unwritten section; addition to Pap. IV B 19:

. . . . . *to be specific, if doubt is merely a composite of contradictions, then the question is: What, then, is thinking? That whereby the difference between doubt and pure thinking is manifested is the interest[57] involved.—*Pap.* IV B 13:20 *n.d.*, 1842-43

From sketch for unwritten section:

Retiring Doubt.[58]

ἐποχή

(a passage in Diogenes Laertius that I marked in my edition).[59]

Inquiring Doubt.

This is really not doubt, least of all *about everything*, since I rather know everything and only doubt how I shall order it, just as the poet does before he catches the intimately known powers of the piece in the poetic idea.

In freedom I can emerge only from that into which I have entered in freedom or in doubt I must be presupposed to have entered. If I am going to emerge from doubt in freedom, I must have entered doubt in freedom. (Act of will.)

—*JP* I 777 (*Pap.* IV B 13:21) *n.d.*, 1842-43

From sketch for unwritten section:

Cognition cannot deceive.[60]

    Aristotle.[61]

    Descartes[62] (his explanation of error).

    Diogenes Laertius[63] (rubric: Epicurus).

           —*Pap.* IV B 13:22 *n.d.*, 1842-43

From sketch for unwritten section:

Descartes teaches that wonder [*Forundring*] (*admiratio*) is the only passion of the soul that has no opposite[64]—therefore one recognizes the correctness of making this the point of departure of all philosophy.—*JP* I 735 (*Pap.* IV B 13:23) *n.d.*, 1842-43

From sketch for unwritten section:

He was rather struck by the fact that Descartes thought that one should make use of probability in acting (Hegel, III, p. 337,[65] and Descartes himself), as if acting were less important than knowing.—*Pap.* IV B 2:14 *n.d.*, 1842-43

EDITORIAL APPENDIX

ACKNOWLEDGMENTS

Preparation of manuscripts for *Kierkegaard's Writings* is supported by a genuinely enabling grant from the National Endowment for the Humanities. The grant includes gifts from the Danish Ministry of Cultural Affairs, the Augustinus Fond, the Konsul George Jorck og Hustru Emma Jorcks Fond, the A. P. Møller og Hustru Chastine Mc-Kinney Møllers Fond, and the Lutheran Brotherhood Foundation.

The translators-editors are indebted to the late Gregor Malantschuk, Grethe Kjær, and Julia Watkin for their knowledgeable observations on crucial concepts and terminology. John Elrod, Per Lønning, and Sophia Scopetéa, members of the International Advisory Board for *Kierkegaard's Writings*, have given valuable criticism of the manuscript on the whole and in detail. Rune Engebretsen, Jack Schwandt, Pamela Schwandt, Michael Daugherty, Steven Knudson, Robert Roberts, Craig Mason, and Kevin Swan have helpfully scrutinized the manuscript. The Greek has been checked by Lloyd Gunderson and James May. Translations of German quotations are by Rune Engebretsen. The index was prepared by Kennedy Lemke. The entire work has been facilitated by George Coulter and Lavier Murray.

Acknowledgment is made to Gyldendals Forlag for permission to absorb notes to *Søren Kierkegaards Samlede Værker*.

Inclusion in the Supplement of entries from *Søren Kierkegaard's Journals and Papers* is by arrangement with Indiana University Press.

The book collection and the microfilm collection of the Kierkegaard Library, St. Olaf College, have been used in preparation of the text, Supplement, and Editorial Appendix. The Royal Library, Copenhagen, has provided photographs of selected manuscript pages.

The manuscript, typed by Dorothy Bolton, has been guided through the press by Gretchen Oberfranc.

COLLATION OF *PHILOSOPHICAL FRAGMENTS*
IN THE DANISH EDITIONS OF
KIERKEGAARD'S COLLECTED WORKS

Vol. IV Ed. 1 Pg.	Vol. IV Ed. 2 Pg.	Vol. 6 Ed. 3 Pg.	Vol. IV Ed. 1 Pg.	Vol. IV Ed. 2 Pg.	Vol. 6 Ed. 3 Pg.
174	198	8	208	233	41
175	199	9	209	234	41
176	199	9	210	235	42
177	200	10	211	236	43
178	201	11	212	237	44
179	203	15	213	238	45
180	203	15	214	239	46
181	204	16	215	241	47
182	205	17	216	242	48
183	206	17	217	243	49
184	207	18	218	244	50
185	209	19	219	245	50
186	210	20	220	246	51
187	211	21	221	247	52
188	212	22	222	248	53
189	213	23	223	249	54
190	214	24	224	250	55
191	215	25	225	251	56
192	216	26	226	252	57
193	217	26	227	254	58
194	218	27	228	255	59
195	219	28	229	256	60
196	220	29	230	257	61
197	221	30	231	259	62
198	223	31	232	260	63
199	224	32	233	261	64
200	225	33	234	262	65
201	226	34	235	264	67
202	227	35	236	264	67
203	228	36	237	265	68
204	230	37	238	266	69
205	231	38	239	267	69
206	231	39	240	268	70
207	232	40	241	269	71

Vol. IV Ed. 1 Pg.	Vol. IV Ed. 2 Pg.	Vol. 6 Ed. 3 Pg.	Vol. IV Ed. 1 Pg.	Vol. IV Ed. 2 Pg.	Vol. 6 Ed. 3 Pg.
242	270	72	257	286	85
243	271	72	258	287	86
244	272	73	259	288	87
245	273	74	260	289	88
246	274	75	261	290	89
247	275	76	262	291	89
248	276	76	263	292	90
249	277	77	264	293	91
250	278	79	265	294	92
251	279	80	266	295	93
252	281	81	267	297	94
253	281	81	268	298	95
254	282	82	269	299	96
255	284	83	270	300	97
256	285	84	271	301	98
			272	302	99

NOTES

PHILOSOPHICAL FRAGMENTS

TITLE PAGE AND EPIGRAPHS

TITLE PAGE. See Supplement, p. 177 (*Pap.* V B 39), for changes in the title page in draft and final copies; see Historical Introduction, pp. xvi-xvii.

EPIGRAPHS. *happiness.* The Danish *Salighed* has a richness of meaning (happiness, bliss, felicity, blessedness, salvation) such that some scholars prefer to keep the word as an especially significant term without translation. Here *Salighed* is translated as "happiness," in keeping with Socratic-Platonic terminology in English. Εὐδαιμονία is usually rendered as "happiness" in the sense of complete well-being, the fulfillment of one's essential human nature rather than pleasurable satisfaction or joyousness. See, for example, Plato, *Phaedo*, 81 a; *Platonis quae exstant opera*, I-XI, ed. Friedrich Ast (Leipzig: 1819-32; *ASKB* 1144-54), I, pp. 530-31; *Udvalgte Dialoger af Platon*, I-VIII, tr. Carl Johan Heise (Copenhagen: 1830-59; *ASKB* 1164-67, 1169 [I-VIII]), I, p. 49; *The Collected Dialogues of Plato*, ed. Edith Hamilton and Huntington Cairns (Princeton: Princeton University Press, 1963), p. 64 (Socrates speaking): "Very well, if this is its condition, then it [the soul] departs to that place which is, like itself, invisible, divine, immortal, and wise, where, on its arrival, happiness awaits it, and release from uncertainty and folly, from fears and uncontrolled desires, and all other human evils, and where, as they say of the initiates in the Mysteries, it really spends the rest of time with God."

Can . . . historical knowledge. See Supplement, pp. 182-83 (*Pap.* V B 1:1-2, 39), for changes in the epigraph on the title page; see also pp. 181-82 (*Pap.* V B 35). The central issue of the relation of historical knowledge and eternal truth is treated by Lessing in "*Ueber den Beweis des Geistes und der Kraft*," *Gotthold Ephraim Lessing's sämmtliche Schriften*, I-XXXII (Berlin, Stettin: 1825-28; *ASKB* 1747-62), V, pp. 80-83; *Lessing's Theological Writings*, ed. and tr. Henry Chadwick (Stanford: Stanford University Press, 1957), pp. 53-55, a portion of which is cited in *Concluding Unscientific Postscript to Philosophical Fragments*, *KW* XII (*SV* VII 74). On this issue, Lessing follows Leibniz, although Lessing's distinction pertains to philosophy of religion and Leibniz's is epistemological and metaphysical. See Gottfried Wilhelm Leibniz, *The Monadology*, para. 33; *God. Guil. Leibnitii opera philosophica . . .*, I-II, ed. Johann Eduard Erdmann (Berlin: 1840; *ASKB* 620), II, p.

707; *Leibniz: The Monadology and Other Philosophical Writings,* tr. Robert Latta (London: Oxford University Press, 1965), pp. 235-36: "There are also two kinds of *truths:* those of *reasoning* and those of *fact.* Truths of reasoning are necessary and their opposite is impossible: Truths of fact are contingent and their opposite is possible."
Better well hanged than ill wed. Hellig Tre Kongers Aften, eller: Hvad man vil, tr. Adolphe Engelbert Boye (Copenhagen: 1829); *Det Kongelige Theaters Repertoire,* I-VI (Copenhagen: 1828-42), I, no. 22, p. 5: "*At blive godt hængt, er mangen Gang bedre end at blive slet givt* [To be well hanged is many times better than to be ill wed]"; *Was ihr wollt,* I, 5, *Shakspeare's dramatische Werke,* I-XII, tr. August Wilhelm v. Schlegel and Ludwig Tieck (Berlin: 1839-41; *ASKB* 1883-88), V, p. 116: "*Gut gehängt ist besser als schlecht verheirathet* [Well hanged is better than ill wed]"; *Twelfth Night,* I, 5, 20-21, *The Complete Works of Shakespeare,* ed. George Lyman Kittredge (Boston, Ginn, 1936), p. 404 (Clown to Maria): "Many a good hanging prevents a bad marriage." In the Preface to *Postscript, KW* XII (*SV* VII, p. v), the line in *Philosophical Fragments* is interpreted: "Undisturbed and in accordance with the motto ('Better well hanged than ill wed'), the hanged, indeed, the well-hanged, author has remained hanging. No one—not even in sport or jest—has asked him for whom he did hang. But that was as desired: better well hanged than by a hapless marriage to be brought into systematic in-law relationship with the whole world."

PREFACE

1. See Supplement, pp. 183-85 (*Pap.* V B 24), for an earlier version of the Preface.
2. A similar kind of expression is found in Cicero, *Philippics,* II, 37; *M. Tullii Ciceronis opera omnia,* I-V, ed. Johann August Ernesti (Halle: 1756-57; *ASKB* 1224-29), II², pp. 1376-77; *Philippics,* tr. Walter Kerr (Loeb, New York: Putnam, 1926), p. 158.
3. In Ludvig Holberg, *Jacob von Tyboe Eller Den stortalende Soldat,* III, 4, *Den Danske Skue-Plads,* I-VII (Copenhagen: 1788; *ASKB* 1566-67), III, no pagination, Magister Stygotius boasts (ed. tr.): "I walk in the footsteps of the ancients, of which proof will be seen the day after tomorrow when I, *volente Deo* [God willing], will defend my thesis."
4. In *Jugurtha,* IV, 4, Sallust writes that it was from justifiable motives rather than from indolence that he would record events instead of engaging in politics. *C. Sallustii Crispi opera,* I-II (Halle: 1828-34; *ASKB* 1269-70), II, p. 22; *Sallust,* tr. J. C. Rolfe (Loeb, New York: Putnam, 1921), pp. 136-37.
5. Xenophon uses the term with reference to Socrates. See *Memorabilia,* III, 11, 16; *Xenophontis memorabilia,* ed. F. A. Bornemann (Leipzig: 1829; *ASKB* 1211), p. 236; *Memorabilia,* tr. E. C. Marchant (Loeb, New York: Putnam, 1923), p. 248. According to Solon's law, an Athenian who refused to participate in civil disputes should lose his rights as a citizen. See Aris-

totle, *The Constitution of Athens*, 8, 4-5; *The Works of Aristotle*, I-XII, ed. J. A. Smith and W. D. Ross (Oxford: Oxford University Press, 1908-52), X; see also Karl Friedrich Becker, *Verdenshistorie*, I-XII, tr. Jacob Riise (Copenhagen: 1822-29; *ASKB* 1972-83), I, p. 427.

6. See Valerius Maximus, VIII, 7, 7; *Valerius Maximus: Sammlung merkwürdiger Reden und Thaten*, I-V, tr. Friedrich Hoffmann (Stuttgart: 1828-29; *ASKB* 1296), V, pp. 514-15. See *The Concept of Anxiety*, p. 23, *KW* VIII *(SV* IV 295); *The Corsair Affair*, p. 165, *KW* XIII *(Pap.* VII¹ B 11).

7. Diogenes of Sinope (c. 413-323 B.C.), prototype of Greek Cynic philosophers. See Lucian, "How to Write History," 3; *Luciani opera*, I-IV (Leipzig: 1829; *ASKB* 1131-34), II, p. 122; *Lucian*, I-VIII, tr. K. Kilburn (Loeb, Cambridge: Harvard University Press, 1959), VI, p. 5.

8. With a reference to Wilhelm Gottlieb Tennemann, *Geschichte der Philosophie*, I-XI (Leipzig: 1798-1819; *ASKB* 815-26), I, p. 355, fn. 6 b, journal entry *JP* V 5618 *(Pap.* IV A 63, 1843) states: "If anyone wants to call my fragment of wisdom Sophistic, I must point out that it lacks at least one characteristic according to both Plato's and Aristotle's definitions: that one makes money by it." See Plato, *Greater Hippias*, 283 b; *Opera*, IX, pp. 6-7; *Collected Dialogues*, p. 1535; Aristotle, *On Sophistic Fallacies*, 165 a, 171 b; *Aristoteles graece*, I-II, ed. Immanuel Bekker (Berlin: 1831; *ASKB* 1074-75), I, pp. 165, 171; *Works*, I.

9. In one of Johan Ludvig Heiberg's plays, Baron Goldkalb of Frankfurt is expected to travel to Copenhagen via Korsør. When the poor Jewish merchant Salomon Goldkalb of Hamburg arrives in Korsør, he is ceremoniously welcomed. *Kong Salomon og Jörgen Hattemager* (Copenhagen: 1825), 14-26, pp. 47-79.

10. See Supplement, pp. 226-27 *(Pap.* X² A 155). In the preface to Hans Lassen Martensen's dissertation, published in Danish translation by Lauritz Vilhelm Petersen, *Den menneskelige Selvbevidstheds Autonomie i vor Tids dogmatiske Theologie* (Copenhagen: 1841; *ASKB* 651), Petersen states (ed. tr.): "It was the first work to appear in this country in the new speculative trend and heralded the era in theology from which we have already begun to reckon."

11. The Danish *Dyrehavstid* is literally "Deer Park time." An area in Deer Park (near Copenhagen to the north), known as Dyrehavsbakken, was and still is the site of a carnival-type amusement park (perhaps the world's oldest) that operates from springtime into autumn.

12. The flip-flopping of the concept refers to Hegel's view, in his criticism of Kant's antinomies, that thought is a unity of opposites and that events proceed through contradictions in a progressive unity of opposites. See, for example, G.W.F. Hegel, *Wissenschaft der Logik*, I, *Georg Wilhelm Friedrich Hegel's Werke. Vollständige Ausgabe*, I-XVIII, ed. Philipp Marheineke et al. (Berlin: 1832-45; *ASKB* 549-65), III, p. 217; *Jubiläumsausgabe [J.A.]*, I-XXVI, ed. Hermann Glockner (Stuttgart: 1927-40), IV, p. 227; *Hegel's Science of Logic* (tr. of *W.L.*, Lasson ed., 1923; Kierkegaard had 2 ed., 1833-34), tr. A. V. Miller (New York: Humanities Press, 1969), p. 191: "But profounder

insight into the antinomial, or more truly into the dialectical nature of reason demonstrates *any* Notion whatever to be a unity of opposed moments to which, therefore, the form of antinomial assertions could be given."

13. Presumably an allusion to David's dancing before the Ark of the Covenant; see II Samuel 6:14-16.

14. With reference to the remainder of the sentence, see Supplement, p. 185 (*Pap.* V B 36:1).

15. An allusion to I Corinthians 9:13.

16. With reference to the following three sentences, see Supplement, p. 185 (*Pap.* V B 36:2).

17. Plato, *Cratylus*, 384 b; *Opera*, V, pp. 108-09; *Collected Dialogues*, p. 383 (Socrates speaking): "Son of Hipponicus, there is an ancient saying that 'hard is the knowledge of the good.' And the knowledge of names is a great part of knowledge. If I had not been poor, I might have heard the fifty-drachma course of the great Prodicus, which is a complete education in grammar and language—these are his own words—and then I should have been at once able to answer your question about the correctness of names. But, indeed, I have only heard the single-drachma course, and therefore I do not know the truth about such matters."

CHAPTER I

1. See Supplement, pp. 185-86 (*Pap.* V B 1:12, 3:1, 40:6), for changes in draft and final copies. See Historical Introduction, p. xvii. The term "Propositio" means "proposal," more specifically here "hypothesis," with the "if/then" form that provides the structure of the entire work.

2. Originally termed "Position II." See Historical Introduction, p. xvii.

3. See p. 91, where the form of *Philosophical Fragments* is called "algebraic," in contrast, for example, to *Either/Or*, "A Fragment of Life," and *Fear and Trembling*, "Dialectical Lyric." The hypothetical ("if/then") character of *Fragments* is signaled again by "Thought-Project" (see note 1 above), in contrast to *Postscript*, which is in "historical costume."

4. See Supplement, pp. 186-87 (*Pap.* V B 3:2, 40:7). The original opening portion was shifted to the end in the final copy.

5. The Danish *læres* may be rendered as "be learned" or as "be taught." See Plato, *Protagoras*, 320 b; *Opera*, I, pp. 28-29; Heise, II, p. 129; *Collected Dialogues*, p. 318 (Socrates speaking): "Protagoras, I do not believe that virtue can be taught." *Gorgias* offers very little on this theme. See *Meno*, 70 a; *Opera*, IX, pp. 194-95; *Collected Dialogues*, p. 354 (Meno speaking): "Can you tell me, Socrates—is virtue something that can be taught?" *Euthydemus*, 276 d; *Opera*, IX, pp. 120-21; *Collected Dialogues*, p. 390 (Euthydemus speaking): "Do the learners learn what they know, or what they don't know?"

6. *Meno*, 80 e; *Opera*, IX, pp. 222-23; *Collected Dialogues*, p. 363 (Socrates speaking): "Do you realize that what you are bringing up is the

trick argument that a man cannot try to discover either what he knows or what he does not know? He would not seek what he knows, for since he knows it there is no need of the inquiry, nor what he does not know, for in that case he does not even know what he is to look for." W. K. Guthrie's translation ("trick argument") of ἐριστικὸν λόγον gives a secondary and narrow meaning of the phrase. Climacus takes the primary meaning of "combative, pugnacious," and in so doing is also close to Ast's Latin *litigiosam orationem*. The position is pugnacious because it apparently ends in a dilemma. It is a trick argument, however, to one who has a third way, the way of recollection, whereby one learns what one once knew and has forgotten but nevertheless in a sense does know and in principle can recollect.

7. See *Meno*, 81 c-d; *Opera*, IX, pp. 224-25; *Collected Dialogues*, p. 364 (Socrates speaking):

> Thus the soul, since it is immortal and has been born many times, and has seen all things both here and in the other world, has learned everything that is. So we need not be surprised if it can recall the knowledge of virtue or anything else which, as we see, it once possessed. All nature is akin, and the soul has learned everything, so that when a man has recalled a single piece of knowledge—*learned* it, in ordinary language— there is no reason why he should not find out all the rest, if he keeps a stout heart and does not grow weary of the search, for seeking and learning are in fact nothing but recollection.
>
> We ought not then to be led astray by the contentious argument you quoted. It would make us lazy, and is music in the ears of weaklings. The other doctrine produces energetic seekers after knowledge, and being convinced of its truth, I am ready, with your help, to inquire into the nature of virtue.

8. See note 7 above. No distinction is made here between Socrates and Plato. Nor is a distinction made in *Fragments* between Socrates-Plato and philosophical idealism nor between them and naturalism and scientific humanism, inasmuch as all of them presuppose an immanental possession of genuine knowledge or of the condition for acquiring it. See *Postscript, KW* XII (*SV* VII 172-74); *JP* II 2274 (*Pap*. III A 5).

9. See Plato, *Phaedo*, 72 e-77 a; *Opera*, I, pp. 508-21: Heise, I, pp. 32-41; *Collected Dialogues*, pp. 55-60, for example, 75 e, p. 59 (Socrates speaking): "And if it is true that we acquired our knowledge before our birth, and lost it at the moment of birth, but afterward, by the exercise of our senses upon sensible objects, recover the knowledge which we had once before, I suppose that what we call learning will be the recovery of our own knowledge, and surely we should be right in calling this recollection." See Supplement, p. 187 (*Pap*. V B 40:8).

10. By "ancient speculation," Climacus may be pointing not only to Plato's views but also to the metempsychosis of the Orphic mysteries and of the Pythagoreans, as well as to medieval thinkers like Origen and John

Scotus Erigena. "Modern speculation" presumably points to Franz Baader, Schelling, and Hegel. See Supplement, p. 181 (*Pap.* II A 448).

11. With reference to the following sentence, see Supplement, p. 187 (*Pap.* V B 40:8).

12. See *The Concept of Irony, with Continual Reference to Socrates, KW* II (*SV* XIII 232-78), in which the treatment of Socrates by Hegel and certain contemporary Hegelians is discussed. The emphasis there is upon Socrates' thought and actions as negative. See *JP* I 754 (*Pap.* III A 7). Cf. *JP* IV 4281 (*Pap.* X³ A 477).

13. The Danish text here and throughout *Fragments* (with few exceptions) has *Guden*, a noun with the definite article. This unusual form emphasizes the Socratic-Platonic context of the hypothesis and its development in the entire work. Although the English quotation in note 15 below uses no definite article in the translation of ὁ θεός, at the time *Fragments* was being written the current German translation employed the definite article. See *Platons Werke*, I-III, tr. Friedrich Ernst Daniel Schleiermacher (Berlin: 1817-28; *ASKB* 1158-63), II¹, p. 202. There was no Danish translation of *Theaetetus* available to Kierkegaard. *Guden* is used in later Danish translations: *Platons Theaitetos*, tr. Bendt Treschow and Frederik Clemens Bendtsen Dahl (Copenhagen: 1869), pp. 22-23; *Platons Skrifter*, I-XI, tr. Carsten Høeg and Hans Ræder (Copenhagen: 1932-41), VII, pp. 108-09. The Jowett translation of the quotation from *Theaetetus* in note 15 below has "the god." In the entire Kierkegaard authorship, *Guden* is very rarely found except in *Fragments* and *Postscript*.

14. *Apology*, 21-23 b, 28 e-30; *Opera*, VIII, pp. 106-13, 126-31; *Collected Dialogues*, pp. 7-9, 15-17, for example, 28 d-e, p. 15 (Socrates speaking): "This being so, it would be shocking inconsistency on my part, gentlemen, if, when the officers whom you chose to command me assigned me my position at Potidaea and Amphipolis and Delium, I remained at my post like anyone else and faced death, and yet afterward, when [the] God appointed me, as I supposed and believed, to the duty of leading the philosophical life, examining myself and others, I were then through fear of death or of any other danger to desert my post. That would indeed be shocking, and then I might really with justice be summoned into court for not believing in the gods, and disobeying the oracle, and being afraid of death, and thinking that I am wise when I am not."

15. *Theaetetus*, 150 b-d; *Opera*, II, pp. 26-29; *Collected Dialogues*, p. 855 (Socrates speaking): "My art of midwifery is in general like theirs; the only difference is that my patients are men, not women, and my concern is not with the body but with the soul that is in travail of birth. And the highest point of my art is the power to prove by every test whether the offspring of a young man's thought is a false phantom or instinct with life and truth. I am so far like the midwife that I cannot myself give birth to wisdom, and the common reproach is true, that, though I question others, I can myself bring nothing to light because there is no wisdom in me. The reason is this. Heaven [ὁ θεός; Jowett translation: "the god"] constrains me

to serve as a midwife, but has debarred me from giving birth. So of myself I have no sort of wisdom, nor has any discovery ever been born to me as the child of my soul. Those who frequent my company at first appear, some of them, quite unintelligent, but, as we go further with our discussions, all who are favored by heaven make progress at a rate that seems surprising to others as well as to themselves, although it is clear that they have never learned anything from me. The many admirable truths they bring to birth have been discovered by themselves from within. But the delivery is heaven's work and mine." See note 16 below.

16. Diogenes Laertius, II, 21. The text has a Danish translation from the Greek, *Diogenis Laertii de vitis philosophorum*, I-II (Leipzig: 1833; *ASKB* 1109), I, p. 70. See *Diogen Laërtses filosofiske Historie*, I-II, tr. Børge Riisbrigh (Copenhagen: 1812; *ASKB* 1110-11), I, p. 66; *Lives of Eminent Philosophers*, I-II, tr. R. D. Hicks (Loeb, New York: Putnam, 1925), I, pp. 150-51: "he discussed moral questions in the workshops and the market-place, being convinced that the study of nature is no concern of ours; and . . . he claimed that his enquiries embraced

Whatso'er is good or evil in an house . . .."

17. See p. 20 and note 43.

18. *Mediering* in its various forms is the Danish rendering of the Hegelian term *Vermittelung*: reconciliation of opposites in a higher unity. See, for example, *Wissenschaft der Logik*, I-III, *Werke*, III, pp. 92, 110, 159, 197, 456; IV, pp. 75-77, 90-91, 107, 117-18, 120-24, 127-29, 167-68; V, pp. 229-30, 233-35, 311-12, 353; *J.A.*, IV, pp. 102, 120, 169, 207, 466, 553-55, 568-69, 585, 596, 599-603, 605-07, 645-46; V, pp. 229-30, 233-35, 311-12, 353; *Science of Logic*, pp. 93 ("For being which is the outcome of *mediation* we shall reserve the term: *Existence*"), 107, 146, 175, 375, 445-47, 456-57, 469, 478 ("This immediacy that is mediated by ground and condition and is self-identical through the sublating of mediation, is *Existence*"), 481-83, 486-87, 516-17 "The truth of the relation consists therefore in the *mediation*; its essence is the negative unity in which both the reflected and simply affirmative [*seiende*] immediacy are sublated"), 749, 752-53, 811, 843-44 ("But in this next resolve of the pure Idea to determine itself as external Idea, it thereby only posits for itself the mediation out of which the Notion ascends as a free Existence that has withdrawn into itself from externality, that completes its self-liberation in the *science of spirit*, and that finds the supreme Notion of itself in the science of logic as the self-comprehending pure Notion").

19. Prodicus of Ceoa was a distinguished Sophist contemporary with Socrates. Plato mentions him in *Protagoras*, 337 a-c, 340-42 a; *Theaetetus*, 151 b; *Cratylus*, 384 b; *Charmides*, 163 d; *Greater Hippias*, 282 c; *Euthydemus*, 305 c; *Meno*, 75 e, 96 d; *Opera*, I, pp. 64-67, 72-77; II, pp. 28-29; VIII, pp. 436-41; IX, pp. 4-5, 186-87, 208-09; Heise, II, pp. 165-66, 171-75; *Collected Dialogues*, pp. 331-32, 333-35, 856, 422, 109, 1535, 418-19, 358, 380. His famous "Choice of Heracles" is related in Xenophon, *Memorabilia*, II, 1, 21-34; Borneman, pp. 91-101; Loeb, pp. 95-103.

20. See Supplement, p. 187 (*Pap.* V B 3:4); *JP* IV 4512 (*Pap.* IV A 44).

21. Presumably προτρεπτικός (encouraging) was intended here. Both forms are used in the dialogue. See *Clitophon,* 410 b-e; *Opera,* IX, pp. 362-65.

22. See Supplement, pp. 231-32 (*Pap.* III A 7) and note 2.

23. In keeping with the context of the hypothesis in *Fragments,* this conception of the eternal echoes classical Greek philosophy, Augustine, and nineteenth-century speculative idealism. See, for example, Plato, *Timaeus,* 37-38; *Opera,* V, pp. 150-55; *Collected Dialogues,* pp. 466-68 ("the past and future are created species of time, which we unconsciously but wrongly transfer to eternal being"); Friedrich Wilhelm Joseph Schelling, *Vom ICH als Prinzip der Philosophie* (Tübingen: 1795), p. 105 ("*Ewigkeit . . . ist Seyn in keiner Zeit* [eternity is being in no time]"); Hegel, *Differenz des Fichteschen und Schellingschen Systems . . . , Werke,* I, p. 225; *J.A.,* I, p. 97 ("*Das wahre Aufheben der Zeit ist zeitlose Gegenwart, d.i. Ewigkeit*"); *The Difference between Fichte's and Schelling's System of Philosophy,* tr. H. S. Harris and Walter Cerf (Albany: State University of New York Press, 1977), p. 134: "The true suspension of time is a timeless present, i.e., eternity."

24. For a discussion of the concept "the moment," see a companion volume to *Fragments, The Concept of Anxiety* (published four days later, June 17, 1844), pp. 81-90, *KW* VIII (*SV* IV 351-60); *JP* III 2739-44 and pp. 821-22; VII, p. 62. See note 25 below.

25. The Danish *blev til* (as well as *tilblive, Tilblivelse, være til,* and *Tilværelse*) refers to temporal and spatial modes of becoming and being. The eternal as timeless being does not come into being but comes into time and space as a specific embodiment of the eternal. The moment, therefore, is an atom of eternity and has a significance qualitatively different from that of transient instants of time. Existence is a mode of being, but not all being is existence. Therefore, for example, in *Postscript, KW* XII (*SV* VII 287), Johannes Climacus states that "God does not think, he creates; God does not exist, he is eternal."

26. See *The Sickness unto Death,* p. 95, *KW* XIX (*SV* XI 206); *JP* I 651 (*Pap.* VIII² B 83).

27. On the concept of human freedom and responsibility in relation to divine omnipotence, see *JP* II 1251 (*Pap.* VII¹ A 181).

28. With reference to the following three paragraphs and footnote, see Supplement, pp. 187-88 (*Pap.* V B 3:8).

29. On the origin and consequences of sin and responsibility for it, see *Anxiety,* passim, *KW* VIII; *JP* IV 3989-4051 and pp. 657-58; VII, pp. 69, 87.

30. With reference to the following six sentences, see Supplement, p. 188 (*Pap.* V B 2).

31. On freedom and the eventuation of misused freedom in unfreedom, see, for example, *Anxiety,* pp. 107-12, *KW* VIII (*SV* IV 376-81); *JP* II 1230-78 and p. 561; VII, p. 39.

32. See, for example, *Either/Or,* I, *KW* III (*SV* I 13).

33. A free but substantially correct rendering of Aristotle, *Nicomachean Ethics,* III, 5, 1114 a; Bekker, II, p. 1114; *Die Ethik des Aristoteles,* I-II, tr.

Christian Garve (Breslau: 1798-1801; *ASKB* 1082-83), II, p. 41; *Works*, IX.
34. A reading note (*Pap.* IV C 49) includes these lines: "Also the way in which the skeptics denied motion. See Diogenes Laertius, IX, 11, para. 99." *Vitis*, II, p. 175; Riisbrigh, I, p. 445; Loeb, II, p. 511. Earlier in Diogenes Laertius (IX, 72; *Vitis*, II, pp. 164-65; Riisbrigh, I, p. 433; Loeb, II, p. 485), Zeno is specifically named as a skeptic: "Furthermore, they find Xenophanes, Zeno of Elea, and Democritus to be skeptics: Xenophanes because he says,
Clear truth hath no man seen nor e'er shall know;
and Zeno because he would destroy motion, saying, 'A moving body moves neither where it is nor where it is not' . . ." (see para. 99). Zeno's paradoxes of motion were the flying arrow, Achilles and the tortoise, and the marching columns.

35. See John 8:34; Galatians 5:1.

36. For a reference to Socrates, see *The Point of View for My Work as an Author*, *KW* XXII (*SV* XIII 541-42).

37. See Galatians 4:4.

38. The Danish term *Discipel* means "pupil," "learner," "apprentice," "follower," and "disciple." Here and elsewhere in *Fragments* (except for references to the relation of teacher and pupil or learner), "follower" is most appropriate.

39. On this theme, see *JP* III 3782-90 and pp. 918-19; VII, p. 81.

40. See Philippians 3:13-14; *Upbuilding Discourses in Various Spirits*, *KW* XV (*SV* VIII 119-20).

41. With reference to the following paragraph, see Supplement, p. 188 (*Pap.* V B 3:11).

42. The judges of the underworld, named by Socrates in *Apology*, 41 a; *Opera*, VIII, pp. 154-55; *Collected Dialogues*, p. 25.

43. See p. 11. With reference to the following three sentences, see Supplement, p. 188 (*Pap.* V B 3:12). While writing the draft of *Johannes Climacus, or De omnibus dubitandum est* in 1842-43, Kierkegaard read Descartes's works and Hegel on Descartes. The text may refer to *Meditations on First Philosophy*, III; *Meditationes de prima philosophia*, *Renati Des-Cartes opera philosophica* (Amsterdam: 1678; *ASKB* 473), pp. 19, 21; *Descartes' Philosophical Writings*, tr. Norman Kemp Smith (London: Macmillan, 1952), pp. 222, 225: "Now among my ideas in addition to the idea which exhibits me to myself . . . there is another which represents God . . . my awareness of God must be prior to that of myself." The same thought is found in Hegel's treatment of Descartes in *Vorlesungen über die Geschichte der Philosophie*, III, *Werke*, XV, p. 350; *J.A.*, XIX, p. 350; *Hegel's Lectures on the History of Philosophy* (tr. of *G.P.*, 2 ed., 1840-44; Kierkegaard had 1 ed., 1833-36), I-III, tr. E. S. Haldane and Frances H. Simson (New York: Humanities Press, 1955), III, p. 237: "In the form of God no other conception is thus here given than that contained in *Cogito, ergo sum*, wherein Being and thought are inseparably bound up . . . ."

44. *Opera*, II, pp. 50-51; *Collected Dialogues*, p. 856: "People have often . . .

been positively ready to bite me for taking away some foolish notion they have conceived."

45. With reference to the following sentence, see Supplement, p. 188 (*Pap.* V B 3:13).

46. With reference to the remainder of the chapter, see Supplement, pp. 188–89 (*Pap.* V B 3:14).

47. In the Danish game *Gnavspil*, if the player who has the counter with the picture of a house does not want to make an exchange, he says, "Go to the next house." See *Fear and Trembling*, p. 100, *KW* VI (*SV* III 147).

CHAPTER II

1. See p. 9 ("Propositio" and "Thought-Project"); *Repetition*, pp. 357–62, *KW* VI. All three terms point to the hypothetical character and form of the imaginary construction elaborating the implications of going beyond Socrates. On "poetical venture," see *Two Ethical-Religious Essays*, *KW* XVIII (*SV* XI 55, 91).

2. In his dissertation (1841), *The Concept of Irony, with Continual Reference to Socrates*, *KW* II (*SV* XIII 231-59), Kierkegaard concludes that Aristophanes' presentation of Socrates is less a caricature than is generally supposed. In Chapter I of *Fragments*, Socrates is treated as symbolic of an epistemological position. In Chapter II, Socrates is depicted positively as a unique practicing pedagogue, a characterization at some variance with the interpretation in *Irony*.

3. Influenced as well as influencing: the teacher is also a learner and the learner is also a teacher.

4. Presumably a reference to Hegel and Hegelians, perhaps also to Schelling. See, for example, Hegel, *Geschichte der Philosophie*, II, *Werke*, XIV, pp. 71, 85; *J.A.*, XIX, pp. 71, 85; *History of Philosophy*, II, pp. 407, 426: "It [the Good] is a principle, concrete within itself, which, however, is not yet manifested in its development, and in this abstract attitude we find what is wanting in the Socratic standpoint, of which nothing that is affirmative can, beyond this, be adduced. Aristophanes regarded the Socratic philosophy from the negative side, maintaining that through the cultivation of reflecting consciousness, the idea of law had been shaken [*added in second German edition, 1840-44:* and we cannot question the justice of this conception]. Aristophanes' consciousness of the one-sidedness of Socrates may be regarded as a prelude to his death; the Athenian people likewise certainly recognized his negative methods in condemning him." The title of Heinrich Eberhard Gottlob Paulus's pirated pre-edition of Schelling's Berlin lectures (1841-42; see Kierkegaard's notes in *KW* II) was *Die endlich offenbar gewordene positive Philosophie der Offenbarung* (Darmstadt: 1843).

5. Jealous of their prerogatives, the gods disciplined, even destroyed, men who in pride (*hybris*) went beyond their proper bounds. This is the central theme of Greek tragedies. In the *Symposium*, 189 d-191 d, Plato has Aris-

tophanes relate the consequences of the moon descendants' encroachment on Mt. Olympus, the home of the gods. *Opera,* III, pp. 468-75; Heise, II, pp. 37-41; *Collected Dialogues,* pp. 542-44.

6. See Plato, *Symposium,* 215 d-e; *Opera,* III, pp. 528-31; Heise, II, pp. 88-89; *Collected Dialogues,* p. 567 (Alcibiades speaking): "And speaking for myself, gentlemen, if I wasn't afraid you'd tell me I was completely bottled, I'd swear on oath what an extraordinary effect his words have had on me—and still do, if it comes to that. For the moment I hear him speak I am smitten with a kind of sacred rage, worse than any Corybant, and my heart jumps into my mouth and the tears start into my eyes—oh, and not only me, but lots of other men."

7. The Corybantes were priests of the Phrygian goddess Cybele, whose rites were conducted with wild music and frenzied dancing.

8. This observation is a remnant of the earlier interpretation of Socrates in *Irony.* See p. 23 and note 2; Supplement, p. 189 (*Pap.* V B 4:3).

9. See *Symposium,* 216-18, where Alcibiades tells of his having tried to influence Socrates in this way. *Opera,* III, pp. 530-37; Heise, II, pp. 89-94; *Collected Dialogues,* pp. 567-69.

10. With reference to the next three sentences, see Supplement, p. 189 (*Pap.* V B 4:4).

11. Aristotle's definition of God. See *Metaphysics,* 1072 b; Bekker, II, p. 1072; *Aristoteles Metaphysik,* I-II, tr. Ernst Wilhelm Hengstenberg (Bonn: 1824; *ASKB* 1084), I, p. 243; *Works,* VIII: "The final cause, then, produces motion as being loved, but all other things move by being moved. Now if something is moved, it is capable of being otherwise than as it is. Therefore if its actuality is the primary form of spatial motion, then in so far as it is subject to change, in *this* respect it is capable of being otherwise,—in place, even if not in substance. But since there is something which moves while itself unmoved, existing actually, this can in no way be otherwise than as it is. For motion in space is the first of the kinds of change, and motion in a circle the first kind of spatial motion; and this the first mover *produces.* The first mover, then, exists of necessity; and in so far as it exists by necessity, its mode of being is good, and it is in this sense a first principle. For the necessary has all these senses—that which is necessary perforce because it is contrary to the natural impulse, that without which the good is impossible, and that which cannot be otherwise but can exist only in a single way. On such a principle, then, depend the heavens and the world of nature." *JP* II 1332 (*Pap.* IV A 157) mentions Schelling's references to Aristotle's discussion of the first and final cause. See also Kierkegaard's account in *Schelling Lecture Notes, KW* II (*Pap.* III C 27, Suppl. XIII, pp. 271-78).

12. Plato, *Gorgias,* 490 c; *Opera,* I, pp. 570-71; Heise, III, p. 110; *Collected Dialogues,* p. 272 (Callicles speaking): "You keep talking about food and drink and doctors and nonsense. I am not speaking of these things."

13. See Plutarch, "Themistocles," XXIX, 3, *Lives; Plutark's Levnetsbeskrivelser,* I-IV, tr. Stephan Tetens (Copenhagen: 1800-11; *ASKB* 1197-1200), II, pp. 59-60; *Plutarchs Werke,* I-VI, tr. J. G. Klaiber (Stuttgart: 1827-30;

ASKB 1190-91), III, p. 352; *Plutarch's Lives,* I-XI, tr. Bernadotte Perrin (Loeb, New York: Macmillan, 1914-26), II, p. 79: "But Themistocles made answer [to King Xerxes] that the speech of man was like embroidered tapestries, since like them this too had to be extended in order to display its patterns, but when it was rolled up it concealed and distorted them. Wherefore he had need of time."

14. The Danish *hoverende* (*overende* in Kierkegaard's manuscript) is related to the Latin *ovatio,* a lesser celebration or ovation in which the victor entered the capital on foot or on horseback and offered only a sheep (*ovis*) in sacrifice; *triumpherende* is related to the Latin *triumph,* a more splendid celebration in which the victor entered in a chariot.

15. See Matthew 22:19-21.

16. See Matthew 9:23, the raising of Jairus's daughter.

17. See Psalm 90:4; II Peter 3:8.

18. See Matthew 6:29.

19. A reference to Exodus 33:20: " 'But,' he [the Lord] said, 'you cannot see my face, for man shall not see me and live.' " Although the Danish text has the Platonic "the god" (*Guden*), the Hebrew "the Lord" or "God" seems more appropriate here.

20. See Luke 15:7.

21. The dash signifies the recurrence of the basic conditional "if/then" formulation of the hypothesis (as on p. 28): "if *the moment* is to have decisive significance (and without this we return to the Socratic, even though we think we are going further), the learner . . . ."

22. With reference to this phrase and the remainder of the paragraph, see Supplement, p. 189 (*Pap.* V B 4:6).

23. See John 8:32.

24. See *Symposium,* 209 e–211 b; *Opera,* III, pp. 514-19; Heise, II, pp. 77-80; *Collected Dialogues,* pp. 561-62. In his speech, Socrates recalls the Eros-inspired ascent as told to him by Diotima:

> Well now, my dear Socrates, I have no doubt that even you might be initiated into these, the more elementary mysteries of Love. But I don't know whether you could apprehend the final revelation, for so far, you know, we are only at the bottom of the true scale of perfection.
>
> Never mind, she went on, I will do all I can to help you understand, and you must strain every nerve to follow what I'm saying.
>
> Well then, she began, the candidate for this initiation cannot, if his efforts are to be rewarded, begin too early to devote himself to the beauties of the body. First of all, if his preceptor instructs him as he should, he will fall in love with the beauty of one individual body, so that his passion may give life to noble discourse. Next he must consider how nearly related the beauty of any one body is to the beauty of any other, when he will see that if he is to devote himself to loveliness of form it will be absurd to deny that the beauty of each and every body is the same.

Having reached this point, he must set himself to be the lover of every lovely body, and bring his passion for the one into due proportion by deeming it of little or of no importance.

Next he must grasp that the beauties of the body are as nothing to the beauties of the soul, so that wherever he meets with spiritual loveliness, even in the husk of an unlovely body, he will find it beautiful enough to fall in love with and to cherish—and beautiful enough to quicken in his heart a longing for such discourse as tends toward the building of a noble nature. And from this he will be led to contemplate the beauty of laws and institutions. And when he discovers how nearly every kind of beauty is akin to every other he will conclude that the beauty of the body is not, after all, of so great moment.

And next, his attention should be diverted from institutions to the sciences, so that he may know the beauty of every kind of knowledge. And thus, by scanning beauty's wide horizon, he will be saved from a slavish and illiberal devotion to the individual loveliness of a single boy, a single man, or a single institution. And, turning his eyes toward the open sea of beauty, he will find in such contemplation the seed of the most fruitful discourse and the loftiest thought, and reap a golden harvest of philosophy, until, confirmed and strengthened, he will come upon one single form of knowledge, the knowledge of the beauty I am about to speak of.

And here, she said, you must follow me as closely as you can.

Whoever has been initiated so far in the mysteries of Love and has viewed all these aspects of the beautiful in due succession, is at last drawing near the final revelation. And now, Socrates, there bursts upon him that wondrous vision which is the very soul of the beauty he has toiled so long for. It is an everlasting loveliness which neither comes nor goes, which neither flowers nor fades, for such beauty is the same on every hand, the same then as now, here as there, this way as that way, the same to every worshiper as it is to every other.

Nor will his vision of the beautiful take the form of a face, or of hands, or of anything that is of the flesh. It will be neither words, nor knowledge, nor a something that exists in something else, such as a living creature, or the earth, or the heavens, or anything that is—but subsisting of itself and by itself in an eternal oneness, while every lovely thing partakes of it in such sort that, however much the parts may wax and wane, it will be neither more nor less, but still the same inviolable whole.

25. See *Symposium*, 220 a-b; *Opera*, III, pp. 538-41; Heise, II, p. 97; *Collected Dialogues*, p. 571. Alcibiades tells of the winter expedition to Potidaea: "Then again, the way he got through that winter was most impressive, and the winters over there are pretty shocking. There was one time when the frost was harder than ever, and all the rest of us stayed inside, or if we did go out we wrapped ourselves up to the eyes and tied bits of felt and sheepskins over our shoes, but Socrates went out in the same old

coat he'd always worn, and made less fuss about walking on the ice in his bare feet than we did in our shoes. So much so, that the men began to look at him with some suspicion and actually took his toughness as a personal insult to themselves."

26. See Luke 9:58.
27. See Matthew 4:6; Psalm 91:11-12.
28. See, for example, Matthew 4:24, 9:36.
29. See Philippians 2:8.
30. See Matthew 4:2.
31. See Matthew 27:46.
32. Ecce homo! See John 19:5.
33. See Luke 7:37-38.
34. See Luke 10:39-42.
35. See John 2:4.
36. See Matthew 4:10, 16:23.
37. With reference to the following paragraph, see Supplement, p. 189 (*Pap.* V B 4:7).
38. See Luke 2:35.
39. See Matthew 26:38.
40. See Matthew 26:39.
41. See Matthew 27:48.
42. Faith or offense.
43. The Danish *digte* (nouns: *Digt,* poem, and *Digter,* poet) means "to write a poem," "to compose a literary work." It also means "to fabricate" or "to fictionize." In all cases, it signifies that the project is a making, as does the English "poem" (from the Greek *poiema,* derived from *poiein:* "to make," "to compose," "to write"). Here and elsewhere in *Fragments, digte* and *Digt* are rendered as the context requires. See note 1 above.
44. See Matthew 9:17.
45. See Exodus 19:16-19.
46. With reference to the remainder of the chapter, see Supplement, pp. 189-90 (*Pap.* V B 4:2).
47. See Plato, *Apology* 27 b-c; *Opera,* VIII, pp. 122-23; *Collected Dialogues,* p. 13 (Socrates speaking): "Is there anyone in the world, Meletus who believes in human activities, and not in human beings? Make him answer, gentlemen, and don't let him keep on making these continual objections. Is there anyone who does not believe in horses, but believes in horses' activities? Or who does not believe in musicians, but believes in musical activities? No, there is not, my worthy friend. If you do not want to answer, I will supply it for you and for these gentlemen too. But the next question you must answer. Is there anyone who believes in supernatural activities and not in supernatural beings?"
48. See *JP* V 5222 (*Pap.* II A 92).
49. See I Corinthians 2:9; *Sickness unto Death,* pp. 84, 118, *KW* XIX (*SV* XI 195, 228).

CHAPTER III

1. On the theme of "paradox," see *JP* III 3070-3102 (especially 3073-74) and pp. 845-46; VII, p. 69.

2. See Plato, *Phaedrus*, 229 d–230 a; *Opera*, I, pp. 130-31; *Collected Dialogues*, p. 478 (Socrates speaking):

> For my part, Phaedrus, I regard such theories [a scientific account of how Boreas seized Orythia from the river] as no doubt attractive, but as the invention of clever, industrious people who are not exactly to be envied, for the simple reason that they must then go on and tell us the real truth about the appearance of centaurs and the Chimera, not to mention a whole host of such creatures, Gorgons and Pegasuses and countless other remarkable monsters of legend flocking in on them. If our skeptic, with his somewhat crude science, means to reduce every one of them to the standard of probability, he'll need a deal of time for it. I myself have certainly no time for the business, and I'll tell you why, my friend. I can't as yet 'know myself,' as the inscription at Delphi enjoins, and so long as that ignorance remains it seems to me ridiculous to inquire into extraneous matters. Consequently I don't bother about such things, but accept the current beliefs about them, and direct my inquiries, as I have just said, rather to myself, to discover whether I really am a more complex creature and more puffed up with pride than Typhon, or a simpler, gentler being whom heaven has blessed with a quiet, un-Typhonic nature.

3. See *Postscript*, *KW* XII (*SV* VII 84); *JP* III 3566 (*Pap.* X¹ A 609): "Take the paradox away from a thinker—and you have a professor. A professor has at his disposal a whole line of thinkers from Greece to modern times; it appears as if the professor stood above all of them. Well, many thanks—he is, of course, the infinitely inferior."

4. For the analogy of laughing and crying to walking and falling, see *Either/Or*, I, *KW* III (*SV* I 5).

5. See p. 12 and note 18.

6. See, for example, *Stages on Life's Way*, *KW* XI (*SV* VI 161-62); *Postscript*, *KW* XII (*SV* VII 178).

7. One source of information about Democritus's thought is the work of Sextus Empiricus (fl. A.D. 200), Greek skeptic and author of *Pyrrhonenses hypotyposes*, a summary history of Greek skepticism, and *Adversus mathematicos*, a skeptical critique of those who claim to know and to teach. See *Outlines of Pyrrhonism*, II, 22-24, 27; *Sexti Empirici opera quae extant* (Avreliana: 1621; *ASKB* 146), pp. 56, 58; *Sextus Empiricus*, I-IV, tr. R. G. Bury (Loeb, New York: Putnam, 1933-49), I, pp. 165-67, 169.

8. See *JP* I 42 (*Pap.* IV C 50).

9. Besides denying universals and thereby the possibility of learning and teaching, Sextus Empiricus argues against that possibility in another way. See *Outlines of Pyrrhonism*, III, 253-54; *Opera*, pp. 162-63; Loeb, I, p. 495:

Thus, for instance, the matter of instruction is either true or false; if false it would not be taught; for they assert that falsehood is non-existent, and of non-existents there could be no teaching. Nor yet if it were said to be true; for we have shown in our chapter "On the Criterion" that truth is non-existent. If, then, neither the false nor the true is being taught, and besides these there is nothing capable of being taught (for no one, to be sure, will say that, though these are unteachable, he teaches only dubious lessons), then nothing is taught. And the matter taught is either apparent or non-evident. But if it is apparent, it will not require teaching; for things apparent appear to all alike. And if it is non-evident, then, since things non-evident are, as we have often shown, inapprehensible owing to the undecided controversy about them, it will be incapable of being taught; for how could anyone teach or learn what he does not apprehend? But if neither the apparent is taught nor the non-evident, nothing is taught.

10. Protagoras (481-411 b.c.) was the leading Greek Sophist. His famous formulation, based upon the privacy of experience, is given in Plato's *Theaetetus*, 152 a (see also *Cratylus*, 385 e); *Opera*, II, pp. 50-51; *Collected Dialogues*, p. 856: " 'man is the measure of all things—alike of the being of things that are and of the not-being of things that are not.' "

The Danish editors take "with everything as the measure of man" as a careless rendition of the Protagorean motto. The unusual formulation may, however, be an echo of a version in Sextus Empiricus, *Outlines of Pyrrhonism*, II, 5, 34-36; *Opera*, pp. 58-59; Loeb, I, pp. 173-75:

Since, then, we are unable to make an agreed statement as to the standard by which the proof itself can be tested (for we are still inquiring about the criterion "By whom"), we shall be unable to pronounce judgement on the proof, and therefore also to prove the criterion, which is the subject of discussion. And if it shall be asserted without proof that objects ought to be judged by Man, the assertion will be disbelieved, so that we shall be unable to affirm positively that the criterion "By whom" (or Agent) is Man. Moreover, who is to be the judge that the criterion of the Agent is Man? For if they assert this without a judgement (or criterion) they will surely not be believed. Yet if they say that a man is to be the judge, that will be assuming the point at issue; while if they make another animal the judge, in what way do they come to adopt that animal for the purpose of judging whether Man is the criterion? If they do so without a judgement, it will not be believed, and if with a judgement, it in turn needs to be judged by something. If, then, it is judged by itself, the same absurdity remains (for the object of inquiry will be judged by the object of inquiry); and if by Man, circular reasoning is introduced; and if by some judge other than these two, we shall once again in his case demand the criterion "By whom," and so on *ad infinitum*. Consequently we shall not be in a position to declare that objects ought to be judged by Man.

The idea of measuring or judging and of being measured or judged is found also in an early note (*Pap*. II C 13) on Hans Lassen Martensen's lectures (1837) on Greek philosophy. Following the heading "Protagoras 'Everything is the measure of man' " is a line from Matthew 7:2 (King James tr.): "with what measure you mete, it shall be measured to you again."

11. See Plato, *Symposium*, 220 c-d; *Opera*, III, pp. 540-41: Heise, II, pp. 97-98; *Collected Dialogues*, p. 571 (Alcibiades speaking):

> And now I must tell you about another thing "our valiant hero dared and did" in the course of the same campaign. He started wrestling with some problem or other about sunrise one morning, and stood there lost in thought, and when the answer wouldn't come he still stood there thinking and refused to give it up. Time went on, and by about midday the troops noticed what was happening, and naturally they were rather surprised and began telling each other how Socrates had been standing there thinking ever since daybreak. And at last, toward nightfall, some of the Ionians brought out their bedding after supper—this was in the summer, of course—partly because it was cooler in the open air, and partly to see whether he was going to stay there all night. Well, there he stood till morning, and then at sunrise he said his prayers to the sun and went away.

12. Cf. a similar expression used by Hegel in connection with *Aufhebung* (contradiction, destruction, and preservation on a higher level) in the dialectic of contradictories in existence. See, for example, *Wissenschaft der Logik*, II, *Werke*, IV, pp. 117-18; *J.A.*, IV, pp. 595-96; *Science of Logic*, pp. 477-78:

> *The fact emerges from the ground*. It is not grounded or posited by it in such a manner that ground remains as a substrate; on the contrary, the positing is the movement of the ground outwards to itself and its simple vanishing. Through its *union* with the conditions, ground receives an external immediacy and the moment of being. But it receives this not as something external, nor through an external relation; on the contrary, as ground, it makes itself into a positedness, its simple essentiality unites with itself in the positedness and is, in this sublation of itself, the vanishing of its difference from its positedness, and is thus simple essential immediacy. Ground, therefore, does not remain behind as something distinct from the grounded, but the truth of grounding is that in it ground is united with itself, so that its reflection into another is its reflection into itself. Consequently, the fact is not only the *unconditioned* but also the *groundless*, and it emerges from ground only in so far as ground has "*fallen to the ground* [*zu Grunde gegangen*]" and ceased to be ground: it emerges from the groundless, that is, from its own essential negativity or pure form.
> This immediacy that is mediated by ground and condition and is self-identical through the sublating [*Aufheben*] of mediation, is *Existence*.

13. See Mark 11:31; *Works of Love, KW* XVI (*SV* IX 34-40).

14. With reference to the parenthetical portion, see Supplement, p. 190 (*Pap.* V B 5:2).

15. See p. 23 and note 2. In the text, the Greek for "than Typhon" is omitted.

16. With reference to the remainder of the paragraph, see Supplement, p. 190 (*Pap.* V B 5:3).

17. See Supplement, p. 190 (*Pap.* V B 5:3) and notes.

18. With reference to the following two paragraphs, see Supplement, pp. 190-91 (*Pap.* V B 5:5). In these paragraphs and in the footnote, Kierkegaard uses *Gud* (God) rather than *Guden* (the god), inasmuch as the language of Spinoza and Leibniz is employed in the discussion of their thought.

19. Cf. *Sickness unto Death*, p. 121, *KW* XIX (*SV* XI 231).

20. See Benedict Spinoza, *Ethics*, Part I, Def. 1, Prop. 7, 11; *Ethica ordine geometrico demonstrata, Opera philosophica omnia*, ed. August Gfroerer (Stuttgart: 1830; *ASKB* 788), pp. 289, 291; *The Chief Works of Benedict de Spinoza*, I-II, tr. R.H.M. Elwes (London: Bell, 1909-12), II, pp. 48, 51: "*Existence belongs to the nature of substance*"; "God, or substance, consisting of infinite attributes, of which each expresses eternal and infinite essentiality, necessarily exists."

21. *Opera*, p. 15; Baruch Spinoza, *Principles of the Philosophy of René Descartes, Earlier Philosophical Writings*, tr. Frank A. Hayes (Indianapolis: Bobbs-Merrill, 1963), p. 37.

22. *Opera*, p. 15, n. II; *Earlier Philosophical Writings*, p. 38. On the front flyleaf of his copy of the Gfroerer edition of Spinoza's *Opera* (University of Copenhagen Library, Fil. 18782), Kierkegaard wrote:

re pg. 15. Lemma 1. Note II. This dissolves in a tautology, since he explains *perfectio* by *realitas, esse*. The more perfect a thing is, he says, the more it is; but in turn he explains the perfection of a thing by saying that it has in itself more *esse*, which therefore says that the more it is the more it is.

In a logical sense, this is correct—the more perfection, the more it is; but here being has an altogether different meaning than that it factually *is*.

Thus, with respect to God, this ends in the old thesis that if God is possible, he is *eo ipso* necessary (cf. Leibniz on this somewhere in the *Theodicy*).

See note 25 below.

23. See *JP* I 1057, 1059; IV 3852 (*Pap.* X² A 328, 439, 416).

24. *Hamlet*, III, 1, 56; Kittredge, p. 1166.

25. See, for example, *Monadology*, para. 44-45; *Opera*, II, p. 708; *Monadology*, p. 242:

44. For if there is a reality in essences or possibilities, or rather in eternal truths, this reality must needs be founded in something existing and ac-

tual, and consequently in the existence of the necessary Being, in whom essence involves existence, or in whom to be possible is to be actual. (*Theod.* 184-189, 335.) 45. Thus God alone (or the necessary Being) has this prerogative that He must necessarily exist, if He is possible. And as nothing can interfere with the possibility of that which involves no limits, no negation and consequently no contradiction, this [His possibility] is sufficient of itself to make known the existence of God *a priori*. We have thus proved it, through the reality of eternal truths. But a little while ago we proved it also *a posteriori*, since there exist contingent beings, which can have their final or sufficient reason only in the necessary Being, which has the reason of its existence in itself.

26. With reference to the following two paragraphs, see Supplement, pp. 190-91 (*Pap.* V B 5:5).

27. See, for example, Anselm, *Proslogium,* II, where, trusting in the pre-supposed ideality, he proceeds to demonstrate its existence. *St. Anselm,* tr. Sidney N. Deane (Chicago: Open Court, 1930), p. 7:

Truly there is a God, although the fool hath said in his heart, There is no God.

And so, Lord, do thou, who dost give understanding to faith, give me, so far as thou knowest it to be profitable, to understand that thou art as we believe; and that thou art that which we believe. And, indeed, we believe that thou art a being than which nothing greater can be conceived. Or is there no such nature, since the fool hath said in his heart, there is no God? (Psalms xiv. I). But, at any rate, this very fool, when he hears of this being of which I speak—a being than which nothing greater can be conceived—understands what he hears, and what he understands is in his understanding; although he does not understand it to exist.

28. An eccentrically weighted tumbler doll that rolls to its feet when released is misnamed for the so-called Cartesian devil (a hollow glass figure, weighted and open at the bottom and partially filled with air), which moves in a partially filled container of water when the pliable top of the container is pressed down.

29. With reference to the Stoic Chrysippus (282-209 B.C.) and Carneades (c. 215-125 B.C.), a skeptic, see Supplement, p. 191 (*Pap.* V B 5:5), and note 26. A sorites (from σωϱός, a heap, of grain, for example) is a compound or chain syllogism, reputedly invented by Chrysippus, whereby an opponent is brought by small degrees from the admission of a self-evident truth to the admission of what is not manifestly true. In the statement of a sorites, all conclusions except the last are suppressed, and the sorites may be thought of as a single valid inference independent of analysis into constituent syllo-gisms. According to the order in which the premises are arranged, the so-rites is called *progressive* (if, in the analysis into syllogisms, each new premise after the first is a major premise and each intermediate conclusion serves as

a minor premise for the next syllogism) or *regressive* (if each new premise after the first is a minor premise and each intermediate conclusion a major premise).

30. Psalms 14:1 and 53:2.

31. For a deletion from the final copy, see Supplement, pp. 191-92 (*Pap.* V B 40:11). See *JP* III 3195 (*Pap.* X¹ A 401).

32. See Xenophon, *Memorabilia*, I, 4, 2-7; Bornemann, pp. 53-56; Loeb, pp. 55-57 (Socrates speaking):

"Tell me, Aristodemus, do you admire any human beings for wisdom?"

"I do," he answered.

"Tell us their names."

"In epic poetry Homer comes first, in my opinion; in dithyramb, Melanippides; in tragedy, Sophocles; in sculpture, Polycleitus; in painting, Zeuxis."

"Which, think you, deserve the greater admiration, the creators of phantoms without sense and motion, or the creators of living, intelligent, and active beings?"

"Oh, of living beings, by far, provided only they are created by design and not mere chance."

"Suppose that it is impossible to guess the purpose of one creature's existence, and obvious that another's serves a useful end, which, in your judgment, is the work of chance, and which of design?"

"Presumably the creature that serves some useful end is the work of design."

"Do you not think then that he who created man from the beginning had some useful end in view when he endowed him with his several senses, giving eyes to see visible objects, ears to hear sounds? . . . With such signs of forethought in these arrangements, can you doubt whether they are the works of chance or design?"

"No, of course not. When I regard them in this light they do look very like the handiwork of a wise and loving creator."

See Hegel, *Beweise für das Daseyn Gottes, Werke*, XII, p. 518; *J.A.*, XVI, p. 518. The reference is to Socrates and the Xenophon passage quoted above. See Supplement, p. 192 (*Pap.* V B 5:6).

33. For continuation of the thought, see Supplement, p. 192 (*Pap.* V B 5:6). For deletion from the final copy, see Supplement, pp. 192-93 (*Pap.* V B 40:12).

34. A reference to the formulation by Gorgias, a Sophist. See Sextus Empiricus, *Against the Logicians*, VII, 65; *Opera*, p. 149; Loeb, II, p. 35: "Gorgias of Leontini belonged to the same party as those who abolish the criterion, although he did not adopt the same line of attack as Protagoras. For in his book entitled *Concerning the Non-existent* or *Concerning Nature* he tries to establish successively three main points—firstly, that nothing exists;

secondly, that even if anything exists it is inapprehensible by man; thirdly, that even if anything is apprehensible, yet of a surety it is inexpressible and incommunicable to one's neighbour."

35. See *The Book on Adler, KW* XXIV (*Pap.* VII² B 235, p. 144); *Sickness unto Death,* pp. 99, 117, 126, 127, *KW* XIX (*SV* XI 209-10, 227, 235, 237).

36. See, for example, *JP* III 3074-77 (*Pap.* IV C 84, A 47, 62, 103).

37. See Matthew 6:26.

38. See Supplement, p. 193 (*Pap.* V B 1:11, 5:7).

39. With reference to the remainder of the paragraph, see Supplement, pp. 193-94 (*Pap.* V B 5:8).

40. With reference to the following paragraph, see Supplement, p. 194 (*Pap.* V B 5:9).

41. With reference to the remainder of the paragraph, see Supplement, pp. 194-95 (*Pap.* V B 5:10).

42. Socrates. See pp. 23, 39.

43. With reference to the following paragraph, see Supplement, p. 195 (*Pap.* V B 5:11).

APPENDIX

1. See Supplement, pp. 195-96 (*Pap.* V B 6:1).

2. See Supplement, p. 196 (*Pap.* V B 11:2).

3. The Danish *lidende* literally means "suffering" or "undergoing," therefore passivity and receptivity in contrast to activity and agency.

4. See, for example, Spinoza, *Ethics,* Part III, Def. III; *Opera,* p. 340; *Works,* II, p. 130:

> By *emotion* I mean the modifications of the body, whereby the active power of the said body is increased or diminished, aided or constrained, and also the ideas of such modifications.
>
> N.B. If we can be the adequate cause of any of these modifications, I then call the emotion an activity, otherwise I call it a passion, or state wherein the mind is passive.

5. See Spinoza, *Ethics,* Part II, Prop. 43, Demonstration; *Opera,* p. 331; *Works,* II, p. 115: "Further, what can there be more clear, and more certain, than a true idea as a standard of truth? Even as light displays both itself and darkness, so is truth a standard both of itself and of falsity."

6. See Xenophon, *Memorabilia,* III, 9, 5; Bornemann, pp. 216-17; Loeb, p. 225:

> He said that Justice and every other form of Virtue is Wisdom. "For just actions and all forms of virtuous activity are beautiful and good. He who knows the beautiful and good will never choose anything else, he who is ignorant of them cannot do them, and even if he tries, will fail. Hence the wise do what is beautiful and good, the unwise cannot and fail

if they try. Therefore since just actions and all other forms of beautiful and good activity are virtuous actions, it is clear that Justice and every other form of Virtue is Wisdom."
See *Irony, KW* II (*SV* XIII 307-08).

7. The final clause has the same form as, for example, the proverb "*Intet er saa galt at det jo er godt for noget* [Nothing is so bad that it is *not* good for something]." For an explication of the idea, see *JP* IV 4297 (*Pap.* XI¹ A 318).

8. See John 8:44.

9. With reference to the remainder of the sentence, see Supplement, p. 196 (*Pap.* V B 11:4).

10. See I Corinthians 1:23.

11. A common version of Tertullian, *De carne Christi,* 5: "*Mortuus est dei filius; credibile est, quia ineptum est*"; *On the Flesh of Christ, The Ante-Nicene Fathers,* I-IX, ed. Alexander Roberts and James Donaldson (Buffalo, N.Y.: Christian Literature Publishing Co., 1885-97), III, p. 525: "And the Son of God died; it is by all means to be believed, because it is absurd [*ineptum*]." In an entry from 1839 (*JP* IV 4095; *Pap.* II A 467), Kierkegaard uses the common version.

12. See Supplement, pp. 195-96 (*Pap.* V B 6:1).

13. A game (*Forundringsstolen;* also, but rarely, named *Beundringsstolen*) sometimes called the "wonder stool" or "wonder game," in which one person sits blindfolded on a stool in the middle of a circle while another goes around quietly asking others what they wonder about the person who is "it." Upon being told what others had wondered about him, he tries to guess the source in each instance. See *Sickness unto Death,* p. 5, *KW* XIX (*SV* XI 117); "To Mr. Orla Lehmann," *Early Polemical Writings, KW* I (*SV* XIII 28).

14. See Supplement, pp. 195-96 (*Pap.* V B 6:1).

15. See Lactantius, *Institutiones divinae,* VI, 9; *Firmiani Lactantii opera,* I-II, ed. O. F. Fritzsche (Leipzig: 1842-44; *ASKB* 142-43), II, p. 19; *The Divine Institutes, The Ante-Nicene Fathers,* VII, pp. 171-72. The idea is usually attributed to Augustine, although the expression is not his. Cf. *The City of God,* XIX, 25; *Aurelii Augustini . . . de civitate Dei,* I-II (Leipzig: 1825), II, p. 267; *The City of God, Basic Writings of Saint Augustine,* I-II, ed. Whitney J. Oates (New York: Random House, 1948), II, p. 504:

> For although some suppose that virtues which have a reference only to themselves, and are desired only on their own account, are yet true and genuine virtues, the fact is that even then they are inflated with pride, and are therefore to be reckoned vices rather than virtues. For as that which gives life to the flesh is not derived from flesh, but is above it, so that which gives blessed life to man is not derived from man, but is something above him; and what I say of man is true of every celestial power and virtue whatsoever.

16. See Shakespeare, *All's Well That Ends Well*, II, 3, 1-3; Kittredge, p. 373 (Lafeu speaking): "They say, miracles are past; and we have our philosophical persons, to make modern and familiar, things supernatural and causeless." The Danish text is based on a German translation, Schlegel and Tieck, XI, p. 297.

17. See Shakespeare, *King Lear*, IV, 6, 97-101; Schlegel and Tieck, XI, pp. 100-01; Kittredge, p. 1230 (Lear speaking): "Ha! Goneril with a white beard? They flatter'd me like a dog, and told me I had white hairs in my beard ere the black ones were there. To say 'ay' and 'no' to everything I said! 'Ay' and 'no' too was no good divinity."

18. For references to the various items, see notes 11, 14-17 above. The particular Luther reference has not been located.

19. Goethe, *"Der Fischer,"* 31, *Goethe's Werke. Vollständige Ausgabe letzter Hand,* I-LX (Stuttgart, Tübingen: 1828-42; *ASKB* 1641-68 [I-LV]), I, p. 186 (ed. tr.). Cf. *Goethe,* ed. and tr. David Luke (Harmondsworth, Middlesex: Penguin, 1964), p. 80.

CHAPTER IV

1. With reference to the opening of the chapter, see Supplement, pp. 196-97 (*Pap.* V B 5:10, 6:3,6).

2. See Philippians 2:7-8.

3. See *JP* III 3077 (*Pap.* IV A 103).

4. See Luke 7:25.

5. See Matthew 26:53.

6. See Matthew 6:25-26.

7. See Matthew 8:20.

8. See Matthew 8:22.

9. With reference to the remainder of the paragraph, see Supplement, p. 197 (*Pap.* V B 12:1).

10. See Luke 24:29.

11. See Matthew 6:28.

12. See John 4:34.

13. See Matthew 12:49.

14. See, for example, Matthew 4:25.

15. See John 3:1-15.

16. See Luke 2:7.

17. With reference to the following paragraph, see Supplement, p. 197 (*Pap.* V B 1:4, 6:4).

18. See title page.

19. With reference to the following paragraph, see Supplement, p. 197 (*Pap.* V B 6:2).

20. See Matthew 27:24.

21. See Matthew 4:4; John 6:12.

22. Plato was a pupil of Socrates for a time, but Socrates' view of knowl-

edge and his method of teaching precluded followers both in principle and in practice. See Chapter I.

23. See p. 24 on Alcibiades.

24. See pp. 10-11.

25. With reference to the following eight paragraphs, see Supplement, p. 197 (*Pap.* V B 6:7).

26. With reference to the remainder of the sentence, see Supplement, p. 197 (*Pap.* V B 12:4).

27. See *JP* I 203 (*Pap.* I A 55).

28. See I John 1:1.

29. See Supplement, p. 198 (*Pap.* V B 12:5); Luke 24:13-32.

30. See Luke 11:27-28.

31. See Luke 13:26.

32. With reference to the remainder of the paragraph and the first five sentences of the next, see Supplement, p. 198 (*Pap.* V B 12:7).

33. See Luke 13:27.

34. See I Corinthians 13:12.

35. Cf., for example, Pliny, *Natural History,* VII, 24, 88; *Natural History,* I-X, tr. H. Rackham (Loeb, Cambridge: Harvard University Press, 1942), II, pp. 563-65:

> As to memory, the boon most necessary for life, it is not easy to say who most excelled in it, so many men having gained renown for it. King Cyrus could give their names to all the soldiers in his army, Lucius Scipio knew the names of the whole Roman people, King Pyrrhus's envoy Cineas knew those of the senate and knighthood at Rome the day after his arrival. Mithridates who was king of twenty-two races gave judgements in as many languages, in an assembly addressing each race in turn without an interpreter.

36. The first edition of *Fragments* has *Guden* here; the article ending is lacking in *Samlede Værker,* editions 1, 2, and 3.

37. With reference to the remainder of the paragraph, see Supplement, p. 198 (*Pap.* V B 6:8).

38. With reference to the remainder of the sentence, see Supplement, p. 199 (*Pap.* V B 12:8).

39. Literally, "the personal act of seeing" (Grk. *autos,* self + *optos,* seen).

40. See Herodotus, *History,* III, 61-69; *Die Geschichten des Herodotos,* I-II, tr. Friedrich Lange (Berlin: 1811; *ASKB* 1117), I, pp. 255-62; *Herodotus,* I-IV, tr. A. D. Godley (Loeb, New York: Putnam, 1921-24), II, pp. 77-91:

> Now after Cambyses son of Cyrus had lost his wits, while he still lingered in Egypt, two Magians, who were brothers, rebelled against him. One of them had been left by Cambyses to be steward of his house; this man now revolted from him, perceiving that the death of Smerdis was kept secret, and that few persons knew of it, most of them believing him to be still alive. Therefore he thus plotted to gain the royal power: he had

a brother, his partner, as I said, in rebellion; this brother was very like in appearance to Cyrus' son, Smerdis, brother of Cambyses and by him put to death; nor was he like him in appearance only, but he bore the same name also, Smerdis. . . .

Cambyses being dead, the Magian, pretending to be the Smerdis of like name, Cyrus' son, reigned without fear for the seven months lacking to Cambyses' full eight years of kingship. . . . but in the eighth month it was revealed who he was, and this is how it was done:—There was one Otanes, son of Pharnaspes, as well-born and rich a man as any Persian. This Otanes was the first to suspect that the Magian was not Cyrus' son Smerdis but his true self; the reason was, that he never left the citadel nor summoned any notable Persian into his presence; and in his suspicion— Cambyses having married Otanes' daughter Phaedyme, whom the Magian had now wedded, with all the rest of Cambyses' wives—Otanes sent to this daughter, asking with whom she lay, Smerdis, Cyrus' son, or another. . . . So Phaedyme, daughter of Otanes, performed her promise to her father. When it was her turn to visit the Magian (as a Persian's wives come in regular order to their lord), she came to his bed, and uncovered the Magian's ears while he slumbered deeply; and having with much ease assured herself that he had no ears, she sent and told this to her father as soon as it was morning.

41. With reference to the following three sentences, see Supplement, p. 199 (*Pap.* V B 12:9).

42. A children's game, a version of blindman's buff.

INTERLUDE

1. See Supplement, p. 199 (*Pap.* V B 6:9).

2. See Supplement, pp. 182, 199 (*Pap.* IV C 62; V B 6:9).

3. See Callicles' complaint in Plato, *Gorgias*, 490 e–491 b; *Opera*, I, pp. 572-73; Heise, III, pp. 111-112; *Collected Dialogues*, p. 273.

CALLICLES: How you keep saying the same things, Socrates!

SOCRATES: Not only that, Callicles, but about the same matters. . . . You see, my good Callicles, that you do not find the same fault with me as I with you. For you claim that I keep saying the same things, and reproach me with it, but I make the opposite statement of you, that you never say the same things about the same subjects.

4. With reference to the remainder of the paragraph, see Supplement, pp. 199-200 (*Pap.* V B 13).

5. For deletions here, see Supplement, pp. 200-09 (*Pap.* V B 14, 41).

6. "Existence," "exist," and "to exist" pertain to temporal and spatial being or actuality. All existence is being, but not all being is existence or actuality. Therefore, for example, in *Postscript, KW* XII (*SV* VII 287), Johannes Climacus states that "God does not think, he creates; God does not

exist, he is eternal. A human being thinks and exists, and existence separates thinking and being, holds them apart from each other in succession."

"To exist" and "exist" also have a special qualitative meaning in *Postscript.* Johannes Climacus (*SV* VII 508) touches on the ordinary meaning (temporal and spatial actuality) and the special meaning (qualitative becoming, in view of which ordinary existence could more accurately be termed "subsistence"): "Sin is the new existence-medium. 'To exist [*at existere*]' generally signifies only that by having come into existence the individual does exist and is becoming; now it signifies that by having come into existence he has become a sinner. 'To exist' generally is not a more sharply defining predicate but is the form of all more sharply defining predicates; one does not become something [qualitative] by coming into existence, but now to come into existence is to become a sinner." In *Fragments* (p. 76), the special qualitative meaning of "to exist" is expressed as a "redoubling," "a coming into existence within its own coming into existence." In *Either/Or,* II, *KW* IV (*SV* II 125), Judge William, in writing about the qualitative possibility of the ethical, states, "Thus, when patience acquires itself in patience, it is inner history." Johannes Climacus in *Postscript, KW* XII (*SV* VII 214), calls it *"gaining a history."* See p. 13 and note 25.

7. With reference to the following four paragraphs, see Supplement, pp. 209-10 (*Pap.* V B 15:1).

8. Motion, change of all kinds. See *JP* I 258 (*Pap.* IV C 47). The views of Aristotle and of Tennemann are in the background of the discussion of change. See Aristotle, *Physics,* 200 b; Bekker, I, p. 200; *Works,* II:

> NATURE has been defined as a "principle of motion and change", and it is the subject of our inquiry. We must therefore see that we understand the meaning of "motion" [κίνησις]; for if it were unknown, the meaning of "nature", too, would be unknown. . . .
>
> We may start by distinguishing (1) what exists in a state of fulfilment only, (2) what exists as potential, (3) what exists as potential and also in fulfilment—one being a "this," another "so much," a third "such," and similarly in each of the other modes of the predication of being.

See Tennemann, III, pp. 125-27 (ed. tr.):

> The word κίνησις had already been used by Plato in a broader and in a narrower sense, namely, for any change and for motion in space. Aristotle uses it in the broader sense. He, of course, could designate all changes with one word, *motion,* because he really treats the science of natural entities that exist in space and every change that happens to them in space. Therefore he declares that motion in space is the basis of every other motion. . . . It should not appear strange that he sometimes regards *production* and *passing away* (γένεσις, φθορά) as kinds of motion. . . . *Change takes place only with actual objects.* Everything that is, is either *possible* or *actual,* and the actual is conceived of as substance of a specific quantity and quality etc. in keeping with the remaining categories. Everything that

changes changes with regard to *the subject*, with regard to its *quantity* and *quality*, or with regard to *place*. There are no other kinds of changes. Because in everything possibility and actuality are distinguishable, the change, then, really is *the actualization of the possible.* . . . The transition, then, from possibility to actuality is change, κίνησις. One could express this more accurately by saying: change, motion, is the actualization of the possible insofar as it is possible. Therefore Aristotle uses the expressions ἐνέργεια [energy] and ἐντελέχεια [entelechy], both of which mean actualization as action in which something becomes actual.

9. See Aristotle, *Posterior Analytics*, 75 a; Bekker, I, p. 75; *Works*, I: "It follows that we cannot in demonstrating pass from one genus to another. We cannot, for instance, prove geometrical truths by arithmetic."

10. See pp. 41-42 fn.

11. The source has not been located. The quotation may refer to phrases already used in the paragraph.

12. See, for example, Hegel, *Wissenschaft der Logik*, I, *Werke*, IV, p. 211; *J.A.*, IV, p. 68; *Science of Logic*, p. 549:

> The *negation* of real possibility is thus its *identity*-with self; in that in its sublating it is thus within itself the recoil of this sublating, it is *real necessity*.
>
> What is necessary *cannot be otherwise;* but what is simply *possible* can; for possibility is the in-itself that is only positedness and therefore essentially otherness. Formal possibility is this identity as transition into a sheer other; but real possibility, because it contains the other moment, actuality, is already itself necessity. Therefore what is really possible can no longer be otherwise; under the particular conditions and circumstances something else cannot follow. Real possibility and necessity are therefore only *seemingly* different; this is an identity which does not have to *become* but is already *presupposed* and lies at their base. Real necessity is therefore a relation pregnant with content; for the content is that implicit identity that is indifferent to the differences of form.

See also Hegel, *Encyclopädia der philosophischen Wissenschaften, Erster Theil, Die Logik*, para. 147, *Werke*, VI, p. 292; *J.A.* (*System der Philosophie*), VIII, p. 330; *Hegel's Logic* (tr. of *L.*, 3 ed., 1830; Kierkegaard's ed., 1840, had the same text, plus *Zusätze*), tr. William Wallace (Oxford: Oxford University Press, 1975), p. 208: "Necessity has been defined, and rightly so, as the union of possibility and actuality."

13. See Aristotle, *On Interpretation*, 21 b-23 a; Bekker, I, pp. 21-23; *Works*, I:

> The contradictory, then, of 'it may *not* be' is not 'it cannot be', but 'it cannot not be', and the contradictory of 'it may be' is not 'it may *not* be', but 'it cannot be'. Thus the propositions 'it may be' and 'it may *not* be' appear each to imply the other: for, since these two propositions are not contradictory, the same thing both may and may *not* be. But the propo-

sitions 'it may be' and 'it cannot be' can never be true of the same subject at the same time, for they are contradictory. Nor can the propositions 'it may not be' and 'it cannot not be' be at once true of the same subject.

The propositions which have to do with necessity are governed by the same principle. The contradictory of 'it is necessary that it should be' is not 'it is necessary that it should not be', but 'it is not necessary that it should be', and the contradictory of 'it is necessary that it should not be' is 'it is not necessary that it should not be'.

Again, the contradictory of 'it is impossible that it should be' is not 'it is impossible that it should not be' but 'it is not impossible that it should be', and the contradictory of 'it is impossible that it should not be' is 'it is not impossible that it should not be'. . . .

Yet perhaps it is impossible that the contradictory propositions predicating necessity should be thus arranged. For when it is necessary that a thing should be, it is possible that it should be. (For if not, the opposite follows, since one or the other must follow; so, if it is not possible, it is impossible, and it is thus impossible that a thing should be, which must necessarily be; which is absurd.)

Yet from the proposition 'it may be' it follows that it is not impossible, and from that it follows that it is not necessary; it comes about therefore that the thing which must necessarily be need not be; which is absurd. But again, the proposition 'it is necessary that it should be' does not follow from the proposition 'it may be', nor does the proposition 'it is necessary that it should not be'. For the proposition 'it may be' implies a twofold possibility, while, if either of the two former propositions is true, the twofold possibility vanishes. . . . Those potentialities which involve a rational principle are potentialities of more than one result, that is, of contrary results; those that are irrational are not always thus constituted. As I have said, fire cannot both heat and not heat, neither has anything that is always actual any twofold potentiality. . . .

Our conclusion, then, is this: that since the universal is consequent upon the particular, that which is necessary is also possible, though not in every sense in which the word may be used.

We may perhaps state that necessity and its absence are the initial principles of existence and non-existence, and that all else must be regarded as posterior to these.

It is plain from what has been said that that which is of necessity is actual. Thus, if that which is eternal is prior, actuality also is prior to potentiality. Some things are actualities without potentiality, namely, the primary substances; a second class consists of those things which are actual but also potential, whose actuality is in nature prior to their potentiality, though posterior in time; a third class comprises those things which are never actualized, but are pure potentialities.

14. See Tennemann, III, p. 407 (ed. tr.): "Judgments (δόξαι) can be either true or false. The criterion of their truth is sensory perception: *negative*, if

no sensory perceptions contradict the judgment; *positive*, if it is actually confirmed by experience. If experience is contrary, the judgment is false." See also Hegel, *Geschichte der Philosophie, Werke,* XIV, pp. 481–82; *J.A.,* XVIII, pp. 481–82; *History of Philosophy,* II, p. 284:

> In the last place, opinion is nothing but the reference of that general conception, which we have within us, to an object, a perception, or to the testimony of the senses; and that is the passing of a judgment. For in a conception we have anticipated that which comes directly before our eyes; and by this standard we pronounce whether something is a man, a tree, or not. 'Opinion depends on something already evident to us, to which we refer when we ask how we know that this is a man or not. This opinion is also itself termed conception, and it may be either true or false:—true, when what we see before our eyes is corroborated or not contradicted by the testimony of the conception; false in the opposite case.' That is to say, in opinion we apply a conception which we already possess, or the type, to an object which is before us, and which we then examine to see if it corresponds with our mental representation of it. Opinion is true if it corresponds with the type; and it has its criterion in perceiving whether it repeats itself as it was before or not. This is the whole of the ordinary process in consciousness, when it begins to reflect. When we have the conception, it requires the testimony that we have seen or still see the object in question.

15. See note 13 above.
16. See note 6 above.
17. A clue to the meaning of "by way of a ground" is suggested by a reading entry in German from the early stage of the writing of *Fragments* (*JP* V 5603; *Pap.* IV C 101, 1842–43):

A.

Essence as Ground of Existence

(a) The Primary Characteristics or
Categories of Existence

(α) Identity (β) Difference (γ) Ground

(b) Existence

(c) The Thing

B.

Appearance

(a) The World of Appearance or
Phenomenal World

(b) Content and Form

(c) Ratio (Relation)

C.

Actuality

See Hegel, *Inhalts-Anzeige, Die Logik, Werke*, VI, p. xlii; *J.A.*, VIII, p. vi; *Hegel's Logic*, p. xxix (an abbreviated table of contents). Hegel identifies thought and being, logic and metaphysics, the becoming of events and the necessity of logical thought. See *Die Logik*, para. 123 *Zusatz*, para. 147 *Zusatz*, *Werke*, VI, pp. 250-52, 294; *J.A.*, VIII, pp. 288-89, 332; *Hegel's Logic*, pp. 180, 209:

The phrase "Existence" (derived from *existere*) suggests the fact of having proceeded from something. Existence is Being which has proceeded from the ground, and has reinstated by annulling its intermediation. The Essence, as Being set aside and absorbed, originally came before us as shining or showing in self, and the categories of this reflection are identity, difference, and ground. The last is the unity of identity and difference; and because it unifies them it has at the same time to distinguish itself from itself. But that which is in this way distinguished from the ground is as little mere difference as the ground itself is abstract sameness. The ground works its own suspension: and when suspended, the result of its negation is existence. Having issued from the ground, existence contains the ground in it; the ground does not remain, as it were, behind existence, but by its very nature supersedes itself and translates itself into existence. This is exemplified even in our ordinary mode of thinking, when we look upon the ground of a thing, not as something abstractly inward, but as itself also an existent. For example, the lightning-flash which has set a house on fire would be considered the ground of the conflagration; or the manners of a nation and the condition of its life would be regarded as the ground of its constitution. Such indeed is the ordinary aspect in which the existent world originally appears to reflection—an indefinite crowd of things existent, which being simultaneously reflected on themselves and on one another are related reciprocally as ground and consequence. In this motley play of the world, if we may so call the sum of existents, there is nowhere a firm footing to be found: everything bears an aspect of relativity, conditioned by and conditioning something else. The reflective understanding makes it its business to elicit and trace these connections running out in every direction; but the question touching an ultimate design is so far left unanswered, and therefore the craving of the reason after knowledge passes with the further development of the logical Idea beyond this position of mere relativity.

The theory however which regards the world as determined through necessity and belief in a divine providence are by no means mutually excluding points of view. The intellectual principle underlying the idea of divine providence will hereafter be shown to be the notion. But the notion is the truth of necessity, which it contains in suspension in itself; just as, conversely, necessity is the notion implicit. Necessity is blind only so long as it is not understood. There is nothing therefore more mistaken than the charge of blind fatalism made against the Philosophy of History, when it takes for its problem to understand the necessity of every event.

18. See Hegel, *Encyclopädie*, II, *Zweiter Theil, Die Naturphilosophie*, para. 254, *Werke*, VII, p. 45; *J.A.*, IX, p. 71; *Hegel's Philosophy of Nature* (tr. of *N.*, 2 ed., 1847; Kierkegaard had 1 ed., 1841), tr. A. V. Miller (Oxford: Oxford University Press, 1970), p. 28, where space is called "a wholly ideal *side-by-sideness*," that is, the self-externality of the Idea. See *Anxiety*, p. 86 fn., *KW* VIII (*SV* IV 356).

19. Presumably a reference to German romantic philosophy of nature, for example, that of Henrich Steffens and of Schelling, both of whom regarded nature as a system of sequential levels.

20. See *JP* III 3660–64 and pp. 908–09; VII, p. 80.

21. See note 6 above.

22. See *JP* V 5593 (*Pap.* IV C 34); Tennemann, II, pp. 155–56; IV, 273 (ed. tr.):

> He claimed that only that is possible which actually is or that actually will happen. Nothing happens that does not happen out of necessity, and whatever can possibly happen is either already actual or will become actual. Just as the truth about what has happened cannot become false, it is also impossible that the truth about the future becomes false. What has happened cannot be made to have not happened. Here the necessity and the unchangeability are so obvious that nobody can deny it.

> Chrysippus had a dispute with the Megarian Diodorus and with his teacher Cleanthes about the possibility of the future and the necessity of the past. He asserted against the one *that everything past, inasmuch as it cannot be changed, is necessary*, and against the other *that even that which will not happen is possible*.

See also Leibniz, *Theodicy*, para. 169–70; *Leibnitzs Theodicee*, tr. Johann Christoph Gottscheden (Hanover, Leipzig: 1763; *ASKB* 619), pp. 333–39; *Opera*, II, pp. 554–55; *Theodicy* (tr. of *T.* in *Philosophische Schriften*, I–VII, 1875–90), ed. Austin Farrer, tr. E. M. Huggard (New Haven: Yale University Press, 1952), pp. 229–33:

> 169. The question of the *possibility of things that do not happen* has already been examined by the ancients. It appears that Epicurus, to preserve freedom and to avoid an absolute necessity, maintained, after Aristotle, that contingent futurities were not susceptible of determinate truth. For if it was true yesterday that I should write to-day, it could therefore not fail to happen, it was already necessary; and, for the same reason, it was from all eternity. Thus all that which happens is necessary, and it is impossible for anything different to come to pass. But since that is not so it would follow, according to him, that contingent futurities have no determinate truth. To uphold this opinion, Epicurus went so far as to deny the first and the greatest principle of the truths of reason, he denied that every assertion was either true or false. Here is the way they confounded him: "You deny that it was true yesterday that I should write to-day; it was therefore false." The good man, not being able to admit this conclusion,

was obliged to say that it was neither true nor false. After that, he needs no refutation, and Chrysippus might have spared himself the trouble he took to prove the great principle of contradictories, following the account by Cicero in his book *De Fato* . . . . M. Bayle observes (*Dictionary,* article 'Epicurus', let. T, p. 1141) 'that neither of these two great philosophers [Epicurus and Chrysippus] understood that the truth of this maxim, every proposition is true or false, is independent of what is called *fatum,* it could not therefore serve as proof of the existence of the *fatum,* as Chrysippus maintained and as Epicurus feared. Chrysippus could not have conceded, without damaging his own position, that there are propositions which are neither true nor false. But he gained nothing by asserting the contrary: for, whether there be free cause or not, it is equally true that this proposition, The Grand Mogul will go hunting to-morrow, is true or false. Men rightly regarded as ridiculous this speech of Tiresias: All that I shall say will happen or not, for great Apollo confers on me the faculty of prophesying. If assuming the impossible, there were no God, it would yet be certain that everything the greatest fool in the world should predict would happen or would not happen. That is what neither Chrysippus nor Epicurus has taken into consideration.' . . .

170. Let us come now to the possibility of things that do not happen, and I will give the very words of M. Bayle, albeit they are somewhat discursive. This is what he says on the matter in his *Dictionary* (article 'Chrysippus', let. S, p. 929): 'The celebrated dispute on things possible and things impossible owed its origin to the doctrine of the Stoics concerning fate. The question was to know whether, among the things which have never been and never will be, there are some possible; or whether all that is not, all that has never been, all that will never be, was impossible. A famous dialectician of the Megaric Sect, named Diodorus, gave a negative answer to the first of these two questions and an affirmative to the second; but Chrysippus vehemently opposed him. . . . Cicero makes it clear enough that Chrysippus often found himself in difficulties in this dispute, and that is no matter for astonishment: for the course he had chosen was not bound up with his dogma of fate, and, if he had known how, or had dared, to reason consistently, he would readily have adopted the whole hypothesis of Diodorus. We have seen already that the freedom he assigned to the soul, and his comparison of the cylinder, did not preclude the possibility that in reality all the acts of the human will were unavoidable consequences of fate. Hence it follows that everything which does not happen is impossible, and that there is nothing possible but that which actually comes to pass. Plutarch (*De Stoicor. Repugn.,* pp. 1053, 1054) discomfits him completely, on that point as well as on the dispute with Diodorus, and maintains that his opinion on possibility is altogether contrary to the doctrine of *fatum.* . . . Take note that Chrysippus recognized that past things were necessarily true, which Cleanthes had not been willing to admit.' . . .

It is sufficiently evident that Cicero when writing to Varro the words that have just been quoted (lib. 9, Ep. 4, *Ad Familiar.*) had not enough comprehension of the effect of Diodorus's opinion, since he found it preferable. He presents tolerably well in his book *De Fato* the opinions of those writers, but it is a pity that he has not always added the reasons which they employed. Plutarch in his treatise on the contradictions of the Stoics and M. Bayle are both surprised that Chrysippus was not of the same opinion as Diodorus, since he favours fatality. But Chrysippus and even his master Cleanthes were on that point more reasonable than is supposed. That will be seen as we proceed. It is open to question whether the past is more necessary than the future. Cleanthes held the opinion that it is. The objection is raised that it is necessary *ex hypothesi* for the future to happen, as it is necessary *ex hypothesi* for the past to have happened. But there is this difference, that it is not possible to act on the past state, that would be a contradiction; but it is possible to produce some effect on the future. Yet the hypothetical necessity of both is the same: the one cannot be changed, the other will not be; and once that is past, it will not be possible for it to be changed either.

23. With reference to the following sentence, see Supplement, p. 211 (*Pap.* V B 15:6).

24. An allusion to the title of Ludvig Holberg's comedy *Hexerie Eller blind Allarm, Danske Skue-Plads,* IV, no pagination.

25. See Supplement, pp. 200-05 (*Pap.* V B 14); Hegel, *Wissenschaft der Logik,* II, *Werke,* V, pp. 329-34; *J.A.,* V, pp. 329-34; *Science of Logic,* pp. 825-30, especially pp. 826-27:

From this course the method has emerged as the *self-knowing Notion that has itself,* as the absolute, both subjective and objective, *for its subject matter,* consequently as the pure correspondence of the Notion and its reality, as a concrete existence that is the Notion itself.

Accordingly, what is to be considered here as method is only the movement of the Notion itself, the nature of which movement has already been cognized; but *first,* there is now the added *significance* that the Notion is *everything,* and its movement is the *universal absolute activity,* the self-determining and self-realizing movement. The method is therefore to be recognized as the unrestrictedly universal, internal and external mode; and as the absolutely infinite force, to which no object, presenting itself as something external, remote from and independent of reason, could offer resistance or be of a particular nature in opposition to it, or could not be penetrated by it. It is therefore *soul and substance,* and anything whatever is comprehended and known in its truth only when it is *completely subjugated to the method;* it is the method proper to every subject matter because its activity is the Notion. This is also the truer meaning of its *universality;* according to the universality of reflection it is regarded merely as the method for *everything;* but according to the universality of the Idea, it is both the manner peculiar to cognition, to the *subjectively* self-knowing

Notion, and also the *objective* manner, or rather the *substantiality*, of things—
that is of Notions, in so far as they appear primarily to *representation* and
reflection as *others*. It is therefore not only the highest *force*, or rather the
sole and absolute *force* of reason, but also its supreme and sole *urge* to find
and cognize *itself by means of itself in everything*.

26. See Hegel, *Philosophie der Geschichte*, *Werke*, IX, pp. 129-35; *J.A.*, XI,
pp. 151-57; *The Philosophy of History* (tr. of *P.G.*, 2 ed., 1840; Kierkegaard
had 1 ed., 1837), tr. J. Sibree (New York: Dover, 1956), pp. 105-10, in which
the phases of the expression of Absolute Mind in history are outlined:
the Orient as unreflected consciousness; the Greek world, the period
of adolescence; the Roman state, the manhood of history, the realm of abstract universality; and the fourth phase of world history, old age as perfect
maturity and strength.

27. See Hegel, *Wissenschaft der Logik*, II, *Werke*, V, pp. 348-49; *J.A.*, V,
pp. 348-49; *Science of Logic*, p. 840: "We have shown that the determinateness which was a result is itself, by virtue of the form of simplicity into
which it has withdrawn, a fresh beginning; as this beginning is distinguished
from its predecessor precisely by that determinateness, cognition rolls on-
wards from content to content. First of all, this advance is determined as
beginning from simple determinatenesses, the succeeding ones becoming
ever *richer and more concrete*. For the result contains its beginning and its
course has enriched it by a fresh determinateness. The *universal* constitutes
the foundation; the advance is therefore not to be taken as a *flowing* from
one *other* to the next *other*. In the absolute method the Notion *maintains* itself
in its otherness, the universal in its particularization, in judgement and reality; at each stage of its further determination it raises the entire mass of its
preceding content, and by its dialectical advance it not only does not lose
anything or leave anything behind, but carries along with it all it has gained,
and inwardly enriches and consolidates itself."

28. The main character in Ludvig Holberg's *Mester Gert Westphaler Eller
den meget talende Barbeer*, *Danske Skue-Plads*, I, no pagination. The reference
to Hegelian Westphalers is presumably to Johan Ludvig Heiberg and
to the Danish jurist Carl Mettus Weiss (1809-1872), who published in J. L.
Heiberg's *Perseus* (II, 1838, pp. 47-99) an article, "*Om Statens historiske Udvi-
kling*," based on Hegel's idea of the four phases of world history (see notes
26, 27 above). In *Pap.* IV B 131, part of a draft of *Prefaces*, *KW* IX, Nicolaus
Notabene writes that the idea of the four world-historical monarchies "has
been taken up now in our time and one hears it everywhere, and at times it
is spoken of in such a way that one would think Gert W. to be the source."

29. See note to subtitle of *Repetition*, pp. 357-62, *KW* VI.

30. "To construct" (from Latin *construere*, to build) is imaginatively to
devise a representation of an idea, a theory. In contrast to a hypothesis,
which purports to represent actuality, a construction is fictional and may be
quite arbitrary. See *Anxiety*, p. 11, *KW* VIII (*SV* IV 283); Friedrich Wilhelm Joseph Schelling, *Vorlesungen über die Methode des academischen Studium*

(Stuttgart, Tübingen: 1830; *ASKB* 764), pp. 91-92; *On University Studies*, tr.
E. S. Morgan (Athens, Ohio: Ohio University Press, 1966), pp. 46-47:

Reality in general, and the reality of knowledge in particular, is not defined exclusively in terms of the universal, nor exclusively in terms of the
particular. Mathematical knowledge is neither of mere abstractions nor of
concrete things, but of the intuitively apprehended Idea. The representation of the universal and the particular in their unity is called construction,
which does not differ from demonstration. The unity is expressed in two
ways. First, underlying all geometrical constructions, such as the triangle,
the square, the circle, etc., is the same absolute form, and to grasp them
in their particularity nothing is required beyond the one universal and
absolute unity. Second, in respect to every figure the universal is identical
with the particular. For instance, what is true of the triangle in general is
also true of any particular triangle, and conversely. The particular triangle
stands for all triangles and is both unity and totality. The same unity is
expressed as form and essence, since the construction, which—in the sense
of a cognition—would seem to be mere form, is also the essence of the
construct itself.

See also Hegel, *Wissenschaft der Logik*, II, *Werke*, V, pp. 311-12; *J.A.*, V, pp.
311-12; *Science of Logic*, pp. 811-12:

Now the *mediation*, which we have next to consider in detail, may be
simple or may pass through several mediations. The mediating members
are connected with those to be mediated; but in this cognition, since mediation and theorem are not derived from the Notion, to which transition
into an opposite is altogether alien, the mediating determinations, in the
absence of any concept of connexion, must be imported from somewhere
or other as a preliminary material for the framework of the proof. This
preparatory procedure is the *construction*.

Among the relations of the content of the theorem, which relations
may be very varied, only those now must be adduced and demonstrated
which serve the proof. This provision of material only comes to have
meaning in the proof; in itself it appears blind and unmeaning. Subsequently, we see of course that it served the purpose of the proof to draw,
for example, such further lines in the geometrical figure as the construction specifies; but during the construction itself we must blindly obey; on
its own account, therefore, this operation is unintelligent, since the end
that directs it is not yet expressed. It is a matter of indifference whether
the construction is carried out for the purpose of a theorem proper or a
problem; such as it appears in the first instance *before* the proof, it is
something not derived from the determination given in the theorem or
problem, and is therefore a meaningless act for anyone who does not
know the end it serves, and in any case an act directed by an external end.

This meaning of the construction which at first is still concealed, comes
to light in the *proof*. As stated, the proof contains the mediation of what

the theorem enunciates as connected; through this mediation this connexion first *appears as necessary*. Just as the construction by itself lacks the subjectivity of the Notion, so the proof is a subjective act lacking objectivity.

See also Frederik Christian Sibbern, *Logik som Tænkelære* (Copenhagen: 1835; *ASKB* 777), pp. 137-63, especially pp. 137-39 (ed. tr.):

> The above-described analytical procedure presupposes *given* or *existing* objects from which the concepts are abstracted in that they are intellectually envisioned in these objects . . . . We have also seen (para. 20) that this analysis itself leads to a construction or a genetic representation, consequently to a synthetic procedure, which as yet has only appeared as an imitation. But in itself it is a free forging and *could* be constructed in other ways. . . . we have examples of the synthesis of actual intuitions for the formation of new intuitions in mathematics, in both arithmetic and geometry, in which the objects, whose nature, characteristics, and relations are to be investigated, must first be constructed by the science itself or be brought into existence, which takes place here independently of all experience.

30a. See *Postscript*, p. 118, *KW* XII.1 (*SV* VII 97)

31. See Supplement, p. 211 (*Pap.* V B 15:7); *Anxiety*, p. 11, *KW* VIII (*SV* IV 283); Schelling, *Philosophie der Offenbarung*, ed. Paulus, p. 611, where "manifestation" refers to the created world as a divine manifestation. Hegel rarely uses the expression but does have a similar concept in his view of the expression and self-objectivization of mind. See also *Encyclopädie*, III, para. 380, 383, 384 *Zusatz*, 386, *Werke*, VII², pp. 12-13, 27, 30-32, 35-36; *J.A.*, X, pp. 18-19, 33, 36-38, 41-42; *Hegel's Philosophy of Mind* (tr. of *E.W.*, III, 3 ed., 1830; Kierkegaard had the same text in *Werke*, 1 ed., 1840-45), tr. William Wallace, *Zusätze* (from *Werke*, 1 ed.), tr. A. V. Miller (Oxford: Oxford University Press, 1971), pp. 7, 16, 18-19, 22:

380

The 'concrete' nature of mind involves for the observer the peculiar difficulty that the several grades and special types which develop its intelligible unity in detail are not left standing as so many separate existences confronting its more advanced aspects. It is otherwise in external nature. There, matter and movement, for example, have a manifestation all their own—it is the solar system; and similarly the *differentiae* of sense-perception have a sort of earlier existence in the properties of *bodies*, and still more independently in the four elements. The species and grades of mental evolution, on the contrary, lose their separate existence and become factors, states, and features in the higher grades of development. . . .

383

This universality is also its determinate sphere of being. Having a being of its own, the universal is self-particularizing, whilst it still remains self-identical. Hence the special mode of mental being is *'manifestation'*. . . .

384

Zusatz. Self-manifestation is a determination belonging to mind as such; but it has three distinct forms. The first mode in which mind, as [only] in itself or as the logical Idea, manifests itself, consists in the direct release [*Umschlagen*] of the Idea into the immediacy of external and particularized existence. This release is the coming-to-be of Nature. . . .

This gives the second form of mind's manifestation. On this level, mind which is no longer poured out into the asunderness of Nature but exists for itself and is manifest to itself, opposes itself to unconscious Nature which just as much conceals mind as manifests it. . . .

Now this limitation is removed by absolute knowledge, which is the third and supreme manifestation of mind. On this level there vanishes, on the one hand, the dualism of a self-subsistent Nature or of mind poured out into asunderness, and, on the other hand, the merely incipient self-awareness of mind which, however, does not yet comprehend its unity with the former. Absolute mind knows that it posits being itself, that it is itself the creator of its Other, of Nature and finite mind, so that this Other loses all semblance of independence in face of mind, ceases altogether to be a limitation for mind and appears only as a means whereby mind attains to absolute being-for-self, to the absolute unity of what it is in itself and what it is for itself, of its Notion and its actuality.

The highest definition of the Absolute is that it is not merely mind in general but that it is mind which is absolutely manifest to itself, self-conscious, infinitely creative mind, which we have just characterized as the third form of its manifestation. . . .

386

The two first parts of the doctrine of Mind embrace the finite mind. Mind is the infinite Idea, and finitude here means the disproportion between the concept and the reality—but with the qualification that it is a shadow cast by the mind's own light—a show or illusion which the mind implicitly imposes as a barrier to itself, in order, by its removal, actually to realize and become conscious of freedom as *its* very being, i.e. to be fully *manifested.* . . .

See also Benedict Franz Xaver v. Baader, *Fermenta Cognitionis,* I–V (Berlin: 1822-24; *ASKB* 394), I, pp. 20-24, 50, 54-55, 65, on manifestation theory, particularly in Jakob Böhme and Hegel.

32. See Supplement, pp. 182, 211 (*Pap.* IV C 62; V B 15:8).

33. Carl Daub, *"Die Form der christlichen Dogmen- und Kirchen-Historie,"* *Zeitschrift für spekulative Theologie* (*ASKB* 354-57), ed. Bruno Bauer, I, 1836, p. 1 (ed. tr.): "The act of looking backward is, just like that of looking into the future, an act of divination; and if the prophet is well called a historian of the future, the historian is just as well called, or even better, a prophet of the past, of the historical."

34. See Supplement, p. 182 (*Pap.* IV C 62); *JP* III 2365, 3549 (*Pap.* IV C

31, 40); Leibniz, *Theodicy*, para. 406-16; *Opera*, II, pp. 620-23; *Theodicy*, pp. 366-73, especially p. 372: "The halls rose in a pyramid, becoming even more beautiful as one mounted towards the apex, and representing more beautiful worlds. Finally they reached the highest one which completed the pyramid, and which was the most beautiful of all: for the pyramid had a beginning, but one could not see its end; it had an apex, but no base; it went on increasing to infinity. That is (as the Goddess explained) because amongst an endless number of possible worlds there is the best of all, else would God not have determined to create any; but there is not any one which has not also less perfect worlds below it: that is why the pyramid goes on descending to infinity."

35. The Danish *Beundring* is literally translated as "admiration," as in "admiration" for Mozart's music (*Either/Or*, I, *KW* III; *SV* I 31). The context, however, and the association with Plato and Aristotle at the end of the next sentence require "wonder," as in "Wonder is the starting point of knowledge" (*Stages, KW* XI; *SV* VI 325). See Plato, *Theaetetus*, 155 d, *Opera*, II, pp. 40-41; *Collected Dialogues*, p. 860: "This sense of wonder [*admiratio in Opera*] is the mark of the philosopher. Philosophy indeed has no other origin . . ."; Aristotle, *Metaphysics*, 982 b; Bekker, II, p. 982; Hengstenberg, I, p. 5; *Works*, VIII: "For it is owing to their wonder that men both now begin and at first began to philosophize . . . ." In *Anxiety*, p. 146, *KW* VIII (*SV* IV 411), *Beundring* is used for "wonder" in connection with Descartes, *De passionibus animae*, II, LIII, *Admiratio; Opera*, p. 27; *The Passions of the Soul, Writings*, p. 306. On the other hand, a draft portion of *Johannes Climacus* (see Supplement, p. 266; *Pap.* IV B 13:23) on the same theme in Descartes has *Forundring* (wonder) as the Danish equivalent of *admiratio*. Benedict Franz Xaver v. Baader, who is mentioned in the sentence following references to Plato and Aristotle (see note 31 above), uses *Bewunderung*, the German cognate of *Beundring*, in his *Fermenta Cognitionis*, I, p. 39, where he discusses the object of admiration, adoration, and devotion. Therefore, Baader's usage does not explain the use of *Beundring* for "wonder." For a twentieth-century English translator of the Latin *admiratio*, the use of "admiration" would come too easily, but a now archaic meaning of "admiration" was "wonder," a direct derivative from the Latin root. Kierkegaard knew very little, if any, English (see *Letters*, Letter 2, p. 40, *KW* XXV). He did, however, know Latin very well, and, under the influence of the double meaning of the Latin *admiratio*, he perhaps conflated the two Danish terms, *Beundring* and *Forundring*, as synonymous (see p. 52 and note 13) with the one Latin word. Whatever the explanation may be, the context and *Pap.* IV B 13:23 make it clear that here and in *Anxiety* the term *Beundring* means "wonder." See *JP* II 2292; III 3284; V 5588 (*Pap.* VII¹ A 34; III A 107; IV C 10).

36. Benedict Franz Xaver v. Baader (1765-1841). The line has not been located.

37. With reference to the remainder of the paragraph, see Supplement, p. 211 (*Pap.* V B 15:9).

38. In Greek, μέθοδος (*methodos*) means "pursuit," "following after."
39. See *Postscript, KW* XII (*SV* VII 335-75).
40. See, for example, Hegel, *Wissenschaft der Logik,* I, *Werke,* III, pp. 64-65; *J.A.,* IV, pp. 74-75; *Science of Logic,* p. 71:

> The essential requirement for the science of logic is not so much that the beginning be a pure immediacy, but rather that the whole of the science be within itself a circle in which the first is also the last and the last is also the first.
>
> We see therefore that, on the other hand, it is equally necessary to consider as *result* that into which the movement returns as into its *ground.* In this respect the first is equally the ground, and the last a derivative; since the movement starts from the first and by correct inferences arrives at the last as the ground, this latter is a result. Further, the *progress* from that which forms the beginning is to be regarded as only a further determination of it, hence that which forms the starting point of the development remains at the base of all that follows and does not vanish from it. The progress does not consist merely in the derivation of an other, or in the effected transition into a genuine other; and in so far as this transition does occur it is equally sublated again. Thus the beginning of philosophy is the foundation which is present and preserved throughout the entire subsequent development, remaining completely immanent in its further determinations.

41. In its immediacy, experience prior to judgments is simply what it is. Truth/falsity pertains to judgments. See Supplement, p. 266 (*Pap.* IV B 13:22); *JP* II 1243 (*Pap.* IV C 56). Cf. *Irony, KW* II (*SV* VIII 285); *Postscript, KW* XII (*SV* VII 271).
42. Danish: *Tro* (belief, faith). Here, and in the following three pages, *Tro* is rendered as "belief," that is, "faith . . . in its direct and ordinary meaning," distinguished from faith "in the wholly eminent sense." See p. 87.
43. Cf. Hebrews 11:1.
44. See pp. 17, 38 and notes 34, 9.
45. See, for example, Hegel, *Geschichte der Philosophie,* II, *Werke,* XIV, p. 69; *J.A.,* XVIII, p. 69; *History of Philosophy,* I, p. 406: "Philosophy must, generally speaking, begin with a puzzle in order to bring about reflection; everything must be doubted, all presuppositions given up, to reach the truth as created through the Notion." See *Johannes Climacus,* p. 132 and notes 14, 15.
46. See Supplement, p. 265 (*Pap.* IV B 13:21); Sextus Empiricus, *Outlines of Pyrrhonism,* I, 30; *Opera,* I, p. 9; Loeb, I, pp. 20-21: "Hence we say that, while in regard to matters of opinion the Sceptic's End is quietude, in regard to things unavoidable it is 'moderate affection [μετριοπάθεια].' But some notable Sceptics have added the further definition 'suspension of judgement [ἐποχή] in investigations.' " See also Supplement, p. 261 (*Pap.* IV B 10:17) and note 48.
47. See note 46 above. Here the Greek word is not the equivalent of the

Danish *nægte Bifald* (deny assent) but designates the consequence of declined assent, that is, moderate feeling. See *JP* I 774, 776; II 1243, 1244 (*Pap.* IV A 72, B 5:13, C 56, 60).

48. See, for example, Diogenes Laertius, IX, 102-04; *Vitis,* II, pp. 176-77; Riisbrigh, I, pp. 446-47; Loeb, II, pp. 513-15:

> The dogmatists answer them by declaring that the Sceptics themselves do apprehend and dogmatize; for when they are thought to be refuting their hardest they do apprehend, for at the very same time they are asseverating and dogmatizing. Thus even when they declare that they determine nothing, and that to every argument there is an opposite argument, they are actually determining these very points and dogmatizing. The others reply, "We confess to human weaknesses; for we recognize that it is day and that we are alive, and many other apparent facts in life; but with regard to the things about which our opponents argue so positively, claiming to have definitely apprehended them, we suspend our judgement because they are not certain, and confine knowledge to our impressions. For we admit that we see, and we recognize that we think this or that, but how we see or how we think we know not. And we say in conversation that a certain thing appears white, but we are not positive that it really is white. As to our 'We determine nothing' and the like, we use the expressions in an undogmatic sense, for they are not like the assertion that the world is spherical. Indeed the latter statement is not certain, but the others are mere admissions. Thus in saying 'We determine nothing,' we are *not* determining even that."

49. See Sextus Empiricus, *Outlines of Pyrrhonism,* I, 119; *Opera,* p. 24; Loeb, I, p. 71: "These effects are due to distances; among effects due to locations are the following: the light of a lamp appears dim in the sun but bright in the dark; and the same oar bent when in the water but straight when out of the water . . .."

50. See Sextus Empiricus, *Outlines of Pyrrhonism,* I, 7; *Opera,* p. 2; Loeb, I, pp. 5-7:

> The Sceptic School, then, is also called "Zetetic" from its activity in investigation and inquiry, and "Ephectic" or Suspensive from the state of mind produced in the inquirer after his search, and "Aporetic" or Dubitative either from its habit of doubting and seeking, as some say, or from its indecision as regards assent and denial, and "Pyrrhonean" from the fact that Pyrrho appears to us to have applied himself to Scepticism more thoroughly and more conspicuously than his predecessors.

See also Diogenes Laertius, IX, 69-70; *Vitis,* II, pp. 163-64; Riisbrigh, I, p. 432; Loeb, II, pp. 482-83:

> All these were called Pyrrhoneans after the name of their master, but Aporetics, Sceptics, Ephectics, and even Zetetics, from their principles, if we may call them such—Zetetics or seekers because they were ever seek-

ing truth, Sceptics or inquirers because they were always looking for a solution and never finding one, Ephectics or doubters because of the state of mind which followed their inquiry, I mean, suspense of judgement, and finally Aporetics or those in perplexity, for not only they but even the dogmatic philosophers themselves in their turn were often perplexed. Pyrrhoneans, of course, they were called from Pyrrho.

51. See, for example, Sextus Empiricus, *Outlines of Pyrrhonism*, I, 14-15; *Opera*, p. 4; Loeb, I, p. 11:

Moreover, even in the act of enunciating the Sceptic formulae concerning things non-evident—such as the formula "No more (one thing than another)," or the formula "I determine nothing," or any of the others which we shall presently mention,—he does not dogmatize. For whereas the dogmatizer posits the things about which he is said to be dogmatizing as really existent, the Sceptic does not posit these formulae in any absolute sense; for he conceives that, just as the formula "All things are false" asserts the falsity of itself as well as of everything else, as does the formula "Nothing is true," so also the formula "No more" asserts that itself, like all the rest, is "No more (this than that)," and thus cancels itself along with the rest. And of the other formulae we say the same.

See also Diogenes Laertius, IX, 74-75; *Vitis*, II, p. 166; Riisbrigh, I, pp. 434-35; Loeb, II, pp. 488-89:

Thus by the expression "We determine nothing" is indicated their state of even balance; which is similarly indicated by the other expressions, "Not more (one thing than another)," and the like. But "Not more (one thing than another)" can also be taken positively [θετικῶς], indicating that two things are alike; for example, "The pirate is no more wicked than the liar." But the Sceptics meant it not positively but negatively, as when, in refuting an argument, one says, "Neither had more existence, Scylla or the Chimera."

52. *Vitis*, II, p. 178; Riisbrigh, I, p. 448; Loeb, II, pp. 517-19:

Against this criterion of appearances the dogmatic philosophers urge that, when the same appearances produce in us different impressions, *e.g.* a round or square tower, the Sceptic, unless he gives the preference to one or the other, will be unable to take any course; if on the other hand, say they, he follows either view, he is then no longer allowing equal value to all apparent facts. The Sceptics reply that, when different impressions are produced, they must both be said to appear; for things which are apparent are so called because they appear. The end to be realized they hold to be suspension of judgement [ἐποχή], which brings with it tranquillity [ἀταραξία] like its shadow: so Timon and Aenesidemus declare.

53. With reference to the following footnote, see Supplement, pp. 211-12 (*Pap.* V B 15:11).

54. See Supplement, p. 212 (*Pap.* V B 40:14).

55. With reference to the following six sentences, see Supplement, p. 212 (*Pap.* V B 15:12).

56. See *JP* III 3658 (*Pap.* IV C 89).

57. See, for example, *Von den Göttlichen Dingen und ihrer Offenbarung, Friedrich Heinrich Jacobi's Werke,* I-VI (Leipzig: 1812-25; *ASKB* 1722-28), III, pp. 367-68; *Ueber die Lehre des Spinoza in Briefen an Herrn Moses Mendelssohn,* IV[1], pp. 210-11 (ed. tr.):

> Dear Mendelssohn, we all are born in faith and must remain in faith, just as we all are born in society and must remain in society. How can we strive for certainty if certainty is not known to us beforehand, and how can it be known to us except through something that we already know with certainty? This leads to the concept of an immediate certainty, which not only needs no proof but totally excludes all proofs and is purely and simply the representation itself in harmony with the presented things (accordingly, this certainly has its ground in itself). The persuasion through proofs is a certainty at second hand, rests on comparison, and can never be thoroughly certain and perfect. Now, if every truth determination that does not originate in rational argument is faith, then persuasion and rational argument themselves must come from faith, and their power must be received solely from it.

A reference to David Hume might have been made in the text of *Fragments* in connection with Jacobi. Martensen had lectured on Hume (*Pap.* II C 18-19); Hamann wrote on Hume; and Jacobi not only touches on Hume at times but has a long piece on Hume and faith: *David Hume über den Glauben, Werke,* II, pp. 3-310. See *JP* II 1539-40 (*Pap.* I A 100, 237); *Pap.* II C 18-19, pp. 329-30, 25 (vol. XII, pp. 283-84), 27 (vol. XIII, p. 279).

58. With reference to the following sentence, see Supplement, p. 212 (*Pap.* V B 15:13).

59. See p. 83 and note 50.

60. See *Either/Or,* II, *KW* IV (*SV* II 158-59).

61. See, for example, *Wissenschaft der Logik, Werke,* IV, p. 69; *J.A.,* IV, p. 547; *Science of Logic,* p. 440; *Philosophie der Geschichte, Werke,* IX, p. 70; *J.A.,* XI, p. 92; *Philosophy of History,* pp. 56-57:

> External, sensuous motion itself is contradiction's immediate existence. Something moves, not because at one moment it is here and at another there, but because in this 'here', it at once is and is not. The ancient dialecticians must be granted the contradictions that they pointed out in motion; but it does not follow that therefore there is no motion, but on the contrary, that motion is *existent* contradiction itself.
>
> Similarly, internal self-movement proper, *instinctive urge* in general (the appetite or *nisus* of the monad, the entelechy of absolutely simple essence), is nothing else but the fact that something is, in one and the same respect, *self-contained and deficient, the negative of itself.* Abstract self-identity is not

as yet a livingness, but the positive, being in its own self a negativity, goes outside itself and undergoes alteration. Something is therefore alive only in so far as it contains contradiction within it, and moreover is this power to hold and endure the contradiction within it.

Universal History exhibits the *gradation* in the development of that principle whose substantial *purport* is the consciousness of Freedom. The analysis of the successive grades, in their abstract form, belongs to Logic; in their concrete aspect to the Philosophy of Spirit. . . .

Here we have only to indicate that Spirit begins with a germ of infinite possibility, but *only* possibility—containing its substantial existence in an undeveloped form, as the object and goal which it reaches only in its resultant—full reality. In actual existence Progress appears as an advancing from the imperfect to the more perfect; but the former must not be understood abstractly as *only* the imperfect, but as something which involves the very opposite of itself—the so-called perfect—as a *germ* or impulse.

62. See p. 81 and note 42.

63. See *JP* III 3085 (*Pap.* VI B 45).

CHAPTER V

1. See Supplement, p. 213 (*Pap.* V B 6:18). Chapters IV and VI in the draft became Appendix (p. 49) and Interlude (p. 72) in the final copy, and Chapter VII became Chapter V.

2. With reference to the remainder of the paragraph, see Supplement, p. 213 (*Pap.* V B 18).

3. See p. 43 and note 29.

4. See *Anxiety*, p. 3, *KW* VIII (*SV* IV 276).

5. Systematically (in principle) and compactly. See *Either/Or*, II, *KW* IV (*SV* II 193); *Anxiety*, pp. 113, 128, 137, *KW* VIII (*SV* IV 382, 395, 403); *JP* V 6137 (*Pap.* VIII¹ A 652).

6. With reference to the following paragraph, see Supplement, p. 213 (*Pap.* V B 6:19).

7. A reference to the legend of the seventy-two (rounded off to seventy) translators of the Septuagint (sometimes written LXX), a Greek version of the Old Testament made (c. 270 B.C.) for Ptolemy II by emissaries from Jerusalem.

8. In this case, however, it is the paradoxical historical fact of the eternal in time.

9. Danish: *opdrage* (to bring up, educate). Kierkegaard frequently uses verbs with the prefix *op*, for example, *opelske* (to love up, to love forth), *opbygge* (to build up). See *Works of Love*, *KW* XVI (*SV* IX 204-09).

10. With reference to the following two paragraphs and the footnote, see Supplement, p. 213 (*Pap.* V B 19).

11. See Diogenes Laertius, X, 124-26 (letter to Menoeccus); *Vitis*, II, pp. 235-36; Riisbrigh, I, pp. 501-02; Loeb, II, pp. 651-53:

Accustom thyself to believe that death is nothing to us, for good and evil imply sentience, and death is the privation of all sentience; therefore a right understanding that death is nothing to us makes the mortality of life enjoyable, not by adding to life an illimitable time, but by taking away the yearning after immortality. For life has no terrors for him who has thoroughly apprehended that there are no terrors for him in ceasing to live. Foolish, therefore, is the man who says that he fears death, not because it will pain when it comes, but because it pains in the prospect. Whatsoever causes no annoyance when it is present, causes only a groundless pain in the expectation. Death, therefore, the most awful of evils, is nothing to us, seeing that, when we are, death is not come, and when death is come, we are not. It is nothing, then, either to the living or to the dead, for with the living it is not and the dead exist no longer. But in the world, at one time men shun death as the greatest of all evils, and at another time choose it as a respite from the evils of life. The wise man does not deprecate life nor does he fear the cessation of life.

12. With reference to the following paragraph and the first two sentences of the next, see Supplement, p. 214 (*Pap.* V B 6:15, 17:2).

13. See *JP* I 452 (*Pap.* V A 10). Cf. Hans Lassen Martensen, *Den christelige Daab* (Copenhagen: 1843; *ASKB* 652), p. 23 (ed. tr.): "It is clear in and by itself that in the period when the essential task was to establish the Church in the world, much had to take forms different from those in later times, when the Church had put out its firm roots in the world, where God's kingdom had become just like nature."

14. See *JP* II 1335 (*Pap.* V A 8).

15. Ludvig Holberg, *Den Stundesløse*, I, 6, *Danske Skue-Plads*, V, no pagination (ed tr.): "A sailor's wife in the *Neuen Buden* [*Nyboder*, since 1631 quarters for naval personnel] had at one time brought thirty-two children into the world and was nevertheless no stouter than an ordinary pregnant woman. How can your grace comprehend this? . . . I can tell the story with details; the children were all baptized but straightway died."

16. A Greek neo-Pythagorean (first century A.D.) who held the Pythagorean-Platonic view of pre-existence and claimed that in an earlier life he had been the captain of an Egyptian ship. See *JP* III 3289 (*Pap.* IV A 19); Flavius Philostratus, *Apollonius of Tyana*, VI, 21, *Werke*, I-V, tr. Friedrich Jacobs (Stuttgart: 1828; *ASKB* 1143), V, p. 537; *Life of Apollonius of Tyana*, I-II, tr. F. C. Conybeare (Loeb, New York: Macmillan, 1912), II, p. 91.

17. See, for example, Hegel, *Philosophie der Geschichte*, *Werke*, IX, pp. 393, 407-08, 547; *J.A.*, XI, pp. 415, 429-30, 569; *Philosophy of History*, pp. 323-24, 335, 457:

The recognition of the identity of the Subject and God was introduced into the World when *the fulness of Time was come:* the consciousness of this identity is the recognition of God in his true essence. The material of Truth is *Spirit* itself—inherent vital movement. The nature of God as pure Spirit is manifested to man *in the Christian Religion.*

But what is Spirit? It is the one immutably homogeneous Infinite—pure Identity—which in its second phase separates itself from itself and makes this second aspect its own polar opposite, viz. as existence for and in self as contrasted with the Universal. But this separation is annulled by the fact that atomistic Subjectivity as simple relation to itself [as occupied with self alone] is itself the Universal, the Identical with self.

Reason in general is the Positive Existence [*Wesen*] of Spirit, divine as well as human. The distinction between Religion and the World is only this—that Religion as such, is Reason in the soul and heart—that it is a temple in which Truth and Freedom in God are presented to the conceptive faculty: the State, on the other hand, regulated by the selfsame Reason, is a temple of Human Freedom concerned with the perception and volition of a reality, whose purport may itself be called divine. Thus Freedom in the State is preserved and established by Religion, since moral rectitude in the State is only the carrying out of that which constitutes the fundamental principle of Religion. The process displayed in History is only the manifestation of Religion as Human Reason—the production of the religious principle which dwells in the heart of man, under the form of Secular Freedom. Thus the discord between the inner life of the heart and the actual world is removed.

That the History of the World, with all the changing scenes which its annals present, is this process of development and the realization of Spirit—this is the true *Theodicæa*, the justification of God in History. Only *this* insight can reconcile Spirit with the History of the World—viz., that what has happened, and is happening every day, is not only not "without God," but is essentially His Work.

18. See p. 37 and note 1.

19. Danish: *Afgrund* (without + ground: bottomless pit, abyss).

20. In Greek-Roman mythology, Clotho spins the thread of life, Lachesis measures it out, and Atropos cuts it.

21. Danish: *primitivt.* In Kierkegaard's writings, the term in its various forms does not mean "undeveloped" or "ancient" but pertains rather to an individual's freshness and authenticity in thinking, feeling, acting, and responding. It designates the opposite of habit, external conformity, and aping. See *JP* III 3558-61 and pp. 887-88; VII, p. 76.

22. With reference to the following paragraph, see Supplement, p. 214 (*Pap.* V B 6:16).

23. See Supplement, p. 214 (*Pap.* V B 6:22). In grammar, *casus* (case) is the relation of a noun, pronoun, or, in inflected languages, an adjective to other words in the sentence or the form indicating the relation. In Hebrew grammar, the genitive or possessive case is indicated by placing the noun

possessed directly before the noun that is the possessor, as in the English construction "the hand of the man." The noun possessed is said to be in the *status constructus*. The second noun or possessor is in the *status absolutus*.

24. With reference to the following four paragraphs, see Supplement, pp. 214-15 (*Pap.* V B 6:10, 12).

25. See Supplement, p. 215 (*Pap.* V B 22).

26. With reference to the remainder of the sentence and the following two sentences, see Supplement, p. 215 (*Pap.* V B 23:1).

27. With reference to the remainder of the paragraph, see Supplement, p. 215 (*Pap.* V B 6:17).

28. See p. 70 and note 39; Supplement, p. 198 (*Pap.* V B 6:8).

29. See I Corinthians 1:23.

30. With reference to the following paragraph, see Supplement, p. 216 (*Pap.* V B 6:14).

31. See Ludvig Holberg, *Erasmus Montanus Eller Rasmus Berg,* IV, 2, *Danske Skue-Plads,* V, no pagination. Berg (hill) is the name of the main character and also the name of the place where the comedy is set. Per Degn, in a discussion of Erasmus's view that the earth is round, argues that the good people of the town believe that the earth is flat and that "one must believe more in what so many say than in what one alone says. *Ergo,* you are wrong" (ed. tr.).

32. A legendary narrator of tall tales, which were based on the anecdotes of Karl Friedrich Hieronymus Freiherr von Münchhausen (1720-1797) of Bodenwerder, Hanover, Germany.

33. With reference to the following sentence, see Supplement, p. 216 (*Pap.* V B 6:13). See *JP* I 294, 343 (*Pap.* II A 369; X¹ A 624).

34. Surgeon Brause says of his assistant, Saft: "How like the devil he twists and turns so that he ends up either in the pantry or in the wine cellar." Adam Oehlenschläger, *Sovedrikken,* I (Copenhagen: 1808), p. 27 (ed. tr.).

35. See John 16:7.

36. See *JP* I 1008-18; VII, p. 31.

37. A conflation of the account (Plutarch, "Nicias," 30, *Lives*; Loeb, III, pp. 309-11) of the barber who spread word of the defeat in Sicily (413 B.C.) and the legend of the runner who fell dead after bringing news of the Marathon victory (490 B.C.) to Athens. See *Prefaces, KW* IX (*SV* V 18-19).

38. With reference to the following sentence, see Supplement, p. 216 (*Pap.* V B 6:21).

39. See John 21:25.

40. See John 19:30.

41. Danish: *ølnordisk,* literally "beer-Nordic," a play on *oldnordisk* and presumably an allusion to Nicolai Frederik Severin Grundtvig's interest in Norse mythology. See *JP* V 5740, 5819, 5832 (*Pap.* V A 58; VI A 73, B 235).

42. An allusion to N.F.S. Grundtvig's *Christelige Prædikener eller Søndags-Bog,* I-III (Copenhagen: 1827-30; *ASKB* 222-24), III, p. 614: "So there is singing and ringing among you" (a translation of Ephesians 5:19).

43. See Gotthilf Heinrich von Schubert, *Die Symbolik des Traumes* (Bamberg: 1821; *ASKB* 776), p. 38 (ed. tr.): ". . . voice of nature, the air music on Ceylon, which sings a frightful, merry minuet in the tones of a profoundly plaintive, heartrending voice." See *Irony, KW* II (*SV* XIII 329); *Postscript, KW* XII (*SV* VII 287).

44. With reference to the remainder of the paragraph, see Supplement, p. 216 (*Pap.* V B 6:20).

45. See *Anxiety*, p. 3, *KW* VIII (*SV* IV 276).

46. See, for example, Hegel, *Wissenschaft der Logik*, I, *Werke*, IV, pp. 57-73; *J.A.*, IV, pp. 535-51; *Science of Logic*, pp. 431-43, especially p. 433:

> *Contradiction resolves itself.* In the self-excluding reflection we have just considered, positive and negative, each in its self-subsistence, sublates itself; each is simply the transition or rather the self-transposition of itself into its opposite. This ceaseless vanishing of the opposites into themselves is the *first unity* resulting from contradiction; it is the null.

See also Hegel, *Encyclopädie*, I, *Logik, Werke*, VI, p. 242; *J.A.*, VIII, p. 280; *Hegel's Logic*, p. 174:

> Contradiction is the very moving principle of the world: and it is ridiculous to say that contradiction is unthinkable. The only thing correct in that statement is that contradiction is not the end of the matter, but cancels itself. But contradiction, when cancelled, does not leave abstract identity; for that is itself only one side of the contrariety. The proximate result of opposition (when realized as contradiction) is the Ground, which contains identity as well as difference superseded and deposited to elements in the completer notion.

See also *Either/Or*, II, *KW* IV (*SV* II 154-55, 200); *Postscript, KW* XII (*SV* VII 261, 264, 271, 284, 301, 365-66, 497).

47. See *Metaphysics*, 1005 b–1006 a, 1007 b, 1008 a; Bekker, II, pp. 1005-06, 1007, 1008; Hengstenberg, I, pp. 60, 65, 67; *Works*, VIII:

> For a principle which every one must have who understands anything that is, is not a hypothesis; and that which every one must know who knows anything, he must already have when he comes to a special study. Evidently then such a principle is the most certain of all; which principle this is, let us proceed to say. It is, that the same attribute cannot at the same time belong and not belong to the same subject and in the same respect; we must presuppose, to guard against dialectical objections, any further qualifications which might be added. This, then, is the most certain of all principles, since it answers to the definition given above. . . .
> —Some indeed demand that even this shall be demonstrated, but this they do through want of education, for not to know of what things one should demand demonstration, and of what one should not, argues want of education. For it is impossible that there should be demonstration of absolutely everything (there would be an infinite regress, so that there would

still be no demonstration); but if there are things of which one should not demand demonstration, these persons could not say what principle they maintain to be more self-evident than the present one.

Again, if all contradictory statements are true of the same subject at the same time, evidently all things will be one.

Also all things would on this view be one, as has been already said, and man and God and trireme and their contradictories will be the same. For if contradictories can be predicated alike of each subject, one thing will in no wise differ from another; for if it differ, this difference will be something true and peculiar to it. And . . . if one may with truth apply the predicates separately, the above-mentioned result follows none the less, and, further, it follows that all would then be right and all would be in error, and our opponent himself confesses himself to be in error.

48. A reference to a possible sequel, namely, *Concluding Unscientific Postscript* to Philosophical Fragments. See Supplement, pp. 185, 217-19 (*Pap.* V B 1:5-10, 12, 7-9, 20). In the Introduction to *Postscript, KW* XII (*SV* VII 1-8), Johannes Climacus discusses the relation of *Fragments* and *Postscript*.

49. See *Irony, KW* II (*SV* XIII 191).

50. See I Corinthians 2:7-9.

51. See Johann Georg Hamann's letter to Lavater, *Hamann's Schriften*, I-VIII, ed. Friedrich Roth and G. A. Wiener (Berlin, Leipzig: 1821-43; *ASKB* 536-44), V, p. 274 (ed. tr.): *"der weiseste Schriftsteller und dunkleste Prophet, der Executor des neuen Testaments, Pontius Pilatus* [the wisest author and most obscure prophet, the executor of the New Testament, Pontius Pilate]."

52. With reference to the following paragraph, see Supplement, p. 219 (*Pap.* V B 23:6).

JOHANNES CLIMACUS, OR
DE OMNIBUS DUBITANDUM EST

TITLE PAGE AND EPIGRAPH

TITLE PAGE. See Supplement, p. 234 (*Pap.* IV B 2:1, 3a:1).

Narrative. See Supplement, pp. 234–35 (*Pap.* IV B 16, 6).

EPIGRAPH. Benedict Spinoza, *On the Improvement of the Understanding; Opera philosophica omnia,* ed. August Gfroerer (Stuttgart: 1830; *ASKB* 788), p. 511; *The Chief Works of Benedict de Spinoza,* I–II, tr. R.H.M. Elwes (London: Bell, 1909–12), II, p. 29. See Supplement, p. 235 (*Pap.* IV B 2:13).

PLEASE NOTE

1. The Hegelian system of philosophy.

2. A common Danish expression about any extraordinary situation or imminent overwhelming event. See Ludvig Holberg, *Jule-Stue,* V, and *Hexerie Eller Blind Allarm,* I, 3, *Den Danske Skue-Plads,* I–VII (Copenhagen: 1788; *ASKB* 1566–67), II, IV, no pagination. See also *Postscript, KW* XII (*SV* VII 314).

3. The phrases "without authority" and "does not have authority" appear in many of Kierkegaard's works. See, for example, *Eighteen Upbuilding Discourses, KW* V (*SV* III 11, 271; IV 7, 73, 121; V 79).

INTRODUCTION

1. Presumably Hafnia (harbor), the Latin name for Copenhagen (in Danish, København: market harbor). See Supplement, p. 235 (*Pap.* IV B 2:2).

2. See *Fragments,* title page.

3. See Historical Introduction, p. ix and note 2.

4. Frederiksberg Castle and Gardens, on the west side of what is now greater Copenhagen.

5. With reference to the following two sentences, see Supplement, p. 235 (*Pap.* IV B 3a:7); *Stages, KW* XI (*SV* VI 194).

6. With reference to the following sentence, see Supplement, p. 236 (*Pap.* IV B 5:2).

7. Frederik O. Lange taught Greek in the Borgerdydsskole, which Kierkegaard attended. His doctoral dissertation was *De casuum universis causis et rationibus commentatio grammatica* (Copenhagen: 1836; *ASKB* 610). His Greek grammar for use in Danish schools, *Det græske Sprogs Grammatik* (3 ed., Copenhagen: 1830; *ASKB* 992), pp. 243–44, 249, 250, 262–64, covers the relations referred to in the following sentences.

8. With reference to the remainder of the paragraph, see Supplement, p. 236 (*Pap.* IV B 3a:9).

9. See Supplement, p. 236 (*Pap.* IV B 3a:10); also, for example, *Anxiety,* pp. 32, 129-32, *KW* VIII (*SV* IV 304, 396-99); *Stages, KW* XI (*SV* VI 171, 307, 353, 355).

10. With reference to the following sentence, see Supplement, p. 236 (*Pap.* IV B 3a:11).

11. With reference to the following two sentences, see Supplement, p. 237 (*Pap.* IV B 3a:12).

12. See *JP* III 2309-15.

13. See *Point of View, KW* XXII (*SV* XIII 565).

14. Cf. *Postscript, KW* XII (*SV* VII 279-80, 335-36).

15. With reference to the following seven lines, see Supplement, p. 237 (*Pap.* IV B 3c).

PARS PRIMA

INTRODUCTION

1. See Supplement, p. 238 (*Pap.* IV B 2:18).

2. With reference to the following paragraph, see Supplement, p. 238 (*Pap.* IV B 4, 5:1).

3. With reference to the remainder of the paragraph and the following two paragraphs, see Supplement, p. 238 (*Pap.* IV B 5:2).

4. With reference to the remainder of the paragraph, see Supplement, p. 239 (*Pap.* IV B 7:1).

5. See John 16:21.

6. With reference to the remainder of the paragraph, see Supplement, p. 239 (*Pap.* IV B 5:10).

7. With reference to the following sentence, see Supplement, p. 239 (*Pap.* IV B 5:3, 7:2).

8. With reference to the following sentence, see Supplement, p. 239 (*Pap.* IV B 7:3).

9. With reference to the following sentence, see Supplement, pp. 239-40 (*Pap.* IV B 5:4).

10. See Supplement, pp. 239-40 (*Pap.* IV B 5:4); G.W.F. Hegel, *Vorlesungen über die Geschichte der Philosophie,* III, *Georg Wilhelm Friedrich Hegel's Werke. Vollständige Ausgabe,* I–XVIII, ed. Philipp Marheineke et al. (Berlin: 1832-45; *ASKB* 549-65), XV, p. 335; *Jubiläumsausgabe [J.A.],* I-XXVI, ed. Hermann Glockner (Stuttgart: 1927-40), XIX, p. 335; *Hegel's Lectures on the History of Philosophy* (tr. of *G.P.,* 2 ed., 1840-44; Kierkegaard had 1 ed., 1833-36), I-III, tr. E. S. Haldane and Frances H. Simson (New York: Humanities Press, 1955), III, p. 224:

Descartes expresses the fact that we must begin from thought as such alone, by saying that we must doubt everything (*De omnibus dubitandum est*); and that is an absolute beginning. He thus makes the abolition of all determinations the first condition of Philosophy. This first proposition has not, however, the same signification as Scepticism, which sets before it no other aim than doubt itself, and requires that we should remain in this indecision of mind, an indecision wherein mind finds its freedom.

For Descartes's view of doubt, see, for example, *Discourse on Method*, II, and *Meditations on First Philosophy*, I; *Renati Des-Cartes opera philosophica* (Amsterdam: 1678; *ASKB* 473), pp. 8, 11-12, 5; *Descartes' Philosophical Writings*, ed. and tr. Norman Kemp Smith (London: Macmillan, 1952), pp. 126, 129, 196:

> In respect, however, of the opinions which I have hitherto been entertaining, I thought that I could not do better than decide on emptying my mind of them one and all, with a view to the replacing of them by others more tenable, or, it may be, to the readmitting of them, on their being shown to be in conformity with reason.

> So, in like manner, in place of the numerous precepts which have gone to constitute logic, I came to believe that the four following rules would be found sufficient, always provided I took the firm and unswerving resolve never in a single instance to fail in observing them.
> The first was to accept nothing as true which I did not evidently know to be such, that is to say, scrupulously to avoid precipitance and prejudice, and in the judgments I passed to include nothing additional to what had presented itself to my mind so clearly and so distinctly that I could have no occasion for doubting it.

> It is now several years since I first became aware how many false opinions I had from my childhood been admitting as true, and how doubtful was everything I have subsequently based on them. Accordingly I have ever since been convinced that if I am to establish anything firm and lasting in the sciences, I must once for all, and by a deliberate effort, rid myself of all those opinions to which I have hitherto given credence, starting entirely anew, and building from the foundations up.

11. With reference to the following two sentences, see Supplement, p. 240 (*Pap.* IV B 5:5).

12. See Aristotle, *Politics*, 1312 a; *Aristoteles graece*, I-II, ed. Immanuel Bekker (Berlin: 1831; *ASKB* 1074-75), II, p. 1312; *The Works of Aristotle*, I-XII, ed. J. A. Smith and W. D. Ross (Oxford: Oxford University Press, 1908-52), X; *JP* IV 4418 (*Pap.* IV A 10).·

13. See, for example, Hans Lassen Martensen, in a review article (*Maanedsskrift for Litteratur*, XVI, 1836, pp. 518-19) on Johan Ludvig Heiberg's *Indledningsforedrag til det i November 1834 begyndte logiske Cursus paa den kongelige militaire Høiskole* (ed. tr.): "doubt is the beginning of wisdom. . . . Descartes had indeed expressed this thought and advanced the demand for a presuppositionless philosophy, but a long time was needed before the thought could be developed into a concept and before the expressed demand

for a presuppositionless philosophy could actually be realized. The demand '*de omnibus dubitandum est*' is not as easily done as said, because it does not demand a finite doubt, the popular doubt about this or that, whereby one always keeps something in reserve that is not drawn into the doubt."

Kierkegaard's notes (*Pap.* II C 18, p. 328) on Martensen's lecture (Nov. 29, 1837) on Kant's predecessors begin with a reference to Descartes: "*Descartes* (d. 1650) said: *cogito ergo sum* and *de omnibus dubitandum est*. He thereby produced the principle for modern Protestant subjectivity. By means of the latter proposition—*de omnibus dubitandum est*—he gave his essential watchword, for he thereby denoted a doubt not about this or that but about everything . . . ."

14. See, for example, Hegel, *Phänomenologie des Geistes, Werke,* II, pp. 64-65; *J.A.,* II, pp. 72-73; *The Phenomenology of Mind* (tr. of *P.G.,* 3 ed., 1841; Kierkegaard had 2 ed., 1832), tr. J. B. Baillie (New York: Harper, 1967), pp. 136-37:

> If we stick to a system of opinion and prejudice resting on the authority of others, or upon personal conviction, the one differs from the other merely in the conceit which animates the latter. Scepticism, directed to the whole compass of phenomenal consciousness, on the contrary, makes mind for the first time qualified to test what truth is; since it brings about a despair regarding what are called natural views, thoughts, and opinions, which it is a matter of indifference to call personal or belonging to others, and with which the consciousness, that proceeds straight away to criticize and test, is still filled and hampered, thus being, as a matter of fact, incapable of what it wants to undertake. . . . —The scepticism which ends with the abstraction "nothing" or "emptiness" can advance from this not a step farther, but must wait and see whether there is possibly anything new offered, and what that is—in order to cast it into the same abysmal void. When once, on the other hand, the result is apprehended, as it truly is, as *determinate* negation, a new form has thereby immediately arisen; and in the negation the transition is made by which the progress through the complete succession of forms comes about of itself.

See Supplement, p. 246 (*Pap.* IV B 2:4).

15. See, for example, Hegel, *Geschichte der Philosophie,* III, *Werke,* XV, pp. 334-35; *J.A.,* XIX, pp. 334-35; *History of Philosophy,* III, pp. 223-24:

> In Philosophy Descartes struck out quite original lines; with him the new epoch in Philosophy begins, whereby it was permitted to culture to grasp in the form of universality the principle of its higher spirit in thought, just as Boehme grasped it in sensuous perceptions and forms. Descartes started by saying that thought must necessarily commence from itself; all the philosophy which came before this, and specially what proceeded from the authority of the Church, was for ever after set aside. . . . In order to do justice to Descartes' thoughts it is necessary for us to be assured of the necessity for his appearance; the spirit of his philosophy is simply knowl-

edge as the unity of Thought and Being. . . . Descartes expresses the fact that we must begin from thought as such alone, by saying that we must doubt everything (*De omnibus dubitandum est*); and that is an absolute beginning. He thus makes the abolition of all determinations the first condition of Philosophy.

CHAPTER I

1. For a draft version of the opening of Chapter I, see Supplement, p. 240 (*Pap.* IV B 7:5).

2. See Supplement, p. 240 (*Pap.* IV B 7:6).

3. With reference to the following sentence, see Supplement, pp. 240-41 (*Pap.* IV B 7:7).

4. With reference to the remainder of the paragraph and the first line of the next paragraph, see Supplement, p. 241 (*Pap.* IV B 7:8).

5. With reference to the remainder of the sentence, see Supplement, p. 241 (*Pap.* IV B 7:9).

6. See Supplement, p. 241 (*Pap.* IV B 7:10).

7. With reference to the following sentence, see Supplement, p. 241 (*Pap.* IV B 5:7).

8. According to legend, purple or violet-red dye was discovered by a dog rooting among sea-snails. See *Practice in Christianity, KW* XX (*SV* XII 191).

9. On the concept of "leap" in Kierkegaard's writings and in his journals and papers, see *JP* III 2338-59 and p. 794; VII, p. 56.

10. With reference to the following three sentences, see Supplement, p. 242 (*Pap.* IV B 7:11).

11. With reference to the following two paragraphs, see Supplement, p. 242 (*Pap.* IV B 2:10).

12. With reference to the remainder of the paragraph, see Supplement, p. 242 (*Pap.* IV B 7:12).

13. With reference to an extended draft version of the following sentence, see Supplement, p. 242 (*Pap.* IV B 7:13).

14. The Danish term here is *Moment*, not *Øieblik*, which is usually translated "moment" and usually has a special meaning in Kierkegaard's writings (see *JP* III 2739-44 and p. 821; VII, p. 62). Here "moment" is used as it is found in Hegel's works: an element, a factor, or a particular in a whole, a constituent or a part of a unity. See, for example, *Wissenschaft der Logik, Werke,* III, pp. 108, 111, 121; *J.A.,* IV, pp. 118, 121, 131; *Hegel's Science of Logic* (tr. of *W.L.*, Lasson ed., 1923; Kierkegaard had 2 ed., 1833-34), tr. A. V. Miller (New York: Humanities Press, 1969), pp. 105, 107, 116:

MOMENTS OF BECOMING: COMING-TO-BE
AND CEASING-TO-BE

Becoming is the unseparatedness of being and nothing, not the unity which abstracts from being and nothing; but as the unity of *being* and *nothing* it is this *determinate* unity in which there *is* both being and nothing. But in so far as being and nothing, each unseparated from its other, *is,* each *is not.* They *are* therefore in this unity but only as vanishing, sublated moments. They sink from their initially imagined *self-subsistence* to the status of *moments,* which are still *distinct* but at the same time are sublated.

Grasped as thus distinguished, each moment is in this *distinguishedness* as a unity with the *other.* Becoming therefore contains being and nothing as *two* such unities, *each* of which is itself a unity of being and nothing; the one is being as immediate and as relation to nothing; and the other is nothing as immediate and as relation to being; the determinations are of unequal values in these unities.

Something is sublated only in so far as it has entered into unity with its opposite; in this more particular signification as something reflected, it may fittingly be called a *moment.* In the case of the lever, weight and distance from a point are called its mechanical moments on account of the sameness of their effect, in spite of the contrast otherwise between something real, such as a weight, and something ideal, such as a mere spatial determination, a line. We shall often have occasion to notice that the technical language of philosophy employs Latin terms for reflected determinations, either because the mother tongue has no words for them or if it has, as here, because its expression calls to mind more that is immediate, whereas the foreign language suggests more what is reflected.

The more precise meaning and expression which being and nothing receive, now that they are *moments,* is to be ascertained from the consideration of determinate being as the unity in which they are preserved.

This mediation with itself which something is *in itself,* taken only as negation of the negation, has no concrete determinations for its sides; it thus collapses into the simple oneness which is *being.* Something *is,* and *is,* then, also a determinate being; further, it is *in itself* also *becoming,* which, however, no longer has only being and nothing for its moments. One of these, being, is now determinate being, and, further *a* determinate being. The second is equally a *determinate* being, but determined as a negative of the something—an *other.* Something as a *becoming* is a transition, the moments of which are themselves somethings, so that the transition is *alternation*—a becoming which has already become *concrete.*

15. With reference to the remainder of the sentence and the following sentence, see Supplement, p. 242 (*Pap.* IV B 7:14).

16. The issues of possibility and necessity, past, present, and future, only touched upon here, become an important part of *Fragments.* See especially "Interlude," pp. 73-88 (*SV* IV 235-51).

17. For a continuation of the paragraph, see Supplement, p. 243 (*Pap.* IV B 7:15).

18. With reference to the end of the paragraph and the following chapter heading, see Supplement, p. 243 (*Pap.* IV B 7:16).

CHAPTER II

1. With reference to the chapter title and the following three paragraphs, see Supplement, pp. 239-40, 243 (*Pap.* IV B 5:4, 2:17).

2. With reference to the following sentence, see Supplement, p. 243 (*Pap.* IV B 7:17).

3. See p. 80 and note 35; *Anxiety*, p. 146, *KW* VIII (*SV* IV 411).

4. With reference to the remainder of the paragraph, see Supplement, p. 243 (*Pap.* IV B 2:6).

5. See Supplement, pp. 239-40 (*Pap.* IV B 5:4).

6. With reference to the remainder of the paragraph, see Supplement, p. 244 (*Pap.* IV B 7:19).

7. See Diogenes Laertius, IX, 63; *Diogenis Laertii de vitis philosophorum*, I-II (Leipzig: 1833; *ASKB* 1109), II, pp. 160-61; *Diogen Laërtses filosofiske Historie*, I-II, tr. Børge Riisbrigh (Copenhagen: 1812; *ASKB* 1110-11), I, p. 429; *Lives of Eminent Philosophers*, I-II, tr. R. D. Hicks (Loeb, New York: Putnam, 1925), II, p. 477.

8. With reference to the remainder of the paragraph, see Supplement, p. 244 (*Pap.* IV B 7:20).

9. See p. 95 and note 11.

10. See Supplement, p. 244 (*Pap.* IV B 7:21).

11. With reference to the remainder of the paragraph and the following paragraph, see Supplement, p. 246 (*Pap.* IV B 2:4).

12. With reference to the following two sentences, see Supplement, p. 245 (*Pap.* IV B 7:22).

13. See Peter Michael Stilling, *Philosophiske Betragtninger over den spekulative Logiks Betydning for Videnskaben* (Copenhagen: 1842), pp. 9-11, 19-21, 38-42, 68-69.

14. See Johan Ludvig Heiberg, *Perseus*, no. 1, 1837 (*ASKB* 569), pp. 36-37, 39-40.

15. See, for example, Hegel, *Phänomenologie, Werke*, II, pp. 402-03; *J.A.*, II, pp. 410-11; *Phenomenology*, pp. 554-55:

. . . here the first and foremost moment is Absolute Being, spirit absolutely self-contained, so far as it is simple eternal substance. But in the process of realizing its constitutive notion, which consists in being spirit, that substance passes over into a form where it exists for an other; its self-identity becomes actual Absolute Being, actualized in self-sacrifice; it becomes a self, but a self that is transitory and passes away. Hence the third stage is the return of self thus alienated, the substance thus abased, into its first primal simplicity. Only when this is done is spirit presented and manifested as spirit.

16. See Hegel, *Encyclopädie der philosophischen Wissenschaften, Erster Theil, Die Logik*, para. 86, *Werke*, VI, p. 165; *J.A.* (*System der Philosophie*), VIII, p. 203; *Hegel's Logic* (tr. of *L.*, 3 ed., 1830; Kierkegaard's ed., 1840, had the

same text, plus *Zusätze*), tr. William Wallace (Oxford: Oxford University Press, 1975), p. 124:

> Pure *Being* makes the beginning: because it is on one hand pure thought, and on the other immediacy itself, simple and indeterminate; and the first beginning cannot be mediated by anything, or be further determined. All doubts and admonitions, which might be brought against beginning the science with abstract empty being, will disappear if we only perceive what a beginning naturally implies.

17. A servant in Ludvig Holberg's *Jean de France, Danske Skue-Plads*, I, no pagination. See *Irony, KW* II (*SV* XIII 325, 484); *Stages, KW* XI (*SV* VI 88).

18. With reference to the following two sentences, see Supplement, p. 245 (*Pap.* IV B 7:26).

19. On the theme of authority, see *JP* I 182-92; VII, p. 8.

20. With reference to the following sentence, see Supplement, p. 245 (*Pap.* IV B 7:27).

21. With reference to the following sentence, see Supplement, p. 245 (*Pap.* IV B 7:28).

22. See Supplement, p. 246 (*Pap.* IV B 2:9).

23. See Supplement, p. 246 (*Pap.* IV B 2:4).

24. See Supplement, p. 246 (*Pap.* IV B 2:16).

25. See *JP* V 5209 (*Pap.* II 'A 36).

26. See p. 99 and note 21.

CHAPTER III

1. With reference to the following eight sentences, see Supplement, pp. 246-47 (*Pap.* IV B 2:3, 8:2,11).

2. See Diogenes Laertius, VIII, 10; *Vitis*, II, pp. 94-95; Riisbrigh, I, p. 368; Loeb, II, p. 329: "For five whole years they had to keep silence, merely listening to his discourses without seeing him, until they passed an examination, and thenceforward they were admitted to his house and allowed to see him."

3. Diogenes of Sinope (c. 4 B.C.), archetype of the Greek Cynics. See Diogenes Laertius, VI, 36-37; *Vitis*, I, pp. 264-65; Riisbrigh, I, pp. 244-45; Loeb, II, pp. 37-39.

4. With reference to the following two sentences, see Supplement, p. 247 (*Pap.* IV B 8:4).

5. With reference to the following sentence, see Supplement, p. 247 (*Pap.* IV B 8:6).

6. The source of this line has not been located. See *Stages, KW* XI (*SV* VI 163); *Christian Discourses, KW* XVII (*SV* X 77). Cf. *Pap.* X² A 442; *JP* IV 4460 (*Pap.* X² A 642).

PARS SECUNDA

INTRODUCTION

1. See Supplement, pp. 247-48 (*Pap.* IV B 13:1, 9:2).

2. Theodor Gottlieb von Hippel, *Lebensläufe nach aufsteigender Linie*, I-III (Berlin: 1778-81; *ASKB* 1706-09).

3. For a continuation of the paragraph, see Supplement, p. 248 (*Pap.* IV B 9:3).

4. With reference to the following four sentences, see Supplement, p. 248 (*Pap.* IV B 8:13).

5. With reference to the following two sentences, see Supplement, pp. 248-49 (*Pap.* IV B 5:9, 8:5, 8:12).

6. With reference to the remainder of the Introduction, see Supplement, p. 249 (*Pap.* IV B 8:10).

7. See Supplement, pp. 249-50 (*Pap.* IV B 2:5,7, 8:9).

CHAPTER I

1. See Supplement, pp. 250-51 (*Pap.* IV B 5:6, 13:4,12).

2. With reference to the remainder of the sentence, see Supplement, p. 252 (*Pap.* IV B 14:1).

3. With reference to the following ten paragraphs, see Supplement, p. 252 (*Pap.* IV B 10:6).

4. See Supplement, p. 252 (*Pap.* IV B 14:3).

5. With reference to the remainder of the paragraph and the following eleven paragraphs, see Supplement, pp. 252-53 (*Pap.* IV B 10a).

6. With reference to the following seven paragraphs, see Supplement, p. 254 (*Pap.* IV B 10:1,9).

7. See pp. 81-83.

8. See Plato, *Sophist*, 236 e-264 b; *Platonis quae exstant opera*, I-XI, ed. Friedrich Ast (Leipzig: 1819-32; *ASKB* 1144-54), II, pp. 266-351; *The Collected Dialogues of Plato*, ed. Edith Hamilton and Huntington Cairns (Princeton: Princeton University Press, 1963), pp. 979-1011, especially 237 a-b, 264 a-b, pp. 979-80, 1011:

> STRANGER: . . . It is extremely hard, Theaetetus, to find correct terms in which one may say or think that falsehoods have a real existence, without being caught in a contradiction by the mere utterance of such words.
> THEAETETUS: Why?
> STRANGER: The audacity of the statement lies in its implication that 'what is not' has being, for in no other way could a falsehood come to have being. But, my young friend, when we were of your age the great Parmenides from beginning to end testified against this, constantly telling us what he also says in his poem, 'Never shall this be proved—that things

that are not are, but do thou, in thy inquiry, hold back thy thought from this way.

So we have the great man's testimony, and the best way to obtain a confession of the truth may be to put the statement itself to a mild degree of torture. So, if it makes no difference to you, let us begin by studying it on its own merits.

STRANGER: Well then, since we have seen that there is true and false statement, and of these mental processes we have found thinking to be a dialogue of the mind with itself, and judgment to be the conclusion of thinking, and what we mean by 'it appears' a blend of perception and judgment, it follows that these also, being of the same nature as statement, must be, some of them and on some occasions, false.

9. See Friedrich Ernst Daniel Schleiermacher, *Der christliche Glaube*, I-II (3 ed., Berlin: 1835; *ASKB* 258), I, pp. 27-30; *The Christian Faith*, tr. H. R. MackIntosh and J. S. Stewart (Edinburgh: Clark, 1960), pp. 22-24. On feelings and truth, see Schleiermacher, *Ueber die Religion* (Berlin: 1843; *ASKB* 271), p. 91; *On Religion: Addresses in Response to Its Cultured Critics*, tr. Terrence N. Tice (Richmond: Knox, 1969), p. 99: "Everything caught up in the immediacy of religion is true, for how could it be otherwise? But what is immediate? Only what has not yet been filtered through concepts but has emerged in feeling, fresh and uncontaminated."

10. *Zeitschrift für spekulative Theologie*, 1838 (*ASKB* 354-57).

11. See Aristotle, *Metaphysics*, 1012 a; Bekker, II, p. 1012; *Aristoteles Metaphysik*, I-II, tr. Ernst Wilhelm Hengstenberg (Bonn: 1824; *ASKB* 1084), I, p. 77; *Works*, VIII: "While the doctrine of Heraclitus, that all things are and are not, seems to make everything true, that of Anaxagoras, that there is an intermediate between the terms of a contradiction, seems to make everything false; for when things are mixed, the mixture is neither good nor not-good, so that one cannot say anything that is true." See Supplement, p. 254 (*Pap.* IV B 2:15).

12. Wilhelm Gottlieb Tennemann, *Geschichte der Philosophie*, I-XI (Leipzig: 1798-1819; *ASKB* 815-26).

13. With reference to the following paragraph, see Supplement, p. 254 (*Pap.* IV B 10:10).

14. With reference to the following paragraph, see Supplement, p. 255 (*Pap.* IV B 10:14).

15. *Vitis*, I, p. 16; Riisbrigh, I, p. 15; Loeb, I, pp. 35-39, especially p. 37:

He held there was no difference between life and death. "Why then," said one, "do you not die?" "Because," said he, "there is no difference." To the question which is older, day or night, he replied: "Night is the older by one day." Some one asked him whether a man could hide an evil deed from the gods: "No," he replied, "nor yet an evil thought." To the adulterer who inquired if he should deny the charge upon oath he replied that perjury was no worse than adultery. Being asked what is difficult, he replied, "To know oneself." "What is easy?" "To give advice to another." "What is most pleasant?" "Success." "What is the divine?" "That which has neither beginning nor end."

16. With reference to the following three paragraphs, see Supplement, p. 255 (*Pap.* IV B 14:6). With reference to the remainder of the chapter, see Supplement, pp. 255-56 (*Pap.* IV B 10:11).

17. In *De omnibus,* Johannes Climacus uses "actuality" and "reality" (*Virkelighed, Realitet*) synonymously, a practice not followed in the other pseudonymous and signed works. Here "reality" signifies "actuality" (the spatial-temporal). See *JP* III 3651-55 and pp. 900-03.

18. With reference to the following five paragraphs, see Supplement, p. 256 (*Pap.* IV B 13:18).

19. See *JP* III 3281 (*Pap.* III A 11).

20. In *Fragments,* pp. 46, 101, 108-09, and *Postscript, KW* XII (*SV* VII 20, 170-72, 261, 264, 271, 284, 287, 299, 301, 365-66, 389, 497, 526), Johannes Climacus uses the terms "contradiction" (*Modsigelse*), "principle of contradiction" (*Contradictionsprincip, Modsigelsens Grundsætning*), and "self-contradiction" (*Selvmodsigelse*) to designate a logical principle governing the relation of ideas. Here in *De omnibus,* Climacus uses "contradiction" in discussing the nature of consciousness and the relation of thought (and language) and thing, ideality and reality (actuality).

In discussing "the purely ideal" and the "object of immediate perception or intuition," the abstract (ideal) and the concrete (real), Frederik Christian Sibbern (1785-1872), professor of philosophy at the University of Copenhagen when Kierkegaard was a student, used the term "opposition" or "contrast" (*Modsætning*) rather than "contradiction" in his *Logik som Tænkelære* (Copenhagen: 1835; *ASKB* 777), pp. 61-64, 89-90. Inasmuch as "contrast" rather than "contradiction" seems to be a more appropriate term here in *De omnibus,* a clue to the use of "contradiction" must be sought elsewhere than in Sibbern. The most likely source is Hegel's *Phänomenologie, Werke,* II, p. 67; *J.A.,* II, p. 75; *Phenomenology,* p. 139, to which Climacus refers without mentioning the title (see note 26 below). The first section is on "consciousness," and in the Introduction Hegel states that the entire work is concerned with "relating science to phenomenal knowledge," which in other terms is Climacus's question.

This exposition, viewed as a process of relating science to phenomenal knowledge, and as an inquiry and critical examination into the reality of knowing, does not seem able to be effected without some presupposition which is laid down as an ultimate criterion. For an examination consists in applying an accepted standard, and, on the final agreement or disagreement therewith of what is tested, deciding whether the latter is right or wrong; and the standard in general, and so science, were this the criterion, is thereby accepted as the essence or inherently real *(Ansich)*. But, here, where science first appears on the scene, neither science nor any sort of standard has justified itself as the essence or ultimate reality; and without this no examination seems able to be instituted.

This *contradiction* [ed. italics] and the removal of it will become more definite if, to begin with, we call to mind the abstract determinations of knowledge and of truth as they are found in consciousness. Consciousness, we find, *distinguishes* from itself something, to which at the same time it *relates* itself; or, to use the current expression, there is something *for* consciousness; and the determinate form of this process of relating, or of there being something for a consciousness, is knowledge. But from this being for another we distinguish being in itself or *per se;* what is related to knowledge is likewise distinguished from it, and posited as also existing outside this relation; the aspect of being *per se* or in itself is called Truth.

21. With reference to the following sentence, see Supplement, p. 256 *(Pap.* IV B 14:7).

22. See note 17 above.

23. For an extension of the sentence, see Supplement, p. 256 *(Pap.* IV B 14:8).

24. With reference to the following two sentences, see Supplement, p. 257 *(Pap.* IV B 14:9).

25. With reference to the following three sentences, see Supplement, p. 257 *(Pap.* IV B 10:5,7). With reference to the following paragraph and footnote, see Supplement, pp. 257-58 *(Pap.* IV B 10:12).

26. See Hegel, *Phänomenologie, Werke,* II, pp. 73, 131, 174; *J.A.,* II, pp. 81, 139, 182; *Phenomenology,* pp. 147, 215, 269: "A Consciousness"; "B Self-Consciousness"; "C [Free Concrete Mind] (AA) Reason."

27. With reference to the following sentence, see Supplement, p. 258 *(Pap.* IV B 10:2,13; 13:2).

28. With reference to the following three sentences, see Supplement, p. 258 *(Pap.* IV B 10:15).

29. See, for example, *Postscript, KW* XII *(SV* VII 161, 165, 269-72); *JP* I 197; II 2283 *(Pap.* IV C 100, 99).

30. With reference to the remainder of the paragraph, see Supplement, pp. 259-60 *(Pap.* IV B 2:12; 5:8,13,15; 13:2,9,10,18,19). Cf., for example, *JP* I 778 *(Pap.* VIII[1] A 7): "It is claimed that arguments against Christianity arise out of doubt. This is a total misunderstanding. The arguments against Christianity arise out of insubordination, reluctance to obey, mutiny against all authority. Therefore, until now the battle against objections has been shadowboxing, because it has been intellectual combat with doubt instead of being ethical combat against mutiny."

31. See pp. 81-83.

32. With reference to the following sentence and the next paragraph, see Supplement, p. 260 (*Pap.* IV B 10:3,4,8).

33. On the Hegelian term "moment," see p. 140 and note 14.

34. The work was not completed. For items from sketches of contemplated portions, see Supplement, pp. 260–66.

SUPPLEMENT

PHILOSOPHICAL FRAGMENTS

1. Gottfried Wilhelm Leibniz, *Theodicy*, para. 182; *Leibnitzs Theodicee*, tr. Johann Christoph Gottscheden (Hanover, Leipzig: 1763; *ASKB* 619), pp. 355-56; *God. Guil. Leibnitii opera philosophica*, I-II, ed. Johann Eduard Erdmann (Berlin: 1840; *ASKB* 620), II, p. 560; *Theodicy* (tr. of *T.* in *Philosophische Schriften*, I-VII, 1875-90), ed. Austin Farrer, tr. E. M. Huggard (New Haven: Yale University Press, 1952), pp. 240-41.

2. Plato, *Euthyphro*, 6 d–15 c; *Platonis quae exstant opera*, I-XI, ed. Friedrich Ast (Leipzig: 1819-32; *ASKB* 1144-54), VIII, pp. 66-92; *The Collected Dialogues of Plato*, ed. Edith Hamilton and Huntington Cairns (Princeton: Princeton University Press, 1963), pp. 174-85.

3. Leibniz, *Theodicy*, para. 181; Gottscheden, pp. 354-55; *Opera*, II, pp. 559-60; *Theodicy*, p. 240.

4. See, for example, p. 109.

5. See Hebrews 7:3.

6. See Historical Introduction, p. xi and notes 7-8.

7. Boethius, *The Consolation of Philosophy*, V, 4; *De consolatione philosophiae* (Agriae: 1758; *ASKB* 431), pp. 126-27; *The Consolation of Philosophy*, tr. V. E. Watts (New York: Penguin, 1969), pp. 155-59.

8. See Leibniz, *Theodicy*, para. 369, 377; Gottscheden, pp. 582-83, 594-95; *Opera*, II, pp. 611, 613-14; *Theodicy*, pp. 346, 351-52:

> When one asserts that a free event cannot be foreseen, one is confusing freedom with indetermination, or with indifference that is complete and in equipoise; and when one maintains that the lack of freedom would prevent man from being guilty, one means a freedom exempt, not from determination or from certainty, but from necessity and from constraint. This shows that the dilemma is not well expressed, and that there is a wide passage between the two perilous reefs. One will reply, therefore, that Adam sinned freely, and that God saw him sinning in the possible state of Adam, which became actual in accordance with the decree of the divine permission. It is true that Adam was determined to sin in consequence of certain prevailing inclinations: but this determination destroys neither contingency nor freedom.
>
> . . . I think I have sufficiently proved that neither the foreknowledge nor the providence of God can impair either his justice or his goodness, or our freedom.

9. G. E. Lessing, *"Ueber den Beweis des Geistes und der Kraft,"* *Gotthold Ephraim Lessing's sämmtliche Schriften*, I-XXXII (Berlin, Stettin: 1825-28; *ASKB*

1747-62), V, pp. 80-83; *Lessing's Theological Writings,* ed. and tr. Henry Chadwick (Stanford: Stanford University Press, 1957), pp. 53-55. See *Postscript, KW* XII (*SV* VII 74-78).

10. For entries and references regarding this important concept, see *JP* III 2338-59 and p. 794; VII, p. 56.

11. Lessing, *"Ueber den Beweis des Geistes und der Kraft," Schriften,* V, p. 83; *Theological Writings,* p. 55. See *Postscript, KW* XII (*SV* VII 74-85).

12. See *Postscript, KW* XII (*SV* VII 47).

13. See p. 6 and note 8.

14. See p. 8 and note 17.

15. See Historical Introduction, p. xvii.

16. Ibid.

17. Ibid.

18. Ibid., p. xviii.

19. Ibid.

20. See Wilhelm Gottlieb Tennemann, *Geschichte der Philosophie,* I-XI (Leipzig: 1798-1819; *ASKB* 815-26), VI, pp. 383-95, 403-23, with an emphasis on Plotinus.

21. Tennemann, quoting the Greek expression by Chrysippus, explains the Stoic view that the passions are falsified perceptions of good and evil. The four main passions are pleasure and sadness, desire and fear, which are a weakness and sickness of the soul.

22. See *JP* II 1335; III 3793 (*Pap.* V A 8; IV A 156).

23. Cherubim in Beaumarchais (Pierre-Augustin Caron), *Le Mariage de Figaro,* I, 7; *Figaros Givtermaal,* tr. Niels T. Bruun (Copenhagen: 1817), p. 21.

24. Kant does not use the term *accessorium* in maintaining that the concept is one thing and existence adds nothing to the concept. The two are related as possibility and actuality. See *Critik der reinen Vernunft* (4 ed., Riga: 1794; *ASKB* 595), pp. 625-26; *Critique of Pure Reason* (tr. of *C.V.,* 2 ed., 1787), tr. Norman Kemp Smith (London: Macmillan, 1933), pp. 503-04:

> My answer is as follows. There is already a contradiction in introducing the concept of existence—no matter under what title it may be disguised—into the concept of a thing which we profess to be thinking solely in reference to its possibility. If that be allowed as legitimate, a seeming victory has been won; but in actual fact nothing at all is said: the assertion is a mere tautology. We must ask: Is the proposition that *this or that thing* (which, whatever it may be, is allowed as possible) *exists,* an analytic or a synthetic proposition? If it is analytic, the assertion of the existence of the thing adds nothing to the thought of the thing; but in that case either the thought, which is in us, is the thing itself, or we have presupposed an existence as belonging to the realm of the possible, and have then, on that pretext, inferred its existence from its internal possibility—which is nothing but a miserable tautology. The word 'reality', which in the concept of the thing sounds other than the word 'existence' in the concept

of the predicate, is of no avail in meeting this objection. For if all positing (no matter what it may be that is posited) is entitled reality, the thing with all its predicates is already posited in the concept of the subject, and is assumed as actual; and in the predicate this is merely repeated. But if, on the other hand, we admit, as every reasonable person must, that all existential propositions are synthetic, how can we profess to maintain that the predicate of existence cannot be rejected without contradiction? This is a feature which is found only in analytic propositions, and is indeed precisely what constitutes their analytic character.

I should have hoped to put an end to these idle and fruitless disputations in a direct manner, by an accurate determination of the concept of existence, had I not found that the illusion which is caused by the confusion of a logical with a real predicate (that is, with a predicate which determines a thing) is almost beyond correction. Anything we please can be made to serve as a logical predicate; the subject can even be predicated of itself; for logic abstracts from all content. But a *determining* predicate is a predicate which is added to the concept of the subject and enlarges it. Consequently, it must not be already contained in the concept.

'*Being*' is obviously not a real predicate; that is, it is not a concept of something which could be added to the concept of a thing. It is merely the positing of a thing, or of certain determinations, as existing in themselves. Logically, it is merely the copula of a judgment.

25. See G.W.F. Hegel, *Vorlesungen über die Geschichte der Philosophie*, III, *Georg Wilhelm Friedrich Hegel's Werke. Vollständige Ausgabe*, I-XVIII, ed. Phillip Marheineke et al. (Berlin: 1832-45; *ASKB* 549-65), XV, pp. 582-84; *Sämtliche Werke. Jubiläumsausgabe [J.A.]*, I-XXVI, ed. Hermann Glockner (Stuttgart: 1927-40), XIX, pp. 582-84; *Hegel's Lectures on the History of Philosophy* (tr. of *G.P.*, 2 ed., 1840-44; Kierkegaard had 1 ed., 1833-36), I-III, tr. E. S. Haldane and Frances H. Simson (New York: Humanities Press, 1955), III, pp. 451-53; *Wissenschaft der Logik*, I, *Werke*, III, pp. 83-88; *J.A.*, IV, pp. 93-98; *Hegel's Science of Logic* (tr. of *W.L.*, Lasson ed., 1923; Kierkegaard had 2 ed., 1833-34), tr. A. V. Miller (New York: Humanities Press, 1969), pp. 86-90.

26. Tennemann (ed. tr.): "Carneades had good reason to laugh at the escape (to hesitate with his answer) that Chrysippus had thought of under pressure of the question of the first link of the relationship in a series of relative things. As far as I am concerned, he said, you may not only rest but sleep, too. What good does it do you? There will follow another who wakes you with the question 'At what number do you stop?' "

27. Ludvig Holberg, *Erasmus Montanus*, II, 3, IV, 2, *Den Danske Skue-Plads*, I-VII (Copenhagen: 1788; *ASKB* 1566-67), V, no pagination. Erasmus Montanus demonstrates that Nille is a stone by asserting that a stone cannot fly, that Nille cannot fly—ergo, Nille is a stone. Then, when she cries, he argues that since a stone cannot cry she is not a stone. He tells Per Degn that a rooster has certain characteristics that distinguish it from other

animals: "It awakens people, it sounds the hours, it boasts of its voice, and it has a comb. You waken people, you sound the hours, you boast of your voice, and you wear a jagged wig—*ergo*, you are a rooster" (ed. tr.). Per Degn cries, but he is not restored, as was Nille.

28. Cf. Luke 5:4; John 21:6.

29. Pp. 23-36.

30. See Johann Georg Hamann, *Hamann's Schriften*, I-VIII, ed. Friedrich Roth and G. A. Wiener (Berlin, Leipzig: 1821-43; *ASKB* 536-44), I, p. 425; *JP* II 1540 (*Pap.* I A 237).

31. See *Hamann's Schriften*, I, p. 497. See *JP* I 265, p. 117; II 1542, 1722 (*Pap.* II A 12, 2; III A 49).

32. See Romans 9:16.

33. Herostratus (fl. c. 356 B.C.) was the Greek incendiary of the temple of Diana at Ephesus.

34. Johann Christoph Friedrich Schiller, *Die Worte des Glaubens, Schillers sämmtliche Werke*, I-XII (Stuttgart, Tübingen: 1838; *ASKB* 1804-15), I, pp. 403-04. *Einhalt* in *einhaltsschwer* is an old spelling of *Inhalt*, according to the Grimms' *Wörterbuch*, III, col. 194-95.

35. See p. 78 fn. and note 25.

36. See p. 78 fn.

37. See Aristotle, *Nicomachean Ethics*, 1139 b; *Aristoteles graece*, I-II, ed. Immanuel Bekker (Berlin: 1831; *ASKB* 1074-75), II, p. 1139; *Die Ethik des Aristoteles*, I-II, tr. Christian Garve (Breslau: 1798-1801; *ASKB* 1082-83), II, pp. 164-65; *The Works of Aristotle*, I-XII, ed. J. A. Smith and W. D. Ross (Oxford: Oxford University Press, 1908-52), IX: "Now what *scientific knowledge is, if we are to speak* exactly and not follow mere similarities, is plain from what follows. We all suppose that what we know is not even capable of being otherwise; of things capable of being otherwise we do not know, when they have passed outside our observation, whether they exist or not. Therefore the object of scientific knowledge is of necessity. Therefore it is eternal; for things that are of necessity in the unqualified sense are all eternal; and things that are eternal are ungenerated and imperishable." See *JP* II 2281 (*Pap.* IV C 23).

38. Plato, *Sophist*, 248 a; *Opera*, II, p. 300; *Collected Dialogues*, p. 992.

39. See note 34 above.

40. See note 35 above.

41. See note 36 above.

42. With reference to the following two paragraphs, see pp. 76-77.

43. See, for example, Hegel, *Wissenschaft der Logik*, I, *Werke*, IV, p. 211; *J.A.*, IV, p. 689; *Science of Logic*, p. 549:

The *negation* of real possibility is thus its *identity*-with self; in that in its sublating it is thus within itself the recoil of this sublating, it is *real necessity*.

What is necessary *cannot be otherwise*; but what is simply *possible* can; for possibility is the in-itself that is only positedness and therefore essentially otherness. Formal possibility is this identity as transition into a sheer other; but real possibility, because it contains the other moment, actuality, is already itself necessity. Therefore what is really possible can no longer be otherwise; under the particular conditions and circumstances something else cannot follow. Real possibility and necessity are therefore only *seemingly* different; this is an identity which does not have to *become* but is already *presupposed* and lies at their base.

44. See note 7 above.

45. See note 48 below.

46. See p. 83 fn.; Aristotle, *De anima,* 427 b; Bekker, I, p. 427; *Works,* III: "perception of the special objects of sense is always free from error." On the front flyleaf of his copy of the August Gfroerer edition of Spinoza's *Opera* (Stuttgart: 1830; *ASKB* 788; University of Copenhagen, Fil. 18782), Kierkegaard wrote: "re pg. 19. Every necessary cognition is true (to this could be compared Aristotle's teaching that in cognition there is never error but only in ignorance). The error lies in the will. Now, that is all right, but what is the relation between cognition and will (the example that Spinoza himself adduces at the end of the same pg. about the [winged] horse); here the middle term is lacking, how cognition is effective, whether it is so compelling that I cannot abstain from giving it my approval and I thereby commit an error?—the whole cognition principle cannot be explained."

47. René Descartes, *Principles of Philosophy*; *Renati Des-Cartes opera philosophica* (Amsterdam: 1678; *ASKB* 473), pp. 9, 11; *The Meditations and Selections from the Principles of Philosophy,* tr. John Veitch (LaSalle, Ill.: Open Court, 1937), pp. 146, 151:

XXXI. That our errors are, in respect of God, merely negations, but, in respect of ourselves, privations.

But as it happens that we frequently fall into error, although God is no deceiver, if we desire to inquire into the origin and cause of our errors, with a view to guard against them, it is necessary to observe that they depend less on our understanding than on our will, and that they have no need of the actual concourse of God, in order to their production; so that, when considered in reference to God, they are merely negations, but in reference to ourselves, privations.

XLII. How, although we never will to err, it is nevertheless by our will that we do err.

But now since we know that all our errors depend upon our will, and as no one wishes to deceive himself, it may seem wonderful that there is any error in our judgments at all. It is necessary to remark, however, that there is a great difference between willing to be deceived, and willing to yield assent to opinions in which it happens that error is found. For though there is no one who expressly wishes to fall into error, we will yet hardly find any one who is not ready to assent to things in which, unknown to himself, error lurks; and it even frequently happens that it is the desire itself of following after truth that leads those not fully aware of the order in which it ought to be sought for, to pass judgment on matters of which they have no adequate knowledge, and thus to fall into error.

48. See Plato, *Theaetetus,* 195 c-d; *Opera,* II, p. 152; *Collected Dialogues,* p. 902.

49. See Poul Martin Møller, *Udkast til Forelæsninger over den ældre Philosophies Historie, Efterladte Skrifter,* I-III (Copenhagen: 1839-43; *ASKB* 1574-76), II, p. 470 (ed. tr.): "Aristotle makes the right relations of words the object of his inquiry, because the single idea is not true or false but only the relation of ideas in propositions. The ideas are the results of the impressions that similar things have made upon men (shepherd, man, white); but the true and the false first appear when men link such ideas with the concepts of being and non-being."

50. See, for example, Leibniz, *Theodicy,* para. 23, 61; Gottscheden, pp. 130, 166; *Opera,* II, pp. 486, 496; *Theodicy,* pp. 88, 107.

For I observed at the beginning that by REASON here I do not mean the opinions and discourses of men, nor even the habit they have formed of judging things according to the usual course of Nature, but rather the inviolable linking together [*enchainement*] of truths.

That which contradicts a proposition of Euclid is contrary to the *Elements* of Euclid. That which in us is contrary to the Mysteries is not reason nor is it the natural light or the linking together [*enchainement*] of truths; it is corruption, or error, or prejudice, or darkness.

See *JP* III 3073 (*Pap.* IV C 29).

51. See, for example, Leibniz, *Theodicy,* para. 44; Gottscheden, pp. 153-54; *Opera,* II, pp. 491-92; *Theodicy,* pp. 98-99.

Now we have no need of revealed faith to know that there is such a sole Principle of all things, entirely good and wise. Reason teaches us this by infallible proofs; and in consequence all the objections taken from the course of things, in which we observe imperfections, are only based on false appearances. For, if we were capable of understanding the universal harmony, we should see that what we are tempted to find fault with is connected with the plan most worthy of being chosen; in a word, we *should see,* and should not *believe* only, that what God has done is the best. I call "seeing" here what one knows *a priori* by the causes; and "believing" what one only judges by the effects, even though the one be as certainly known as the other.

52. See p. 100 and note 23.
53. See John 16:7.

54. See Historical Introduction, p. xvii; *Postscript, KW* XII (*SV* VII 6).

55. Ibid.

56. Ibid. (*SV* VII 47).

57. See, for example, Ludwig Andreas Feuerbach, *Das Wesen des Christenthums* (Leipzig: 1843; *ASKB* 488), pp. iii, xii–xiii, 275–413.

58. See *Postscript, KW* XII (*SV* VII 17-20).

59. Ibid. (*SV* VII 25-26).

60. See Supplement, p. 217 (*Pap.* V B 9).

61. A play on the literal meaning of the elements of Feuerbach's name.

62. *"Neue Wendung der deutschen Philosophie," Anekdota zur neuesten deutschen Philosophie und Publicistik,* I-II, ed. Arnold Ruge (Zurich, Winterthur: 1843; *ASKB* 753), II, pp. 23, 27-28, 53.

63. See *Postscript, KW* XII (*SV* VII 28).

64. Ibid. (*SV* VII 24).

65. Ibid. (*SV* VII 28).

66. Ibid. (*SV* VII 28-29).

67. Ibid. (*SV* VII 27-28).

68. Ibid. (*SV* VII 26, 32).

69. Cf. *Fear and Trembling*, p. 11, *KW* VI (*SV* III 64).

70. See pp. 45-46, 55-58.

71. The amusement park in what is now the center of Copenhagen.

72. *Neues Repertorium für die theologische Literatur und kirchliche Statistik* (Berlin), II, 1, April 30, 1845, pp. 44-48, especially p. 45. See Historical Introduction, p. xx *Postscript, KW* XII (*SV* VII 233-36).

73. See *Repetition*, pp. 357-62, *KW* VI.

74. See note 72 above.

75. The entire entry is a listing of titles of works contemplated or in progress during 1844-1845, after Kierkegaard had completed the writing of *Fragments*. "Logical Problems" was the initial title of *Postscript*. See *JP* V 5850-51 (*Pap.* VI B 89-90).

76. The theme of the Christian art of speaking, or religious address, was of live concern to Kierkegaard throughout his life. It involved the use of Aristotle's *Rhetoric* and the making of crucial distinctions between it and his projected work. "The Dialectic of Ethical and Ethical-Religious Communication" (*JP* I 648-57 [*Pap.* VIII² 79-89]) was begun but never finished or published. The substance, however, appears throughout the authorship, including *Fragments*, an instance of the indirect method.

77. The pseudonymous author of *Fear and Trembling*.

78. Aristotle, *Rhetoric*, 1399 a; Bekker, II, p. 1399; *Aristoteles Rhetoric*, tr. Karl Ludwig Roth (Stuttgart: 1833; *ASKB* 1092), p. 197; *Works*, XI.

79. See *JP* V 5813-17 (*Pap.* VI A 55-59).

80. Danish: *Experiment*. See *Repetition*, pp. 357-62, *KW* VI.

81. See *JP* V 5759 (*Pap.* VI B 194).

82. A declaration by the chorus in Johan Ludvig Heiberg's *Kong Salomon og Jörgen Hattemager* (Copenhagen: 1825), 23, p. 68.

83. See p. 87.

84. In *Theologisk Tidsskrift, Ny Række*, IV, 1 (Vol. X), May 1846, pp. 175-82, there appeared a review of *Fragments* signed '80' (Johan Frederik Hagen) and dated October 1845. See Historical Introduction, p. xix.

85. See Chapter V, pp. 89-105.

86. In June 1844, four of Kierkegaard's writings, pseudonymous or signed, were published: *Three Upbuilding Discourses, Fragments, Anxiety,* and *Prefaces.* In 1846, Adolph Peter Adler (1812-1869), Danish theologian with Hegelian and gnostic leanings, published *Nogle Digte, Studier og Exempler, Forsøg til en kort systematisk Fremstilling af Christendommen i dens Logik,* and *Theologiske Studier.*

87. Hans Lassen Martensen (1808-1884), professor of theology at the University of Copenhagen and subsequently Bishop Mynster's successor, returned to Denmark in the autumn of 1836 after a two-year period of study and travel. In Berlin, he studied with Henrich Steffens and Philipp Marheineke and read Hegel's works. In Heidelberg, he studied with Carl Daub. He visited David Strauss in Tübingen and Franz Baader in Munich, where he also heard Schelling lecture. See *JP* II 1570; V 5200 (*Pap.* II A 52, 7).

88. See pp. 6-7 and note 10.

89. See Julius Müller, *Die christliche Lehre von der Sünde*, I-II (Breslau: 1849: *ASKB* 689-90), II, pp. 310-43, especially p. 335.

90. See Immanuel Hermann Fichte, *Sätze zur Vorschule der Theologie* (Stuttgart, Tübingen: 1826; *ASKB* 501), p. 214.

91. See pp. 74-75.

92. Carl Edvard Marius Levy (1808-1865), Danish physician, expert on children's diseases and obstetrics. He published articles in *Hospitals Meddelelser*, I, III, 1848, 1850, and in *Ugeskrift for Læger, 2 Række*, X, 1849, in which he criticized the theories of Ignaz Semmelweis (Vienna) on the transmission of childbed fever.

93. See *Postscript, KW* XII (*SV* VII 115, 119-20, 271, 276, 278).

JOHANNES CLIMACUS

1. See Historical Introduction, p. ix and note 2.

2. See Plato, *Apology,* 40 e–41 d; *Opera*, VIII, pp. 154-57; *Collected Dialogues,* p. 25:

If on the other hand death is a removal from here to some other place, and if what we are told is true, that all the dead are there, what greater blessing could there be than this, gentlemen? If on arrival in the other world, beyond the reach of our so-called justice, one will find there the true judges who are said to preside in those courts, Minos and Rhadamanthus and Aeacus and Triptolemus and all those other half-divinities who were upright in their earthly life, would that be an unrewarding journey? Put it in this way. How much would one of you give to meet

Orpheus and Musaeus, Hesiod and Homer? I am willing to die ten times over if this account is true. It would be a specially interesting experience for me to join them there, to meet Palamedes and Ajax, the son of Telamon, and any other heroes of the old days who met their death through an unfair trial, and to compare my fortunes with theirs—it would be rather amusing, I think. And above all I should like to spend my time there, as here, in examining and searching people's minds, to find out who is really wise among them, and who only thinks that he is. What would one not give, gentlemen, to be able to question the leader of that great host against Troy, or Odysseus, or Sisyphus, or the thousands of other men and women whom one could mention, to talk and mix and argue with whom would be unimaginable happiness? At any rate I presume that they do not put one to death there for such conduct, because apart from the other happiness in which their world surpasses ours, they are now immortal for the rest of time, if what we are told is true.

You too, gentlemen of the jury, must look forward to death with confidence, and fix your minds on this one belief, which is certain—that nothing can harm a good man either in life or after death, and his fortunes are not a matter of indifference to the gods.

3. See II Corinthians 10:5.
4. See p. 97 and note 16.
5. Ibid.
6. See René Descartes, *Meditations on First Philosophy*, IV; *Opera*, pp. 27-28; Veitch, pp. 67-69.

Whereupon, regarding myself more closely, and considering what my errors are (which alone testify to the existence of imperfection in me), I observe that these depend on the concurrence of two causes, viz., the faculty of cognition which I possess, and that of election or the power of free choice,—in other words, the understanding and the will. For by the understanding alone, I [neither affirm nor deny anything, but] merely apprehend (*percipio*) the ideas regarding which I may form a judgment; nor is any error, properly so called, found in it thus accurately taken. And although there are perhaps innumerable objects in the world of which I have no idea in my understanding, it cannot, on that account, be said that I am deprived of those ideas [as of something that is due to my nature], but simply that I do not possess them, because, in truth, there is no ground to prove that Deity ought to have endowed me with a larger faculty of cognition than he has actually bestowed upon me; and however skilful a workman I suppose him to be, I have no reason, on that account, to think that it was obligatory on him to give to each of his works all the perfections he is able to bestow upon some. Nor, moreover, can I complain that God has not given me freedom of choice, or a will sufficiently ample and perfect, since, in truth, I am conscious of will so ample and extended as to be superior to all limits. And what appears to me here to be highly remarkable is that, of all the other properties I possess, there is none so great and perfect as that I do not clearly discern it could be still greater and more perfect. For, to take an example, if I consider the faculty of understanding which I possess, I find that it is of very small extent, and greatly limited, and at the same time I form the idea of another faculty of the same nature, much more ample and even infinite; and seeing that I can frame the idea of it, I discover, from this circumstance alone, that it pertains to the nature of God. In the same way, if I examine the faculty of memory or imagination, or any other faculty I possess, I find none that is not small and circumscribed, and in God immense [and infinite]. It is the faculty of will only, or freedom of choice, which I experience to be so great that I am unable to conceive the idea of another that shall be more ample and extended; so that it is chiefly my will which leads me to discern that I bear a certain image and similitude of Deity. . . .

From all this I discover, however, that neither the power of willing, which I have received from God, is of itself the source of my errors, for it is exceedingly ample and perfect in its kind; nor even the power of understanding, for as I conceive no object unless by means of the faculty that God bestowed upon me, all that I conceive is doubtless rightly conceived by me, and it is impossible for me to be deceived in it.

Whence, then, spring my errors? They arise from this cause alone, that I do not restrain the will, which is of much wider range than the understanding, within the same limits, but extend it even to things I do not understand, and as the will is of itself indifferent to such, it readily falls into error and sin by choosing the false in room of the true, and evil instead of good.

7. Descartes, *Principles of Philosophy*, I, para. 10; *Opera*, p. 2 ("*ego cogito, ergo sum*"); Veitch, p. 134: "I *think*, therefore I am."

8. Tennemann, *Geschichte der Philosophie*.

9. See *JP* V 5634 (*Pap.* IV A 234).

10. See Matthew 23:4.

11. See *Postscript, KW* XII (*SV* VII 215, 265-67).

12. Benedict Spinoza, *Renati Descartes principiorum philosophiae, Opera philosophica omnia*, ed. August Gfroerer (Stuttgart: 1830; *ASKB* 788), pp. 1-49; *Earlier Philosophical Writings*, tr. Frank A. Hayes (Indianapolis: Bobbs-Merrill, 1963), pp. 11-103.

13. See Supplement, p. 264 (*Pap.* IV B 13:16).

14. See note 7 above.

15. See Descartes, *Principles of Philosophy*, I, para. 29; *Opera*, p. 8; Veitch, p. 145. See also Hegel, *Geschichte der Philosophie*, III, *Werke*, XV, pp. 352-53; *J.A.*, XIX, pp. 352-53; *History of Philosophy*, III, pp. 238-39.

16. See Hegel, *Geschichte der Philosophie*, III, *Werke*, XV, p. 335 (where reference is made to Spinoza, *Principia philosophiae Cartesianae, Benedicti de Spinoza opera*, I-II, ed. Heinrich Eberhard Gottlob Paulus [Jena: 1802-03], I, p. 2); *J.A.*, XIX, p. 335; *History of Philosophy*, III, pp. 224-25.

17. Cf. *Fear and Trembling*, p. 6, *KW* VI (*SV* III 58).

18. See p. 157 and note 2.

19. See p. 97 and note 16.

20. Ibid.

21. A Gnostic sect, founded in the second century by Carpocrates of Alexandria, that advised experience of all possible good and evil in order to achieve perfection. See *Anxiety*, p. 103, *KW* VIII (*SV* IV 372); *JP* V 5227 (*Pap.* II A 599).

22. See p. 70 and note 42.

23. See Diogenes Laertius, *Lives of Eminent Philosophers*, V, 37; *Diogenis Laertii de vitis philosophorum*, I-II (Leipzig: 1833; *ASKB* 1109), I, p. 223; *Diogen Laërtses filosofiske Historie*, I-II, tr. Børge Riisbrigh (Copenhagen: 1812; *ASKB* 1110-11), I, p. 207; *Lives of Eminent Philosophers*, I-II, tr. R. D. Hicks (Loeb, New York: Putnam, 1925), I, p. 483.

24. See Supplement, p. 226 (*Pap.* X² A 155) and note 87.

25. See p. 167 and note 8.

26. See p. 167 and note 9.

27. See p. 167 and note 10.

28. See pp. 167-68 and note 17.

29. In Leibniz's thought, the Principle of the Identity of Indiscernibles: no two monads can be exactly alike. Entities completely alike would be indistinguishable. See Leibniz, *Monadology*, 8, 9; *Opera*, II, p. 705; *The Monadology*, tr. R. Latta (London: Oxford University Press, 1965), p. 222. See also Frederik Christian Sibbern, *Logik som Tænkelære* (Copenhagen: 1835; *ASKB* 777), p. 129.

30. See pp. 82-83.

31. See Aristotle, *Metaphysics*, 1050 b; Bekker, II, p. 1050; *Aristoteles Metaphysik*, I-II, tr. Ernst Wilhelm Hengstenberg (Bonn: 1824; *ASKB* 1084), I, p. 179; *Works*, VIII: "Obviously, therefore, the substance or form is actuality. According to this argument, then, it is obvious that actuality is prior in substantial being to potency; and as we have said, one actuality always precedes another in time right back to the actuality of the eternal prime mover."

32. See pp. 37-39.

33. See pp. 167-68 and note 17.

34. Ibid.

35. Ibid.

36. Ibid.

37. Ibid.

38. See *Pap.* II C 25 (*Pap.* XII, p. 282) for these terms in notes from Hans Lassen Martensen's lectures, "The History of Philosophy from Kant to Hegel," University of Copenhagen, first semester 1838-1839; Hegel, *Geschichte der Philosophie*, II, *Werke*, XIV, p. 552; *J.A.*, XVIII, p. 552; *History of Philosophy*, II, p. 332:

The result of the older Scepticism is indeed the subjectivity of knowledge only, but this is founded on an elaborately thought out annihilation of everything which is held to be true and existent, so that everything is made transient.

According to this, the function of Scepticism is wrongly termed the inculcation of proneness to doubt; nor can we translate σκέψις by Doubt, if Scepticism was also called by Sextus (Pyrrh. Hyp. I. 3, 7) ephectic (ἐφεκτική) because one of its chief points was that judgment must be suspended. Doubt, however, is only uncertainty, irresolution, indecision, the thought which is opposed to something held to be valid. Doubt proceeds from the fact of there being two; it is a passing to and fro between two or more points of view, so that we neither rest at the one nor the other—and yet we ought to remain at one point or another.

39. See p. 82.
40. Ibid.
41. Ibid.
42. See pp. 81-83.
43. See p. 83 fn.
44. See Diogenes Laertius, X, 31-32; *Vitis,* II, p. 196; Riisbrigh, I, p. 464; Loeb, II, p. 561:

Now in *The Canon* Epicurus affirms that our sensations and preconceptions and our feelings are the standards of truth; the Epicureans generally make perceptions of mental presentations to be also standards. His own statements are also to be found in the *Summary* addressed to Herodotus and in the *Sovran Maxims.* Every sensation, he says, is devoid of reason and incapable of memory; for neither is it self-caused nor, regarded as having an external cause, can it add anything thereto or take anything therefrom. Nor is there anything which can refute sensations or convict them of error: one sensation cannot convict another and kindred sensation, for they are equally valid; nor can one sensation refute another which is not kindred but heterogeneous, for the objects which the two senses judge are not the same; nor again can reason refute them, for reason is wholly dependent on sensation; nor can one sense refute another, since we pay equal heed to all. And the reality of separate perceptions guarantees the truth of our senses.

45. See notes 6 and 15 above.
46. See note 16 above.
47. Tennemann, *Geschichte der Philosophie.*
48. See pp. 245-46; Diogenes Laertius, IX, 107-08; *Vitis,* II, pp. 178-79; Riisbrigh, I, p. 448; Loeb, II, pp. 517-19: "The Sceptics reply that, when different impressions are produced, they must both be said to appear; for things which are apparent are so called because they appear. The end to be realized they hold to be suspension of judgement, which brings with it tranquillity like its shadow: so Timon and Aenesidemus declare. For in matters which are for us to decide we shall neither choose this nor shrink from that; and things which are not for us to decide but happen of necessity, such

as hunger, thirst, and pain, we cannot escape, for they are not to be removed by force of reason." See Tennemann, II, pp. 175, 179; V, pp. 61-62, 98-100, 278.

49. See note 16 above.

50. See pp. 81-85.

51. See Diogenes Laertius, IX, 104–05; *Vitis*, II, p. 177; Riisbrigh, I, p. 447; Loeb, II, p. 515: " 'We admit the apparent fact,' say they, 'without admitting that it really is what it appears to be.' We also perceive that fire burns; as to whether it is its nature to burn, we suspend our judgement. We see that a man moves, and that he perishes; how it happens we do not know. We merely object to accepting the unknown substance behind phenomena."

52. Cf. pp. 81-85.

53. See Tennemann, V, pp. 62-64. Aenesidemus gives ten bases for doubting. See Frederick Copleston, *A History of Philosophy*, I-IX (London: Burns Oates & Washbourne; New York: Newman Press, 1947-75), I, P. 443 (ed. adaptation):

(1) Differences among types of living beings imply different ideas of same object.

(2) Differences among individual men imply the same.

(3) Different structures and presentations of our various senses.

(4) Differences among our various states: e.g., waking or sleeping, youth or age.

(5) Differences of perspective: e.g., the stick immersed in water appears bent; the square tower appears round from a distance.

(6) The objects of perception are never presented in their purity, but a medium is always involved, such as air.

(7) Differences in perception due to differences of quality: e.g., one grain of sand appears rough, while if sand is allowed to slip through the fingers it appears smooth and soft.

(8) Relativity in general.

(9) Differences in impressions due to frequency or infrequency of perception.

(10) Different ways of life, moral codes, laws, myths, philosophic systems, etc.

54. See Hegel, *Geschichte der Philosophie*, III, *Werke*, XV, p. 334 ("*in ihrer Darstellung etwas sehr Populares und Naives . . . er geht ganz einfach und kindlich dabei zu Werke*"); *J.A.*, XIX, p. 334; cf. *History of Philosophy*, III, p. 224.

55. Cf. Hegel, *Geschichte der Philosophie*, I, III, *Werke*, XIII, p. 52, XV, p. 335; *J.A.*, XVII, p. 68, XIX, p. 335; *History of Philosophy*, I, p. 38, III, p. 224: "The Cartesian principles, for instance, are very suitable for application to mechanism, but for nothing further . . .." "And yet on the whole there is little to say about his philosophy."

56. See p. 170.

57. Ibid.

58. See pp. 81-83, 169-71.

59. See Supplement, p. 261 (*Pap.* IV B 10:17) and note 48.

60. See pp. 81-83.

61. See p. 83 fn. and note 54.

62. See Supplement, pp. 232-33 (*Pap.* IV C 11) and note 6.

63. See note 44 above.

64. See p. 80 and note 35.

65. Hegel, *Geschichte der Philosophie*, III, *Werke*, XV, p. 337; *J.A.*, XIX, p. 337 (where Descartes, *Principia philosophiae*, I, 1-6, *Opera*, pp. 1-2, is cited); *History of Philosophy*, III, pp. 225-26.

BIBLIOGRAPHICAL NOTE

For general bibliographies of Kierkegaard studies, see:
Jens Himmelstrup, *Søren Kierkegaard International Bibliografi*. Copenhagen: Nyt Nordisk Forlag Arnold Busck, 1962.
Aage Jørgensen, *Soren Kierkegaard-litteratur 1961-1970*. Aarhus: Akademisk Boghandel, 1971. *Søren Kierkegaard-litteratur 1971-1980*. Aarhus: priv. publ, 1983. *"Søren Kierkegaard-litteratur 1981-1990. Udkast til bibliografi,"* Uriasposten, VIII, 1989.
Bruce H. Kirmmse, *Kierkegaard in Golden Age Denmark*. Bloomington: Indiana University Press, 1990.'
François H. Lapointe, *Sören Kierkegaard and His Critics: An International Bibliography of Criticism*. Westport, Connecticut: Greenwood Press, 1980.
International Kierkegaard Newsletter, ed. Julia Watkin. Copenhagen: 1979—.
Kierkegaard: A Collection of Critical Essays, ed. Josiah Thompson. New York: Doubleday (Anchor Books), 1972.
Kierkegaardiana, XII, 1982; XIII, 1984; XIV, 1988.
Søren Kierkegaard's Journals and Papers, I, ed. and tr. Howard V. Hong and Edna H. Hong, assisted by Gregor Malantschuk. Bloomington: Indiana University Press, 1967.

For topical bibliographies of Kierkegaard studies, see *Søren Kierkegaard's Journals and Papers*, I-IV, 1967-75.

INDEX

ADVISORY BOARD

KIERKEGAARD'S WRITINGS